Geographica's
FAMILY ATLAS

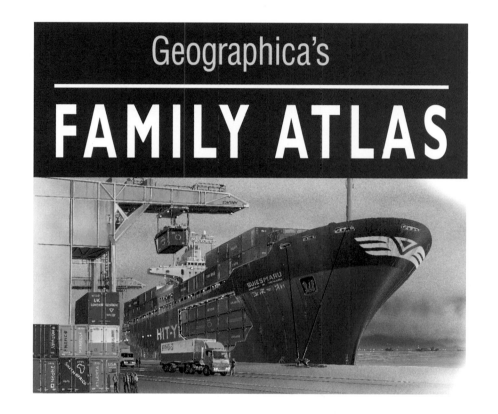

This edition published in 2001 by Whitecap Books
351 Lynn Avenue, North Vancouver, British Columbia V7J 2C4

First published in 2000 by Random House Australia Pty Ltd

Children's Publisher: Linsay Knight
Managing Editor: Marie-Louise Taylor
Editor: Loretta Barnard
Art Director: Ivan Finnegan
Cartographers: Grahame Keane, Andrew Dunlop, David Morris, of Cartodraft (Australia) Pty Ltd
Cartographic Co-ordinator: James Mills-Hicks
Production Manager: Linda Watchorn
Publishing Co-ordinator: Pia Gerard
Photo Library: Susan Page
Picture Research: Loretta Barnard, Marie-Louise Taylor
Flags supplied by: Flag Society of Australia

Illustrators: Jenny Black pages 20 (bottom), 22; Greg Bridges page 170; Wendy de Paauw pages 32, 64–5; Garry Fleming pages 21 (bottom), 37, 39 (bottom), 46, 50–1, 53, 104, 183; Kim Graham pages 44, 72–3; Helen Halliday pages 24–5; David Kirshner pages 19, 45, 98; Frank Knight pages 20 (top), 97; Kevin Stead pages 15, 16–17, 20–1, 41; Mark Vesey pages 73, 112; Spike Wademan pages 1, 4, 10–11, 12–13, 26–7, 31, 39 (top), 55, 60, 61, 63; David Wood page 15.

Writers: Stephen Murray, Mark Lamont, Margaret McPhee & Judith Simpson

Film separation by Pica Colour Separation Overseas Pte Ltd, Singapore
Printed by Sing Cheong Printing Co. Ltd. Hong Kong

Page 1: Container ship
Page 3: Great Barrier Reef (top); penguins (middle); school boys in Pakistan (bottom)
Page 4 : Pluto and its moon (left); cleaning up after a radioactive spill (top right); African wild dogs (bottom right)
Page 5: New York

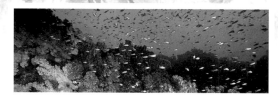

Geographica's
FAMILY ATLAS

Consultant: Stephen Murray

WHITECAP BOOKS

Vancouver/Toronto/New York

Contents

PART 3: COUNTRIES OF OUR WORLD

How this book works

Geographica's Family Atlas **is an authoritative guide to today's world. It will take you from the solar system and Earth's beginnings to an exploration of how the world might be in the future. And, of course, it provides comprehensive maps on the nations of the world.**

Part 1 looks at our world and beyond into the exciting frontier of space exploration. Part 2 provides informative, interesting discussions of some of the major issues facing our world today. How are we dealing with the problems of waste and pollution? What is happening to our climate? Can we stop the destruction of our environment and ensure the survival of endangered species?

LEGEND

—— — —— —	International border
– – – – –	Disputed or undefined border
————	Administrative border
● **Nairobi**	City
● **Nakuru**	Town
● Bura	Other Settlement
◉ **Sydney**	Capital City
	River
	Lake, dam or reservoir
▲ Mt Adams 3751 m	Peak (height in metres)
	2,000 metres
	4,000 metres
	6,000 metres
AUSTRALIA	Country name
TIROL	Administration name
MOUNTAINS	Mountain range name
Ivory Coast	Coastal name
VALLEY	Valley name
FLORIDA KEYS	Major island group
Comerong Island	Island name
Comerong Point	Point name
Susquehanna	River name
Lake Erie	Lake name
ATLANTIC	Ocean name
TIMOR SEA	Sea name
Small Bay	Bay name

FACT FILE

FLAG

COUNTRY NAME

PHOTOGRAPH

FACT FILE

BRAZIL

Capital Brasilia
Population 171,853,126
Official language Portuguese
Main religions Roman Catholic 89%, Protestant 7%
Currency Real
Form of government Federal republic
Record holder Largest country in South America in both area and population; World's largest producer of coffee; The Amazon carries more water than any other river in the world

Brazil

The Iguaçu Falls, on the border with Argentina, from the Brazilian side. The falls form a curtain of water almost 3 kilometres (1½ miles) wide.

A bountiful rainforest

The Amazon Basin—once an inland sea—extends over more than 8 million square kilometres (3 million square miles), mainly in Brazil. Drained by the mighty Amazon and its more than 1,000 tributaries, it contains over a quarter of the planet's rainforests and a wider variety of plant and animal life than any other part of the world. There are over a thousand species of birds alone!

European colonists established huge sugarcane plantations on the fertile coastal plains, so until recently the Amazon Basin was virtually untouched. Today, however, logging, mining, clearing for cattle farms and the resettlement of Brazil's landless peasants is reducing the Amazon rainforest by up to 4 per cent each year. Raging forest fires in 1998 caused even more destruction. [*See Habitat destruction; Resource depletion; The industrial frontier; World Cultures*]

The dye arrow-poison frog lives in the forests of Central and South America.

Brazil takes up almost half the continent of South America and is the fifth largest country in the world. It is also one of the most populous countries of the world. Its vast tropical northern half is covered in dense rainforest and is sparsely populated. Valuable trees found here include mahogany, kapok, rosewood, rubber and the towering Brazil nut tree, which can grow to 45 metres (148 feet) in height. High rainfall feeds a network of mighty rivers, including the Amazon, which flow through the forests to the Atlantic. More than 3,000 fish species live in the inland waterways, including the flesh-eating piranha. Anacondas are found along the forested banks. Other rainforest animals include spider monkeys, brightly coloured parrots, sloths and thousands of insect species. The Brazilian Highlands, in the centre and south, are made up of an immense plateau of hard, ancient rock, weathered into deep river valleys with spectacular waterfalls. Much of the interior is covered by savanna woodland. By contrast, much of the northeast region suffers from drought.

98

LOCATOR GLOBE

MAIN ENTRY

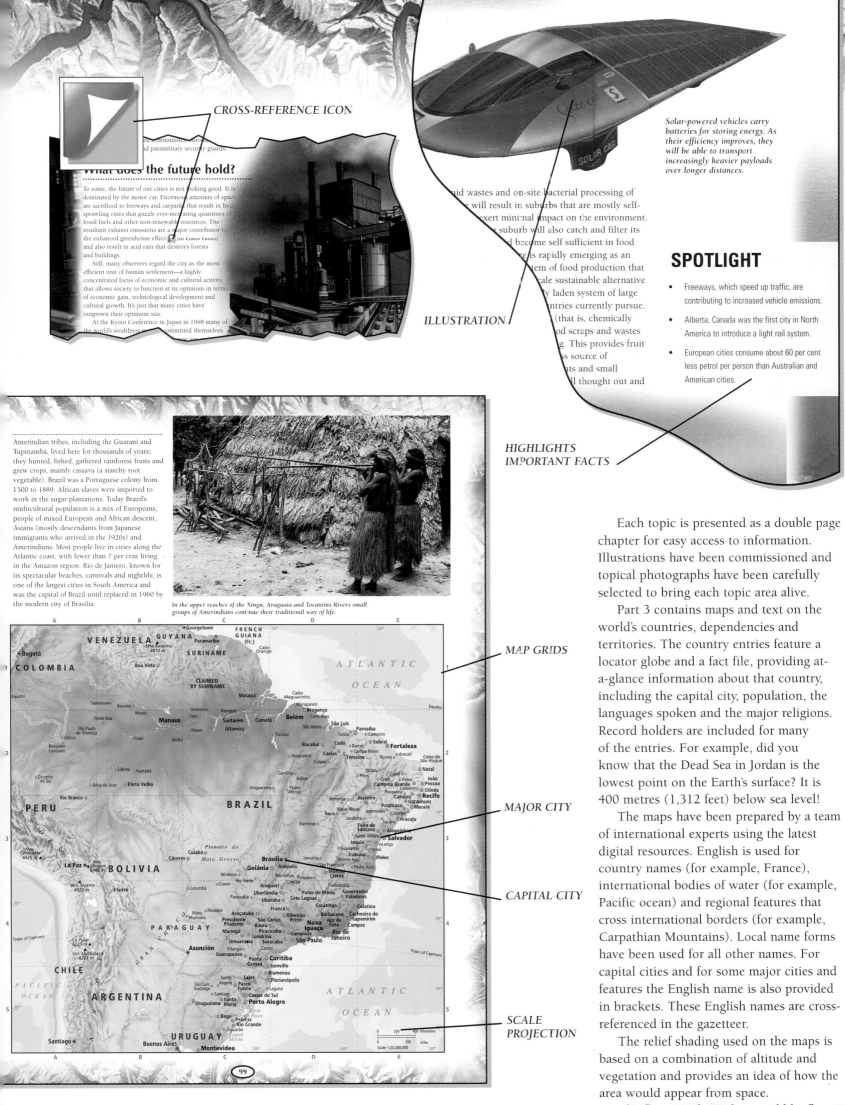

CROSS-REFERENCE ICON

What does the future hold?

To some, the future of our cities is not looking good. It is dominated by the motor car. Enormous amounts of space are sacrificed to freeways and carparks that result in huge, sprawling cities that guzzle ever-increasing quantities of fossil fuels and other non-renewable resources. The resultant exhaust emissions are a major contributor to the enhanced greenhouse effect [SEE CLIMATE CHANGE] and also result in acid rain that destroys forests and buildings.

Still, many observers regard the city as the most efficient unit of human settlement—a highly concentrated focus of economic and cultural activity that allows society to function at its optimum in terms of economic gain, technological development and cultural growth. It's just that many cities have outgrown their optimum size.

At the Kyoto Conference in Japan in 1998 many of the world's wealthiest nations committed themselves

...id wastes and on-site bacterial processing of ... will result in suburbs that are mostly self-... exert minimal impact on the environment. ... suburb will also catch and filter its ... become self sufficient in food ... is rapidly emerging as an ... tem of food production that ... cale sustainable alternative ... laden system of large ... ntries currently pursue. ... (that is, chemically ... od scraps and wastes ... g. This provides fruit ... s source of ... ts and small ... l thought out and

Solar-powered vehicles carry batteries for storing energy. As their efficiency improves, they will be able to transport increasingly heavier payloads over longer distances.

ILLUSTRATION

SPOTLIGHT

- Freeways, which speed up traffic, are contributing to increased vehicle emissions.

- Alberta, Canada was the first city in North America to introduce a light rail system.

- European cities consume about 60 per cent less petrol per person than Australian and American cities.

HIGHLIGHTS IMPORTANT FACTS

Amerindian tribes, including the Guaraní and Tupinambá, lived here for thousands of years; they hunted, fished, gathered rainforest fruits and grew crops, mainly cassava (a starchy root vegetable). Brazil was a Portuguese colony from 1500 to 1889. African slaves were imported to work in the sugar plantations. Today Brazil's multicultural population is a mix of Europeans, people of mixed European and African descent, Asians (mostly descendants from Japanese immigrants who arrived in the 1920s) and Amerindians. Most people live in cities along the Atlantic coast, with fewer than 7 per cent living in the Amazon region. Rio de Janiero, known for its spectacular beaches, carnivals and nightlife, is one of the largest cities in South America and was the capital of Brazil until replaced in 1960 by the modern city of Brasilia.

In the upper reaches of the Xingu, Araguaia and Tocantins Rivers small groups of Amerindians continue their traditional way of life.

MAP GRIDS

MAJOR CITY

CAPITAL CITY

SCALE PROJECTION

Each topic is presented as a double page chapter for easy access to information. Illustrations have been commissioned and topical photographs have been carefully selected to bring each topic area alive.

Part 3 contains maps and text on the world's countries, dependencies and territories. The country entries feature a locator globe and a fact file, providing at-a-glance information about that country, including the capital city, population, the languages spoken and the major religions. Record holders are included for many of the entries. For example, did you know that the Dead Sea in Jordan is the lowest point on the Earth's surface? It is 400 metres (1,312 feet) below sea level!

The maps have been prepared by a team of international experts using the latest digital resources. English is used for country names (for example, France), international bodies of water (for example, Pacific ocean) and regional features that cross international borders (for example, Carpathian Mountains). Local name forms have been used for all other names. For capital cities and for some major cities and features the English name is also provided in brackets. These English names are cross-referenced in the gazetteer.

The relief shading used on the maps is based on a combination of altitude and vegetation and provides an idea of how the area would appear from space.

The flags are those that would be flown by a citizen of that country in their own backyard.

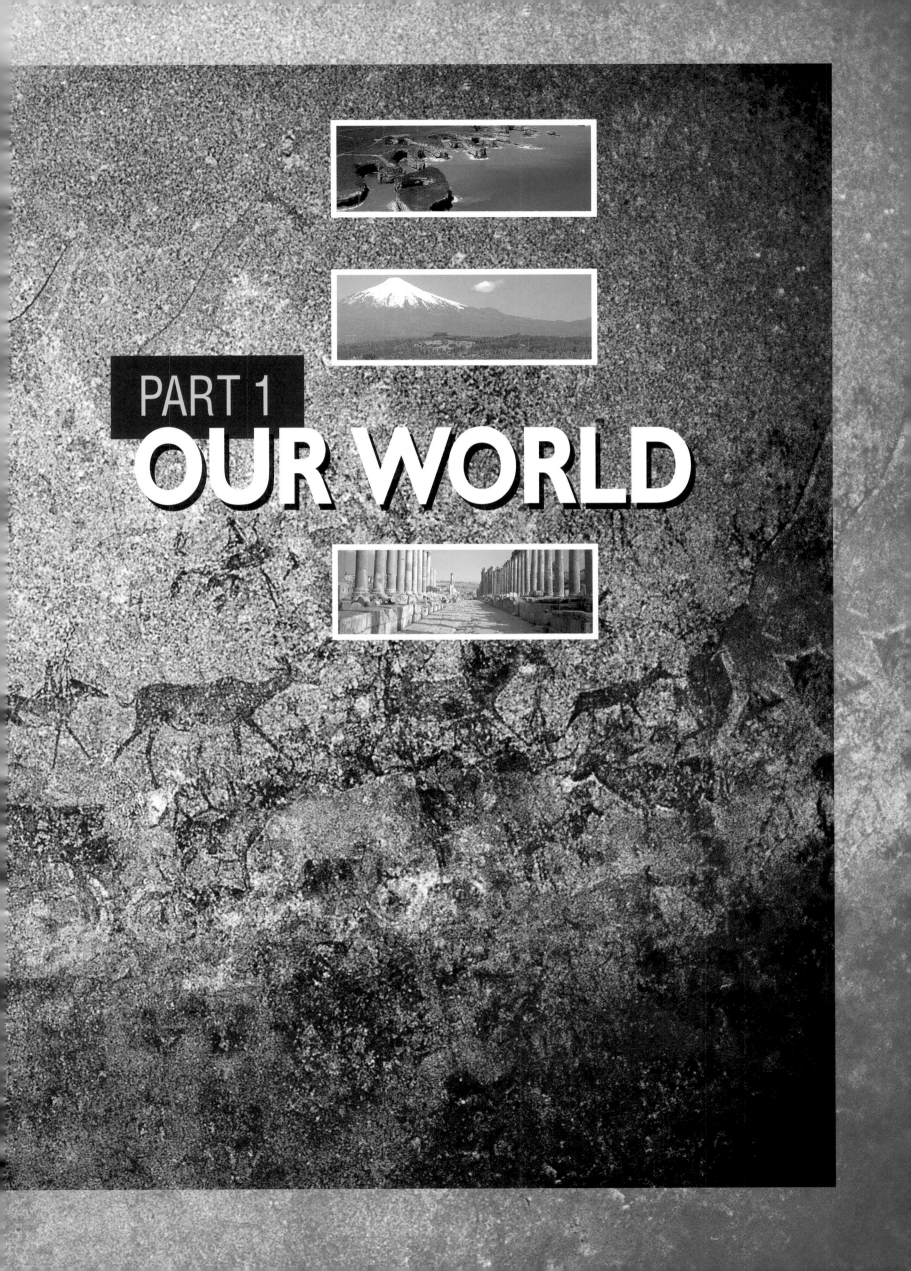

PART 1
OUR WORLD

THE
Solar system

Five billion years ago

The Sun was formed in a huge cloud of gas a little less than five billion years ago. The infant Sun was surrounded by a cooling disc of gas and dust known as the solar nebula, where pieces of material were forming, colliding, breaking and merging. The larger pieces, called planetesimals, grew from the merging of smaller pieces until a few large planetesimals dominated.

The planetesimals from the warm inner parts of the cooling disc became small rocky planets. Further out in a cooler region, where ices of water, ammonia and methane could condense, larger planets formed. They created deep atmospheres and rocky cores. The giant planets copied the Sun's solar nebula process on a smaller scale and created their moons.

Newborn planets

As the Sun settled into its present stable state, the pressure of radiation and the gas of the solar wind streaming outward blew away the remains of the solar nebula. Newborn planets swept up larger debris. In the process they were intensely bombarded, resulting in the craters of the rocky surfaces of the inner solar

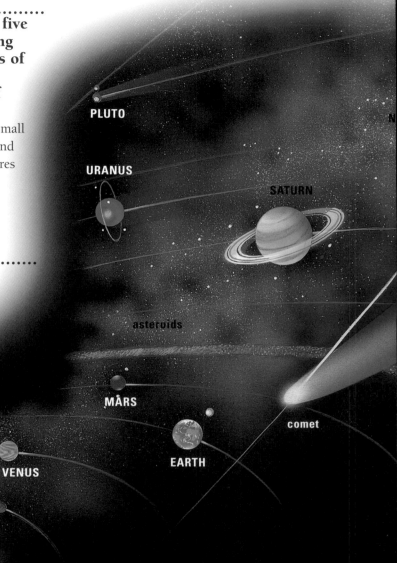

PLUTO

URANUS

SATURN

asteroids

MARS

comet

EARTH

VENUS

MERCURY

FASCINATING FACTS

- The solar system consists of numerous asteroids, sixty-three known moons, nine planets, one sun and a lot of space.
- Jupiter's diameter is more than ten times the Earth's diameter.
- Pluto is almost 40 times as far from the Sun as Earth.

- Among more than 100 billion stars in the Milky Way galaxy, one is unique. It is the Sun—the only star we know that has a system of planets, including one planet that sustains life as we know it. That planet is, of course, Earth; the 'jury' is yet to be convinced about Mars.

    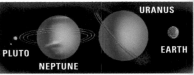

EARTH VENUS   EARTH MARS   JUPITER EARTH   SATURN EARTH   PLUTO NEPTUNE URANUS EARTH

system and the icy surfaces of the moons of the outer solar system. The solar system today has been largely swept clean of the debris of its formation. It is dominated by the Sun, which constitutes almost 99.9 per cent of the solar system's mass. Most of the remainder is contained in the two giant planets Jupiter and Saturn. Earth is less than 0.0003 per cent of the Sun's mass. The area of space inhabited by the planets is a flat plane centred on the Sun and about 15 billion kilometres (just under 10 billion miles) across. That's almost fifty times the span of Earth's orbit.

The void between each planet is sparsely populated by debris that orbits the Sun. The debris ranges from dust particles to rocky asteroids and icy comets—these can be hundreds of kilometres across.

The inner planets

The inner rocky planets and asteroids and Earth's moon share a common heritage, yet there are significant differences in their features. Mercury and the moon are geologically dead worlds with little or no atmosphere. Mars has had more geological activity and features Olympus Mons, the solar system's largest volcano. Venus and Earth are similar in size but are different beneath the surface. Both show evidence of volcanic activity, but Earth's activity includes moving plates of rock causing mountains to be built; this has not occurred on Venus. Earth, Venus and Mars each have thin atmospheres but the atmospheres of Venus and Mars are mostly carbon dioxide.

The solar system. Evidence suggests the Sun, planets and moons were all formed at the same time.

JUPITER

The outer planets

The atmospheres of the giant outer planets are quite different from those of the inner planets. Jupiter and Saturn are surrounded by deep atmospheres of ammonia compounds, and layers of water. Each of these planets is made of liquid metallic hydrogen overlying a rocky core. High-speed winds and cyclonic storms that may last centuries circulate the atmospheres of these planets.

Uranus and Neptune are colder. Their blue-green appearance is caused by methane in their atmospheres. The outer planets all have moons, the moons of the larger planets tending to be larger and more numerous. The largest moons, Jupiter's Ganymede and Saturn's Titan, are actually larger than the planet Mercury.

Most of the moons of the outer planets are pitted with craters from bombardment that occurred at the same time as the inner planets were created. Distant Pluto only gains planet status because it has an elongated orbit around the Sun.

Fury & fizz

The future of the solar system depends on the Sun's evolution. It is predicted that in 5 billion years, the Sun will suddenly increase in size and brightness, swallowing up most of the inner planets and baking the rest with temperatures about 1,000 times greater than they are now. Within a few hundred million years however, the Sun is expected to shrivel up with barely enough energy to illuminate the remains of its family.

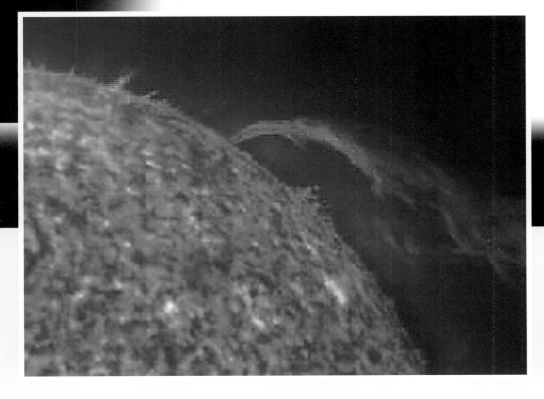

The leaping flare shown is a gaseous explosion known as a prominence. Prominences can sometimes be seen rising from sunspots, which are cooler spots on the Sun. Sunspots send out magnetic fields that can effect electrical equipment like computers.

Space exploration

This small craft, known as the Lander, was built to explore the surface of Mars in great detail. Using a robotic arm, the Lander samples Martian dust for analysis.

moons. Their journeys have shaped civilisation's progress. The heavens were our masters and rulers and dictated our daily lives, prescribing how we governed ourselves, planned our journeys and crusades and when we could harvest our crops or bury our dead.

The frontier beyond

The last great frontier for exploration lies beyond the Earth's boundary— space—a frontier that has captured the imagination of humans from the moment our ancestors turned skyward and stood gazing at the stars. Throughout history the spectre of what lies beyond Earth has captured the imagination of scientists and scholars, and spawned the creation of elegant theories of astrophysics, the origins of our universe, religion, mathematics and navigation, geology and medicine.

For hundreds of thousands of years, our spiritual identity has been driven by the endless patterns and cycles of the stars and planets and their

A changing view of space

A simple telescope invented by Galileo Galilei in 1609 transformed our view of space. It revealed mountains on the moon, Jupiter's moons and countless stars in the Milky Way. These were amazing discoveries, and the next 250 years of astronomy was devoted to measuring positions and cataloguing the stars and planets.

New technologies in navigation, surveying and cartography, driven by exciting new discoveries of our planetary system, not only assisted in our settlement and colonisation of the planet but at the same time heightened our curiosity in what lay 'beyond'. The radio telescope extended our view of space to distances once thought impossible. Stunning new developments in fuel and jet propulsion technologies and telecommunications opened up the prospect of travelling vast distances to planets within our own solar system.

The space age

The space age began with the beeping voice of *Sputnik 1* circling Earth in 1957, and over the next ten years the exploration of planets using unmanned spacecraft was underway with attempts to reach Venus and Mars in the early 1960s. In 1973 the United States *Mariner 10* spacecraft successfully flew past Venus and then onto Mercury where it captured what are still the only close-up images we have of the surface of that planet. By 1975 Soviet spacecraft had successfully captured images of the landscape of Venus and revealed a rocky desolate surface.

Today, United States space shuttle flights assume the mantle of ordinary everyday occurrences, but their payloads contain increasingly sophisticated technologies for the purposes of further studying our universe and the dynamics of the Earth's surface.

Pluto has a small moon called Charon. In the future, Pluto Express will visit these worlds.

A telescopic view

Trying to view space from the surface of the Earth is like looking through a dirty window—the dust and moisture in Earth's atmosphere prevent scientists from gaining a clear picture of distant galaxies and even the planets of our own solar system. Orbiting space stations such as Salyut and Mir enabled scientists to observe previously unrecorded features of our universe. The best known unmanned telescope is the Hubble Telescope, a 2.4 metre (8 feet) aperture telescope 600 kilometres (373 miles) above the Earth's surface, which captures exceptionally high quality pictures in infra-red, visible and ultraviolet light.

Some astronomical satellites, such as the Cosmic Background Explorer (COBE), have probed the glow of the Big Bang. In recent years scientists have pointed the Solar Heliospheric Observer (SOHO) directly at the sun 1.5 million kilometres (933,000 miles) from Earth in order to study the evolution of the sun and the dynamics of its surface, and so better understand the origin of our universe and solar system. Ninety-two sun grazing comets discovered by SOHO appear to have come from the breakup of a single gigantic comet more than 2,000 years ago.

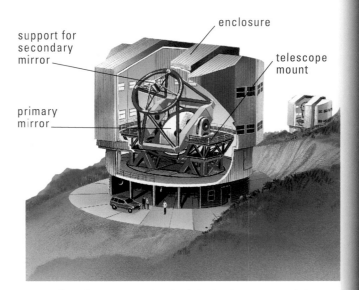

support for secondary mirror

enclosure

telescope mount

primary mirror

One of the four 8 metre (26 foot) high telescopes in Chile, called the Very Large Telescope.

The International Space Station is the biggest structure ever built in space. When it is completed in 2004 it will have as much room inside as the passengers do on a 747 jumbo jet.

SPOTLIGHT

- Since 1969, ten people have walked on the moon—all from the United States *Apollo* moon missions. The last mission, *Apollo 17*, was in 1972.

- The *Apollo* lunar landings have returned 382 kilograms (840 pounds) of lunar rock and soil, as well as photographs and other data which have shaped our understanding of the moon's history and our solar system.

- *Voyager 2* was launched in 1977. It passed Jupiter two years later and flew past Neptune in 1989. In mid-1998 it was 8.3 billion kilometres from Earth and still going!

As part of the Pathfinder mission, the unmanned Sojourner rover took X-ray measurements of Martian rocks.

FASCINATING FACTS

• Recent satellite probes to Jupiter have revealed that Europa, one of Jupiter's moons, may have a warm ocean of water under its icy crust and could support some form of life.

If evidence of other forms of life such as *Cyanobacteria* is found, scientists are in a much stronger position to explain the evolution of our solar system and the emergence of life on Earth.

OUR
Remarkable planet

Rock...

Earth is a giant ball of rock that is 12,756 kilometres (7,925 miles) in diameter. Its rotation causes it to be flattened slightly at the Poles, but if Earth were reduced to the size of a ping-pong ball, its surface would be smoother than modern technology could reproduce. Earth is the largest of the rocky planets in the solar system and because it is so bulky, it retains a hot interior. In fact, the temperature may reach 6000°C (10,830°F) at the core—as hot as the surface of the Sun!

...'n' roll

Earth's orbit around the Sun is almost circular, ranging between 147 million and 152 million kilometres (92 and 95 million miles) from the Sun. The point of closest approach occurs on 2 January each year during the southern hemisphere's summer. It is a common misconception that the small change in distance between Earth and Sun causes seasons. Looking from above the North Pole, Earth spins on its axis in a counter-clockwise direction, and it orbits the Sun in the same counter-clockwise direction.

The four seasons

Earth's axis of rotation is tilted at an angle of 23.5°. This angle is calculated relative to Earth's plane of orbit. The axis of rotation remains pointed in the same direction as the Earth orbits the Sun, and this holds the key to explaining the seasons. The northern hemisphere experiences summer in the middle of the year when the tilt of Earth's axis faces it more directly in view of the Sun. Meanwhile the southern hemisphere experiences its winter as it is tucked away from the Sun until the end of the year when it experiences summer, with Earth on the opposite side of its orbit.

Tummy rumbles

Down below Earth's surface, a mix of metallic nickel and iron form a solid inner core, and an outer fluid zone that reaches halfway to the surface. Surrounding this is Earth's mantle. The dense rocks in this zone flow over millions of years under intense heat and pressure.

Earth's skin is made up of lightweight rocks and is only 60 kilometres (37 miles) deep at the thickest point. Actually, the crust is a set of interlocking plates called tectonic plates [SEE NATURAL DISASTERS]. Heat in the mantle causes constant movement and flexing of these surface plates.

When pressure builds up between plates they fold along the edges to form mountains like the Andes, the Rocky Mountains and the Himalayas. Some of the largest 'mountains' sit just below the surface of oceans.

At times Earth's inner heat exerts so much pressure on the crust, that the crust opens up at points of weakness (typically along the edges of plates) and releases molten rock as lava from volcanoes.

Planet Earth travels around its orbit at about 30 kilometres per second (18 miles per second). At this speed it takes 365.25 days to complete one circuit. This is one calendar year. The '.25' explains the leap year every four years where a day is added to the month of February.

Volcan Villarrica is located in the Lake District of Chile. This volcano, like most others, sits on the border of two tectonic (interlocking) plates, awaiting the next 'bump'.

On the surface

The atmosphere tapers off into space and is all but gone 100 kilometres (62 miles) above the surface. Oxygen and nitrogen are the atmosphere's main ingredients. Oxygen only developed in the atmosphere when early life forms began the oxygen producing process of photosynthesis some 500 million years ago. The atmosphere keeps Earth warmer than it would be otherwise, permitting oceans of liquid water on the surface.

Above the atmosphere is the magnetosphere, a magnetic field that deflects most magnetic particles flowing from the Sun. Some, however, do penetrate the magnetosphere, and are channelled towards the Poles forming glowing auroras as shown below.

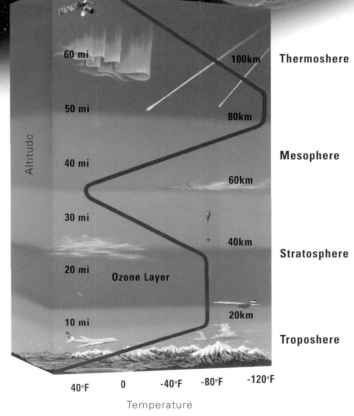

The atmosphere. The troposphere is the layer where life exists. The stratosphere is the next layer. The ozone layer, which absorbs most of the Sun's harmful ultraviolet rays, is in the stratosphere. The next layer is the mesosphere. The thermosphere is the outer layer of the atmosphere. Gases are very thin here, and this is where auroras and meteors are seen. The red line shows the increases and decreases in temperature through each layer of the atmosphere.

Temperature scale: 40°F 0 -40°F -80°F -120°F
0 -20°c -60°c -80°c

Altitude: 60 mi, 50 mi, 40 mi, 30 mi, 20 mi, 10 mi
100km Thermoshere, 80km, 60km Mesophere, 40km, 20km

Stratosphere
Ozone Layer
Troposhere

An aurora glowing in the magnetosphere, as seen from a space shuttle.

OUR
Dynamic Earth

Changing the Earth's surface

Not long ago people cleared forests from the slopes of the world's highest mountain range. Heavy rain washed exposed soil down the slopes into the river system. So much soil was carried downstream that a large silt island formed at the river mouth. Neighbouring countries then argued about who owned the island.

Apart from highlighting conflict, the story shows that Earth's surface changes, especially after human activity. Earth's surface is also being constantly transformed by falling rain, glaciers, rivers, underground water, wind and waves. Land is eroded, debris is washed away and deposited in low-lying areas. Erosion, transportation and deposition mould the landscape, often creating new features.

Ice rip

Glaciers carve out mountainsides and valleys mainly in cold, high-altitude environments. Made of solid ice, some of the longest glaciers remaining are between 39 and 73 kilometres long (24 and 46 miles) and are found in the Karakoram ranges in the Himalayas. Glaciers rip up rocks along the valley floor as they slide down the slope with the spring melt. Although they generally move slowly—2 to 3 centimetres ($3/_4$ to $1^1/_2$ inches) per day—glaciers are powerful carving tools and can move 4 to 5 metres (13 to $16^1/_2$ feet) a day. Glacial mountains

are easily recognisable with their steep slopes and pointed features, the legacy of years of ice erosion.

Situated in the high country of equatorial Irian Jaya is a remarkable 'tropical glacier', a remnant of widespread glaciation that occurred during the last Ice Age (11,000 years ago). Global warming has caused this unique ice environment to shrink in recent years *[SEE CLIMATE CHANGE]*.

Waterworks

Rainfall and water flow also change landforms.

Wherever water flows, it tends to erode and carry loose soil, sand and rock fragments with it. Rivers transport soil and rock material in a form known as 'solution'—a little like dissolving a sugar cube in water. Stones and rock fragments are also carried downstream by currents and they add to the abrasive force of stream flow. The outside bends of waterways experience higher levels of erosion as water travels faster around the outside bank. The slow inside bend on the other hand tends to attract a build up of sediment.

Rivers in mountainous areas flow rapidly because they have a steep course to follow. Such rivers are often highly erosive, and may cut their channels vertically, producing V-shaped valley profiles. Rivers slow down along coastal flood plains, especially where they meet the sea. Slower flows encourage suspended soil and rock particles to settle on the river floor, which often becomes quite shallow and broad as a result. This, in part, explains why floodplains become flooded.

River sediment deposited downstream sometimes develops into a series of small islands, called a delta. Plant communities often develop on delta islands. Deposition snowballs, as initial sediment deposits cause river flows to slow,

Aerial view of a river showing the build up of sediment that has been transported downstream.

in turn causing further deposition and so on. Sometimes deposition is so great that a river becomes blocked altogether.

Rivers themselves are constantly trying to find balance. Rivers bend (meander) to accommodate a larger water load, particularly if there is long-term rainfall increase, or when there is an increase in the stream's slope. Rivers however also 'straighten' when the climate becomes drier. Curved ponds to the side of a river are called oxbow lakes and are evidence of meandering in a wetter, flatter period of history.

Slip, slump, slope

Slopes are particularly dynamic parts of the Earth's surface as they are at the mercy of gravity. High rainfall on a slope, especially a cleared slope, results in slope soil becoming waterlogged. Waterlogged slopes are heavy and lubricated. Typically soil slips, slumps or creeps down the slope in this situation. Leaning trees and fences on slopes are a sign of such processes. In the worst case, an earthquake or storm can make a slippery slope cave in altogether with mudslides and rock-falls.

Wind & waves

Winds lift and transport sand and soil particles. Sandy deserts and coastal dunes migrate under the power of wind. Wind has been wearing, shifting and shaping deserts for tens of millions of years.

Waves and salt spray etch receding rocky coastlines. Waves pack a heavy punch and they just keep rolling in, chewing away rock, adding and sometimes subtracting sand from beaches, dunes and spits. Waves also shift sand along a beach and are responsible for the formation of spectacular coastal features.

Lateral moraine slumping, Tasman Glacier, New Zealand.

The features of glacial areas:
1. Cirque basin. 2. Hanging valley in a glacial trough.
3. Outwash basin from glacial meltwater.
4. Terminal moraine of a valley glacier. 5. Lateral moraine. 6. Medial moraine. 7. Ground moraine.
8. Arête or sharp-crested ridge.
9. Horn or sharp peak.

Wave action carved this work of art—a series of spectacular rocky outcrops.

Earth's ecosystems

Q: What do rainforests, temperate forests, coniferous forests, savanna woodlands, shrublands, grasslands, wetlands, deserts, coastal and alpine areas have in common?

A: They are all ecosystems.

Actually, a grouping of any one of these ecosystem types is called a biome. For example, while each tropical rainforest ecosystem around the world is unique, all rainforests share general characteristics, and so they are collectively referred to as a tropical rainforest biome. The world distribution of different biomes is shown in the map at the bottom of the facing page.

Atomic forest

Let's 'unpack' an ecosystem. Inside an ecosystem are different communities: plants, insects, animals and so on. Each species in a community is part of a breeding group known as a population. Each plant or animal in a population is a living system known as an organism. For example, a frog is an organism. Inside each organism we find organ systems and these are made up of organ tissues. Organ tissues are groups of cells, which in turn are made up of protoplasm. Inside protoplasm are compounds and inside these we find molecules, which in turn are made up of atoms. Each atom consists of sub-atomic particles.

So a grand coniferous forest is really a collection of sub-atomic particles!

Ecosystems are based on the interaction of their living (biotic) and non-living (abiotic) parts, each relying on the other for nourishment and protection. Energy and materials are transferred across ecosystems at different levels, ranging from the transfer of rain-bearing clouds across continents, to the latest opportunity for young plants to soak up sunlight after a nearby tree falls.

The right conditions

Ecosystems develop according to the conditions and limiting factors of their location. For example, tropical rainforests thrive, despite poor equatorial soils, because trees have adapted their root systems to draw nutrients from the surface of the moist, leafy forest floor. Open woodlands and grasslands tend to emerge in lower rainfall areas where seasonal variations are more striking. Desert ecosystems have produced their very own plant and animal adaptations. The Australian frill-necked lizard is well adapted to its dry environment, as are cacti that store moisture. It is even thought that some animals develop small brains to conserve energy, thus increasing their chances of survival in harsh conditions.

Plugged in!

Most life on Earth is supported by the continuous flow of energy from the Sun into the biosphere. A tiny proportion of this radiant energy is used by plants and is then released as sugars and other forms of chemical energy. Left over energy accumulates as organic material and supports further plant growth. It also provides a home for bugs, food for animals, and decomposition for fungi and bacteria. As only plants are 'plugged in' to solar energy,

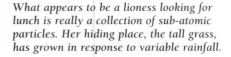

What appears to be a lioness looking for lunch is really a collection of sub-atomic particles. Her hiding place, the tall grass, has grown in response to variable rainfall.

their productivity determines energy levels in the surrounding ecosystem. Tropical rainforests have the highest energy levels. On land, ecosystem productivity is mainly controlled by the availability of water. In aquatic environments, the availability of nutrients is vital. Generally, land-based ecosystems are more efficient than aquatic ecosystems and this explains why forests do not grow underwater.

Who's for breakfast?

Life is tough in the animal kingdom. It's a fox eat bird world. Each animal and insect has a place in nature's menu. At the top a few privileged species like the wolf have few worries apart from humans. As shown in the illustration below, further down the menu are small animals, insects and vegetation. Unlike a restaurant however, ecosystems do not function properly unless the entire menu is available. 'No vegetation' eventually means 'no fox'. Food chains are important to the flow of nutrients and energy throughout an ecosystem.

Humans have made, and continue to make, many attempts to remedy past and present ecosystem damage *[SEE ENDANGERED SPECIES; HABITAT DESTRUCTION; POLLUTION].*

The food chain in the tundra. At the top of the chain is the wolf, who has no predators. At the bottom is the vegetation. In between are insects, small mammals (such as lemmings, ground squirrels and Arctic hares) and birds, followed by other larger mammals (such as caribou and Arctic foxes).

Fern leaves are spread out like huge solar panels, soaking up energy for the forest. Worms will one day feed on the fern's energy. Each part of the ecosystem depends on the other parts.

BIOMES

- Tropical rainforest
- Tropical savanna and forest
- Temperate grasslands and scrub
- Broadleaf forest—evergreen
- Broadleaf forest—deciduous
- Mediterrean shrubland
- Warm desert shrubland
- Cold desert shrub and grassland
- Coniferous (needle leaf) forest
- Tundra
- Undifferentiated mountain zones
- Ice

Life on Earth

Give or take a million

It's hard to believe that the Earth is about 4,500 million years old, but it's only in the last 600 million years that life on Earth has really blossomed. Animals familiar to us only appeared in the last 60 million years. Humans (*Homo sapiens*) emerged a mere 0.2 million years ago.

In the beginning

The first bacteria-like fossils are 3,500 million years old and blue-green algae appeared at this time. Algae was the main life form for a long time, and over millions of years, it slowly contributed oxygen to the atmosphere.

This build-up of oxygen stimulated the development of more complex organisms. About 13,000 million years ago, organisms began reproducing sexually, which allowed for evolutionary change. As more oxygen was generated, the ozone layer eventually developed. The development of the ozone layer meant that further biological evolution became possible.

The earliest animals, which existed about 800 million years ago, were simple protozoans that ate living organisms. By 680 million years ago, protozoans were a diverse and more complex set of multi-celled animals—mostly coral or worm-like life forms.

The 'backbone' of evolution

During the late Proterozoic Eon, animals without spinal columns (invertebrates) appeared. The oceans housed a diversity of animals, some with central nerve cords. Trilobites were a dominant form of marine life.

Then came the Ordovician Period (500 to 435 million years ago), which was characterised by increased species diversity. Animals with backbones (vertebrates) appeared. The primitive jawless fish of 485 million years ago were the first ancestors of fish, amphibians, reptiles, birds and mammals.

Flowers, fungi & forests

Mossy, fungal plants emerged on land about 450 million years ago. During the Silurian Period (435 to 395 million years ago), algae diversified and major fish groups appeared. Plants with systems for moving nutrients developed. Plants of the late Silurian to early Devonian Period are very similar worldwide and provide evidence that the super continent Pangaea existed. From 395 to 345 million years ago plants underwent a remarkable diversification, resulting in Devonian 'forests'.

Amphibians and fern-like foliage soon emerged. Fossils from the Carboniferous Period (345 to 280 million years ago) suggest that mossy forests were filled with spiders, scorpions and centipedes. Vertebrates began reproducing on land.

An ice age approached in the late Carboniferous Period, leading to less diverse flora dominated by seed ferns. Conifers (pine-like plants) dominated the Permian Period (280 to 245 million years ago). Reptiles with bone structures similar to mammals were present.

Scorpions and their relatives, spiders, have been on the Earth for over 300 million years.

1,000 mya

800 mya

PROTEROZOIC EON

570 mya

EDIACARAN FAUNA

600 mya

PALAEOZOIC ERA

544 mya

245 mya

MESOZOIC ERA

200 mya

The turtle on the left is from the Triassic Period; the turtle on the right is a modern turtle. It's interesting to note that apart from the fact that the turtle lost its tail through evolution, there's very little difference between them.

Bring on the reptiles

During the Mesozoic Era (245 to 65 million years ago), reptiles, flowering plants, birds and mammals appeared. The Triassic Period (245 to 200 million years ago) saw the appearance of lizards and dinosaurs along with turtles, crocodiles and flying reptiles (pterosaurs).

From about 220 million years ago dinosaurs dominated land habitats. They maintained this dominant position for almost 160 million years. Mammals, initially small, perhaps nocturnal creatures, possibly adapted from mammal-like reptiles. After mass extinction, frogs and toads appeared.

When Pangaea broke up, ocean currents and the global climate altered. This limited animal migration and determined the distribution and characteristics of the plants and animals seen today.

Even more life

Jurassic rocks include fossils of flies, wasps, bees, mosquitos, ants and marine crustaceans. Birds such as the Archaeopteryx evolved either from dinosaurs or earlier reptiles.

Flora was complex in the early Cretaceous Period (145 to 65 million years ago). From about 80 million years ago, conifers and flowering plants expanded at the expense of palms and ferns. Mammals also become dominant. Monotremes, marsupials and the first predatorial mammals evolved.

The age of mammals

An extinction event at the end of the Cretaceous Period caused the demise of dinosaurs. This marked the start of the Cenozoic Era (65 million years ago to the present) and saw the formation of the world's mountains; a cooling trend; and the positioning of continents as we know them today. Once dinosaurs died out, mammals 'took over', adapted and soon came to dominate.

The Tertiary Period (65 to 1.8 million years ago) saw major new vegetation groups developing. Grasses appeared about 50 million years ago, and grazing animals emerged. Hoofed animals appeared 85 million years ago; rodents about 40 million years ago. Major bird groups evolved by 50 million years ago.

Some 2.5 million years ago, stone tool users emerged. *Homo erectus* dates from 1.8 million years ago. *Homo sapiens* evolved in Africa about 200,000 years ago and migrated worldwide in the past 100,000 years.

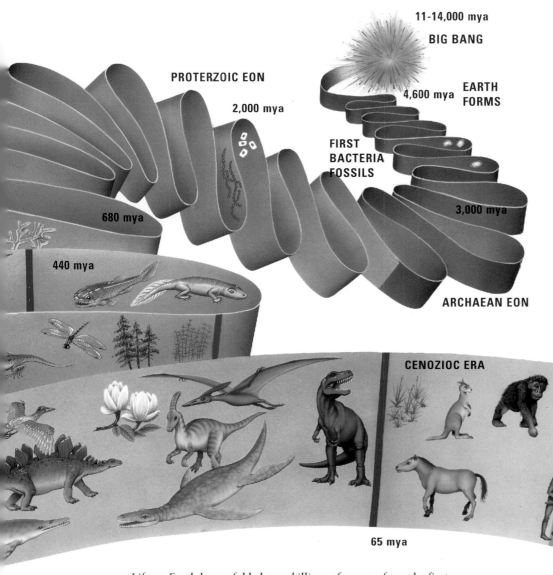

Life on Earth has unfolded over billions of years—from the first bacteria-like organisms, around 3,500 million years ago, to humans, who first appeared 0.2 million years ago.

SPOTLIGHT

- If the time since Earth was formed represented twenty-four hours, dinosaurs would have lasted less than one hour and human existence would make up less than the last four seconds.

- Life is defined as a closed system of molecules that can reproduce from generation to generation. Hydrogen, carbon, oxygen and nitrogen—elements that make up most living tissues—were available in Earth's early history. Energy abounded but the atmosphere needed more oxygen for life to develop.

They don't make pets like they used to! This furry, meat-eating land mammal about the size of a dog is an ancestor of whales. It lived more than 50 million years ago.

THE
Human journey

A different route

People have long known that humans and apes share a common ancestor, but this common ancestry goes back some 15 million years! At that time, Asian and African hominids (the earliest known ancestors of humans and apes) diverged, taking their development along very different pathways.

The African hominids adapted to woodland and savanna habitats and developed the ability to walk on two legs, while the Asian hominids continued their tree-climbing existence. Although the fossil record is incomplete, scientists believe that a later divergence probably occurred among African hominids between gorillas and the common ancestors of humans and chimpanzees.

Fossil finds

The earliest hominid fossils were found in the Olduvai Gorge in the Great Rift Valley of Tanzania. The anthropologist Louis Leakey began excavations there in the 1930s, and in the ensuing years, he and others found a large number of hominid fossils and stone tools.

Other hominid fossils found at Olduvai Gorge were identified as tool users and were classified as *Homo habilis* or 'handy man'. Tools similar to those found at Olduvai have been found at sites elsewhere in Africa and dated at between 1,800,000 and 2,340,000 years old!

Fossil remains of early humans in Europe were discovered in 1865 in the Neander Valley near Düsseldorf in Germany and were named Neanderthals. This find caused widespread excitement as it was the first discovery of an extinct ancestor of modern humans. The Neanderthals lived in Europe and Western Asia approximately 35,000 to 130,000 years ago, overlapping with the modern human species, *Homo sapiens sapiens*.

Increased brain capacity allowed *Homo sapiens sapiens* to develop greater intelligence and problem-solving capabilities. This resulted in the development of tools and, more significantly, speech and language. These skills enabled modern humans to develop strategies for coping with harsh environments, such as campfires, clothing, natural food storage facilities and simple cooking methods.

Archaeological evidence reveals a dramatic change in the development of modern humans around 40,000 years ago. Not only did tools become more sophisticated, but art became an important form of social expression. Art usually took the form of jewellery, figurines, paintings and engravings (often depicting hunting scenes). The widespread use of raw materials that could only have been obtained from distant sources suggest that trade networks had expanded. Campsites show evidence of more settled living, including artificial shelters, food storage pits, and well-built, regularly used fireplaces. Burial sites became more elaborate, containing ornaments and other cultural objects.

Archaeologists take many years of slow and meticulous digging to uncover the secrets of the human journey.

This ancient cave painting was found in Rhodes-Matapos National Park in Zimbabwe, Africa. It depicts the animals that were important sources of food.

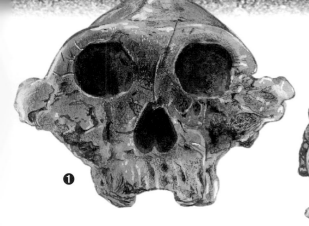

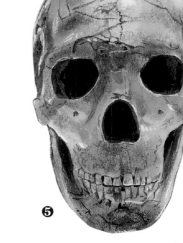

Rubbing stone and base. Australian Aborigines developed a highly effective hunting and gathering culture based on the production of efficient stone blades and points created by stone rubbing and grinding.

Human fossil skulls: 1. Australopithecus boisei. 2. Homo habilis. 3. Homo ergaster. 4. Homo erectus. 5. Homo sapiens neanderthalensis. 6. Homo sapiens sapiens. See how the thick brow ridges gradually disappeared, and the cranium grew larger, indicating an increasing brain capacity and intelligence.

Out of Africa

Fossil and genetic evidence suggests that hominids migrated out of Africa on many occasions, probably beginning with *Homo erectus, Homo habilis,* or the taller and more slender *Homo ergaster,* more than 2 million years ago. Changes in the climate may have been a major factor in these early migrations. One theory suggests that between 2 to 3 million years ago, a widespread drop in temperature led to the replacement of the tropical woodlands in eastern Africa by savanna grassland. The *Homo* species adapted readily to the open terrain and soon began to roam widely, following the animals as they moved north and east with the expansion of the grasslands.

To date, early *Homo* sites have been discovered at several Asian sites in the Republic of Georgia, in China, and on the island of Java in Indonesia. Early humans did not appear in Europe until some time later (around 1 to 1.5 million years ago), and this region remained sparsely populated until 500,000 years ago.

Colonisation on the scale undertaken by *Homo sapiens sapiens* required all of the species' newfound technical and social skills. Its success depended not just on tools and an ability to plan ahead, but also on the existence of extensive social structures which could provide the support and co-operation necessary for the completion of long, hazardous journeys into unknown lands.

Compared with the migrations made by archaic populations, the spread of modern humans during the last 100,000 years occurred remarkably quickly. Furthermore, *Homo sapiens sapiens* ventured much farther than earlier hominids, eventually reaching the Americas and Australia. These more extensive migrations were made possible by their greater adaptability and by the exposure of numerous land bridges during the last ice age.

SPOTLIGHT

- The first hominids (the earliest ancestors of modern human beings not also related to modern great apes) developed about 5 to 6 million years ago.

- In 1959 a hominid fossil was uncovered in the Olduvai Gorge. Named Zinjanthropus, it is believed to be 1,750,000 years old.

- Recent studies by molecular biologists have shown that there is a much closer genetic link between humans and the African great apes, especially chimpanzees, than was previously thought.

Many people believe that the invention and use of tools marked out the early humans from other hominids. We can see the development of human technology in these tools: 1. Scraper from Swanscombe, England: 300,000–200,000 BP. 2. Sidescraper from Le Moustier, France: 70,000–35,000 BP. 3. Bone point from Aurignac, France: 35,000–23,000 BP. 4. Bifacial stone knife from Solutré, France: 20,000–17,000 BP. 5. Bone harpoon from Le Moron, France: 16,000–8,000 BP.

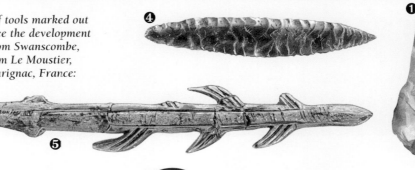

THE
Impact of civilisation

Remarkable progress

Civilisation has made many leaps forward over the last few thousand years, but what exactly has driven this remarkable progress? Cities! As cities developed and grew, they became centres of technological innovation, scientific knowledge and cultural enrichment, and provided a great diversity in social life.

Yet civilisation also brought with it many unwelcome consequences, such as the increasing destructiveness of warfare, the spread of disease, and the life-long bondage imposed on certain classes of people.

Innovation & adaptation

Farming had long been a way of life for many people, and the adoption of a sedentary lifestyle, that is, settling in a particular area rather than roaming about the countryside, produced many positive developments. An invention devised in one location rapidly dispersed to other locations, especially if the invention was useful. The wheel, for example, appears to have been invented near the Black Sea around 3400 BC, and within a few hundred years, it was being used throughout Europe and Asia.

Local needs were catered for and often new inventions were adapted for specific purposes. So, shortly after the emergence of the wheel, innovations based on this technology—such as pulleys, water wheels and windmills—appeared, and then spread quickly along ever expanding trade routes. With such ingenious innovations, no wonder the growth in technology was so rapid.

Technology & warfare

This growth in technology led to an increase in the size of urban settlements, and as cities grew bigger, conflict over land with neighbouring agricultural and pastoral people often resulted in warfare.

This stimulated the manufacture of weaponry. Early weapons were made of bronze, but by the beginning of the first millennium BC, iron weapons were being widely produced in the Fertile Crescent. By 500 BC, iron tools and weapons were widespread. Interestingly, ironworking in the Americas did not appear until after the Spanish conquests of the sixteenth century.

Science & health

Archaeological records indicate that early civilisations made careful observations of natural phenomena. The Mayans developed a calendar based on the solar year and lunar month, and could predict eclipses—a feat that required advanced mathematical skills. The Egyptians acquired considerable medical knowledge and surgical skills such as the cutting of bone in the skull to relieve pressure on the brain resulting from a skull fracture, or to treat headaches.

Permanent settlements had a significant impact on the health of their communities. People generally lived in close proximity to domestic animals, as well as to each other. This created a perfect environment for the spread of disease. When human populations are small and move frequently, the opportunities for parasitic infections to spread are limited. By contrast, urban lifestyles, with their permanent housing and large refuse dumps, attract vermin and insects, and

Spinning llama fleece in Ecuador. Simple technologies such as the spinning wheel enabled cultures throughout the world to convert animal fleece to cloth.

The principles of modern day architecture can be traced back thousands of years to sites such as these ancient ruins at Bosra in Syria.

Agriculture brought sedentary lifestyles and permanent settlements, such as this small rural village of Marou in Cameroon, Central Africa.

parasites spread much more quickly. Even more significant was the domestication of animals. These days, people associate animals with diseases such as rabies, anthrax and parasitic worms, but domestic animals were also the original source of infections that are now commonly transmitted by humans, such as measles and influenza.

Trade, migration and conquest encouraged the spread of disease. The bubonic plague was spread to other parts of the world by traders from Asia. Diseases carried by conquering armies were often more destructive than their military campaigns. For example, in 1520, the Spaniards inadvertently brought smallpox to the Aztecs, causing a massive epidemic that killed more than half the population and led to the demise of the empire.

Social hierarchies

The increasing division of labour and the steady enhancement of specialised skills in urban communities led to the development of more sophisticated social hierarchies. People directly involved in food production were often obliged to provide tribute payments (a type of tax) to a centralised authority. However, as urban populations increased and relationships became more complex, so the social distinctions became more marked.

The pyramids at Giza in Egypt were built during the Fourth Dynasty to house the remains of the rulers Khufu, Khafra and Menkau-re.

SPOTLIGHT

- Horses were domesticated around 4000 BC.

- In 1532 the conquistador Pizzaro defeated the Inca army of 10,000 men with only 168 soldiers.

- Smallpox was eliminated in 1977 and now exists only as carefully guarded samples in secure laboratories.

Horses and donkeys continue to be the main form of transport in many cultures.

FASCINATING FACTS

- The first major European civilisation emerged in Crete at the end of the third millenium BC.

- Classical Greek civilisation emerged during the first millenium BC in a number of self-governing cities, such as Athens and Sparta.

Traders & travellers

The spread & decline of empires

Long before written records ever existed, humans moved from place to place, either individually or in groups. The earliest records show they were driven by such motives as a desire to occupy more fertile areas, to trade, to fulfil religious duty and to seek new knowledge. Some people moved because of the fear of invasion.

The growth of empires fostered trade and treaties, both with neighbours and with more distant powers. The Han Empire in China, for example, had strong contacts with Phoenicians, Carthaginians, Syrians and the Roman Empire, trading in silks, iron, furs, glass and other exotic goods. Merchants also brought back knowledge. In the first century AD, a Greek navigator wrote of the Indian Ocean, where Hindu traders competed with merchants from the Red Sea and described Arabs dealing in wax and ivory, rhinoceros horns, tortoiseshell, and palm oil.

The Arab Empire

While Western Europe was fragmented and trade was declining, the Byzantine Empire in the East was the spearhead of Christianity against the rising Arab Empire. Mohammed's followers were spurred on by the idea of a 'holy war', which combined religion with military exploits. After taking Syria and Egypt, they swept along the North African coast and crossed into Spain. When the Arabs succeeded in dominating Africa, they then pushed east across the Indian Ocean, carrying Islam to India and overwhelming the Hindu trading colonies of Sumatra, Java, and Borneo, eventually acquiring a firm footing in Canton and other Chinese cities.

The Chinese Empire

In the period after the Han, successive empires had been established in China, some ruled by nomadic invaders. The Tang had subdued their neighbours and ruled from Korea to the frontiers of Persia. They also had extensive links with the West. When Canton was sacked in 879, the slaughtered included large numbers of Christians, Arabs, Jews and other ethnic and religious groups.

Western Europe

In the eighth century, driven by population pressure, the Vikings of Scandinavia set out in longboats to prey upon the coasts of Northern Europe. Sturdy fighters and skilled sailors, the Vikings explored the western routes via Iceland and Greenland towards the American continent, perhaps even landing there. In time, they settled in parts of Scotland, Ireland, northern England and Normandy and turned to trading. After the spread of the Arab Empire had been halted in the West, a new and fragile balance of power saw trade reviving in Western Europe. In 1095, the West felt strong enough to challenge Islam for possession of Jerusalem, and two centuries of Crusades began. The Crusades, however, did not hinder the growing trade in the Mediterranean. Merchants sought protection behind city walls and, by the twelfth century, fought for the right to govern themselves as independent communities.

The Mongols

The Mongols reopened the great land trade routes to the West and enabled Western merchants and missionaries

Ancient Roman ruins at Jerash in Syria. The Roman Empire reached its zenith in the first and second centuries AD. During this time, the empire covered much of modern-day Europe, from Britain to as far south as Egypt.

Vikings are said to be the first people to discover America. Here we see them coming across the coast of Labrador. They carried their shields on the side of the boat to provide protection against the weather, and for convenient storage.

to visit the East. The nomads who inhabited the great steppes were united by Genghis Khan (c.1162–1227) in the first part of the thirteenth century into a powerful empire, with its capital at Korokaras. The Mongol hordes provided an extremely effective army, whose tactics left all who faced it outmatched. They annexed Russia, ravaged Hungary, overwhelmed China, and set up the Mongol Empire. This empire was ruled in Marco Polo's time by Kublai Khan, whose ambitions stretched to conquering Java and Japan.

In 1258, the Mongols defeated the Turks and took Iraq and Persia. They controlled communications between these centres and enticed or forced skilled workers and traders to live with them.

It was only when the Mongols were eventually converted to Islam and became more sedentary that the Ottoman Turks were able to retake the Arabic Empire and once again cut off Western travellers from land routes to India and China.

A Viking graveyard in Denmark. The Vikings were great adventurers, sailing great distances across the seas in their quest for wealth and glory.

Remains of a Byzantine mosaic in Madaba, Jordan. The area in the Middle East now known as Jordan has been ruled by Assyrians, Babylonians, Persians, Greeks, Romans, Muslim Arabs and Ottoman Turks. This succession of rulers has left Jordan with many valuable ancient ruins.

World religions

Many faiths

Religion is one feature of the human experience that most cultures have. Religion has been the inspiration for much of the world's great art, music, literature and architecture. There are many forms of religious belief and they vary widely. Most religions involve the worship of a supreme being, although in some faiths such as Theravada Buddhism, the supreme beings play only a minor role. Some religions, such as Hinduism, allow great diversity within their practices, core doctrines and moral codes.

Religion has also been the source of long-standing disputes and local, regional and international conflicts. Religious beliefs have often been, and continue to be, the cause of great social conflict, particularly where two or more religions are in competition. Even within religions that have a core doctrine, comparatively minor differences of faith or practice can cause bitter divisions. Past tensions between Christian denominations, such as the tension between Catholics and Protestants in Northern Ireland, are are good examples of this.

The top five

The main religions in the world today are:

> *Christianity*
> *Islam*
> *Buddhism*
> *Hinduism*
> *Judaism*

One-third of the world's population identify themselves as Christians, with about half belonging to the Roman Catholic Church. The next largest religious group is Islam, which includes nearly one-fifth of the world's population. These two major faiths are monotheistic, that is, they are based on the belief that there is only one God. Both Christianity and Islam have their roots in Judaism.

Buddhism, the third largest religion, has approximately 325 million followers.

Hinduism is followed by almost 13 per cent of the world's population.

Judaism was originally the tribal religion of a people who traced themselves back to Canaan in the eastern Mediterranean. Although Judaism has a comparatively small number of followers (around 14 million), it is significant both for its role in the development of Christianity and Islam, and for its continuing influence on cultural and historical events.

Christianity originated as a movement within Judaism. Fundamental to its doctrine is the belief that Jesus Christ is the Messiah. After Christ's crucifixion, Christian doctrines were disseminated throughout the Mediterranean by Christ's apostles and by missionaries. Christianity then spread throughout the Roman Empire, first among Jewish communities and then into the general population.

Islam was founded early in the seventh century AD by Muhammad, a merchant from the prosperous Arabian city of Mecca. Muhammad had contact with both Jewish and Christian communities, and he came to regard the Judaeo-Christian prophets, including Christ, as forerunners of Islam. After his death in AD 632, Muslims expanded their territory beyond the Arabian peninsula. At its peak, the Arabic empire stretched from Spain and Morocco in the west, to Afghanistan and Central Asia in the east, but the Islamic religion was carried even further into Asia and Africa by Muslim traders.

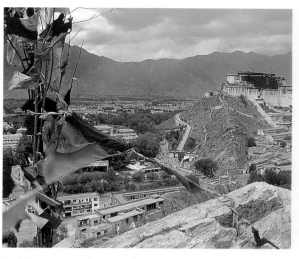

Buddhist prayer flags in Lhasa, Tibet. The Potala Palace can be seen in the background.

Muslim girls from Malaysia. Religion continues to exert a significant influence on the social and reproductive role of women in many cultures. The Islamic religion dictates very strict expectations in relation to social roles and responsibilities, starting at an early age.

Sikhism 0.4%
Judaism 0.3%
Christianity 33%
Ethnic religions 4%
Other 4.7%
Islam 19.6%
Buddhism 6%
Chinese folk religions 6.2%
No religion 13%
Hinduism 12.8%

This pie chart shows the percentage of the world's population belonging to the major religions.

Eastern deities

Hinduism has its roots in Vedism, the religion of the Indo-European peoples who inhabited northern India during the second millennium BC. The religion's sacred texts are the Vedas, which explore humankind's place in the cosmos and describe the roles played by various gods in the functioning of the universe. Hinduism has a large and faithful following among the diverse peoples of the Indian subcontinent, but it has relatively few adherents elsewhere.

Like Christianity and Islam, Buddhism is also based on the religious enlightenment experienced by one man. However, it has much earlier origins. According to tradition, Siddhartha Gautama lived in northeastern India in the sixth century BC, and was reared in the royal household. In his adulthood, Siddhartha is said to have sought enlightenment, which he achieved through a night of meditation, thereby becoming the Buddha or Awakened One. For 45 years he travelled India as an itinerant teacher while formalising his religious ideas. His teachings spread into southern Asia, where the first Buddhist tradition, the Theravada (meaning 'doctrine of the elders'), still prevails in Sri Lanka, Myanmar, Cambodia, Laos and Thailand.

Buddhism also spread to the east (Tibet, China and Japan), where the second tradition, Mahayana (meaning 'great vehicle') Buddhism, emerged in the second century BC. A more liberal tradition, Mahayana is said to express greater compassion and social concern than the more aloof Theravada Buddhism.

Ancient Hindu temples, such as this one in Sri Lanka, illustrate the ornate and extravagant architecture that was devoted to the worship of many Hindu gods and spirits. Few of these ancient temples have survived in their original form and condition, and many continue to decay or fall victim to looters and vandals.

SPOTLIGHT

- Only 13 per cent of the world's population have no religious beliefs.

- An increasing number of people in Western cultures are adopting Eastern religious beliefs.

MAJOR RELIGIONS

	Christian
	Jewish
	Muslim (Sunni and Shiite)

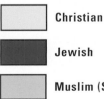

	Hindu
	Buddhist (including Shintoist, Confucianist and Taoist)
	Indigenous
	None

THE
Agricultural frontier

The first farmers

Farming is humanity's oldest productive activity and there is no doubt that farming changed the way people lived. The transition from a mobile life of hunting and gathering to a sedentary farming lifestyle in settled communities evolved slowly over many thousands of years.

It is probable that between 7,000 to 11,000 years ago, the cultivation of crops developed independently in a number of different regions, including the Fertile Crescent (a region stretching from present-day central Turkey southeastward through Iraq to the Persian Gulf), China, Mesoamerica (roughly present-day Mexico and Guatemala), and the Central Andes.

Agriculture's legacy

Agriculture has transformed both human societies and landscapes. The need to make cultivation more efficient encouraged rapid technological change. The use of clay, which was already known in pre-agricultural times, became widespread and people began to make large receptacles for holding and storing food and water. Other innovations that emerged were metal-working, the wheel (which improved the making of pots and stimulated progress in transport), and the use of sails on boats.

Early agricultural societies were based on small village communities. As the range of domesticated plants and animals grew, village economies began to diversify and food production techniques improved. These developments led to specialisation and to trade with other communities. Social divisions also increased. In many areas, elite classes emerged who were able to devote their time to religious, cultural and military pursuits, while living off the surplus produced by subordinate peasant farmers. The development of grain farming, some 10,000 years ago, ensured food production for large populations. It led to sedentary settlements and, ultimately, to some of the great ancient civilisations such as Egypt, northern China, and the Indus Valley. Since the 1800s, agriculture has seen the development of mechanisation, the use of fertilisers and pesticides, and improved varieties of both plant and animal species.

The green revolution

The population explosion in several developing countries within the past 50 years greatly increased the demand for food, and it became necessary to increase crop yields per unit of land. This ushered in the so-called green revolution, which involved using high-yielding seeds, fertilisers and pesticides. Although these products increased grain output, the increase has been at some environmental and social cost.

Brazil: a case study

Some of the impacts of agricultural change can be seen in Brazil. Before becoming a colony, Brazil's agriculture was of the slash-and-burn type practised by forest Indians. This involves clearing a forest patch, then burning to fertilise the soils: cultivation only lasts a few seasons as the soils become depleted of nutrients. The exhausted patches are then abandoned and a new patch of forest is cleared.

Grain silos in Alberta, Canada. Huge areas of farming land are devoted to grain crops in the North American grain belt. More and more grain is being grown to feed livestock to sustain dairy, beef and pork production. Such food production systems consume ever-increasing amounts of energy and other resources.

Secondary forests grow in these abandoned sites and, after some years, the reafforested areas can be used again. This rotating system can only support small numbers of people. It is not suitable for the type of food production that is needed for large, or growing, populations. Great increases in Brazil's population placed pressure on the Amazon rainforest where large tracts of forest are still being transformed by people wishing to establish farms. Currently, more than 10 million hectares (24.7 million acres) of forests are being lost each year.

Rice fields in Bali, Indonesia. Food production began independently in China when rice was cultivated about 9,000 years ago. From here, rice cultivation spread throughout Southeast Asia, reaching Indonesia about 4,000 years ago.

Monoculture

Modern-day agriculture is characterised by large-scale highly mechanised production with heavy reliance on fertilisers and chemicals. Parallel with this development has been the rise of monoculture—the reliance on a small number of varieties of a particular grain or plant. The genetic characteristics of plant and animal species is increasingly being modified to resist disease, increase yields and satisfy consumer tastes—technical and expensive processes.

Consequently the global agricultural system is being transformed both in terms of what is produced and how, but also in terms of who owns the farm. More and more, it is large transnational corporations that are gaining control of all stages of the agricultural production process from the farm to the table, thus creating a new 'feudal system' of corporate 'food barons' and dependent farmers.

Many farmers today use small planes to spray pesticides over their crops. Pesticides and fertilisers are used to greatly increase crop yields.

FOODS & THEIR ORIGINS

wheat	Fertile Crescent	**tea**	China
potatoes	Central Andes	**apples**	Western Europe
rice	China	**oranges**	Southeast Asia
corn	Mesoamerica	**sheep**	Fertile Crescent
sugar	New Guinea	**turkey**	Mexico
coffee	Ethiopia		

EARLY AGRICULTURAL CENTRES

Centres where food production arose independently

Centres where food production may have arisen independently

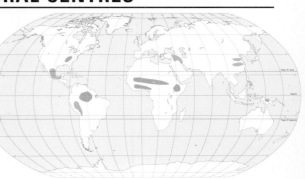

31

Industrial production prior to the Industrial Revolution relied on hand methods and energy provided by animals and flowing water.

THE
Industrial frontier

Impact of the Industrial Revolution

In the second half of the eighteenth century, Great Britain found itself at the centre of a monumental change in human history—the Industrial Revolution! This period was marked by massive and rapid advances in technology, and humankind has never looked back.

There were a number of factors that made Britain ripe for industrial development. Improvements in agricultural methods had reduced the number of workers required to produce sufficient food for the population, so these workers were available to work in the increasing number of factories. A growing class of artisans and tradesmen possessed a high level of expertise in particular technologies, such as machinery, that could be readily applied to production processes. Continuing improvements in inland transportation, particularly river canal, and road transport, allowed the rapid distribution of goods. Finally, Britain's growing empire provided it with access to vast overseas markets.

The first phase of the Industrial Revolution took place between the 1780s and 1830s and was based on the early mechanisation of production processes. The new industrial

When stored under pressure, steam provided a newfound form of energy that could move large numbers of people and heavy payloads.

The planning and architecture of industrial towns, like Huddersfield in England with its textile mill next to a canal, were influenced by manufacturing and transport links.

Old 'smokestack' industries of early industrial Britain, such as the Ebbow Vale British Steelplate mill in Wales, have all but disappeared from the industrial landscape.

system focused on textiles (especially cotton) and textile machinery, and employed water power as its principal source of energy.

The second phase of the Industrial Revolution occurred between the 1840s and 1880s. The manufacture of iron and steel was a major innovation at this time. Another big change was the powering of factories by steam engines. When this technology was used to develop railroads and steamships, the country entered a new phase of production and transport. The effects of this iron-and-steel-based Industrial Revolution were remarkable. Factories now employed thousands of workers, rather than hundreds. Wages and living standards increased significantly, and British exports, which included foreign investments in railroads, rose rather dramatically. The revolution soon spread, with Germany and the United States among the first nations to industrialise on a large scale.

Industry today

The Industrial Revolution's third phase began in the last decades of the nineteenth century. By now, the emphasis was on electrical and heavy engineering, and steel alloys and heavy chemicals were used. New factory systems combined electricity with new production methods and better materials. Giant firms, cartels and monopolies became the leading commercial organisations. Germany, the United States and Japan began to rival the United Kingdom for industrial supremacy.

The advance of the Industrial Revolution continues, with the rapid industrialisation in the last few decades of nations such as Taiwan, Korea, Singapore, Mexico, Brazil and Thailand.

Consequences of industrialisation

When industrial technology is applied to an economy, it generally results in a population shift from rural to urban areas, as agricultural employment dwindles and people move to cities to look for work. This process is known as urbanisation. In the nineteenth century, the population of the city of London, for example, rose from approximately 1 million in 1800 to almost 7 million by 1900. While new industries raised living standards for many, the urban poor suffered overcrowding, poor sanitation and pollution. There are many parallels between the social conditions in nineteenth century United Kingdom cities and those in rapidly growing, newly industrialised cities today. For example, the rapid expansion of an urban area such as Mexico City, which has grown from 3 million inhabitants in 1950 to about 10 million today, has resulted in acute social problems, including regular water shortages, severe air pollution, and a chronic lack of adequate housing.

Recently, the industrialisation of certain developing countries has had an interesting effect on the economies of the world's first industrial nations. Newly industrialised nations, particularly in Southeast Asia, have attracted manufacturing investment from the older developed countries to such an extent that there has actually been a decline in manufacturing jobs in the countries where the first and second phases of the Industrial Revolution occurred.

The United Kingdom, Germany and the United States have all reindustrialised to some extent. But today's era of industrialisation differs significantly from its earlier phases. New forms of technology, particularly in transport and communications, has meant that the contemporary industrial system extends to all comers of the globe, and encompasses most commodities. The Industrial Revolution is now in its worldwide phase, integrating selected localities as workshops of emerging global factories.

FASCINATING FACTS

- The main form of energy used in the first stages of the Industrial Revolution was water power.
- In 1994, over 33 per cent of the Toyota Corporation's car production was outside Japan. This is expected to increase to 60 per cent by 2025.

- World steel demand is increasing. Most of this demand is sourced in developing countries.
- The United States has the largest share of the world's total manufacturing output, followed by Japan, Germany, France, the United Kingdom and Italy.

PART 2
ISSUES FACING OUR PLANET

OUR
Watery planet

A drop in the ocean

Rivers, lakes and marshes make up only 0.03 per cent of the world's water. Polar ice caps make up about 2 per cent and less than 1 per cent of water is underground or in the air. Salty oceans account for an enormous 97 per cent of the world's water.

Clearly, the amount of fresh water available for all the species on Earth, including humans, is 'a drop in the ocean'. Fresh water is a precious resource that we must respect.

Water issues

Water is vulnerable to human activity because it is so mixed up with elements of the environment and everyday life. When vegetation is removed, water is affected. Air pollution affects rainwater *[SEE POLLUTION]*. Sometimes when farmers fertilise and over-irrigate crops, algae and salt infest rivers. Waste disposal at landfill and sewerage treatment sites often places a strain on nearby water systems during heavy rainfall *[SEE THE WORLD'S WASTE]*.

As polar ice melts, the low-lying Marshall Islands in the Pacific Ocean are drowning.

Time & tide

Sea levels are rising and most scientists see this as a result of global warming related to the enhanced greenhouse effect *[SEE CLIMATE CHANGE]*. Each decade, low-lying coastal areas such as the Marshall Islands are 'going under'. Even coral reefs cool down and change as sea waters rise.

Ice ahead!

B-10A is the name given to a giant slab of ice that snapped off Antarctica and is floating at sea near the southern tip of South America. It covers an area of over 730 square kilometres (450 square miles) and is 60 metres (200 feet) thick in some places. B-10A is a hazard to shipping and is seen by many as evidence that climate change is affecting the watery planet.

The Zambezi River takes a plunge at Victoria Falls, Zimbabwe. Rivers may be a 'drop in the ocean', but they are vital to life on the continents.

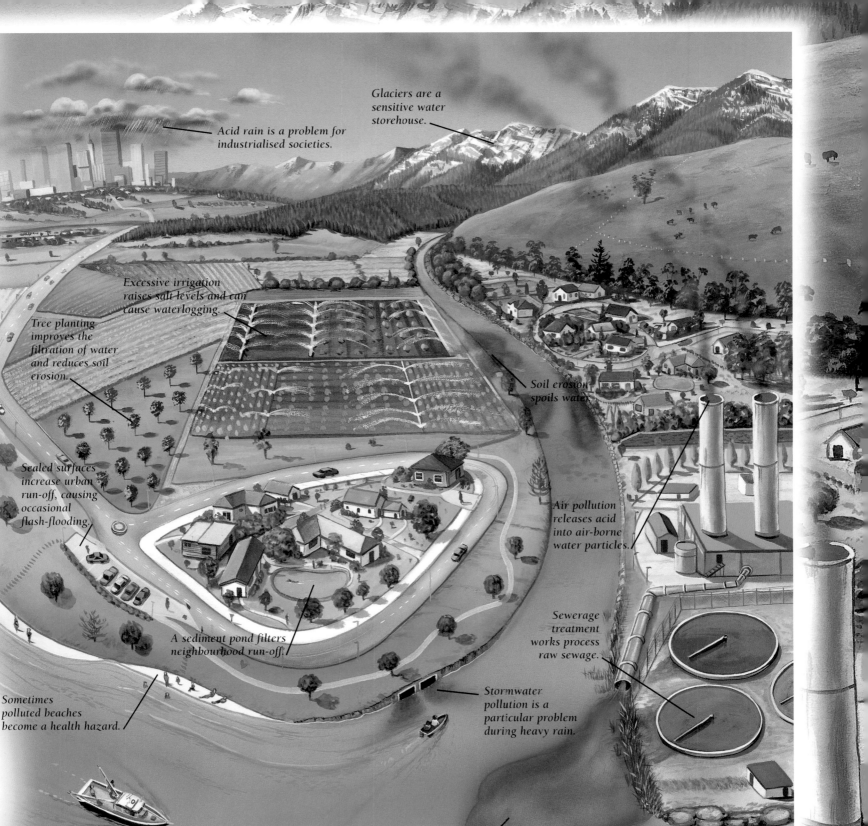

Acid rain is a problem for industrialised societies.

Glaciers are a sensitive water storehouse.

Excessive irrigation raises salt levels and can cause waterlogging.

Tree planting improves the filtration of water and reduces soil erosion.

Soil erosion spoils water.

Sealed surfaces increase urban run-off, causing occasional flash-flooding.

Air pollution releases acid into air-borne water particles.

A sediment pond filters neighbourhood run-off.

Sewerage treatment works process raw sewage.

Sometimes polluted beaches become a health hazard.

Stormwater pollution is a particular problem during heavy rain.

An industrial plant discharges liquid wastes.

The Himalayas. Some 11,000 years ago glacial mountains like these were more widespread. Today, the remnants of temperate and even tropical glaciers are shrinking.

SPOTLIGHT

- If the Arctic and Antarctic ice caps melted completely, there would be an 80 metre (262 foot) rise in sea level on average. If that were to happen, most of the world's major cities would become fish habitats like the mythical lost city of Atlantis!

- About 13,000 million tonnes of water 'floats' in the atmosphere. That's equivalent to 2.5 centimetres (1 inch) of water covering Earth's surface.

- A massive 200,000 cubic metres of water flows from South America's Amazon River every second.

- The Pacific Ocean contains an amazing 707.5 million cubic kilometres of salt water.

THE World's oceans

Mysterious places

Ever since civilisation began, oceans and seas have dominated where and how humanity lives. The oceans cover more than 70 per cent of the Earth's surface, yet we know very little of the dynamics of the oceans and the possibilities of harnessing them as a source of energy. One thing is for sure—the oceans are one of our planet's most valuable resources.

Because all oceans and seas are different, each has its own unique ecology. Ecological richness is governed by the ocean's proximity to land, the depth of the water, and the presence of warm or cold ocean currents. Certain species of fish, whales and other marine life can only be found in certain waters. Yet our oceans are rapidly becoming badly depleted of fish and other animal and plant life, and are commonly used as a dumping ground for large quantities of toxic chemical and nuclear waste materials.

Fishing

Fishing is the most important resource gathering activity of the seas. In recent decades however, overfishing of the seas has reached—in some places—crisis proportions. For example, the once highly productive cod fishing industry in Canada employing an estimated 40,000 people, collapsed in 1992.

Several nations grant licences to foreign fishing fleets to fish in their waters and this has accelerated the loss of fish stocks, as has been the case with the southern bluefin tuna from the waters of New Zealand and Australia and the Southern Ocean.

Resources

In recent decades, rich petroleum and natural gas deposits have been discovered in the continental shelves. The petroleum deposits originated millions of years ago, from the debris of marine organisms in oxygen-free shelf bottoms. Among the well-known deposits that are currently being exploited are those in the North Sea, the Gulf of Mexico, and off the city of Bombay on India's west coast. Improvements in drilling technology have enabled exploration in ever-deeper seas;

Fishing boats and trawlers can now venture further and stay longer at sea using sophisticated radar technologies to increase their catch.

drilling for natural gas deposits is currently being carried out at depths of more than 1,700 metres (5,700 feet) in the Marlim field, off Brazil.

Waste disposal

Unfortunately, the seas have long been considered convenient dumping grounds for waste—anything from urban sewage to nuclear materials. Chemicals from factories, fertilisers and pesticides from agricultural areas, and oil slicks from ships are also being released, often illegally, into the seas. Ballast water taken on by large ships on one side of the world is released on the other, with all its attendant marine organisms thus finding their way into other environments.

The effects of this pollution are quite severe already in some areas, particularly in the semi-enclosed waters of the Mediterranean Sea. Pollution threatens the existence of marine life, and thus, because marine ecological systems are entwined with land-based ecological systems, it will eventually affect life on land, including human life. There are more immediate effects, too, in some cases. Dangerous oil spills, such as that from the *Exxon Valdez*

Forests of giant kelp near New Zealand's southern coast. Kelp provides a rich source of nutrients and trace elements for the rapidly growing global health food industry.

in Alaska in 1989, threaten the livelihood of the nearby fishing communities who depend on the sea for their economic existence. Fishing communities in the Gulf of Mexico have also experienced this threat following oil spills from offshore petroleum wells.

Extending land boundaries

Many nations, realising the potential riches of the oceans, have declared resource boundaries under the United Nations' Law of the Sea Convention. Territorial seas are normally set at 12 nautical miles (22 kilometres). Exclusive economic zones, which include the resource-rich continental shelves, extend to 200 nautical miles (370 kilometres).

A nation can legitimately claim all its adjacent continental shelf, even if that shelf extends beyond 200 nautical miles (370 kilometres), as is the case with the United States and Australia. This law means that some small island nations, such as in those in the South Pacific, have maritime claims that far exceed their land areas.

No doubt, the oceans are an essential part of the world's ecosystem, and oceanographers are just beginning to unravel the dynamics of ocean currents and the impact they have on world climates. In an era of global warming perhaps our next frontier of colonisation and settlement will be the oceans.

Exploration of the ocean depths is now made possible by deep-sea submersibles, such as Alvin *pictured here. These craft can withstand depths of thousands of metres.*

FASCINATING FACTS

- The build-up of warm waters can have significant effects on weather patterns such as cyclones (also known as hurricanes or typhoons).

- Cold ocean currents originate in the polar regions and rise to the surface when they collide with warm surface waters.

A newborn humpback whale calf is pulled along in its mother's slipstream to save energy.

Climate change

Climates over time

For centuries the weather has been viewed as chaotic and unpredictable— a weapon of the gods—and it is true that the world's climates are indeed changing. Using sophisticated technologies, scientists gather information from rocks and fossils, the growth rings of trees, ocean and lake sediments and tiny bubbles of air trapped in ancient ice deep beneath the South Pole to build a fascinating picture of the Earth's past climates and to try to predict what changes may be in store for us in the future. The questions they are seeking to answer are: 'By how much is climate changing?' and 'What are the causes for such change?'. And although we have long been aware of the long-term variability of climate, as evidenced by El Niño and La Niña, there is still much for scientists to discover.

Climate change has had a huge impact on humanity since civilisation began. Archaeological records reveal periods of great drought that laid waste entire cultures, forcing massive population movements and devastating loss of crops and livestock. The interior of Australia, for instance, has passed through eras of lush tropical forests to icy wastelands to searing desert. Australian Aborigines, for example, had to adapt to these environmental extremes or perish.

Some causes of climatic change

The water cycle is the Earth's 'climate engine'—it transfers or exchanges moisture and heat energy from the Equator to the Poles in an endless cycle. The daily and seasonal variations in winds, temperatures and rainfall are part of this cycle; and in addition, regular cycles of climatic change have also occurred. These cycles range from thousands to millions of years.

Continental drift is the process by which the continents change their positions. Changing continental positions not only altered a continent's proximity to the Poles, but also involved changes in the differential heating of land and sea. This in turn influenced the distribution of air masses and the deflection of ocean currents.

Another cause of climatic change is the slight 'wobble' in the tilt of the Earth's axis —an event that occurs every 20,000 to 40,000 years. This wobble sets up tiny variations in the amount of solar energy reaching Earth's surface; just enough to trigger a slight cooling and the onset of a new period of glaciation—a new Ice Age. Changes in the Earth's orbit also occur approximately every 100,000 years with similar impacts.

Over the last 4 billion years the Sun has been getting hotter. But despite this, records show that the Earth's surface has remained remarkably cool, with temperatures altering very little since life began. The Earth's surface has even experienced periods of extensive glaciation and widespread freezing of oceans and lakes, called ice ages.

How then have temperatures remained more or less constant while the Sun has been getting hotter? The answer rests with the Earth's natural protective cover, the greenhouse effect—a gaseous blanket of carbon dioxide (CO_2) that keeps the Earth's temperatures constant, any surplus CO_2 being stored in 'carbon sinks' such as forests and the oceans and seas.

Global warming reduces the number of ice floes in the Arctic. This results in a significant loss of habitat for many Arctic species such as the polar bear.

The city of Venice faces an uncertain future with continued global warming. As sea levels rise many areas of the city will be lost through flooding, forcing large-scale evacuations of the city's population. The city's priceless architecture, such as the Grand Canal shown here, also faces certain ruin.

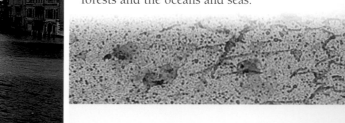

SPOTLIGHT

- The Arctic has warmed by twice as much as the rest of the planet over the last 150 years, but 50 per cent of this took place more than 60 years ago and was caused entirely by nature.

- The Earth's oceans have been completely frozen over about four times between 600 and 750 million years ago.

- Climate doesn't change gradually or smoothly; it changes rapidly and often with extreme events.

- About 100,00 years ago, in what is now Berlin, summer temperatures would have been 3° Celsius warmer than they are now.

Cataclysmic events such as giant meteor collisions with Earth can trigger extreme and sudden changes in climate. Many scientists think that such an event probably caused the extinction of dinosaurs about 65 million years ago.

Global warming

Since the industrial era, humans have altered the balance of CO_2 in the atmosphere, by burning fossil fuels and clearing large areas of forest. This has resulted in a slight warming of the atmosphere (approximately 0.5° Celsius over the last 300 years) known as the 'enhanced greenhouse effect'. This warming is expected to climb to approximately 2–3.5° Celsius over the next 200 years, which is enough to precipitate a major shift in the Earth's climates.

As global warming continues, sea levels rise, placing many of the world's coastal cities, such as Venice, and low-lying island communities, such as New Caledonia, at great risk. Bangladesh will probably experience a higher incidence of devastating floods.

Global warming will also affect the world's agricultural patterns. Crop growth will be enhanced by higher CO_2 levels, but plants will consume more water, leaving the production potential of the world's grain belts at risk of repeated crop failure.

The issue of climate change is one that affects us all!

Amadee Island in New Caledonia, like many islands in the Pacific, will disappear as sea levels rise, causing widespread destruction of local cultures.

FASCINATING FACTS

- Cows fart many times during a day. Given the large cow population, on a global scale, they deposit an enormous amount of methane—a greenhouse gas—into the atmosphere. To combat this scientists have developed the 'moo plug', a suppository that contains a high-powered bacterial 'counterpunch' that reduces the amount of methane produced in the cow's stomach.

- El Niño (Spanish for 'little child') occurs every four to seven years. It refers to the onset of severe drought along the western coast of South America. At the same time, across the Pacific Ocean, sea temperatures rise causing torrential drought-breaking rain and floods along Australia's east coast and in Southeast Asia. When the opposite weather patterns occur, it is called La Niña.

Natural disasters

Splitting headaches

Earthquakes, tidal waves and volcanic eruptions come and go like headaches. Your skull, like the Earth, is made up of several separate yet interlocking plates. When pressure builds up, disturbance occurs. With the Earth, the pressure between the plates (tectonic plates) is released through a sudden flinch: a quake. It is no coincidence that mountain ranges and strings of islands (archipelagoes) often exist along plate borders. These features form as plates fold against one another and lava is released. Modern-day lava-flows, quakes and tidal waves (tsunamis) like those in the Pacific 'ring of fire' indicate that Earth is still under construction.

Approximately 1.5 million people lost their lives in tectonic events in the twentieth century, yet this number is small when it is compared with losses through storms, floods and fires.

Blow-out!

Hurricanes, typhoons, cyclones and tornadoes have similarities: they are all caused by air rushing from an area of high air pressure to an area of low air pressure—like air rushing from a punctured tyre. They are strong, destructive winds that move unpredictably, usually bringing heavy rain until they eventually 'fizz out'. Tornadoes are different from the others, because they have a narrow path in the hundreds of metres they travel; they also have higher wind speeds, often exceeding 400 kilometres (249 miles) per hour. Hurricanes, typhoons and cyclones have a wider path than tornadoes, and their winds reach 200 kilometres (124 miles) per hour.

The monsoon season brings flooding rains to Vietnam.

Scorched lands

Bushfire and drought are often, but not always, 'natural'. Fires can cause major damage and air pollution. Wildfires across Indonesia in 1997 covered the wider region in thick smoke, making it unsafe to go outside.

Logging, agriculture and arson are the main causes of bushfires. Some vegetation, such as turpentine, is more flammable than others. Indigenous communities in the past were more widespread across the world and often managed fire through the use of small controlled fires for hunting. This form of fire management is now less common, especially in many remote areas.

Burnt out bushland. The land management practices of many indigenous peoples prevented destructive high-intensity natural fires.

A dramatic eruption at Mount Ruapehu on the North Island of New Zealand.

Drought is often measured by farm failure, but many areas simply do not have rainfall reliable enough for intensive farming. One decade of steady rain can be followed by years of drought. Such areas are referred to as marginal lands and often come under great stress when used for commercial farming. Drought and resulting land degradation have led to many farms being deserted.

Trees down, rivers up!

Flat, low-lying areas obviously suffer most flooding. Bangladesh is virtually a flood plain nation. In 1988, 90 per cent of the country was under flood water. Neighbouring China and India have also suffered major recent floods. The clearing of forests upstream in the Himalayas was a major cause of these floods as the removal of the forest meant less water soaked into the ground.

It is evident that some disasters are not so 'natural' after all, and there is a need for us to continue to learn about the limits of nature.

A bushfire rages on the far shore, lighting up the night sky.

The town of Lahar is buried under huge mud slides after the eruption of Mount Pinatabu in the Philippines.

SPOTLIGHT

Intense bushfires cause:

- species loss
- soil erosion
- air pollution
- property damage

Small fires cause:

- rapid regrowth of some species, for instance some species of acacia rely on fire for reproduction
- gradual species adaptation, such as the spread of eucalyptus trees across Australia

EARTHQUAKES
Devastation over the past century (selected events)

DATE	PLACE	DEATH TOLL	RICHTER SCALE
1906	San Francisco, USA	700	7.9
1908	Messina, Italy	83,000	7.5
1920	Gansu, China	200,000	8.6
1932	Gansu, China	70,000	7.6
1935	Quetta, Pakistan (previously India)	50,000	7.5
1970	North Peru	66,000	7.8
1976	Tangshan, China	255,000	8.0
1995	Kobe, Japan	5,500	6.9
1999	Northwest Turkey	15,700 +	7.4

Habitat destruction

In just fifty years...

Monkeys in Lombok, Indonesia. Their home is being destroyed to make furniture for our homes.

North and Central African deserts are spreading, burying crops, towns and villages. The Amazon rainforests of South America are disappearing, as 'ghost ranchers' clear them for cattle grazing. In northern Europe, forests are being eaten alive by acid rain. Extensive logging in Southeast Asia has resulted in the loss of unknown species and millions of tonnes of soil are washed down brown rivers like the Yangtze.

Pockets of wetlands—places of new life—have been filled in for housing, waste and industry around the world. Dolphins choke on plastic bags strewn across oceans, and each year fish and birds are washed ashore in oil slicks. Animals flee native forests as bulldozers and chainsaws move in.

Tree preservation poster. Trees are vital to the circle of life.

SPOTLIGHT

- With global warming, little known glaciers in equatorial Irian Jaya have shrunk rapidly in recent decades, destroying an astounding habitat.

- Each year, an area of native forest the size of Norway is lost.

As the Earth warms up in the Industrial Age, ice around the world melts. This results in altered habitats.

The atmosphere is warming up. 'B-10A', a giant iceberg, has broken off Antarctica, and the Marshall Islands of the South Pacific are drowning as sea levels rise.

Humans, through rapid industrialisation and commercial lifestyles, have brought more destruction upon the natural environment in the last half-century than over previous millennia.

Bigger feet

The ecological footprint is the area of land required to support the lifestyle of a nation. Japan's footprint is four times the area of the country itself. The ecological footprint per person in the United States is about 10.3 hectares (26 acres) compared with India's per person footprint of less than 1 hectare (2.5 acres). The ecological footprints of countries such as Japan and the United States are so large that resources from other parts of the world must be used to support their lifestyle. This puts pressure on habitats beyond the borders of the nations that require the resources. So large areas of land are cleared or disturbed for farming, mining and other activities required to produce the resources for growing 'footprints'.

Forms of destruction

For many places, soil erosion is the most serious form of habitat destruction. It usually occurs as a result of land clearing. When machines rip out trees, soils become exposed. With heavy rain the soil is washed away. Leaf litter and root systems no longer hold soil in place. In rural areas large gullies often form, destroying habitats and farmland. Soil is the building block and food source for plants. When rich topsoil is lost, it is difficult for native or introduced trees to grow. It is virtually impossible to re-create a rainforest.

Salt is an underground menace that destroys many habitats. Sometimes when farmers use

Logging is a much debated subject; there are opposing views on the way we should use forests. Tall forests and rainforests are home to millions of species and these forests cannot simply be replanted.

large amounts of irrigation water for crops, water soaks into the ground and sits in underground channels known as the water table. As water is added the water table rises. As the water table rises it carries natural salts in deep soil closer to the surface to the roots of trees and plants. Many trees and plants cannot cope with this salt and so they die. So habitats are lost. Animals and insects that relied on the plants no longer have a home. Ironically, the ground may become so affected that even the crops die.

The salt problem often spreads when rain washes salt-affected soil into waterways. Salt can spoil fresh water supplies, marine vegetation and fisheries. Industry also adds chemicals to rivers, destroying marine habitats. Europe's Rhone River releases about 3,000 tonnes of ammonia, 5,000 tonnes of chlorides, and 400 tonnes of arsenic into the Mediterranean Sea each year.

Logging and land clearing require removal of native vegetation; and although logging is now usually accompanied by replanting, an artificial forest is not the same as a native one. Complex and often ancient parts of forests are lost once they have been cleared, even though the new forest may appear the same as the old growth. At the same time, logging has become an essential part of modern societies, although recycling and the use of alternative products do reduce the extent of logging. Land clearing for agriculture requires the virtual removal of habitat.

The way ahead

Some conservationists argue that even the best recycling, replanting and education programs will not prevent increasing habitat loss. At the same time, these practices are encouraged and are certainly a step towards more sustainable use of the natural habitat we share with other species. There is a growing awareness of the need for industrial societies to consider their 'footprint' and the habitat destruction it causes. Technology and the fast growing environmental industry have produced great improvements in land management, but the bulldozers are still out there.

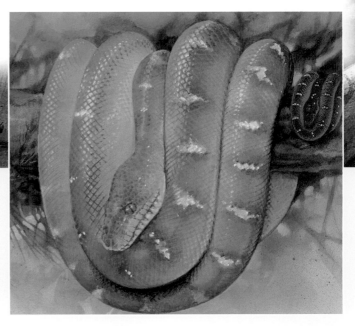

The emerald tree boa from South America (seen here with its young) lives high in the trees of tropical rainforests. Its habitat is fast disappearing.

Endangered species

Going, going...

Species are vanishing before we even get a chance to set eyes on them. While scientists estimate there are over 30 million species in the world, only 1.5 million species have so far been identified. It is a sad fact that many species will become extinct before they are even identified. A century ago, it was estimated that one species per year was lost. Now some 40,000 species are lost each year!

Once, thousands of slender-billed curlews made their annual migration across Europe and northern Africa, but in 1999, only three were officially sighted. Deterioration in the quality of its habitat has resulted in there being fewer than 50 mature northern hairy-nosed wombats in Australia. Their only habitat is an area smaller than 100 square kilometres. It is believed that there are only eight Vietnamese rhinoceroses left in the whole world.

Islands generally have a high number of endemic species ('endemic' means unique to a particular place). For example, over 95 per cent of the invertebrates and plants in the Hawaiian Islands are endemic, and over half of Hawaii's habitats are endangered. The Laysan duck only exists on a 360 hectare (900 acre) island 1,280 kilometres (800 miles) west of Hawaii. Hunting, and the damage caused to its habitat by rabbits (which were introduced there) has left an unfortunate legacy—its numbers have fallen to only 150 in recent years. Madagascar, an island off the east coast of Africa, has the highest endangered species rate in the world.

Most endangered species attention focuses on animals, yet the most significant losses actually occur among insects, small plants and mosses.

A mother beluga whale and her calf. Beluga whales are protected by international conventions.

What are the causes of extinction?

Extinctions do occur naturally, but the activities of humans cause extinctions at over fifty times the rate of natural extinctions. Species have become endangered over the last few centuries because of land clearing, forestry, hunting, poaching, land and water degradation, and the introduction of exotic species and diseases.

In the Amazon Basin of South America species are being lost as huge areas of tropical rainforest are cleared for cattle grazing, which supplies cheap beef to the United States and European fast food markets.

The northeast Australian state of Queensland has one of the world's highest rates of land clearing and this continues to threaten species. Recent tourist development at Hinchinbrook on Queensland's north coast has created controversy, with claims that the local dugong population is being threatened.

In Asia and other parts of the world, dugongs are hunted for meat, oil and leather. Their bones and teeth are carved into ivory ornaments. Some Asian cultures value dugong products for their alleged medicinal properties.

What is being done to save species?

Many countries have banned the hunting or poaching of endangered species, and international conventions protect threatened species like the beluga whale. Governments are increasingly developing laws that restrict the destruction of habitats vital to particular species. Local laws now prevent the removal of trees in some places, and people have been imprisoned for crimes against species and the environment.

The highlands of Rwanda in Central Africa are home to endangered mountain gorillas.

Another positive change is in the management of zoos around the world. Years ago, zoos were places filled with cages showcasing strange animals from far away places. These days, zoos promote conservation and rescue endangered species through breeding programs and research.

World Heritage areas and biosphere reserves have been designated to protect species and their habitats. Major political parties now include policies on environmental conservation as part of their election campaigns; and environmentally based parties have attracted growing support for the protection of species. They have representatives in parliaments around the world.

Schools teach the next generation the value of wildlife conservation. New environmental groups are formed each week. There are even websites that invite visitors to sponsor an endangered species.

Unfortunately, despite all the programs, laws, restrictions and public concern, the rate of species extinction is now the highest it has been since the last days of the dinosaurs.

A male (left) and female African wild dog. Extermination, disease and even attacks by domestic dogs have reduced the number of African wild dogs to between 3,000 and 5,000.

SPOTLIGHT

- Tropical rainforests only make up 7 per cent of the Earth's surface, yet they contain over 50 per cent of the world's species.

- Indonesia has one sixth of the world's bird species and one of the highest rates of logging.

- Steller's sea cow lived in the Arctic waters of the Bering Strait until being hunted to extinction in 1768, just twenty-seven years after its discovery.

Secrecy is sometimes used as a way of protecting endangered species. The ancient Wollemi pine is only found in a single valley in the Blue Mountains of New South Wales, Australia. To ensure its protection, its exact location has not been revealed.

Resource depletion

Valuing our natural resources

A century ago, gold was cheaper than aluminium. In the colonial period that swept the world in the eighteenth and nineteenth centuries, forests were seen as a nuisance to be tamed. Now forests are more valued as places of peace, beauty and heritage. Natural resources change in value over time for all sorts of reasons. Sometimes their value is not fully appreciated until they start to run out.

A report card

Research shows that one-third of Earth's natural wealth has been lost in just the last twenty-five years. An area of native forest the combined size of England and Wales has been lost each year for the past thirty years.

While the developed (financially wealthy) countries make up only a quarter of the world's population, they place more than twice as much pressure on natural resources as the poorer nations do. The pressure on natural resources is estimated to be growing by around 5 per cent each year.

Unsustainable mining

Minerals such as coal, uranium, oil, sand and iron ore have become the building blocks of industrial societies. More of these resources were mined in the twentieth century than in all previous centuries.

As the world consumes more and more, finite resources become more scarce and often more expensive. Mineral resources like gas are non-renewable—that is, once they are used they are gone forever. Sometimes other parts of the environment suffer when minerals are extracted in mining operations. While there have been general improvements in attempts to restore areas affected by mining, current rates of mineral consumption are not sustainable.

Oil and gas rigs, like the one pictured here in the Otway Basin off Australia's southern coast, have a 'use by' date.

What's green, fifty years old and changed the world?

Farming and food production across the world has been transformed over the past fifty years by the Green Revolution. Forests and land resources have been cleared and adapted for high output farming, particularly monoculture (growing a single crop like wheat over a large area). Scientific developments like fertilisers and genetically engineered seeds have boosted crop output and have encouraged a shift away from traditional farming customs in many parts of the world. This has had a significant impact environmentally, as many poor growing areas eventually fail to sustain crops, even with technology. As a result, deserts have spread across parts of Africa and Australia.

In addition, the control of community-based farms has shifted into the hands of large international companies, and traditional land care is often lost in the process.

Survival

Water resources are increasingly under strain  [SEE A WATERY PLANET]. Ecosystem resources like timber are often the topic of community debate. Some people argue that even when

Life on Mars? Queenstown, Tasmania, Australia, used to be covered in forest. Once most trees were cleared for timber, copper smelter fumes poisoned most of what remained.

trees are planted after the logging of native forest, full recovery rarely occurs.

Some people point out that plantations in many countries are harvested sustainably. Some biologists report that fast growing plantation operations may not necessarily restore biodiversity as they rely on the harvesting of a single tree species.

An elephant carrying fuel wood. Wood for fuel is becoming very scarce in some places.

In traditional societies, the gathering of wood for fires has become a major natural resource issue. As forests are cleared, less fuel wood is available and this has placed a strain not only on environments, but also on the livelihood of some of the traditional communities.

What can be done?

Different points of view on the issue of resource depletion are constantly put forward [SEE HABITAT DESTRUCTION]. Society, particularly wealthier societies, will have to decide whether to continue current levels of resource use. Some people are already coming together to live in more sustainable ways. Solar panels are a more common sight and technologies continue to improve the efficiency of other energy alternatives such as wind farms.

Alternative energy sources could be used more extensively to short-circuit resource depletion. Wind farms and geothermal energy are used increasingly in suitable areas.

Our shared future depends on the sustainable use of natural resources.

Once removed, native forest is difficult, sometimes impossible, to restore.

SPOTLIGHT

In thirty years:

- Marine fish consumption has more than doubled.

- Global wood and paper consumption have increased by about 65 per cent.

Hau Wui wind farm, New Zealand. Alternative energy sources could be used more extensively to short-circuit resource depletion. Wind farms and geothermal energy are used increasingly in suitable areas. Our shared future depends on the sustainable use of natural resources.

Pollution

A gasping world

India's cities are suffocating. In a single year over 51,000 city dwellers across the country died from lung diseases and other illnesses linked to air pollution. A recent study revealed that in just one year, 10,000 people in New Delhi died from the effects of air pollution. Most of New Delhi's air pollution is caused by cars.

Next door in China, Beijing's urban district is home to 7 million people. It is estimated that if the city's air pollution levels were reduced to World Health Organisation limits, there would be around 10,000 fewer premature deaths, 81,000 fewer cases of chronic bronchitis, and 270 million fewer symptoms of respiratory illness per year!

Air pollution

Air pollution is made up of nasty gases, particles and molecules. From a distance we see them as a haze. In fact, chemical reactions are taking place. These reactions are often made more intense by direct sunlight. Some air pollution hangs around all day due to temperature inversions. This is where warm air sits on cooler air and traps smog.

Using public transport can help to reduce pollution and congestion evident here in San Diego, California.

Pollutants like sulfur mix with moisture in the air to produce 'acid clouds'. These clouds eventually release acid rain. Some forests and stone buildings across Europe and North America are particularly at risk from this form of pollution.

This platypus was lucky to be saved after getting a rubber seal from a jar caught around its belly. Ocean and waterway litter is a serious problem for wildlife.

International conventions now discourage the use of chlorofluorocarbons (CFCs), because they greatly increase air pollution—CFCs cut holes in the ozone layer high in the atmosphere. As a result, Earth now receives larger doses of radiation from the sun. Pollution from CFCs has been linked to the gradual warming of Earth and higher rates of skin cancer in some countries. CFCs are released from certain pressure pack cans, fire extinguishers, refrigerators and some factory processes. Fortunately, 'friendly' chemicals have now replaced many uses of CFCs.

Water pollution

By far the most serious water pollution is 'invisible'. Heavy metals like mercury, lead and copper are unseen— and deadly—in stream and river ecosystems. Mining is a significant cause of heavy metal water pollution. For example, the Ok Tedi River in Papua New Guinea has suffered due to the heavy concentration of mining in the area.

Highly visible oil slicks, soiled brown water or algae-affected green water recovers faster than water containing heavy metals.

The saying 'It's always greener on the other side' is certainly true when it comes to lawns,

crops and nearby streams and ponds. People's desire for nice green lawns and fast growing crops is satisfied with fertilisers that nourish the soil, boosting growth. The problem is that a great deal of fertiliser nutrients are washed into waterways and turn the water even greener. Golf courses often show the signs of this problem where green slime or abundant water lilies form on the surface of ponds, thriving on the greenkeeper's fertiliser.

The global toilet

Sewerage systems around the world vary in their ability to dispose of waste. Often sewerage systems break down in heavy rains where storm water mixes and causes raw sewage to overflow into rivers or the ocean. Even deep-sea sewage outlets kilometres out to sea cause problems for deep-sea habitats. Sewage so far down takes a long time to break down and can spread over a large area with ocean currents.

On the ocean surface, litter such as plastic bags and discarded fishing lines often entangle, gag and choke dolphins, sharks and seabirds, like the wandering albatross.

On the fringes of many cities, car bodies and roadside litter are a

Signs and billboards may be good for business along Nanjing Road, Shanghai, but visual pollution competes with air pollution visible in the background.

significant pollution problem. Inner suburbs often deal with yet another form of pollution—noise.

Carrots & sticks

The preferred method of dealing with pollution in most places is to encourage people to 'do the right thing' by educating and changing attitudes. 'Carrots' like tax cuts and bus express lanes are often used to promote 'green' lifestyles. Many habits, such as burning household rubbish, are now unacceptable in many places where it was an everyday practice. Technology, such as the development of unleaded petrol, has gone some way to combat pollution. Many countries have enacted laws to penalise polluters and make polluting products like fuel more expensive. However, there is still much to be done to clean up the planet.

The many faces of pollution. On the water, under the water; on the ground and beneath it; on the streets and in the air. The age of mass consumption has seen the production of more pollution than ever before. Modern, anti-pollution technology has not yet reversed this disturbing general trend.

SPOTLIGHT

- About 1,091 million litres (240 million gallons) of oil is dumped down drains in backyard car oil changes each year in the United States. That's nearly the same amount as two *Exxon Valdez* spills each month.

- In 1998 alone, approximately 4,305,000 litres (947,000 gallons) of chemicals and 4,023,000 litres (885,000 gallons) of oil were spilt into United States' waterways.

THE World's waste

Toxic city

Little hands pry open floating remains. Black stench fills towering grey skies that cover a sick city. His eyes look into the oily deep of blood, fish gut, and chemicals. Braced knees resist the rushing red sludge; hands return to search. The young boy's cousin lines up fish heads along the sandy bank. Poverty has stolen their playtime. The boy is six and his dad sells the rotting pieces as fertiliser. Downstream, men without jobs guide the sludge into stinking holes dug in sand. Oil settles on top. This too will be sold.

The city of Chimbote reeks of fishmeal. Fish stench even falls in the rain, staining clothes. It is inescapable. The taste fills the air.

Chimbote is 400 kilometres (250 miles) north of Lima, Peru, on South America's desert coastline. Once a busy fishing port, it is now one of the world's most contaminated cities. Forty fishmeal factories constantly spew toxic waste into the air, soil and water.

Not surprisingly, residents of Chimbote live 10 years less on average than others in Peru. Lung disease is very common, especially among children. The natural environment suffers too— pushed to the edges of stark concrete streets, tin slums and ugly billboards.

People in the community have rallied, forming local action groups for which some were sent to jail. Thousands planted a forest that now makes up half the city's green space. Families travel to the new forest and wetland picnic grounds to escape the smell.

Many factory owners are millionaires who do not live in the city. Most refuse to 'clean up their act' or meet with concerned residents. Some factory owners however are now working with residents to convince other owners to take responsibility for their waste. 'Chimbote' is a story of waste, injustice and hope. The world has many 'Chimbotes'.

Toxic waste at Panguna copper mine, Bougainville. Too often, those with less power are left with the waste created by large, powerful corporations.

What a waste!

Waste comes in many forms. Industrial wastes include toxic sludge, liquids and gases; contaminated ballast water; packaging, and general solid waste. Many industrial wastes are released into the air and water as pollutants. Domestic, or household, waste includes sewage, packaging, food waste, disposable items and general solid items like old fridges or cars. Packaging floating in waterways can choke or strangle wildlife. *[SEE POLLUTION]*

But it is the waste we don't see that is often the most serious. Industrial heavy metal wastes containing mercury, lead and copper are the unseen killers of many waterways.

Plastic bags and packaging adrift at sea tangle and kill fish and birds. Increasingly, sewage is dumped in the deep sea away from beaches. This causes deep-sea habitats to suffer because the dark, cold water is slow to break down bacteria. The waste drifts across the world in currents.

While the impact of waste on the natural environment is a growing concern, its impact on 'human' environments is often significant, as shown here in a poor neighbourhood of Rio de Janeiro, Brazil.

While oil spills are usually unintended, they are deadly to marine life and very wasteful.

Deadly waste

Waste sometimes leaks or overflows from waste dumps (landfill) and sewerage treatment works, especially during heavy rains. Nuclear waste leaks have produced a number of environmental and human tragedies, making the issue particularly controversial. Radioactive waste has the potential to contaminate areas for hundreds of thousands of years. Military waste, such as unexploded bombs and mines, continues to take lives decades after wars have ended.

Throw away places

Consumers are increasingly 'seduced' by fancy packaging. An item in a scratched box is usually the last one to sell. Two 'skins' are expected in throw-away societies. Wares are packaged then wrapped. On the other hand, fast food is wrapped then packaged, even if only for a ten-second walk to the bin or a table.

Disposable razors, plates, cups, nappies and utensils, and junk mail, have taken their toll on the environment, even in the face of increased recycling.

In stark contrast, many people in poorer nations live in waste dumps, gathering food and other recyclable items from rubbish, and raising small sums of money to survive.

Some people argue that continued recycling efforts and smarter technology would solve waste problems. Others believe there is a need to simplify consumer lifestyles in wealthy societies so that they do not produce as much waste in the first place.

Consumer societies are big producers of waste, but recycling is becoming part of the household routine.

The woman photographed here with her two children is part of a group advocating the rights of women who pick waste in her community at Pune, India.

GLOBAL
Nuclear industry

Costs of human error

'Good evening comrades. All of you know that there has been an incredible misfortune; the accident at the Chernobyl nuclear plant. It has painfully affected the Soviet people and shocked the international community. For the first time we confront the real force of nuclear energy, out of control.'

Soviet President Mikhail Gorbachev, 26 April 1986

The world's worst nuclear power accident occurred at Chernobyl, located 100 kilometres (62 miles) north of Kiev in the former USSR (now Ukraine). While testing a reactor, many safety procedures were disregarded, and so the chain reaction in the reactor went out of control. This created an explosion that blew off the reactor's heavy steel and concrete lid, spewing out a huge cloud of radioactive smoke and dust.

The Chernobyl accident killed more than thirty people immediately and, because of the high radiation levels in the surrounding 60 kilometre (37 mile) radius, 135,000 people had to be evacuated within hours. Thousands more later died from effects of the accident. Over the period 27 April to mid-August 1986, about 116,000 people were evacuated to protect them against high levels of radiation. An 'exclusion zone' was established on the most contaminated territories and was extended into the nearby countries of Belarus, Russia and Ukraine.

Nuclear fallout

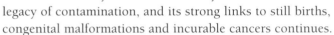

As the fallout spread, Europe was plunged into an environmental crisis for which it was completely unprepared. Milk from Sweden to the Netherlands was declared unfit for human consumption; sugar beet—the principal source of sugar in Europe—was declared inedible; and millions of tonnes of agricultural produce was dumped as a result of radioactive contamination. Health authorities across Europe were placed on red alert, as helpless onlookers watched the toxic cloud of radioactive dust being blown across one of the most populated regions on Earth. Fifteen years later Chernobyl's legacy of contamination, and its strong links to still births, congenital malformations and incurable cancers continues.

A nuclear medicine scanner detects radiation emitted from minute quantities of a radioactive substance. The tracer targets a particular part of the body such as a bone or vital organ and is then scanned, providing detailed data about the disease.

A better industry?

The nuclear energy industry is an infant industry—born out of the convenient marriage of a dwindling fossil fuel base and a powerful new energy technology developed at the end of World War II.

The nuclear fuel cycle is a remarkably simple process. It begins with the extraction of uranium from the ground. This is refined to produce the raw material required by nuclear reactors. A reactor produces heat, which converts water to steam, which spins the turbines of electricity generators. The cycle ends with radioactive waste. To some degree, this waste can be reprocessed and reused in fast breeder reactors. Ultimately though, the resultant waste is extremely toxic and so it is not only difficult to store and handle, but also expensive.

Today, the nuclear power industry is increasingly being regarded as an outmoded and dangerous technology that has cost trillions of dollars for very little benefit—investment that might have been better spent on developing the offshore wind industry, photovoltaics or other forms of 'clean energy', such as tidal power or geothermal energy.

The industry has been dogged by unfulfilled promises of an

Protesters at a proposed uranium mine site at Jabiluka in Australia's Northern Territory. The mine site is near the ecologically sensitive Kakadu National Park and near the Ranger uranium mine. In mid 2000, it was revealed that uranium has in fact leaked into the Park from the Ranger mine.

inexhaustible, clean and cheap source of energy. Consequently there have been no new reactors constructed in Europe or the United States since the 1970s. To many observers, a disturbing trend is the continued refurbishment of old and highly dangerous Soviet-designed reactors in Eastern Europe, as well as the construction of reactors in developing countries whose expertise in waste management and reactor security is frequently inadequate.

But despite these drawbacks associated with the use of nuclear energy in reactors to produce electricity, nuclear energy also has a multitude of highly beneficial uses, such as X-rays in medicine and scientific research. X-rays are also used to detect minute stress fractures in the wings and fuselage of jet aircraft and space vehicles.

High standards of control of radioactive materials used in the nuclear power industry are essential. When spillages or leaks occur, specialist teams of workers in protective clothing are required to contain and minimise the spread of radioactive dust or liquids.

FASCINATING FACTS

- Naturally occurring radioactive materials are widespread throughout the environment, although concentrations are very low and they are not normally harmful.

- The annual fuel requirement for a 100 MWe light water reactor is about 25 tonnes of enriched uranium oxide. This requires the mining and milling of some 50,000 tonnes of ore to provide 200 tonnes of uranium oxide concentrate (U_3O_2) from the mine.

THE
Population explosion

More & more of us

Amazingly, the number of people born since 1950 is higher than the number born all throughout history prior to 1950. Over 6 billion people now live on Earth and the figure is doubling every forty years or so.

Prior to the Industrial Revolution ▶ *[SEE THE INDUSTRIAL FRONTIER]*, the world's population grew very slowly and sometimes declined. Even though women commonly gave birth to eight to twelve children, one out of every four children died before their first birthday and another would die before reaching the age of five. This was mostly due to infectious diseases and poor diet.

Today, population growth is fastest in poorer, developing nations. India and China alone make up one-third of the world's population. In contrast, the populations of many wealthier nations, such as Australia and Italy, would actually decrease if it were not for immigration.

While some European cities are experiencing population decline, overall there has been a massive movement of people into major cities, especially in Asia, South America and Africa ▶ *[SEE THE URBAN EXPLOSION]*. Over 25 million people now live in Mexico City!

Population debate

There is much debate about today's rapid population growth and the issue of poverty.

Some argue that resource shortages and world poverty would be reduced if poor nations planned smaller families to slow down population growth. Others disagree, pointing out that while three-quarters of the world's population is poor, they only have access to one-quarter of the world's resources. So it is wealthy nations—with lower population growth rates—that are responsible for resources running out, because they use up so much.

It is argued that poverty is related to the uneven share of food, energy, water and other goods and services, rather than to population growth. It is also argued that rapid population growth can be a result of poverty rather than the cause. Poor parents know that a larger family is needed to increase the chance of some children surviving to support them in old age.

These children from Sudan are victims of famine. Even though an estimated 36,000 children die each day due to poor health and diet, the world's population continues to rise.

Young societies; old societies

While the child populations of developing nations increase rapidly, life expectancy in such countries is often only forty to fifty years. On the other hand, wealthy, developed nations have pro-portionately smaller youth populations. This is because parents are choosing to have fewer children. They also have ready access to affordable contraception. At the same time,

Millions of people have moved into cities over the past fifty years, as evident here in Bangladesh. Usually the move is encouraged by hopes of finding a job. Unfortunately, there are usually not enough jobs to go around. Despite this, most people stay in the city, often trying to earn money as cleaners, porters or as taxi or rickshaw drivers.

improved health standards and technology-assisted medical services have enabled people in developed countries to live far longer than ever before.

Transport services in Sudan, Africa, have not kept pace with population growth.

Will we have a baby?

The number of births in a population in a given year (the fertility rate) obviously has a major influence on population size. Fertility rates vary from place to place and over time due to many factors. The table below details eight major fertility factors.

The future?

Academics predict that the world's population will be 12 billion by 2050. Africa, Asia and South and Central America will more than ever be home to most of the world's people.

A growing world population provides more opportunities for sharing.

FERTILITY FACTORS

Health conditions	Diet, sanitation and access to medical treatment have a large influence on fertility levels.
Economic conditions	Generally, developed societies experience faster population growth rates in times of prosperity, and vice versa. For example, fertility declined during the hardship of the Great Depression in 1930–31.
	Famine increases poverty and can dramatically reduce fertility rates for a time due to poor diet. This has been experienced in Africa in recent decades.
Wealth	While the wealthy may be able to 'afford' to raise more children, the poor usually have more children.
Contraceptives and education	Education about the use of contraceptives is more widespread in developed countries.
War	When large numbers of men go to war, fertility rates drop. On returning from war, however, fertility rates increase dramatically. This was experienced in the late 1940s after World War II, producing a generation known as 'Baby Boomers'.
Cultural attitudes	In some communities it may be common for parents to have two children. In others, eight to ten children may be the norm.
Religious reasons	There may be religious expectations for parents to have larger numbers of children. This was particularly the case for Roman Catholics in previous generations. There may also be prohibitions on the use of contraception.
Political requirements	Government decisions to encourage smaller families through the promotion of contraceptives have affected rates of population growth. China's 'one child' policy forbids parents from having more than one child. This has not been enough to stop China's population increasing beyond 1.2 billion, but it has slowed down the rate of growth.

THE Urban explosion

A growing trend

For four millennia, cities have been centres of religion, culture and economic activity. Yet cities accounted for a very small percentage of the global population until the last half of the nineteenth century. Only two hundred years ago, most people lived in rural settlements. These were usually small and self-sufficient. A tiny 3 per cent of the world's people lived in large urban areas or cities, but by 1950, the urban–rural balance had shifted and some 30 per cent of people lived in cities. By 2025, it is expected that large urban areas will account for a massive 60 per cent of the world's population!

For the first time in history, the concentration of a growing population in cities around the world constitutes a crucial turning point in the long-term outlook for humanity.

The city's changing role

Cities have long been the centrepoint of social power, culture and religion, and they have now assumed a new economic role as centres of production, consumption and exchange—a consequence of the evolution and spread of industry that began with the Industrial Revolution between the 1780s and 1830s. London's population, for example, grew by over 6 million people between 1800 and 1900, as new industries attracted poor and unemployed rural workers.

More recently, the process of industrialisation has transformed the economies of developing nations, triggering staggering rates of urban

Karachi, Pakistan, is a city choked by narrow streets unable to cope with modern motor transport—a problem common to many rapidly growing cities in developing countries.

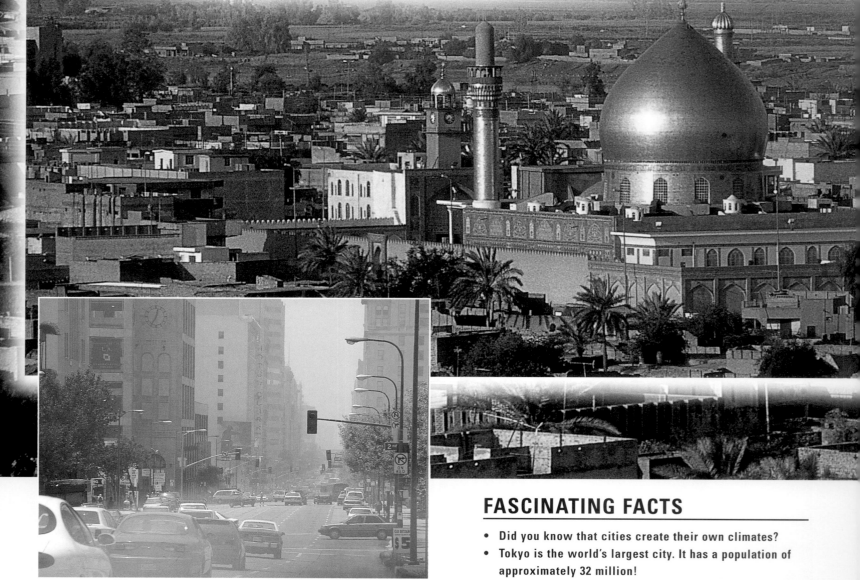

Los Angeles, United States, a sprawling city characterised by heavy dependence on the motor car, produces high levels of smog—a deadly combination of fog and exhaust fumes.

FASCINATING FACTS

- Did you know that cities create their own climates?
- Tokyo is the world's largest city. It has a population of approximately 32 million!
- Children born in large cities in developing countries have about a 30 per cent higher risk of dying before they reach the age of five than those born in smaller cities.

growth in Asia, Latin America and Africa.

'World cities' such as Tokyo, New York, London and Berlin are no longer 'smokestack' industrial cities. As a result of the technological revolution in telecommunications and transport, they have been reborn as 'information cities'. Cities now form a global network controlling the flow of resources, money and information, as well as people and their skills, across the globe. Such cities can even dictate the life chances of the poorest rural peasant in Africa or Asia.

The developing world

War, famine and changing economic conditions in the countryside have all contributed to the spectacular increase in city populations in the developing world. Massive numbers of rural workers have flocked to cities in the hope of finding work and prosperity.

Many of these cities are already unable to cope with these migrations and are experiencing critical environmental degradation. The urban poor are the most vulnerable group. They are forced to live in squatter settlements in sub-standard housing with little or no access to clean water, sanitation or primary health care. Squatter settlements such as the *bustees* of Calcutta or the *favelas* of Rio de Janeiro are frequently found in

areas of the city that are most prone to natural hazards, such as flooding, and so provide little protection for the inhabitants.

Sustainable cities

Cities have become synonymous with growth, and they are increasingly in crisis, struggling to meet the most basic needs of their inhabitants. Some of the challenges facing cities include:

- **the emergence of a growing underclass of unemployed**
- **insufficient housing**
- **overloaded and overcrowded transport systems**
- **air, water and noise pollution**
- **inadequate sanitation and water supplies**
- **increasing social problems of rising crime rates, suicide, drug and alcohol abuse**
- **homelessness.**

The concept of 'the sustainable city' is being raised by urban planners as the most effective means of addressing the problems of urban explosion. A sustainable city is one that delivers a balance between population size and use of resources with minimal waste and pollution. It also has an efficient physical and social infrastructure, such as transport and health care. A sustainable city can also deliver safe and healthy work, and recreation opportunities for its occupants.

La Paz is Bolivia's largest city. La Paz's population is increasing by 3 per cent every year. High rates of growth create many problems, including lack of jobs, inadequate housing, poor drinking water and public transportation, and pollution.

SPOTLIGHT

A mosaic of rooftops in the city of Samara in Iraq is dominated by two mosques, indicating the importance of cities as centres of culture and religion in the Islamic world.

Increasing poverty in rural life in developing countries such as Rajasthan, India, has meant many men move to the cities to find work. The time this girl takes to collect melons to feed the goats leaves less time for village maintenance (a role previously undertaken by men) resulting in lowered standards of housing and greater poverty.

Globalisation

A world of uniformity

Imagine a world where identical consumer goods are produced and marketed across the globe, from Los Angeles to Cairo to Tokyo. Imagine a world where school students in Rio de Janiero worship the same pop stars as their counterparts in London and Beijing. Imagine the same fashion items in demand in Paris being sought after in Glasgow, Cape Town or Reykjavík. This is globalisation—and it's been happening for some time!

The rapid, worldwide changes in manufacturing, agriculture, tourism, finance and banking that occurred midway through the twentieth century, were catalysts for globalisation. And the dramatic developments in transport and communications technologies brought even the most remote parts of the world to ordinary people.

Familiar icons and symbols of transnational corporations transcend geographical and cultural barriers. This fast food outlet is in Dubai, United Arab Emirates.

The global village

The world is frequently described as 'the global village' or 'the global community'—terms that suggest that the world is now a smaller and more closely knit place—where all other parts of the world are within easy reach.

SPOTLIGHT

- Every day approximately 240,000 new subscribers become connected to the World Wide Web or Internet.

- Over 70 per cent of all world agriculture is now controlled by large transnational corporations.

- Coca-Cola is sold in all but two or three of the world's countries.

FASCINATING FACTS

• Demonstrations against the World Trade Organization (WTO) in Seattle in 1999 transformed the WTO into the world's most prominent icon of globalisation. The WTO was established in 1995 to set global trade rules. Some say it has helped usher in an era of economic prosperity, but critics charge the WTO puts economic progress above human rights and environmental protection.

These days, it takes commuters only 3½ hours to travel from London to New York on the British Airways Concorde (above). Given the 5½ hours' time difference, passengers effectively arrive in New York before they leave London!

Global television broadcasts of sporting competitions such as the Olympic Games or FIFA European Cup, or cultural events such as the annual Academy Awards are watched on television by people in almost all the world's countries—an audience of between 1 and 2 billion people.

One effect of globalisation is that the importance of an individual country's sovereignty or nation status is diminishing. International boundaries are gradually becoming less important, as large organisations and corporations expand their presence through commerce and trade, environmental management, peace-keeping forces and political alliances. With an ever increasing number of people now involved in maintaining the global village, the question that comes to mind is: Will globalisation result in the development of a single culture throughout the world?

The global economy

The global economy is actually a network of smaller tightly linked economies. Within this network, some economies such as the United States, Germany or Japan dominate and are able to dictate terms to the rest of the world. Trans-national corporations (TNCs)—companies that operate in a number of countries—are the movers and shakers of the modern global economy. Among the firms with operations that are nearly worldwide are Exxon and Royal Dutch Shell in petroleum; McDonald's, Coca-Cola, Sara Lee, Nabisco and Nestlé in food and beverages; BMW, Ford, Volkswagen and General Motors in automobiles; and Mitsubishi and Mitsui in banking, manufacturing and trade.

The flow of money from country to country is also encouraging the surge in economic globalisation. National boundaries are no barrier to the movement of funds. Thanks to modern telecommunications and computer technology, funds can be transferred to any part of the globe.

The phenomenal growth of the Internet has created opportunities for even very small companies to operate at a global level. By selling goods or services via the World Wide Web, a firm can now compete in markets where it could not previously have even dreamed of establishing a presence, whether for geographical, political or financial reasons.

It is anticipated that globalisation will completely transform the world economy, leaving no national products, no national corporations, no national industries, and no national economies. To succeed in the global marketplace, countries will have to depend entirely on the skills of their inhabitants, and will need to deal with powerful external forces that could create an ever-widening gulf between skilled, globally aware citizens and a growing unskilled, out-of-touch underclass.

Yet globalisation has delivered unequal benefits to many of the world's people. For many, particularly in the 'two-thirds' world (that is, developing nations), globalisation has meant the loss of local culture and employment, and accelerated environmental damage resulting in both economic hardship and social and cultural deprivation [SEE DISAPPEARING CULTURES]. For these nations, globalisation has resulted in a widening gap between rich nations and poor nations.

In these cases, the saying 'act locally' should perhaps include the use of small scale, locally based technologies using local materials. These could deliver environmentally friendly outcomes at lower costs, and may be of more benefit to affected communities than the 'think big' strategies that frequently come with globalisation.

Globalisation reaches into the smallest and most remote communities around the world, such as this small village near Napier in New Zealand.

Global tourism

How far can we go?

In the not-too-distant future, rapid advances in transport and communications technologies will open up the possibility of hypersonic jet travel at high altitudes, making Berlin less than two hours' travelling time from Manila in the Philippines! Perhaps even joy flights to the Moon and beyond will become a reality sometime this century. And, of course, we're likely to see theme parks that provide 'cyber holidays' to fantasy lands somewhere in cyberspace.

So what is the future of tourism? Holiday makers are constantly seeking new and exciting destinations and people now enjoy rapid, cheap and safe access to virtually all points on the globe. Tourism is revolutionising how we view the world, value its natural resources and even how we move about from place to place.

The world at large

Tourism has flourished the world over since the end of World War II. It has become one of the world's largest industries and so has emerged as a major and dynamic sector of the global economy. Tourism, however, brings with it new and complex pressures to bear on natural environments as well as local economies and cultures. Increasingly many tourist destinations fall victim to the 'paradox of tourism', that is, they become so popular that over time they lose their appeal because their original attractions

become spoiled or degraded through overuse. One such location is the Costa del Sol.

Most international tourists come from the wealthy nations of Europe (particularly Germany), the United States and Japan. It is interesting to discover that Australia ranks ahead of the United States and Germany with the most international travellers per 1,000 of the population.

Europe remains the dominant host region for tourists followed by the Americas, Asia and the Pacific, Africa and the Middle East and South Asia. Many new tourist destinations are also emerging in Africa, Latin America and Oceania, and especially in Australia which, in recent years, has become the world's most popular tourist destination.

These days, tourists with high disposable incomes are aware of the environmental and social issues confronting communities around the world, and the tourist experience has since taken on new dimensions. Ecotourism and wilderness adventures are just two of the 'new wave' tourist experiences that many thousands of Europeans seek every year in the remotest corners of the Earth such as the Australian Outback, Antarctica or the Himalayas. Guided tours into active volcanoes in Africa, or undersea visits to shark infested waters off Madagascar, or 'bungy jumping' in New Zealand are also new forms of tourist activity geared to the thrill seeker.

In some parts of the world tourism has been inhibited because of wars and civil unrest, natural disasters and health

Bungy jumping in New Zealand. More and more travellers are venturing into destinations that provide specialised activities for thrill seekers.

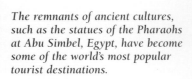

A holiday on Mars? Interplanetary travel is now coming closer to reality as new technologies of space travel and space station construction are realised.

The remnants of ancient cultures, such as the statues of the Pharaohs at Abu Simbel, Egypt, have become some of the world's most popular tourist destinations.

concerns such as tuberculosis, malaria and inadequate sewage and drinking water supplies. Yet the future of tourism is bright, and many economists predict that tourism will be the new frontier productive activity as leisure time and disposable incomes rise.

The other side of tourism

Unfortunately, tourism has also brought some unwelcome impacts for some destinations. Over-development of local resources has resulted in severe pollution and loss of natural habitat. In some instances, local culture has been lost and local workers exploited. In many Asian localities, prostitution has emerged as a major source of exploitation and corruption and is also a highly significant source of sexually transmitted diseases,

especially HIV/AIDS. In some cases, local cultures have become heavily commercialised and their arts and crafts have been replaced by mass-produced, cheap souvenirs that bear little resemblance to the original.

However, tourism does offer many positive opportunities such as balancing the rights of indigenous peoples with tourism development. In the Kakadu Region of Northern Australia, Aboriginal people have assumed responsibility for the management of their ancient homeland which has been listed as a World Heritage Area. This is a good example of management strategies being developed to protect fragile ecosystems and at the same time provide opportunities for people to access their pristine beauty.

Tourism also provides governments with opportunities to 'showcase' their national cultures and highlight significant aspects of their natural and cultural heritage.

Increasing leisure time and higher incomes combined with new technologies in communications and survival equipment have enabled many tourists to visit some of the world's most remote and harshest environments, such as Mount Everest and the Himalayas.

Global guardians

The New World Order

We are frequently reminded that we have entered a period in world history known as the 'New World Order'— a new era of peace and stability that promises an improved quality of life for all the world's people. Yet there is no doubt that there is, in fact, much conflict and instability in many parts of the globe.

The twilight of the twentieth century saw the dimensions of world power reshaped by pressing global developments that affected the entire planet. Some of the issues raised are:

- *the transnationalisation of production*
- *the globalisation of money and finance*
- *the spread of infectious diseases*
- *global environmental degradation, and*
- *the proliferation of weapons of mass destruction.*

Many people believe that political, military, economic, technological and cultural power lie in the hands of a few 'elite' states and corporations located predominantly in wealthy nations. The 'New World Order' was meant to bring everyone into the 'global market' through its free trade policies; instead it has produced intense conflict over the form and direction of economic development. This conflict is both regional and global, and is threatening many developing nations' access to key resources. The result is national, regional and international insecurity. And the power is certainly still in the hands of the elite.

So the New World Order is regarded as a recipe for disorder and anarchy. Fragmented and weak nation states are being overwhelmed by problems such as ethnic conflicts, massive migrations, and environmental degradation. Recent ethnic conflicts may lead to the very real prospect of weapons of mass destruction—nuclear or biochemical—slipping into the hands of angry and desperate minority groups and their sometimes fanatical leaders.

The sale of weapons continues to fuel armed conflicts around the globe. These conflicts cause untold hardship on civilians, and siphon off scarce social and economic resources for weapons purchases. The legacy is massive violations of international humanitarian and human rights laws. Some of these wars, notably in Afghanistan, Angola, Colombia, Somalia, Sri Lanka and Sudan, have dragged on for years without any peaceful resolution in sight.

Keeping the peace

During the second half of the twentieth century, international organisations, including inter-government and non-government bodies, have grown significantly in both number and stature to ensure peace and co-operation between nations. International organisations create sets of rules, norms and procedures and formulate these in international law, particularly in the form of treaties and conventions signed by nation-states. These treaties and conventions define the conduct expected of participants in the international community.

International relief organisations, such as Medecins Sans Frontieres, provide urgently needed medical assistance in many parts of the world, such as here in Sudan.

United Nations security forces and other international organisations now play key roles in reconstructing communities torn apart by war or civil unrest in many parts of the world.

Refugees in Sudan have been transported long distances from their homeland to 'collection centres', where makeshift accommodation is provided.

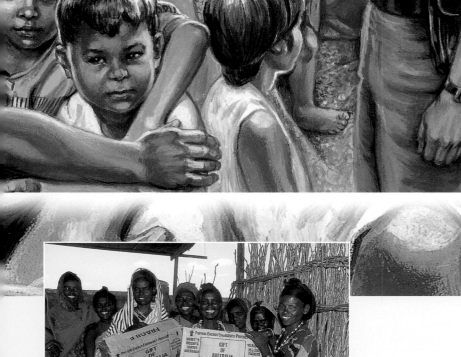

Food parcels from Australia provide short-term relief for a famine-afflicted community in Somalia.

The United Nations

The largest and most influential inter-government organisation is the United Nations (UN) which was established in 1946, and has its headquarters in New York. The main motivation for the creation of the UN was collective security following the end of World War II. Half a century later, the membership of the UN has grown to 185 nations. On the world stage, the UN is critically important, but relatively weak and often controversial. At times it has appeared to be an impotent and ineffective institution that has failed to meet expectations.

NGOs

Non-government organisations (NGOs) are private organisations that are today regarded as legitimate players on the world stage alongside nation-states and inter-government organisations. Most NGOs are primarily concerned with the empowerment of marginal and impoverished sectors of the world's population, so they generally have significantly less power and far fewer financial resources than inter-government bodies. Non-government organisations tend to focus upon specific issues. For example, Greenpeace raises awareness of environmental issues, while groups such as the International Federation of the Red Cross and the Red Crescent Societies provide disaster relief and medical care.

Protecting human rights

Human rights is one highly significant area where international organisations have created the emerging rules, norms and legal instruments that link nations and their citizens together in the 'global community'. Human rights are the laws, customs and practices that have evolved to protect individuals, minorities, groups and races from oppressive rulers and governments. Although the UN has been prominent in human rights legislation, private individuals and NGOs such as Amnesty International have frequently provided the political pressure that has persuaded inter-government and national agencies to act.

SPOTLIGHT

- Today, there are about 500 inter-government organisations around the world, such as the United Nations and the International Monetary Fund (IMF), and approximately 5,000 non-government organisations, including the Red Cross and Amnesty International. This is roughly five times the number that were active at the end of the World War II.

- In 1999 there were 28 major armed confrontations around the world. Of these, 25 were internal, pitting the government against organised groups from among its population.

Gender inequities

Women in society

Quality of life is usually measured by such factors as access to clean water, health care, housing and education, and there is no doubt that there is a growing gap between countries in terms of quality of life. Economic development rarely delivers equitable outcomes between countries. Rapid industrialisation and shifts in the organisation and control of agriculture are radically changing the livelihoods of many millions of people in poorer countries—with growing poverty being the principal outcome.

The process of development has also resulted in different social, economic and political outcomes for men and women, in which women are usually marginalised or 'distanced' from the benefits of development. Development planners typically acknowledge the social roles of women as wives and mothers, yet they continue to underestimate and undervalue the economic roles of women, leaving them out of many development equations.

On the land

In most of sub-Saharan Africa, Southeast Asia and parts of Latin America, women make up the majority of the agricultural labour force—cultivating, weeding and harvesting crops.

Women also process and store the harvest, carry water and fuel, market their farm surplus, care for animals and in many instances play a key role in the conservation and selection of key species of plants that comprise their food supply.

But time is running out. Land degradation and loss of forests have meant that rural women must travel further in search of fuel, wood and water. With fewer hours to devote to other agricultural activities, the food production system begins to break down, and villages go hungry.

Birth abnormalities have jumped enormously in rural areas in many developing countries in recent years. The most likely culprit is the uncontrolled and increased use of chemicals and pesticides in agriculture. Women are the farmers, so they have experienced greater exposure to chemicals, and their reproductive health has declined. Women have also been exploited as a cheap source of labour, frequently having to work in substandard and dangerous factory conditions.

Improved nutrition and health care for women in rural India have achieved higher life expectancies for women and children.

Civil unrest, poverty & disease

Political unrest and civil war in developing countries have caused severe hardships to rural communities. Crops are destroyed, wells are poisoned and livestock is slaughtered. This, combined with agricultural change, has created a flood of migrants and with this highly mobile population has come an unwelcome consequence—an epidemic in sexually transmitted diseases, such as HIV/AIDS, which has had a more devastating impact on women than on men. The widespread practice of polygamy in many cultures stands as a leading cause of the transmission of HIV/AIDS, and women are nearly three times more likely to contract HIV/AIDS than men.

Poverty in many developing countries is entrenched, and it is certainly concentrated on

Rice growing cultures throughout the developing world account for 70 per cent of grain produced, and depend heavily on women as farmers.

women. This concentration of poverty is largely due to the persistence of discrimination based on women's reproductive role. In many cultures, women have little or no control over their fertility, and they face myriad social, cultural and religious barriers in terms of access to contraception, family planning services and health care. Low literacy levels in women compound their low level of reproductive health. So access to information about family planning is poor and prevents informed choices.

Social and cultural traditions also compromise the nutritional health of women in many cultures. In some cultures women always prepare the food and always eat last and so they often do not have as much to eat. Highly nutritious foods such as eggs, vegetables, meats, poultry and fish are often scarce but are offered first to men and guests. There is a strong link between a woman's nutritional and reproductive health. Poor nutritional health leads to poor health standards in both mothers and their children and makes them prime targets for infectious diseases such as measles and tuberculosis.

Such a cycle is difficult to break, but the difficulties faced by women in certain countries needs to be addressed, if any sense of equity is to result.

Women removing sardines from nets in Senegal, Africa. In many cultures around the world, women fulfil important economic as well as social and family roles.

SPOTLIGHT

- An estimated 300 to 400 million women throughout the world have no access to family planning services and have little or no control over their fertility.

- The life expectancy for a female born in the United States in 1975 was 75 years; for a female born in Chad only 44 years. In 1995 a female born in the United States could be expected to live to 82 years of age while her counterpart in Chad could only expect to live to 34 years. A male baby born in Chad in 1995 has a life expectancy of 51 years.

Health counsellors in rural Zimbabwe, Africa, assist local women to realise higher standards of health and nutrition for their children.

Disappearing cultures

Ways of life

What are people interested in these days? What are the 'in' things? Do you wear your hair long or short? Do you wear faded jeans or a silk sarong? Do you eat pork, snail or rice? What music do you listen to: rap, gospel or bluegrass? Our preferences say something about who we are and help to define our culture.

Every group of people has a specific culture. It is their way of life—the sum of beliefs, behaviours and language. Customs, artworks, traditions and fashion are just some aspects of culture. Yet the concept of culture is not static. Culture changes. If a popular youth figure makes it trendy to wear singlets instead of shirts, this fashion may become part of youth culture.

Sometimes the culture of a society can be threatened from outside. For example, popular music from the United States and the United Kingdom has had a tremendous impact on the culture of groups throughout the world, particularly in the twentieth century.

Culture clash

When cultures mix, either by choice, accident or force, some cultural elements may be endangered. Many languages in the world have been lost, due to the domination of one culture over another. It is no surprise that English and Spanish are two of the most widely spoken languages in the world. European language and religion are major cultural forces in Africa, South America, Asia and the Pacific because colonies were established there by Great Britain and Spain. As a dominant culture exerts influence over a weaker one, many of its customs become the normal thing to do.

Before our very eyes

The Huaorani people live deep in the jungles of Ecuador, South America. Their language and crafts designs are unique. Until the 1950s, they lived a subsistence lifestyle, using the forest as their only source of shelter, food and clothing. Oil companies have now acquired Huaorani land, and so the tradition of hunting monkeys will disappear, as will other aspects of Huaorani culture. Some members of the tribe have retreated into the forest; others have begun to explore eco-tourism as a way to maintain some elements of their culture.

Culture creep

Sport is an effective way of transferring culture. It is no coincidence that all cricket-playing nations were once colonies of Great Britain. Through movies, television programs and advertising, countries such as the United States export their culture to many other societies. For instance, American basketball is now replacing cricket as the most popular sport in the West Indies; and some sports stars are heroes all around the world.

Economic development can be a very real threat to culture. As the forests, deserts and oceans of the world are harvested for natural resources, impacts are felt in the fishing village, the nomad's camp and the hunter's lodge.

Migration results in a degree of cultural mixing. For example, an Italian migrant brings her culture to her new country, and can affect the culture of those around her, just as they affect her.

Cultural casualties

Some cultures dominate others intentionally. In many countries, native peoples were forced to assimilate; to live like the Europeans who had settled in their land. Indigenous peoples were made to attend European schools and abandon

A Thai woman with brass neck rings. Along the Thai–Burma border the Karen tradition of 'long-neck' beauty has become a tourist attraction. Some people disagree with the commercialisation of cultural traditions.

their native language, law and religion. Assimilation even extended to taking children away from their parents.

Young people who are caught between cultures can sometimes struggle to find their identity, and sometimes become caught up in a cycle of unemployment, drug and alcohol dependence and self-abuse. Others might become the victims of racism.

One Net: one culture

Imagine everyone in the world speaking the same language, singing the same songs, and dancing the same dances. This is not as far-fetched as it might sound. Television network CNN International is watched by over 149 million households in 212 countries and territories. Such global networks definitely make the world smaller.

Cultures throughout the world are in closer contact than ever before through the use of telephones, satellites, television and the Internet. Some people fear that this ever-increasing contact between regions in the world will eventually lead to the creation of one culture. Some argue that this lack of diversity in culture should be avoided.

I want my identity

A young Maori girl welcomes tourists to her territory; a young Mohawk boy attends his first day at a 'survival school' in Montreal; the Inuit people of the Arctic region develop a conservation strategy aimed at avoiding environmental and economic invasion...

Many efforts are being undertaken to reclaim lost culture. First peoples call for self-determination. This often involves the restoration of access and control of traditional land, respect for customs, and limits on development projects that affect their lifestyle.

Some indigenous groups demand the right to establish their own schools, to protect their own archaeological sites and have a say in issues affecting their cultural heritage. In spite of this, in the third millennium it will become increasingly difficult to maintain a diversity of cultures, as economic and technological developments affect the lives of all people.

A totem pole in Vancouver, Canada. Spirituality is a key aspect of indigenous cultural identity.

More than 200 years on, Aboriginal resistance against the cultural domination of 'white man' continues, as shown here on Australia Day.

World Heritage

What is World Heritage?

World Heritage is what puts a place on the map! Imagine Tibet without the Himalayas, Africa without Mount Kilimanjaro, Europe without the Rhine River, or the United States without the Grand Canyon. The identity of each place is shaped by its natural features. So the protection of natural heritage is vital.

Heritage is part of the 'human environment' as well. Imagine Egypt without its Great Pyramids, or Paris without its Eiffel Tower. Sydney would not be Sydney without its Opera House. What would New York be without the Statue of Liberty? Each of these architectural treasures is recognised worldwide. Their focus in millennium celebrations broadcast to most parts of the globe is an indication of their symbolic value.

Heritage inside the walls

Buildings can take on special significance due to events that take place within their walls. The Kremlin in Moscow, for example, has a long heritage as the national centre of politics in Russia. It has seen the rise and reform of one of the most centralised governments in the modern era. It is a unique reminder of past political systems and maintains its role in world affairs and in the ongoing government of Russia and the Commonwealth of Independent States.

Marine iguanas have become an international symbol of the unique natural heritage of the Galapagos islands.

Cultural links with the past

Many places of World Heritage are recognised for their cultural and religious significance. The Pyramids of Egypt, Aztec ruins, Stonehenge, Jerusalem's Wailing Wall, Mecca, Borobudur Temple, the Taj Mahal and Vatican City are all home to beliefs and customs that have developed over centuries. These places are especially valued for their spiritual significance.

Cape Evans Hut was built by the Scott Antarctic Expedition in 1911. It is now listed as a 'Specially Protected Area' (SPA) under the existing provisions of the International Montreal Treaty. The hut is filled with preserved artefacts from Scott's historic expedition, and is a symbol of discovery and determination.

The Eiffel Tower—in Paris, of course! Some structures are symbols of the modern era and are defining features of places.

Indigenous heritage

Indigenous cultures are another important aspect of World Heritage. Language, traditions and lifestyles that have endured thousands of years in harmony with the environment are increasingly recognised and respected by the world community. Sadly, many areas of the world have lost much of the identity of their first people.

[SEE DISAPPEARING CULTURES]

Natural wonders

Nature provides some of the most striking examples of World Heritage. In 1872, the Yellowstone area of Wyoming in the United States was declared the world's first national park. This was one of the earliest attempts in Western culture to designate and set aside an area of natural beauty.

Places of special natural and cultural significance are now recognised and listed by UNESCO as World Heritage Sites. There are currently over 600 World Heritage Sites across the globe and while many are still threatened, they are usually more protected from human disturbance. World Heritage status places listed sites in the media spotlight and this often leads

to greater conservation efforts. For instance, the highly sensitive Galapagos Islands of Ecuador are listed but the delicate ecological balance is threatened by tourism.

Mount Kenya, at 5,199 metres (17,050 feet), is Africa's second highest peak and is listed as a World Heritage Site. Its impressive glacial summits and surrounding alpine vegetation make it a distinct example of natural heritage for current and future generations to enjoy.

In Africa, Tanzania's Serengeti National Park is a standout World Heritage Site. It is an enormous animal kingdom, complete with wildebeests, giraffes, gazelles, zebras and their predators. The 1.5 million hectare site is unique.

The next generation

Heritage is passed on. Increased attempts to conserve natural and cultural heritage provide greater assurance that future generations will be able to experience and identify with the past. Continued industrial development makes ongoing conservation of World Heritage all the more challenging. It is important that natural and cultural heritage is recognised at a local level as the identity of the world goes well beyond the borders of the sites already chosen.

Stonehenge in England's south is proof that structures can be valued for what they are rather than what they do. No one is absolutely sure what the purpose of the stone circle was. Its religious significance is shrouded in mystery.

The Kremlin in Moscow. This grand building has great political significance for the people of Russia, and the rest of the world.

Global futures

Life in the city

Over the space of just half a millennium we have dramatically changed where and how we live. From an existence built around small isolated rural communities, we have become a highly networked global community of urban dwellers.

Despite the enormous material, social and cultural benefits that large cities provide, they have become very greedy places—reaching into increasingly distant hinterlands to consume vast amounts of energy and resources. Cities are also experiencing many social ills. In the United States, rising crime rates and lawlessness now plague many suburban neighbourhoods, forcing residents to lock themselves away in gated communities, shrouded by high-tech surveillance cameras and paramilitary security guards.

What does the future hold?

To some, the future of our cities is not looking good. It is dominated by the motor car. Enormous amounts of space are sacrificed to freeways and carparks that result in huge sprawling cities that guzzle ever-increasing quantities of fossil fuels and other non-renewable resources. The resultant exhaust emissions are a major contributor to the enhanced greenhouse effect *[SEE CLIMATE CHANGE]* and also result in acid rain that destroys forests and buildings.

Still, many observers regard the city as the most efficient unit of human settlement—a highly concentrated focus of economic and cultural activity that allows society to function at its optimum in terms of economic gain, technological development and cultural growth. It's just that many cities have outgrown their optimum size.

At the Kyoto Conference in Japan in 1998 many of the world's wealthiest nations committed themselves to significantly reduce their greenhouse gas emissions over the next twenty years and beyond. The decisions made at the conference will require a radical rethink by communities across the world about the kind of lifestyles they will need to pursue to achieve their greenhouse targets and ensure a sustainable future for generations to come.

The city that focusses on fossil fuels and the motor car has a limited future compared with the city that focuses on alternative transport and energy systems.

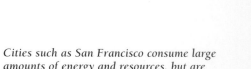

Cities such as San Francisco consume large amounts of energy and resources, but are gradually introducing more energy-efficient means of housing and moving people.

Global warming is not the only issue that raises questions about how we might organise our cities in the future. Technological change in transport and communications is taking place at a breathtaking pace and is dramatically changing our work and leisure patterns. Large scale commerce and industry is being replaced by 'clean' high-tech, small scale industry and commerce where working hours are flexible and workers are highly mobile.

Solar-powered vehicles carry batteries for storing energy. As their efficiency improves, they will be able to transport increasingly heavier payloads over longer distances.

Green suburbs

Such changes will transform the suburb. Increasingly workers will use their homes or apartments as a place of work, functioning as 'telecommuters'. Suburbs will also be characterised by a greater mix of land uses that encourage residents to work locally. That 'sense of community', so clearly absent in many cities, having been destroyed by the motor car, is finding its way back as communities reinvent themselves as smaller and more compact 'urban villages' such as Arabella Park in Munich and Kista in Stockholm. Sites such as disused industrial land will be regenerated into 'green suburbs' where alternative energies are used, such as solar power and bio-energy systems (for example, biogas units that generate methane). Recycling of solid and liquid wastes and on-site bacterial processing of raw sewage will result in suburbs that are mostly self-sufficient and exert minimal impact on the environment.

The new green suburb will also catch and filter its own water supply and become self sufficient in food production. Permaculture is rapidly emerging as an environmentally sound system of food production that offers a low cost and small scale sustainable alternative to the high cost and chemically laden system of large scale agriculture that many countries currently pursue. Permaculture is entirely organic (that is, chemically free) and involves recycling of food scraps and wastes through mulching and composting. This provides fruit and vegetable crops with an endless source of nutrients. The combinations of plants and small animals (such as poultry) will be well thought out and will eliminate plant diseases and pests.

FASCINATING FACTS

- Urban farming makes use of local skills and resources and enables local communities to grow crops according to local need. Sparbrook in Birmingham, England, is an inner city area that is host to an innovative food production system where vegetable gardens provide the mainly Asian and West Indian community with their specialist food needs.
- By the year 2000, there were twenty-five genetically engineered crops in the marketplace. By 2020, this is expected to increase to approximately eighty crops.

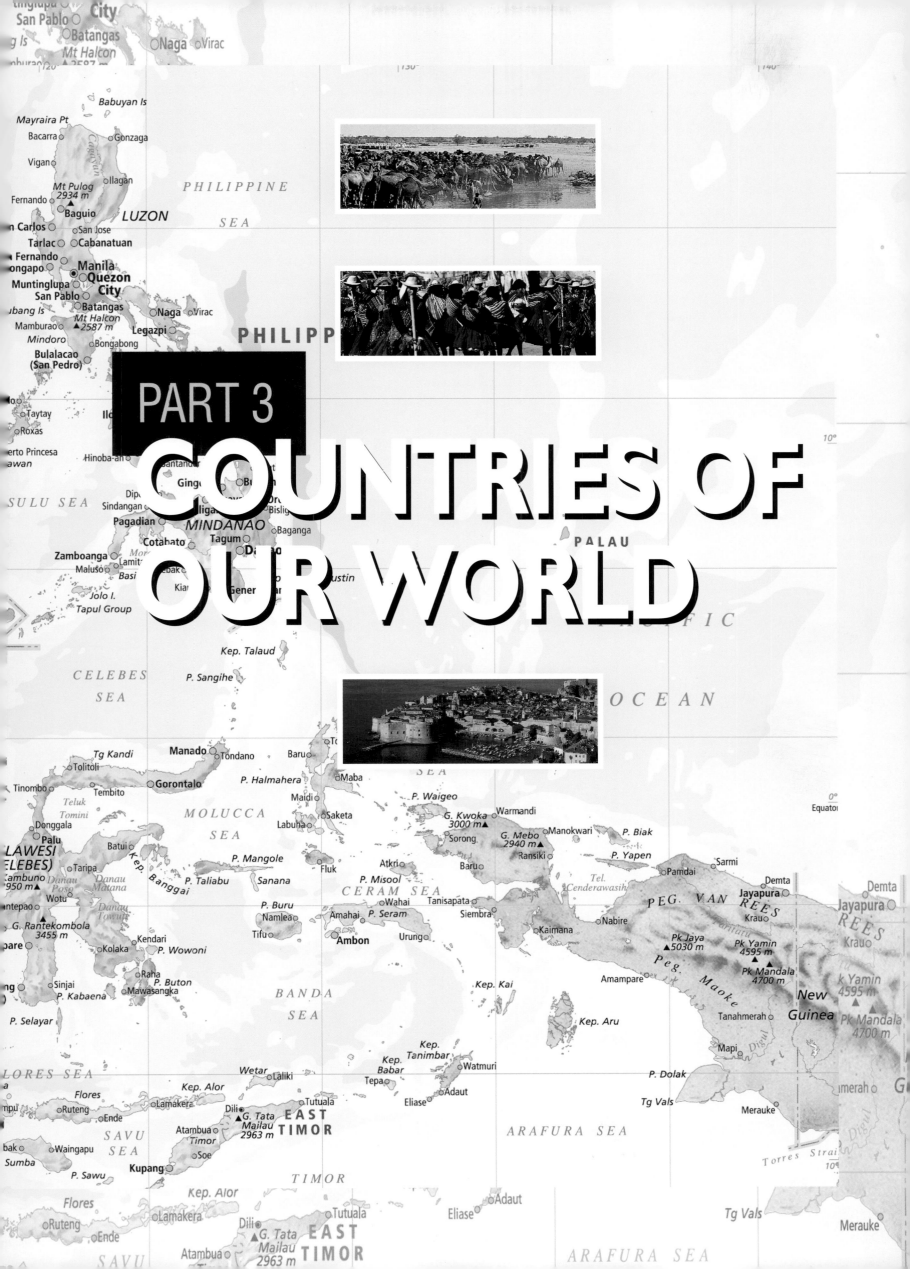

PART 3
COUNTRIES OF OUR WORLD

THE World

ICELAND

JAN MAYEN (Nor.)

Arctic Circle

FAEROE IS (Den.)

SWEDEN

NORWAY
Oslo
Stockholm

BARENTS SEA

Novaya Zemlya

Novosibirskiy Ostrova

R U S S I A N

F E D E R A T I O N

OKHOTSKOY MORE

Ostrov Sakhalin

FINLAND
Helsinki

Tallinn
ESTONIA
Riga LATVIA

Moskva

DENMARK
København

LITHUANIA
Vilnius

Minsk
BELARUS

Astana

ISLE OF MAN (U.K.)
Dublin
IRELAND

UNITED KINGDOM

NETH.
Amsterdam
Berlin

POLAND
Warszawa

Kyyiv

KAZAKHSTAN

Kuril'skiy Ostrov

London
BELG.
Bruxelles
Luxembourg

GERMANY
LUX.
Praha
CZECH REP.

SLOVAKIA
Bratislava
Budapest

UKRAINE
Chişinău
MOLDOVA

Bishkek

Ulaanbaatar

CHANNEL ISLANDS (U.K.)
Paris
Bern

FRANCE
SWITZ.
Ljubljana

LIECH.
Wien
SLOV.
AUST.
HUNG.
Zagreb
CROAT.

ROMANIA
Beograd
Bucureşti

Toshkent
KYRGYZSTAN

MONGOLIA

Beijing

P'yŏngyang
NORTH KOREA

ANDORRA
Madrid

Roma
Tiranë
Sarajevo
YUG.
B.-H.
ITALY

ALBANIA
Skopje
MACE.
Sofiya
BULGARIA

GEORGIA
T'bilisi
ARM.
AZER.
Baki

UZBEKISTAN

Sŏul
SOUTH KOREA
JAPAN
Tōkyō

PORTUGAL
Lisboa

SPAIN

GREECE
Ankara
Yerevan

TURKMENISTAN
Ashgabat

Dushanbe
TAJIKISTAN

C H I N A

GIBRALTAR (U.K.)
Madeira (Port.)
Rabat

Tūnis

MALTA
Valletta

Athína
Lefkosia
CYPRUS

TURKEY
SYRIA
Dimashq
LEBANON
Bayrūt
IRAQ
Baghdād

I R A N
Tehrān

Kābol
AFGHANISTAN

Islāmābād

T'ai-pei
TAIWAN

Islas Canarias (Sp.)

Alger
TUNISIA
Tarābulus

ISRAEL
Yerushalayim
JORDAN
Amman

Al Kuwayt
KUWAIT

PAKISTAN

NEPAL
Kathmandu
BHUTAN
Thimphu

W. SAHARA
Tropic of Cancer

MOROCCO

ALGERIA

LIBYA

EGYPT

Al Qāhirah

Ar Riyāḍ
QATAR
U.A.E.

Al Manāmah
BAHRAIN
Ad Dawhah
Abū Ẓaby
Masqaṭ

New Delhi
I N D I A

BANGLADESH
Dhaka

MAURITANIA
Nouakchott

MALI

NIGER

CHAD

SUDAN

SAUDI ARABIA

OMAN

MYANMAR
LAOS
Ha Nôi

SENEGAL
Dakar
GAMBIA
GUINEA-BISSAU
Conakry

Bamako
Niamey

NIGERIA
Ndjamena

Asmara
ERITREA
Al Khartūm

YEMEN
Şan'ā

ARABIAN SEA

Suquṭrá (Yemen)

Bay of Bengal

Viangchan
VIETNAM

THAILAND
Yangon
Krung Thep
CAMBODIA

NORTHERN MARIANA (U.S.A.)

SIERRA LEONE
Freetown
LIBERIA
Monrovia

CÔTE D'IVOIRE
Ouagadougou
BURKINA

GHANA
TOGO
Abuja
Porto-Novo
BENIN
Accra
Lomé
Malabo
EQ. GUINEA

C.A.R.
Bangui

ETHIOPIA
Ādīs Ābeba

DJIBOUTI
Djibouti

SRI LANKA
Colombo

MALDIVES
Male

Phnum Pénh

Manila
PHILIPPINES

GUAM (U.S.A.)

Yamoussoukro
Yaoundé
CAMEROON

GABON
Libreville

DEM. REP. OF THE CONGO
Kinshasa

Kampala
Kigali
Bujumbura
RWANDA
BURUNDI
KENYA
Nairobi

Muqdisho
SOMALIA

Chagos Archipelago

BRITISH INDIAN OCEAN TERRITORY (U.K.)

MALAYSIA
Kuala Lumpur
SINGAPORE

Bandar Seri Begawan
BRUNEI

Koror
PALAU

MICRONESIA

ASCENSION ISLAND (ST HELENA)
Equator

SÃO TOMÉ & PRÍNCIPE

CONGO
Brazzaville

Luanda

TANZANIA
Dodoma

Victoria
SEYCHELLES

INDONESIA

Jakarta
Dili
EAST TIMOR

PAPUA NEW GUINEA
Port Moresby

ST HELENA (U.K.)

ANGOLA

ZAMBIA
Lusaka
MALAWI
Lilongwe

Moroni
COMOROS
MAYOTTE (Fr.)

CHRISTMAS ISLAND (Aust.)

COCOS (KEELING) ISLANDS (Aust.)

ASHMORE & CARTIER ISLANDS (Aust.)

CORAL SEA ISLANDS (Aust.)

Tropic of Capricorn

NAMIBIA
Windhoek

BOTSWANA
Gaborone

ZIMBABWE
Harare
MOZAMBIQUE

Antananarivo
MADAGASCAR
RÉUNION (Fr.)

MAURITIUS
Port Louis

INDIAN OCEAN

AUSTRALIA

Pretoria
Mbabane
SWAZILAND
Maputo

Bloemfontein
Maseru
LESOTHO

SOUTH AFRICA

Cape Town

Île Amsterdam (Fr.)

Canber

TASMA SEA

SOUTH ATLANTIC OCEAN

FRENCH SOUTHERN & ANTARCTIC ISLANDS (Fr.)

Prince Edward Is (S. Africa)

Îles Crozet (Fr.)

Îles de Kerguélen (Fr.)

Tasmania

Macquari (Aust.)

BOUVERT ISLAND (Nor.)

HEARD & McDONALD ISLANDS (Aust.)

SOUTHERN OCEAN

A N T A R C T I C A

Antarctic Circle

ARCTIC OCEAN

BEAUFORT
SEA

*Ostrov
Vrangelya*

CHUKCHI
SEA

*Banks
Island*

Victoria Island

*Baffin
Bay*

GREENLAND
(KALAALLIT NUNAAT)
(Den.)

Baffin Island

Davis Strait

Arctic Circle

ICELAND
⊛ Reykjavik

U.S.A.

CANADA

*Hudson
Bay*

70°

60°

BERING
SEA

*Gulf of
Alaska*

Aleutian Islands

Newfoundland

Ottawa ⊛

ST PIERRE
AND MIQUELON
(Fr.)

NORTH
ATLANTIC
OCEAN

50°

PACIFIC OCEAN

UNITED STATES OF AMERICA

⊛ Washington D.C.

*Azores
(Port.)*

40°

*Isla Guadalupe
(Mex.)*

*Gulf of
Mexico*

BERMUDA
(U.K.)

30°

MIDWAY ISLANDS
(U.S.A.)

*Hawaiian Islands
(U.S.A.)*

MEXICO

BAHAMAS

La Habana ⊛ Nassau

Tropic of Cancer

WAKE ISLAND (U.S.A.)

*Islas Revillagigedo
(Mex.)*

⊛ México

CUBA

DOMINICAN REPUBLIC
Santo Domingo
HAITI ⊛

20°

JOHNSTON ATOLL
(U.S.A.)

Kingston JAMAICA

ANTIGUA & BARBUDA

CAPE VERDE

ARSHALL ISLANDS

Guatemala BELIZE
GUATEMALA Belmopan
EL SALVADOR HONDURAS
San Salvador ⊛Tegucigalpa

ST KITTS & NEVIS
ST VINCENT DOMINICA
& THE GRENADINES ST LUCIA
BARBADOS
GRENADA

Praia ⊛

⊛ Dalap-Uliga-Darrit

KINGMAN REEF (U.S.A.)
PALMYRA ATOLL (U.S.A.)

Managua ⊛ NICARAGUA
San José PANAMA
COSTA RICA Panamá

TRINIDAD & TOBAGO
Port of Spain
Caracas ⊛ Georgetown
⊛ Paramaribo
FRENCH GUIANA (Fr.)

10°

⊛ Bairiki

BAKER AND
HOWLAND ISLANDS
(U.S.A.)

JARVIS ISLAND (U.S.A.)

Bogotá ⊛ VENEZUELA

NAURU

*Islas Galápagos
(Ecu.)*

COLOMBIA

Equator

Quito ⊛
ECUADOR

0°

oniara KIRIBATI
SOLOMON
ISLANDS Funafuti
TOKELAU
TUVALU (N.Z.)

Îles Marquises

B R A Z I L

PERU

NUATU WALLIS & SAMOA AMERICAN
FUTUNA Apia SAMOA
Port- (Fr.) ⊛ (U.S.A.)
Vila FIJI TONGA NIUE COOK
CALEDONIA (Fr.) Suva Nuku'alofa (N.Z.) ISLANDS
(N.Z.)

*Archipel de
la Société
Tahiti*

Îles Tuamotu

Lima ⊛

La Paz ⊛ ⊛ Brasília

10°

BOLIVIA

Sucre ⊛

*Trindade
(Brazil)*
Tropic of Capricorn

NORFOLK
ISLAND
(Aust.)

FRENCH
POLYNESIA
(Fr.)

PITCAIRN IS.
(U.K.)

*Isla de Pascua
(Chile)*

*Sala y Gómez
(Chile)*

PARAGUAY

Asunción ⊛

20°

*Kermadec Is
(N.Z.)*

*Archipiélago Juan Fernández
(Chile)*

ARGENTINA URUGUAY

30°

North I.

NEW ZEALAND

Santiago ⊛
Buenos Aires ⊛ ⊛ Montevideo

⊛ Wellington
South I.

*Chatham Is
(N.Z.)*

SOUTH
ATLANTIC OCEAN

40°

*Bounty Is
(N.Z.)*

*Auckland Is
(N.Z.)* *Antipodes Is
(N.Z.)*

FALKLAND ISLANDS
(U.K.)

SOUTH GEORGIA &
SOUTH SANDWICH
ISLANDS (U.K.)

50°

*Campbell I.
(N.Z.)*

Cabo de Hornos

*South Shetland
Islands (U.K.)*

*South Orkney
Islands (U.K.)*

60°

0	1500	3000	4000	kilometers
0	1000	2000		miles

Projection: Mercator

*Balleny Is
(N.Z.)*

BELLINGSHAUSEN
SEA

*Antarctic
Peninsula*

Antarctic Circle

70°

Capital Ottawa

Population 31,006,347

Official languages English, French

Main religions Roman Catholic 45%, United Church 12%, Anglican 8%, other 35%

Currency Canadian dollar

Form of government Constitutional monarchy

Record holder Mount Logan, at 5,950 metres (19,521 feet), is the highest point in Canada; Alaska's Mount McKinley, at 6,194 metres (20,321 feet), is the highest point in North America

WESTERN
Canada & Alaska

From the 'Prairie Provinces' to the Arctic Circle

This mighty region stretches from the rolling prairies of mid-west North America to the scattered frozen islands of the Arctic Circle. In the west, Alaska reaches across the Bering Strait almost to Russia. During the last Ice Age, between 35,000 and 12,000 years ago, a land bridge connected the two continents. Humans from Asia crossed here to spread south into the Americas.

Canada is the second largest country in the world. About 90 per cent of Canadians live close to the United States border. The rest of the population is scattered across the vast prairie lands of the west and the frozen wastes of the northwest. With the exception of the populous southwest corner of British Columbia, the sprawling lands of western Canada are the most sparsely settled in North America. Great national parks of forest-covered mountains, rocky peaks, glaciers and high, crystal-clear lakes draw many thousands of tourists each year. The Arctic Archipelago islands range from high mountains in the east to low plains in the west.

Inuit (Eskimo) and First Nation peoples (as indigenous Canadians are called) lived by trapping caribou and bears, and by fishing. The first Europeans into the area were fur traders. The opening of Canada's first transcontinental railway line in the 1880s made the west easier to reach. Today Alberta, Saskatchewan and Manitoba—known as the 'Prairie Provinces'— are covered by wheatfields and cattle ranches. Alberta produces more than 75 per cent of the nation's oil and is an important source of natural gas and coal. Vancouver, in the neighbouring province of British Columbia, is Canada's busiest port. In the 1890s, the discovery of gold in the Yukon, to the north, led to the Klondike gold rush. Nunavut, straddling the Arctic Circle, has been a self-governing Inuit homeland since 1999.

Vast wheatfields stretch across the fertile prairies of Saskatchewan, Canada. High levels of mechanisation have reduced the need for labour.

The spectacular peaks, glacier-fed lakes and extensive stands of evergreen conifers of Banff National Park, on the eastern side of the Canadian Rockies. The layers of shale and limestone banding the barren slopes were laid down on the floor of an ancient inland sea.

An orca being fed at Stanley Park Aquarium, Vancouver. Only natural behaviour is encouraged at the aquarium.

Alaska is both the northernmost state of the United States and its largest state in area. It is a mixture of massive glaciated mountains and broad river valleys. For much of the year, large areas of Alaska are covered in snow.

The most western mainland point of Alaska is only about 80 kilometres (50 miles) from Russia. In the 1700s Russian traders and hunters established outposts along the southeastern shore, and the region was known as Russian America. It was purchased from Russia by the United States in 1867; it became a United States territory in 1912 and a state in 1959.

Alaska is rich in resources, particularly oil and fish. There is also some farming on the lands south of the Arctic Circle where during summer the sun shines for 20 hours a day and crops, mainly barley and potatoes, grow rapidly.

Arrigetch peaks and glacier, Brooks Range, Alaska.

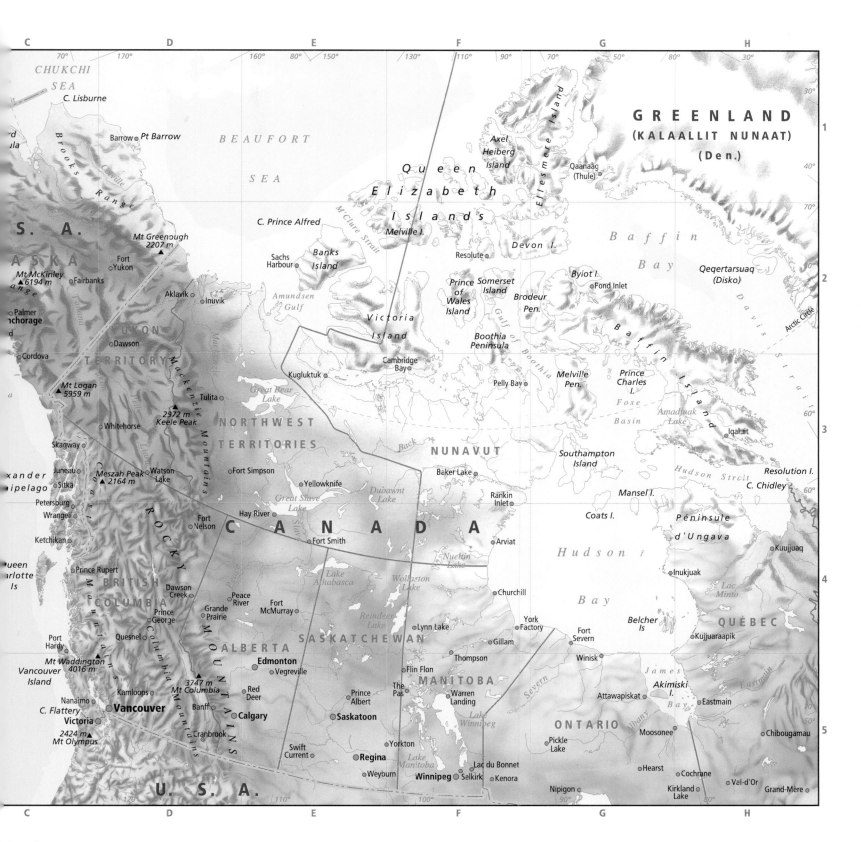

CANADA
SEE PAGE 78

Record holder

- Québec is Canada's only French-speaking province
- Québec City, founded in 1608, is Canada's oldest city
- Toronto's CN Tower, at 553 metres (1820 feet), is the world's tallest free-standing structure

EASTERN
Canada

A 'community of communities'

Although it is basically English-speaking and European in culture, Canada, and especially eastern Canada, is made up of many distinct ethnic communities. They range from its original peoples to the most recent waves of Asian immigrants.

Niagara Falls, on the Canadian–United States border, is actually two waterfalls. The American Falls (left) on the United States side, and the wider Horseshoe Falls (right) which carry about 85 per cent of the flow. The waters drop more than 50 metres (164 feet) into a deep gorge. Constant erosion of the rocky ledge means the falls are moving upstream at the rate of about 5 centimetres (2 inches) a year.

Canada calls itself a 'community of communities'. In the Arctic north is the self-governing Inuit homeland of Nunavut. About 40 per cent of Canadians are descended from the large numbers of Irish and Scottish settlers who began arriving in the 1700s. In recent years the relaxing of Canada's immigration policy has seen an influx of Asian migrants, especially from India and Pakistan. Canada's largest ethnic minority, about 27 per cent of its people, are French-speakers who live mainly in the province of Québec. French settlement began in the 1540s, with explorers pushing inland in search of furs and other trade goods. A British victory in a war with France in 1763 gave Britain control of the region, and following the independence of the United States from Britain in 1783, large numbers of British settlers moved north. The demand of many Québécois (Québec's French-speaking citizens) for autonomy is one of Canada's most difficult and long-standing political problems.

Eastern Canada's St Lawrence–Great Lakes lowlands and the Ontario peninsula are the most heavily populated parts of the nation. Rural settlement in these fertile agricultural lands is more dense than elsewhere in the country; barley, maize and oats are grown and there are a great many dairy farms. The area also includes the large urban centres of Montreal and Toronto, and the St Lawrence Seaway brings huge ocean-going cargo ships inland from the Atlantic Ocean to ports on the Great Lakes.

To the north and west stretches a vast landscape of low hills floored with some of the oldest rocks on Earth. Scattered across it are hundreds of thousands of lakes ranging in size from gigantic to tiny and connected by thousands of rivers and streams. Evergreen forests cover the rolling hills. Here the soil is too poor for agriculture. Timber, pulp and paper, and hydro-electricity are the main industries. The Grand Banks, off the coast of Newfoundland, has for centuries been one of the world's richest and busiest fishing grounds; cod is the main catch.

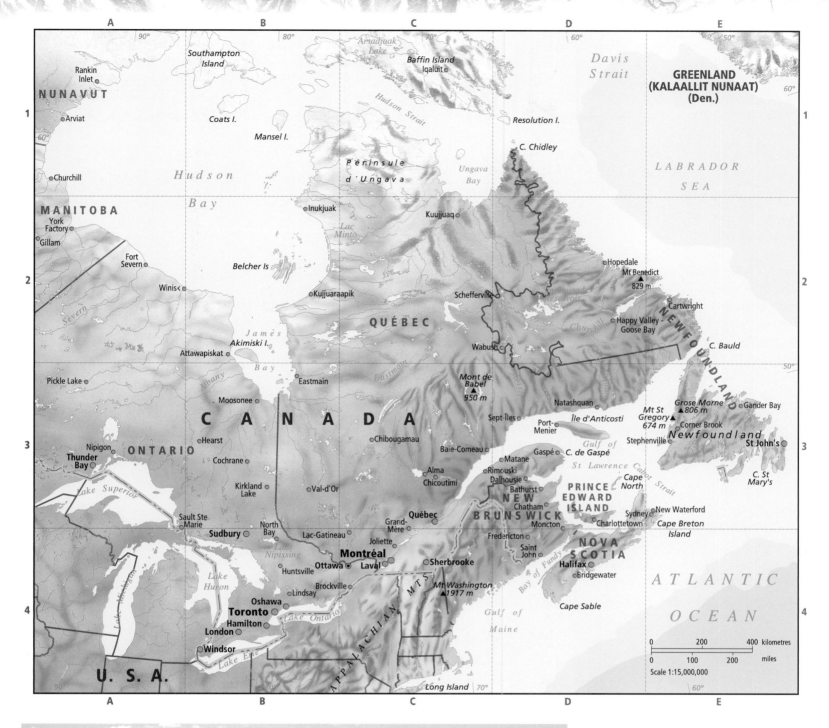

LABRADOR SEA

GREENLAND (KALAALLIT NUNAAT) (Den.)

Davis Strait

NUNAVUT

Rankin Inlet
Arviat
Churchill
York Factory
Gillam
Fort Severn
Winisk

MANITOBA

Southampton Island
Coats I.
Mansel I.
Belcher Is

Hudson Bay

Péninsule d'Ungava

Ungava Bay

Amadjuak Lake
Baffin Island
Iqaluit
Resolution I.
C. Chidley

Hudson Strait

Inukjuak
Kujjuaraapik

Kuujjuaq

Scheffferville

Hopedale
Mt Benedict 829 m
Cartwright
Happy Valley - Goose Bay
C. Bauld

QUÉBEC

Wabush

NEWFOUNDLAND

James Bay

Akimiski I.
Attawapiskat
Pickle Lake

Moosonee

Eastmain

Mont de Babel 950 m

Natashquan

Grose Morne 806 m
Gander Bay
Mt St Gregory 674 m
Corner Brook
Newfoundland
St John's
C. St Mary's

C A N A D A

ONTARIO

Nipigon
Thunder Bay

Hearst
Cochrane

Kirkland Lake

Chibougamau

Val-d'Or

Baie-Comeau

Matane

Gaspé

Sept-Iles
Port-Menier

Île d'Anticosti

C. de Gaspé

Gulf of St Lawrence

Cabot Strait

Stephenville

Alma
Chicoutimi

Rimouski
Dalhousie
Bathurst
Chatham

PRINCE EDWARD ISLAND

Cape North

Cape Breton Island

Sault Ste Marie
Sudbury
North Bay

Lac-Gatineau

Grand-Mère
Québec

NEW BRUNSWICK

Moncton
Charlottetown
Sydney
New Waterford

Lake Superior
Lake Nipissing

Joliette

Montréal
Ottawa Laval

Huntsville

Sherbrooke

Fredericton
Saint John

NOVA SCOTIA

Halifax
Bridgewater

ATLANTIC OCEAN

Lake Huron

Lindsay
Brockville

Mt Washington 1917 m

Bay of Fundy

Cape Sable

Oshawa
Toronto
Hamilton
London
Windsor

Lake Ontario
Lake Erie

APPALACHIAN MTS

Gulf of Maine

Long Island

U.S.A.

0   200   400 kilometres
0   100   200 miles
Scale 1:15,000,000

Ottawa, on the banks of the Ottawa River, grew from an 1820s British military settlement into a trading post and logging town. It was chosen as Canada's capital by Queen Victoria in 1857.

An Inuit woman, Nunavut.

81

United States

World power

The United States of America is the most prosperous and powerful nation on Earth, and its most open multicultural society. It is also the most scientifically advanced nation. Its natural resources are seemingly inexhaustible—it has 20 per cent of the world's known oil reserves, extensive coal deposits, abundant hydro-electricity, as well as being rich in copper, lead, zinc, gold, nickel and silver. A mild climate and good soils and rainfall in most of the United States make it easy to grow food and other crops, and the country is a leading producer of meat, dairy foods, soy beans, maize, oats, wheat, barley, cotton, sugar and forest products.

The **United States** can be divided into three major regions: the ancient Appalachian Mountains and Atlantic coastal plain in the east; the broad basin of the Mississippi and Missouri Rivers in the centre; and in the west, the deserts and young mountain ranges of the Pacific coast.

Washington, Oregon and California share the Pacific shoreline, where coastal ranges trap bountiful rainfall. The huge forests and massive trees of the north are important revenue-earners, primarily for their timber, but also for the tourism attracted to national parks such as Mount Rainier (centred on an inactive volcano) and Olympic. In the south are the spectacular giant redwood forests of northern California and the giant sequoias of the Yosemite area. California's fertile valleys produce most of the nation's fruit, vegetables and wine grapes, while its 'Silicon Valley', a series of new urban developments south of San Francisco, leads the world of high technology. The region lies in an active earthquake zone and has active volcanoes, such as Mount Saint Helens, which erupted violently in 1980.

Montana, Idaho, Wyoming, Utah and Colorado are dominated by the Rocky

A horseback inspection of one of California's numerous vineyards. Although California's first wine grapes were planted by Spanish missionaries near San Diego in the late 1700s, its wine industry really began with the first Napa Valley vineyards in the 1850s and 1860s. Today the state is a major world wine-producing region.

Mountains. In the north are deep gorges cut by the meltwaters of ancient glaciers, and the slopes are forested with magnificent Douglas fir, western hemlock and Sitka spruce. Timber, the mining of gold and silver, beef cattle raising and tourism to wilderness parks and ski resorts such as Aspen, are major revenue-earners. The nation's first transcontinental railway line opened in the 1860s; it cut through the Rocky Mountains, which until that time had formed a barrier to the transport of people and goods across the

A desert landscape in Arches National Park, Utah.

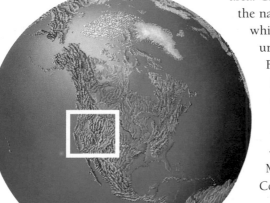

Undulating farming country in Idaho. Potatoes are the state's main crop, followed by hay and wheat.

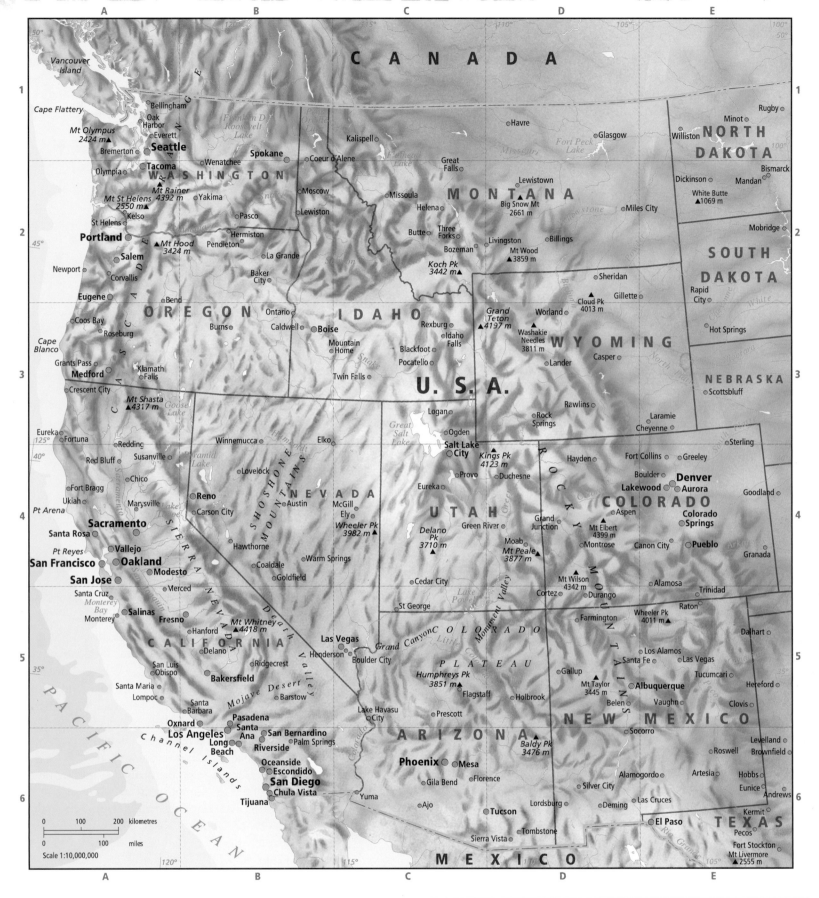

continent. Approximately 70 per cent of Utah's population belong to the Church of the Latter Day Saints (Mormons) which was founded here in the mid-1800s.

In the states of Arizona and New Mexico, huge cattle ranches and fields of cotton are the main farming activities on the dry, warm plains. However, it is the region's large deposits of oil and natural gas that earn most revenue. Natural attractions include the Grand Canyon and the Painted Desert. The influence of early Spanish colonisers can be seen in place names and many customs.

The Navajo of Arizona are noted silversmiths, using patterns from the past to produce jewellery for a modern market. Turquoise, featured in the pieces shown here, is mined locally and regarded as the stone of happiness, health and good fortune.

UNITED STATES OF AMERICA
SEE PAGE 82

Record holder

• Texas is the largest state in the United States

• Missouri River, at 4,090 kilometres (2,545 miles), is the longest river in North America

• Arkansas has the only diamond mine in the United States, near Murfreesboro

Masks on sale for the New Orleans Mardi Gras festival. The city's annual carnival season finishes with a colourful parade on Shrove Tuesday.

Buffalo (bison) are well-adapted to winter on the Great Plains. The mighty herds that once roamed here were destroyed by hunters, not the weather.

CENTRAL
United States

Corn belt and cereal bowl

This region of enormous diversity extends south from the Canadian border and the industrial cities of the Great Lakes, through the vast dry grasslands of the centre to the bayous, swamps and lagoons bordering the Gulf of Mexico. By the mid-1700s much of this land was under the control of the British government, which prohibited settlement west of the Appalachian Mountains. Following the Declaration of Independence in 1776, settlers poured west. There was then more than a century of wars with the Native American peoples who were being forced from the area. The fertile soils of the Great Plains were planted with wheat and corn and, although these crops were highly successful at first, by the 1930s overcropping, dry years and destructive winds had turned vast stretches into a 'dust bowl'. Improved farming methods have since restored its productivity. [*SEE HABITAT DESTRUCTION*]

Draining the centre of the North American continent is the vast basin of the Mississippi–Missouri Rivers, about 2,500 kilometres (1,500 miles) wide and extending south from Canada to empty into the Gulf of Mexico. The Mississippi is a major transport route and also forms the border of a number of states.

The states of North and South Dakota, Nebraska, Iowa, Kansas and Oklahoma spread across the Great Plains, a vast, generally flat, dry grassland that stretches 4,500 kilometres (2,800 miles) from northern Canada into Texas. Today this fertile region is a major wheat-growing area. It also has valuable mineral resources, with one of the world's largest deposits of oil lying under Texas. The Great Plains were once the home of Native American tribes such as the Sioux and Comanche, who lived by hunting buffalo, and the Mandan, Omaha and Kansa, who were farmers. Following the introduction of the horse by the Spanish in the 1500s, the people of the Great Plains became expert at taming, breeding and riding horses. By the end of

The chilly waters of Lake Superior lap the sandstone cliffs of Miners Castle, in Pictured Rocks National Lakeshore, North Michigan.

the 1800s ranchers and farmers had forced most of the Native American peoples off the Great Plains. The once huge buffalo herds also virtually disappeared as their rangelands were ploughed and planted.

Minnesota, Wisconsin and Illinois, bordering the Great Lakes, have densely populated industrial and manufacturing centres, such as Minneapolis, Milwaukee and Chicago, as well as the extraordinary wild beauty of lakes and forested mountains. Missouri, to the south, is an industrial and farming state. Its location on the Mississippi makes it a centre of water transport, and its cities of St Louis and Kansas City are major air, road and rail terminals.

Arkansas and Louisiana lie in the coastal lowlands bordering the Gulf of Mexico. Native American cultures were present from very early times. The rich alluvial soils of the Mississippi give them a strong agricultural base. Cotton and tobacco were once the mainstay, but today a variety of other crops are grown, from vegetables to fruit and peanuts. The region now occupied by these two states was claimed for France in 1682, and control passed to Spain and then back to France. It became part of the United States in 1803, as part of the Louisiana Purchase, when a huge territory bordered by the Gulf, the Mississippi and the Rocky Mountains was bought from France. The purchase doubled the size of the United States.

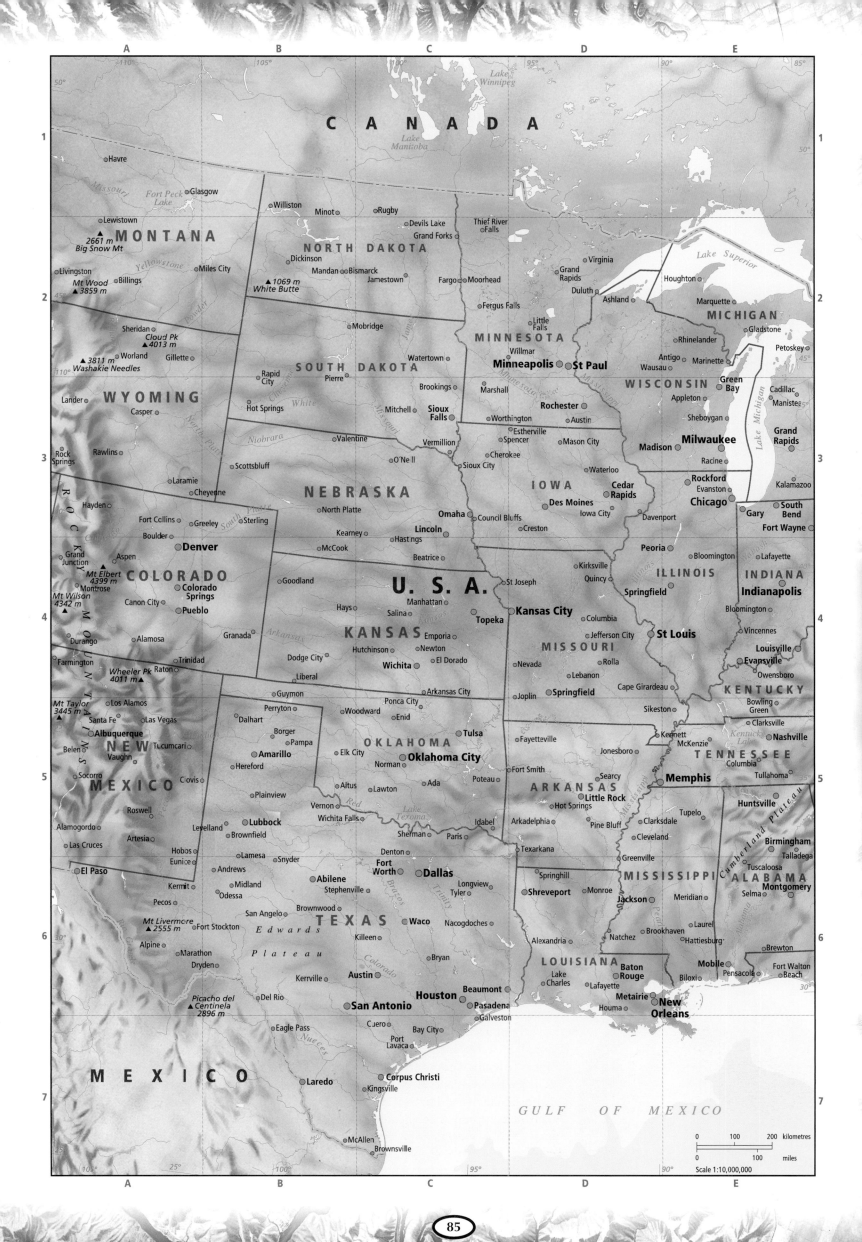

**UNITED STATES
OF AMERICA**
SEE PAGE 82

Record holder

• New York city is the largest city in the
United States

• New York city is the home of the
United Nations

• New Jersey manufactures more chemical
products than any other American state

• Washington is the only city that is not
part of a state. It is a federal district and
lies between the states of Maryland
and Virginia

EASTERN
United States

Colonial heritage, civil war

The east coast of the United States was where the Europeans decided to settle.
First to arrive were the English, in 1607; the Dutch and French followed. The
American War of Independence resulted in the beaten British withdrawing
north, to Canada. The United States became a nation with the Declaration of
Independence in 1776. The most serious threat to its existence came from
within—from 1861 to 1865 it was torn by civil war between the slave-owners
in the south and the slave-liberators in the north.

*The skyscrapers of New York city's borough of Manhattan, as seen at dusk from the Empire State Building.
Manhattan contains the financial centre of Wall Street and the theatrical district of Broadway.*

*'Faces of Honor' sculpture at the
Vietnam Veteran's Memorial,
Washington D.C.*

The Atlantic States are dominated
by coastal lowlands, which stretch south from
Cape Cod to the Florida Keys. Inland are the
Appalachians, an ancient band of sedimentary
mountains and plateaus. They were a barrier to
the westward spread of European settlement until
a way was found up the valley of the Mohawk
River and through the range that opens onto land
bordering the Great Lakes and the interior
plains beyond.

Connecticut, Maine, Massachusetts, New
Hampshire, Rhode Island and Vermont, in the
north of the region, are collectively known as
New England. European settlement here dates
from the English Pilgrim Fathers, who arrived at
Plymouth in 1620. New England is known for its
forested slopes (which have regenerated
in the past century with the decline of
farming), picturesque rural landscapes and
fishing harbours. The area is famous for
its maple syrup. Rhode Island has the
distinction of being the smallest state in
the Union, as well as being home to
some of its oldest buildings.

New York takes its name from its capital
city, which was founded on Manhattan

Island in 1624 by the Dutch as New Amsterdam;
the British changed its name when they captured
it in 1664. New York state was one of the thirteen
original colonies of America. From its earliest
days, it has attracted immigrants from around the
world. The state of Pennsylvania was founded by
Quaker William Penn in 1682 on land granted
to him by King Charles II of England. The
Declaration of Independence was signed in
the city of Philadelphia.

New Jersey was settled by the Dutch in 1660 and
won by the English in 1664; it was the site of
more than ninety battles during the American
War of Independence, and although it is an
important industrial state, its many market
gardens, flower gardens and orchards have also
earned it the nickname of 'Garden State'.

Delaware, Maryland, Virginia, North Carolina,
South Carolina, Georgia and Florida occupy the
low coastal plain, which includes many areas of
swamp. Offshore barrier islands and sandbars are
popular resort areas for the inland population,
despite the threat of hurricanes. Florida is a very
popular tourist destination. The first successful
English settlement in the region was at
Jamestown, Virginia, in 1607.

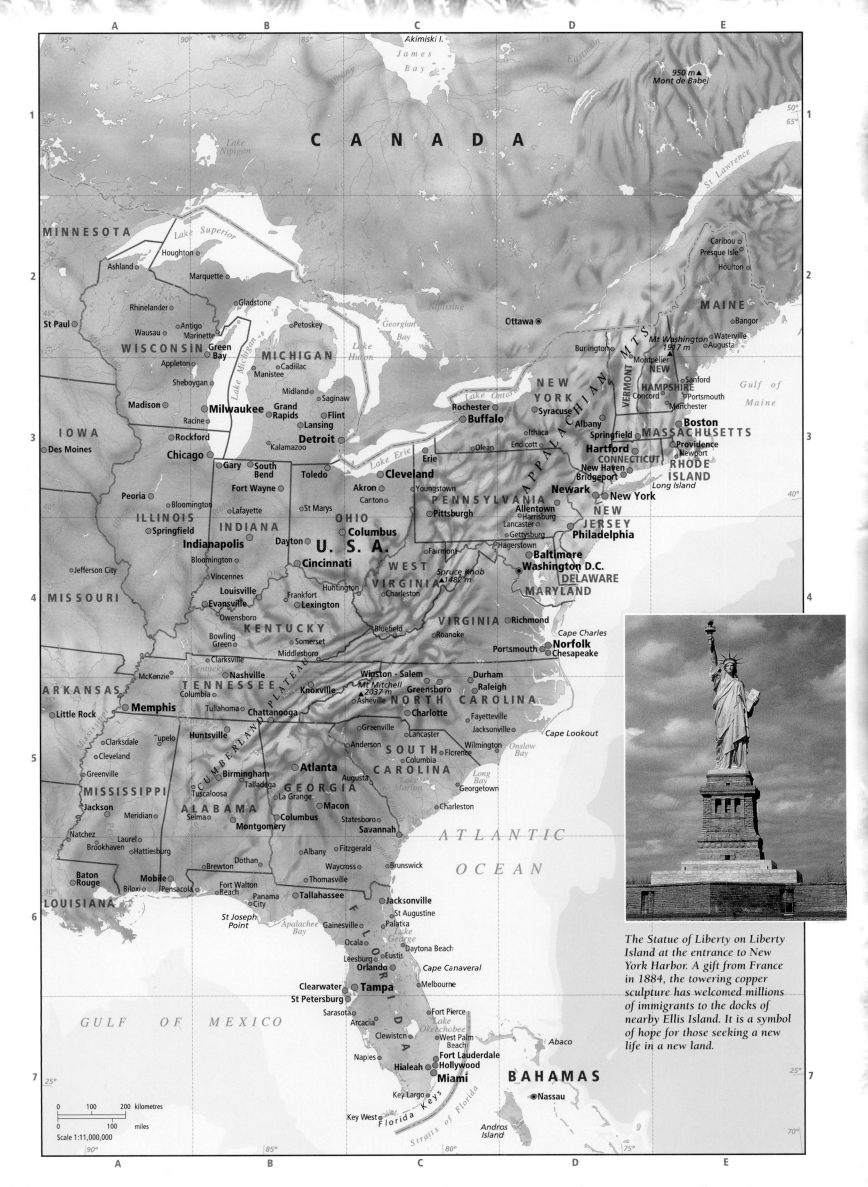

A · B · C · D · E

CANADA

MINNESOTA

Lake Superior

Houghton
Ashland
Marquette
Rhinelander
Gladstone
Petoskey
Georgian Bay
Ottawa

MAINE

Caribou
Presque Isle
Houlton
Bangor

950 m ▲
Mont de Babel

St Paul
Wausau
Antigo
Marinette
WISCONSIN
Green Bay
Appleton
Sheboygan
Madison
Milwaukee
Racine
Rockford
Chicago

MICHIGAN
Cadillac
Manistee
Midland
Saginaw
Lake Michigan
Grand Rapids
Lansing
Flint
Detroit
Kalamazoo

Lake Huron

Nipissing

Burlington
VERMONT
Montpelier
Mt Washington
1917 m
NEW HAMPSHIRE
Concord
Manchester
Sanford
Portsmouth
Waterville
Augusta
Gulf of Maine

NEW YORK
Rochester
Buffalo
Syracuse
Albany
Ithaca
Lake Ontario

Springfield
MASSACHUSETTS
Boston
Hartford
Providence
Newport
CONNECTICUT
RHODE ISLAND
New Haven
Bridgeport
Long Island

IOWA
Des Moines

ILLINOIS
Peoria
Bloomington
Springfield
Indianapolis
Bloomington

INDIANA
Gary
South Bend
Fort Wayne
Lafayette

Toledo
St Marys
Dayton

OHIO
Columbus
Cincinnati

Akron
Canton
Erie
Cleveland
Youngstown
PENNSYLVANIA
Pittsburgh

Olean
Endicott
APPALACHIAN MTS
Newark
New York
Allentown
Harrisburg
Lancaster
Gettysburg
Hagerstown
NEW JERSEY
Philadelphia
Baltimore
Washington D.C.
DELAWARE

U.S.A.

Frankfort
Lexington
Louisville
Evansville
Owensboro
Vincennes

WEST VIRGINIA
Charleston
Huntington
Fairmont
Spruce Knob
▲1482 m

MARYLAND

MISSOURI
Jefferson City

KENTUCKY
Bowling Green
Somerset
Middlesboro
Clarksville

Bluefield

VIRGINIA
Roanoke
Richmond
Cape Charles
Portsmouth
Norfolk
Chesapeake

ARKANSAS
Little Rock

Nashville
Columbia
Tullahoma
Chattanooga
TENNESSEE
Knoxville
McKenzie

Winston - Salem
Greensboro
Durham
Raleigh
Mt Mitchell
▲2037 m
Asheville
NORTH CAROLINA
Charlotte
Fayetteville
Jacksonville
Cape Lookout

Memphis
Clarksdale
Tupelo
Huntsville
Cleveland
Greenville

Talladega
Birmingham
Tuscaloosa

CUMBERLAND PLATEAU

Greenville
Anderson
SOUTH CAROLINA
Columbia
Lancaster
Florence
Wilmington
Onslow Bay

MISSISSIPPI
Jackson
Meridian

GEORGIA
ALABAMA
Selma
Montgomery
La Grange
Atlanta
Augusta
Lake Marion
Columbia
Georgetown
Long Bay

ATLANTIC
OCEAN

Natchez
Laurel
Brookhaven
Hattiesburg

Columbus
Macon
Statesboro
Savannah
Charleston

Baton Rouge
LOUISIANA
Mobile
Biloxi
Pensacola
Dothan
Albany
Fitzgerald
Waycross
Brunswick

Brewton
Fort Walton Beach
Panama City
Tallahassee
Thomasville

St Joseph Point
Apalachee Bay
Gainesville
Ocala
Leesburg
Eustis

FLORIDA
Jacksonville
St Augustine
Palatka
Daytona Beach
Lake George

GULF OF MEXICO

Clearwater
Tampa
St Petersburg
Sarasota
Orlando
Melbourne
Cape Canaveral

Naples
Arcacia
Clewiston
Lake Okeechobee
West Palm Beach
Fort Pierce
Abaco

Fort Lauderdale
Hialeah
Hollywood
Miami
Key Largo

BAHAMAS
Nassau

Key West
Florida Keys
Straits of Florida
Andros Island

0 100 200 kilometres
0 100 miles
Scale 1:11,000,000

The Statue of Liberty on Liberty Island at the entrance to New York Harbor. A gift from France in 1884, the towering copper sculpture has welcomed millions of immigrants to the docks of nearby Ellis Island. It is a symbol of hope for those seeking a new life in a new land.

MEXICO

Capital   Mexico City
Population   100,294,036
Official language   Spanish
Main religion   Roman Catholic 93%
Currency   Mexican peso
Form of government   Federal republic
Record holder   Mexico City has one of
the world's largest metropolitan area
populations; Mexico is the world's leading
producer of silver

Cooking on the streets, Mexico.

Mexico

Ancient empires

**People have lived in the fertile valleys
of central and southeastern Mexico
for more than 10,000 years. From
about 3,000 years ago they began
settling in villages, domesticating
animals and growing crops. Several
civilisations and empires rose and fell
before the arrival of the Spanish in
1500. Most Mexicans today are
descendants of Amerindian peoples
and Spanish colonists.**

Mexico lies at the meeting place of several
of the plates that make up the Earth's surface.
Movement of these plates causes earthquakes
and volcanic eruptions, and Mexico is in an
active earthquake zone with several active
volcanoes. The country has major petroleum
resources and today is one of the world's largest
oil producers. Most oil comes from the Gulf of
Mexico. Agriculture remains important. About a
quarter of the population are farmers, many of
them living by growing maize, beans and squash.
The main agricultural export crops are coffee,
cotton and sugarcane. Meat and fish are also
exported. Mexican forests produce hardwood and
chicle, the gum used in chewing gum. The long
peninsula of Baja California is mostly desert, and
is known for the giant, slow-growing cactus
called saguaro, which can live for up to 200 years
and reach a height of 18 metres (60 feet). Mexico
is the world's leading producer of silver. The
country also boasts mineral reserves that have
yet to be exploited.

*Many vegetables and fruits common throughout the world today, such as tomatoes, corn, avocadoes,
green beans, chilli peppers, red peppers, sweet potatoes and squash, were first cultivated in Central
America. The movement was both ways—radishes, shown here being washed in a Mexican market,
were introduced to the Americas from Europe.*

Agriculture in Mexico began more than 2,500 years ago with crops planted on terraces cut into the fertile volcanic slopes of the central highlands. Networks of irrigation canals made full use of the unreliable rainfall. The Toltecs ruled central Mexico from about AD 1000 to AD 1200. Yucatán, to the east, was part of the Mayan empire, which flourished from AD 250 to AD 900. In the 1300s the Mexica tribe established Tenochtitlan, which became the centre of the Aztec Empire, and is now known as Mexico City. In 1521, when Spanish forces, led by explorer Hernando Cortés, conquered Tenochtitlan and destroyed the empire, the Aztec population may have numbered as many as 15 million. They had a calendar, a counting system and a form of writing. Their cities featured large pyramid-shaped buildings and monumental sculptures. An extensive and highly productive agricultural system drained swampy lakes and turned them into raised fields separated by canals (the chinampas).

Mexico has been dominated by the one political party, the PRI, since 1929. There is growing disatisfaction with the political process, and a number of revolts have occurred in recent years. Rural poverty also contributes to the discontent.

The Temple of the Magician, in the Mayan centre of Uxmal, near Yucatán, Mexico. Mighty stone buildings are all that remain of the Mayan Empire, which collapsed more than six centuries before the arrival of the Spanish.

BELIZE

Capital Belmopan
Population 235,789
Official language English
Main religions Roman Catholic 62%, Protestant 30%
Currency Belizean dollar
Form of government Constitutional monarchy
Record holder Last country in the Americas to achieve independence (formerly known as British Honduras); Longest coral reef in the Americas lies offshore (second only to Australia's Great Barrier Reef)

COSTA RICA

Capital San José
Population 3,674,490
Official language Spanish
Main religion Roman Catholic 95%
Currency Costa Rican colón
Form of government Republic

EL SALVADOR

Capital San Salvador
Population 5,839,079
Official language Spanish
Main religions Roman Catholic 75%, Protestant and other 25%
Currency Colón
Record holder Smallest, most densely populated country in Central America

GUATEMALA

Capital Guatemala
Population 12,335,580
Official language Spanish
Main religions Roman Catholic 75%, Protestant 25%
Currency Quetzal
Record holder Highest peak in Central America is Volcan Tajumulco, 4,220 metres (13,845 feet) high; Largest population of the Central American states

HONDURAS

Capital Tegucigalpa
Population 5,997,327
Official language Spanish
Main religion Roman Catholic 97%
Currency Lempira
Form of government Republic

NICARAGUA

Capital Managua
Population 4,717,132
Official language Spanish
Main religion Roman Catholic 95%
Currency Córdoba
Form of government Republic

PANAMA
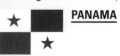

Capital Panama
Population 2,778,526
Official language Spanish
Main religions Roman Catholic 85%, Protestant 15%
Currency Balboa
Record holder Narrowest part of the land bridge between North and South America, 80 kilometres (50 miles) wide; Highest standard of living in Central America

CENTRAL
America

Great plantations

Several of the great plates that make up the Earth's crust meet in this region. The narrow Central American isthmus, washed by the waters of both the Pacific Ocean and the Caribbean Sea, was formed by the collision of the Caribbean and Cocos plates. The islands result from the Caribbean Plate moving against the North American Plate. The many volcanoes—some still active—laid down the fertile soils on which Spanish, British and French colonists established sugar, coffee, cotton and banana plantations from the 1500s on. Countless thousands of slaves were brought from Africa as labour. Plantation products remain major revenue earners, with many of the countries economically dependent on the United States, the main buyer of their exports.

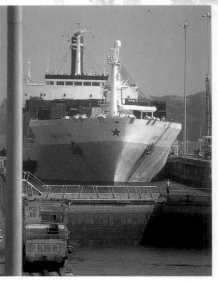

A cargo ship heads east through the Panama Canal.

Belize
was originally inhabited by Mayan Indians. The first European settlers were British who went to Belize to cut the valuable rainforest timber in the 1600s. Sugar plantations worked by African slaves followed. The forests are still logged for rosewood and mahogany and also produce chicle, the gum used for chewing gum. In 1961 a hurricane destroyed the former capital, Belize City.

Costa Rica
was once home to the great Maya and Inca civilisations. Christopher Columbus called this land 'costa rica' meaning 'rich coast'. Coffee is the most important export, followed by bananas.

El Salvador's
main resource is the fertile volcanic soil of its inland plain. From the 1880s much of this has been controlled by only fourteen families. Coffee, sugar and tobacco is grown in vast plantations worked by poorly paid rural labourers. Discontentment at this situation led to civil war from 1979 to 1991.

Guatemala
was the home of the Mayan Amerindian civilisation which flourished between 300 and 900 AD. The Spanish arrived in 1523 and established sugar, coffee and banana plantations on the rich volcanic plains of the Pacific coast.

Honduras
was the world's leading exporter of bananas in the 1920s and 1930s. Coffee is now the main export earner but bananas are still an important commodity. In the west are the historic ruins of Copan, a site of the Mayan civilisation which ended before the arrival of the Spanish in 1522. Most of the workforce are farmers, many at a subsistence level.

Nicaragua
is a former Spanish colony. Its two main exports are coffee and cotton. The 1980s and 1990s saw much violent unrest between the left-wing Sandinistas and the United States-backed 'contras'. Nicaragua's tropical wildlife includes crocodile and jaguar.

Izalco Volcano is one of El Salvador's twenty or so volcanoes. Some are still active.

The jungle-covered temples of the ancient Mayan religious centre of Tikal, in Guatemala, were abandoned long before the Spanish arrived.

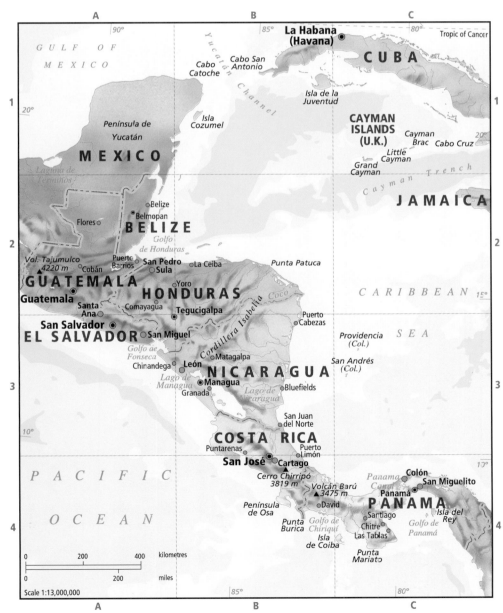

This fruit and vegetable seller has her stall on the road between Honduras' capital Tegucigalpa and Valle des Angeles.

Panama joins the continents of North and South America and, since the opening of the Panama canal, also joins two oceans—the Atlantic and the Pacific. Bananas make up nearly half of the country's exports, but Panama's main revenue earners are financial services and tourism.

ANTIGUA AND BARBUDA

Capital St Johns
Population 64,246
Official language English
Main religions Protestant 90%, Roman Catholic 10%
Currency East Caribbean dollar
Form of government Democracy

BAHAMAS

Capital Nassau
Population 283,705
Official language English
Main religions Baptist 32%, Anglican 20%, Roman Catholic, 19%, Methodist 6%
Currency Bahamian dollar
Form of government Constitutional monarchy

BARBADOS

Capital Bridgetown
Population 259,191
Official language English
Main religions Protestant 67%, Roman Catholic 4%, none 17%
Currency Barbadian dollar
Form of government Parliamentary democracy

CUBA

Capital Havana
Population 11,088,829
Official language Spanish
Main religions Roman Catholic 40%, Protestant and African Spiritist 10%, none 50%
Currency Cuban peso
Form of government Communist state
Record holder Largest island in the Caribbean—it has the same area as all the other islands combined; Cuba has the only communist government in the Americas

DOMINICA

Capital Roseau
Population 64,881
Official language English
Main religions Roman Catholic 77%, Protestant 15%
Currency East Caribbean dollar
Form of government Parliamentary state

THE Caribbean

Islands in the sun

From the 1500s on, Spain, Britain, France and the Netherlands all claimed, fought over and exploited the islands of the Caribbean. The resulting mixture of races (Carib, African and European) and cultures has created national identities marked by different peoples, languages, customs and political systems.

Antigua and Barbuda consists

of three islands. The largest, Antigua, was visited and named by explorer Christopher Columbus in 1493. It became a British colony in 1667, and had vast sugar plantations. Its present Afro-Caribbean population is descended from the original slaves and the original Arawak and Carib Indians.

The Bahamas consists of 700 low-lying

islands and 2,400 cays. Although lacking natural resources, it has one of the highest standards of living in the region, due to income from offshore banking, insurance and financial services that are based there.

Barbados was originally inhabited by

the Arawak Indians, and later settled by the British; its present population is mainly descended from African slaves. The island is ringed by coral and has dazzling white sand beaches and lush, rolling hills in the north and centre. Tourism has recently overtaken sugar-growing and refining as the country's main source of revenue.

Cuba was visited by Christopher Columbus

in 1492. Under Spanish rule, sugar plantations worked by African slaves became the foundation of the island's population and economy. Slavery was only abolished in 1878. Sugar is still Cuba's main export—it is the world's third largest sugar producer—and it also produces tobacco, including the famous Havana cigars.

Dominica was fought over by both

the French and British for years before being colonised by Britain. It is unusual in still having a community of 3,000 Carib Indians, whose warrior ancestors, protected by dense inland forests, held off European colonisation for 250 years.

Lush vegetation meets tropical waters at Port Antonio, on the northeast coast of Jamaica, a British colony from 1655 to 1962. The island is the home of reggae music.

The **Dominican Republic's** mountainous terrain and spectacular beaches have led to a rapid growth in tourism. Sugar is the main export, followed by coffee, cocoa and tobacco.

Grenada's original Carib Indians managed to fend off all invaders until the 1650s, when the island was settled by the French; in 1762 it became British. Today nutmeg and mace, introduced from the Moluccas (Indonesia), are the main crops.

Haiti was used by Spain for growing sugar, then given to France in 1697. Following the French Revolution, a rebellion by slaves in Haiti led to the establishment, in 1804, of the world's first black republic. Since then, the country has endured almost two centuries of instability, violence, dictatorship, military rule, and endemic poverty.

Jamaica became a slave-based sugar-producing plantation society from 1655 when the British seized the island. Over 300 years later, in 1962, Jamaica won independence from Britain. Today tourism and bauxite exports are the main industries.

The image of revolutionary Ché Guevara adorns the wall of a Havana hotel. In the 1960s, Guevara was a minister in Cuba's communist government. He was killed in Bolivia in 1967.

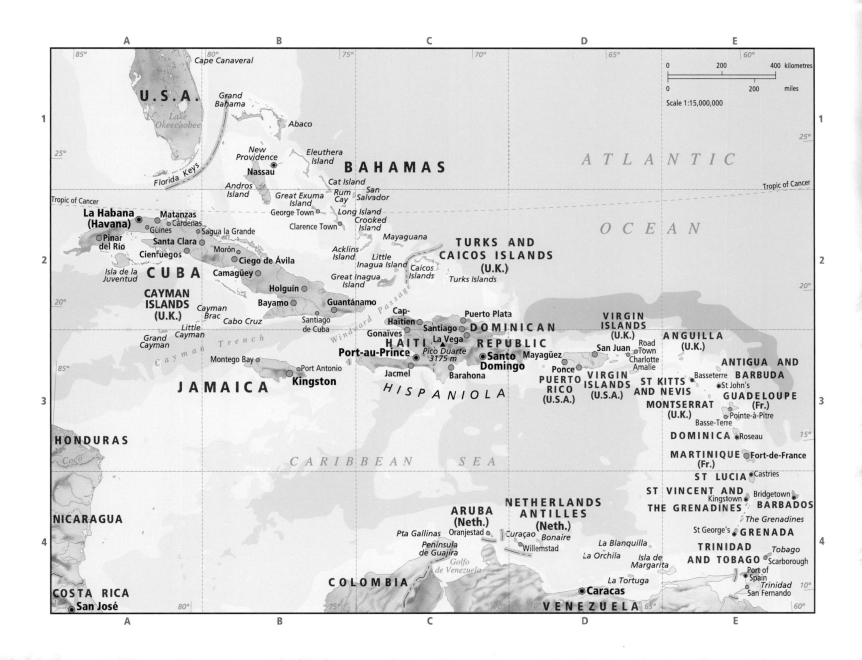

FACT FILE

DOMINICAN REPUBLIC

Capital Santo Domingo
Population 8,129,734
Official language Spanish
Main religion Roman Catholic 95%
Currency Peso
Form of government Republic
Record holder Santo Domingo, founded in 1496 by the brother of Christopher Columbus, is the oldest Spanish city in the Americas; Both the highest and lowest points are in the region—Pico Duarte is 3,175 metres (10,416 feet) high and Lake Enriquillo is 44 metres (144 feet) below sea level

GRENADA

Capital St Georges
Population 97,008
Official language English
Main religions Roman Catholic 64%, Protestant 27%
Currency East Caribbean dollar
Form of government Constitutional monarchy
Record holder World's leading producer of nutmeg and mace

HAITI

Capital Port-au-Prince
Population 6,884,264
Official language French
Main religions Roman Catholic (most of whom also practise Voodoo) 80%, Protestant 16%
Currency Gourd
Form of government Republic
Record holder Poorest country in the western hemisphere; World's highest rate of population growth

JAMAICA

Capital Kingston
Population 2,652,443
Official language English
Main religions Protestant 70%, Roman Catholic 7%, other including Rastafarian 23%
Currency Jamaican dollar
Form of government Constitutional monarchy

ST KITTS AND NEVIS

Capital Basseterre
Population 42,838
Official language English
Main religions Christian 89%, other 11%
Currency East Caribbean dollar
Form of government Constitutional monarchy

ST LUCIA

Capital Castries
Population 154,020
Official language English
Main religions Roman Catholic 90%, Protestant 7%
Currency East Caribbean dollar
Form of government Constitutional monarchy

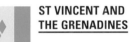

ST VINCENT AND THE GRENADINES

Capital Kingstown
Population 120,519
Official language English
Main religions Anglican 42%, Methodist 21%, Roman Catholic 12%, other 25%
Currency East Caribbean dollar
Form of government Constitutional monarchy

TRINIDAD AND TOBAGO

Capital Port of Spain
Population 1,102,096
Official language English
Main religions Roman Catholic 32%, Hindu 24.5%, Anglican 14.5 %, other Protestant 14%, Muslim 6%
Currency Trinidad and Tobago dollar
Form of government Republic

The rich volcanic slopes of the island of Martinique. Martinique was described by Christopher Columbus in 1493 as 'the most beautiful country in the world'.

There are echoes of bygone plantation days in the gracious lines and landscaped gardens of Devon House, Kingston, Jamaica.

The Caribbean continued...

St Kitts and Nevis was the first part of the Caribbean to be colonised by Britain. Today most islanders are descended from the African slaves who worked the sugar and cotton plantations.

St Lucia's forested mountains and tropical beaches have long been a tourist attraction. As elsewhere in the Caribbean, its population is largely descended from African slaves imported to work in the sugar plantations.

St Vincent and the Grenadines

consist of 32 islands and low cays. The mountainous volcanic island of St Vincent has 89 per cent of the country's land and 95 per cent of its population.

The prosperity of **Trinidad and Tobago** is based on asphalt and oil reserves. Tobago, a detached piece of Trinidad's Northern Range, is known for its abundant wildlife.

There are a number of small dependencies and territories, a legacy of the colonial division of the resource-rich islands. **Anguilla,** the **British Virgin Islands,** the **Cayman Islands, Montserrat** and **Turks and Caicos Islands** are all dependent territories of the United Kingdom. **Guadeloupe** and **Martinique** are both overseas departments of France. **Aruba** and the **Netherlands Antilles** are self-governing parts of the Kingdom of the Netherlands. **Navassa Island** and the **Virgin Islands of the United States** are unincorporated territories of the United States. **Puerto Rico** was ceded by Spain to the United States in 1898.

A colourful shanty town overlooking the ocean in San Juan, the capital and chief port of Puerto Rico. Despite some crowded slums, the standard of living on the island is one of the highest in the region.

South America

Wealth from the soil

Much of this region of South America is rich in precious metals, gemstones, oil, coal and minerals. In the 1500s and 1600s the mines of Colombia were Spain's chief source of gold. Venezuela has valuable oil reserves. Elsewhere bauxite, copper and manganese are mined.

Colombia

Colombia was named after Christopher Columbus, who visited in 1499. It came under Spanish control in 1544, and was mined for its gold. Today its massive coal reserves, the largest in the region, make it a major exporter of coal. Some 80 per cent of the world's emeralds are mined here. Coffee is the country's biggest legitimate earner, but there is little doubt that far more money comes from the illegal trade in cocaine. Colombia's people of mixed indigenous-European or European-African descent make up more than 70 per cent of the population.

Guyana

Guyana was settled by the Dutch in 1616. They cleared coastal land, built dykes and planted sugarcane. The Dutch, and later the British, imported slaves from Africa and labour from India to work the plantations; these two groups now dominate political life in Guyana. Mineral resources include high-quality bauxite, diamonds, oil, uranium and copper. Numerous rivers flow from the mountains through tropical forest rich in wildlife, including the sloth, jaguar, tapir and capybara. In 1995 there was a major cyanide spill at the Omai gold mine, near the Essequibo River, and the effect of mining activities on the wildlife here is of great concern to conservationists. *[See Endangered species; Habitat destruction]*

Suriname

Suriname, formerly known as Dutch Guiana, has an unusual link to New York. In 1667 two colonial powers exchanged territory. The British gave Suriname to the Dutch, and the Dutch gave New Amsterdam, now known as New York, to the British. Suriname's dense forests cover 92 per cent of the nation's total land area and stretch from the coast to the highlands, virtually untouched. Bauxite provides over 65 per cent of Suriname's export earnings.

Venezuela

Venezuela was named 'new Venice' by the Spanish because the rows of Indian stilt houses in the waters of Lake Maracaibo reminded them of the canals of Venice. Today it is one of the region's most urbanised countries with 17 out of every 20 people living in cities, mostly along the fertile coastline and in the hot lowlands. Petroleum products provide more than 70 per cent of the country's export earnings. Iron ore, diamonds and gold are also mined and exported.

River boats in Puerto Colombia on the Caribbean coast of Colombia.

FACT FILE

COLOMBIA

Capital Bogotá
Population 39,309,422
Official language Spanish
Main religion Roman Catholic 95%
Currency Colombian peso
Form of government Republic
Record holder Largest coal exporter in the region

GUYANA

Capital Georgetown
Population 705,156
Official language English
Main religions Protestant 34%, Hindu 34%, Roman Catholic 18%, Muslim 9%
Currency Guyana dollar
Form of government Co-operative republic

SURINAME

Capital Paramaribo
Population 431,156
Official language Dutch
Main religions Hindu 27%, Mus im 20%, Roman Catholic 23%, Protestant 25%
Currency Suriname guilder
Form of government Republic

VENEZUELA

Capital Caracas
Population 23,203,466
Official language Spanish
Main religion Roman Catholic 96%
Currency Bolívar
Form of government Federal republic
Record holder World's highest waterfall, Angel Falls: 979 metres (3,212 feet)

Dependencies & Territories

FRENCH GUIANA

Capital Cayenne
Population 167,982
Official language French
Currency French franc
Form of government Overseas department of France

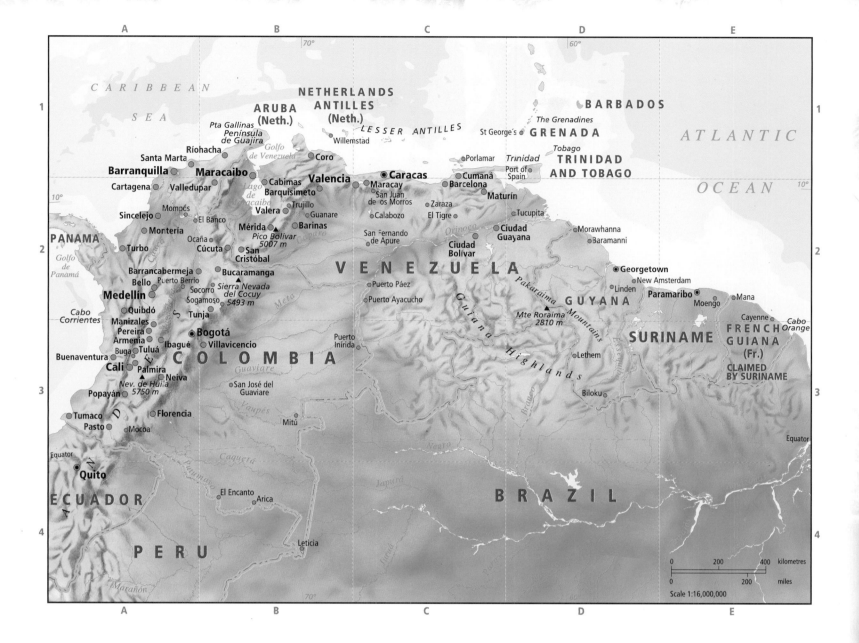

CARIBBEAN SEA

NETHERLANDS ANTILLES (Neth.)

ARUBA (Neth.)

BARBADOS

Pta Gallinas
Peninsula de Guajira

Ríohacha

Golfo de Venezuela

Coro

The Grenadines
St George's **GRENADA**

LESSER ANTILLES

ATLANTIC

Santa Marta

Willemstad

Porlamar

Trinidad **TRINIDAD**

Tobago

Barranquilla

Maracaibo

Valencia

Caracas

Cumaná

Port of Spain

AND TOBAGO

OCEAN

Cartagena

Valledupar

Cabimas

Barquisimeto

Maracay

Barcelona

Maturín

Lago de Maracaibo

Mompós

Valera

Trujillo

San Juan de os Morros

Zaraza

Tucupita

Sincelejo

El Banco

Mérida

Guanare

Calabozo

El Tigre

Montería

Ocaña

Pico Bolívar 5007 m

Barinas

Ciudad Guayana

Morawhanna

PANAMA

Turbo

Cúcuta

San Cristóbal

San Fernando de Apure

Orinoco

Baramanni

Golfo de Panamá

Barrancabermeja

Bucaramanga

V E N E Z U E L A

Ciudad Bolívar

Georgetown

Bello

Puerto Berrío

Puerto Páez

Linden

New Amsterdam

Medellín

Socorro

Sierra Nevada del Cocuy 5493 m

Meta

Puerto Ayacucho

GUYANA

Paramaribo

Moengo

Cabo Corrientes

Quibdó

Sogamoso

Tunja

Mte Roraima 2810 m

Pakaraima Mountains

Mana

Manizales

Pereira

Bogotá

Puerto Inírida

Lethem

SURINAME

Cayenne

Cabo Orange

Armenia

Ibagué

Villavicencio

FRENCH GUIANA (Fr.)

Buenaventura

Buga

Tuluá

Guaviare

Guiana Highlands

Biloku

CLAIMED BY SURINAME

Cali

Palmira

Neiva

Bravo

Nev. de Huila 5750 m

San José del Guaviare

C O L O M B I A

Tumaco

Popayán

Vaupés

Mitú

Equator

Pasto

Florencia

Mocoa

Caquetá

Negro

B R A Z I L

Equator

Equator

Quito

El Encanto

Arica

Japurá

E C U A D O R

Leticia

P E R U

Marañón

0   200   400 kilometres

0   200 miles

Scale 1:16,000,000

French Guiana is an overseas department of France. It is the site of the European Space Agency's rocket base. Sugarcane and bananas are grown on the coast, but the main exports are fish and fish products. French Guiana depends on France for its economic viability. The notorious French penal colony of Devil's Island was here.

The goliath spider can be found on the forest floor in many parts of South America. It hunts for ground birds and bats.

Caracas, capital of Venezuela. The great wealth (unevenly shared) and industrialisation that followed the development of Venezuela's petroleum industry made the country one of the most urbanised in the region.

BRAZIL

Capital Brasília

Population 171,853,126

Official language Portuguese

Main religions Roman Catholic 89%,
Protestant 7%

Currency Real

Form of government Federal republic

Record holder Largest country in South
America in both area and population;
World's largest producer of coffee; The
Amazon carries more water than any other
river in the world

Brazil

The Igaçu Falls, on the border with Argentina, from the Brazilian side. The falls form a curtain of water almost 3 kilometres (1¾ miles) wide.

The dye arrow-poison frog lives in the forests of Central and South America.

A bountiful rainforest

The Amazon Basin—once an inland sea—extends over more than 8 million square kilometres (3 million square miles), mainly in Brazil. Drained by the mighty Amazon and its more than 1,000 tributaries, it contains over a quarter of the planet's rainforests and a wider variety of plant and animal life than any other part of the world. There are over a thousand species of birds alone!

European colonists established huge sugarcane plantations on the fertile coastal plains, so until recently the Amazon Basin was virtually untouched. Today, however, logging, mining, clearing for cattle farms and the resettlement of Brazil's landless peasants is reducing the Amazon rainforest by up to 4 per cent each year. Raging forest fires in 1998 caused even more destruction. *[SEE DISAPPEARING CULTURES; HABITAT DESTRUCTION; RESOURCE DEPLETION; THE INDUSTRIAL FRONTIER]*

Brazil takes up almost half the continent of South America and is the fifth largest country in the world. It is also one of the most populous countries of the world. Its vast tropical northern half is covered in dense rainforest and is sparsely populated. Valuable trees found here include mahogany, kapok, rosewood, rubber and the towering Brazil nut tree, which can grow to 45 metres (148 feet) in height. High rainfall feeds a network of mighty rivers, including the Amazon, which flow through the forests to the Atlantic. More than 3,000 fish species live in the inland waterways, including the flesh-eating piranha. Anacondas are found along the forested banks. Other rainforest animals include spider monkeys, brightly coloured parrots, sloths and thousands of insect species. The Brazilian Highlands, in the centre and south, are made up of an immense plateau of hard, ancient rock, weathered into deep river valleys with spectacular waterfalls. Much of the interior is covered by savanna woodland. By contrast, much of the northeast region suffers from drought.

Amerindian tribes, including the Guaraní and Tupinambá, lived here for thousands of years; they hunted, fished, gathered rainforest fruits and grew crops, mainly cassava (a starchy root vegetable). Brazil was a Portuguese colony from 1500 to 1889. African slaves were imported to work in the sugar plantations. Today Brazil's multicultural population is a mix of Europeans, people of mixed European and African descent, Asians (mostly descendants from Japanese immigrants who arrived in the 1920s) and Amerindians. Most people live in cities along the Atlantic coast, with fewer than 7 per cent living in the Amazon region. Rio de Janiero, known for its spectacular beaches, carnivals and nightlife, is one of the largest cities in South America and was the capital of Brazil until replaced in 1960 by the modern city of Brasília.

In the upper reaches of the Xingu, Araguaia and Tocantins Rivers small groups of Amerindians continue their traditional way of life.

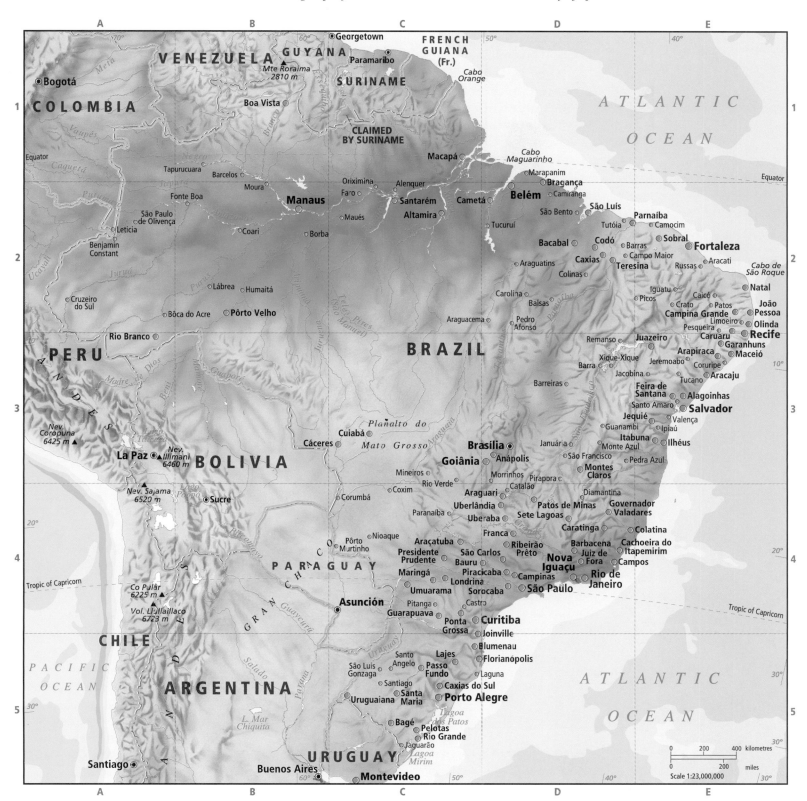

BOLIVIA

Capital Sucre (official),
La Paz (administrative)
Population 7,982,850
Official language Spanish,
Quechua, Aymara
Main religion Roman Catholic 95%
Currency Boliviano
Form of government Republic
Record holder Poorest country in
South America; Highest capital in the
world, La Paz: 3,600 metres (12,000 feet)

ECUADOR

Capital Quito
Population 12,562,496
Official language Spanish
Main religion Roman Catholic 95%
Currency Sucre
Form of government Republic
Record holder Grows more bananas
than any other country in the world

PERU

Capital Lima
Population 26,625,121
Official language Spanish, Quechua
Main religion Roman Catholic 90%
Currency Nuevo sol
Form of government Republic
Record holder Lake Titicaca is the
highest navigable lake in South America;
Iquitos is the furthest inland navigable port
on the Amazon River

CENTRAL
South America

Lost civilisations

Humans have been living in the high plains and valleys of the central Andes for more than 10,000 years. About 3,000 years ago, in Peru, the first of a series of civilisations emerged. It had irrigation to grow maize, potatoes, beans and peppers, fine pottery and expertly woven textiles with striking designs. Last and greatest of the civilisations was the Inca empire, established during the 1400s and extending from Ecuador to central Chile. The Incas built many fine roads, bridges and cities. In the 1530s Spanish conquistadors made their way into the Andes, lured by rumours of the Inca 'kingdom of gold'. The Spanish killed the Inca emperor, bringing the empire to an end.

Llamas grazing on the plains at the foot of Mount Sajama, Bolivia. A relative of the camel, llamas have been kept since prehistoric times for their wool and meat, and were also used to carry goods through the mountains.

Bolivia's mountainous terrain makes it difficult to access. Despite this, the Spanish mined and shipped back to Europe vast wealth from the huge silver deposit at Potosi. The Altiplano region, a high windswept plateau, runs for 400 kilometres (250 miles) from north to south between the parallel Andean ranges. Cold and treeless, it is home to the Quechua and Aymara Indians who make up 55 per cent of the population. Living as subsistence farmers, they grow maize, potatoes and coca, the leaves of which are used to make cocaine, an illegal substance that accounts for much of the country's export earnings.

Rural farmlands near the Inca capital of Cuzco, Peru.

Ecuador's capital Quito was an Inca city before being captured by the Spanish in the 1530s. The Spanish established huge plantations called haciendas on the coastal plains. Although petroleum and natural gas are now the country's main exports, bananas, coffee and cocoa are still important revenue earners. In the highlands, Amerindians continue traditional farming of maize and potatoes. Ecuador owns the Galapagos Islands, home to many remarkable animals, such as marine iguanas and giant tortoise.

Peru has many remarkable ruins from the Inca civilisation. Most famous is Machu Picchu, a site of ceremonial and religious significance built high above the deep Urubamba Valley. When rediscovered in 1912, the temples and other buildings were covered with thick jungle. Cleared and partly rebuilt, the ruins are now Peru's most famous tourist site. On a high desert on the south coast of Peru are the mysterious Nasca lines and figures. They are between 2,200 and 1,300 years old and were made by removing rocks and topsoil. There are huge stylised sculptures of fish, birds and mammals, and ruler-straight lines, some stretching for several kilometres.

Indians dancing at a festival in Peru. About half of the country's population lives in the valleys of the two high Andean ranges; most are subsistence farmers.

Blue-footed boobies on Galapagos Islands.

Spanish conquests

Southern South America is a region of amazing variety in climate and landform, from fertile subtropical plains to snow-capped volcanic peaks, high deserts and slow-moving glaciers. The boundaries of its four mainland countries were drawn by the colonial Spanish who arrived in the 1500s seeking silver, gold and other riches. Today beef production is the most important industry. Although their people come from many different backgrounds, the mainland countries share a common language and have all known major political upheavals in the nineteenth and twentieth centuries. Cattle, sheep and cereal crops are the main industries.

Mountains in the Torres del Paine National Park, on Chile's rugged southern coast.

Autumn colours on Tierra del Fuego, a windswept island divided between Argentina and Chile.

Argentina is the second largest country in South America. Its name comes from the Latin word for 'silver', which the Spanish explorers of the 1500s hoped to find there. In fact, the country lacked sizeable deposits. Instead the Spanish introduced horses, sheep and cattle. By the 1800s the last of the Amerindians were forced from the pampas (fertile grasslands) that became the home of beef cattle and gauchos (part Amerindian, part Spanish cattle herders). Today most Argentinians are of Spanish and Italian descent and live in the cities. Argentinian art, music and literature is strongly European in style.

Chile, hemmed in between the Pacific and the towering Andes, is never more than 180 kilometres (110 miles) wide. The Araucanian Indians fought hard to keep free, first against the Peruvian Indians, and then against the

Spanish. Today 60 per cent of the population lives in the fertile valley around Santiago, which has Chile's main vineyards and manufacturing industries. Chile owns several small Pacific islands, including Easter Island.

Paraguay was originally home to the Guaraní Indians. In 1537 it was settled by the Spanish who hoped to use the Guaraní to work their estates. However, the influence of the Jesuit priests prevented the exploitation of the indigenous Indians that happened elsewhere. Today 95 per cent of the population is of combined Indian and Spanish descent; about half are farmers.

Uruguay is the second smallest country in South America. Rich grasslands cover most of the country, and cattle and sheep farming is very successful. Uruguay is the world's second largest exporter of wool. Its industries are based on animal products, including meat processing. Most of the population is descended from the early Spanish settlers. The majority of the people live in cities and towns.

The **Falkland Islands** consist of East Falkland and West Falkland and about 200 islets. The islands are hilly and windswept, and it rains on an average of one day in two. Most of the population farm sheep. Ownership of the islands is disputed between Argentina and the United Kingdom. In 1982, Argentina waged an unsuccessful campaign to take the Falkland Islands. The three-month conflict cost approximately a thousand lives.

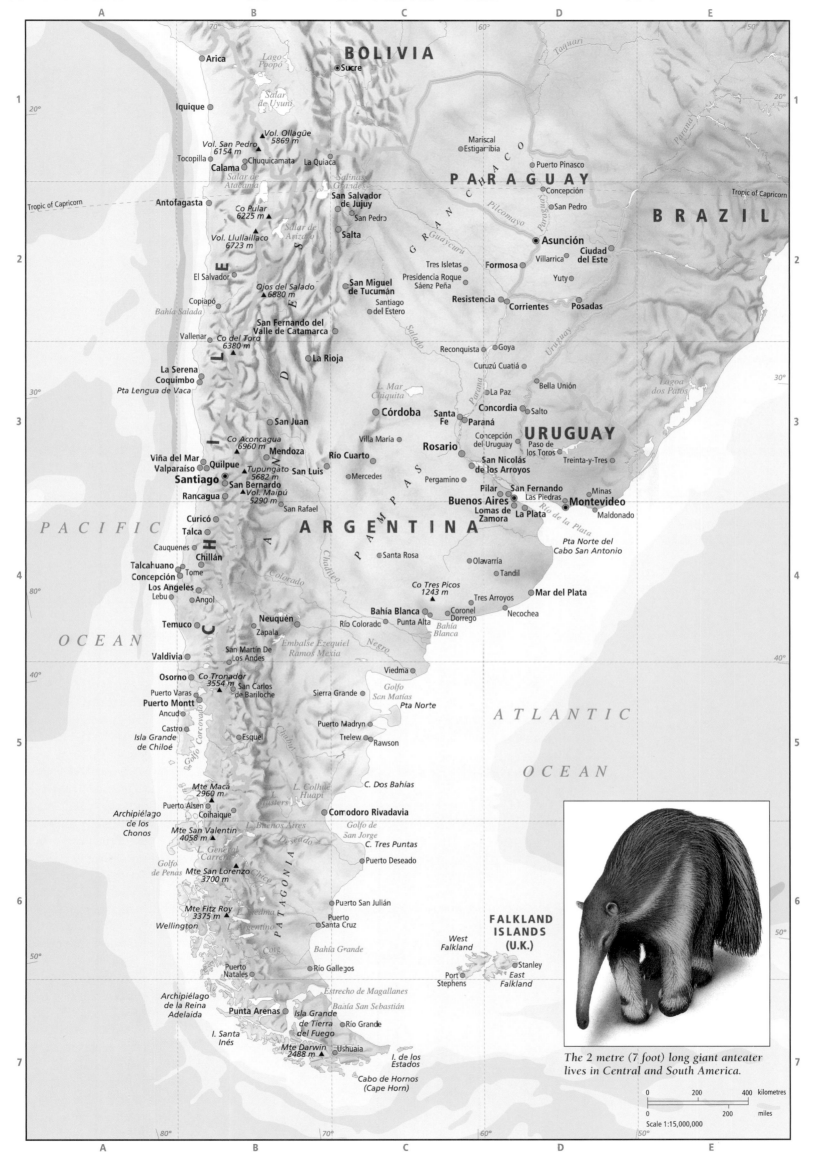

BOLIVIA

Arica
●Sucre

Lago
Poopó

Iquique

Salar
de Uyuni

Vol. San Pedro
6154 m
▲Vol. Ollagüe
5869 m

Tocopilla
Calama
Chuquicamata
La Quiaca

P A R A G U A Y

Mariscal
Estigarribia

●Puerto Pinasco

Salar de
Atacama

Salinas
Grandes

Concepción

Antofagasta

Tropic of Capricorn

Tropic of Capricorn

B R A Z I L

San Pedro

Co Pular
6225 m

**San Salvador
de Jujuy**

San Pedro

Salar de
Arizaro

Vol. Llullaillaco
6723 m

Salta

Formosa

Villarrica
Yuty
**Ciudad
del Este**

El Salvador

Tres Isletas

Presidencia Roque
Sáenz Peña

Asunción

**San Miguel
de Tucumán**

Copiapó

Ojos del Salado
▲6880 m

Santiago
del Estero

Resistencia
Corrientes
Posadas

Bahía Salada

Vallenar

**San Fernando del
Valle de Catamarca**

Co del Toro
6380 m ▲

La Rioja

Reconquista ●Goya

Curuzú Cuatiá

Uruguay

Lagoa
dos Patos

La Serena
Coquimbo
Pta Lengua de Vaca

L. Mar
Chiquita

Córdoba

Santa
Fe

Bella Unión

Concordia
Salto

San Juan

Villa María

Paraná

URUGUAY

**Co Aconcagua
6960 m**

Mendoza

Río Cuarto

Rosario

Concepción
del Uruguay

Paso de
los Toros

Treinta-y-Tres

Viña del Mar
Valparaíso
Quilpue
San Luis

Tupungato
5682 m

Mercedes

**San Nicolás
de los Arroyos**

Pergamino

Santiago
San Bernardo
Rancagua

Vol. Maipú
5290 m

San Rafael

Pilar
Buenos Aires
Lomas de
Zamora
San Fernando
Las Piedras
La Plata

Minas
Montevideo
Maldonado

Curicó
Talca
Cauquenes

A R G E N T I N A

Santa Rosa

Río de la Plata

Pta Norte del
Cabo San Antonio

Chillán
Talcahuano
Tome
Concepción
Los Angeles
Lebu
Angol

Co Tres Picos
1243 m ▲

Olavarría
Tandil

Tres Arroyos
Mar del Plata

Necochea

Neuquén
Zapala

Bahía Blanca
Río Colorado
Punta Alta

Coronel
Dorrego

Bahía
Blanca

Temuco

San Martín De
los Andes

Embalse Ezequiel
Ramos Mexia

Negro

Valdivia

P A C I F I C

O C E A N

Viedma

Osorno
Co Tronador
3554 m ▲
San Carlos
de Bariloche

Sierra Grande

Golfo
San Matías

Pta Norte

Puerto Varas
Puerto Montt
Ancud
Castro

Isla Grande
de Chiloé

Esquel

Puerto Madryn

Trelew
Rawson

A T L A N T I C

O C E A N

C. Dos Bahías

Mte Maca
2960 m ▲
Puerto Aisen
Coihaique

Archipiélago
de los
Chonos

Mte San Valentin
4058 m ▲

Golfo
de Penas

Mte San Lorenzo
3700 m ▲

L. Buenos
Aires

Comodoro Rivadavia

Golfo
de San Jorge

C. Tres Puntas

Puerto Deseado

Mte Fitz Roy
3375 m ▲

Wellington

Puerto San Julián

**FALKLAND
ISLANDS
(U.K.)**

Puerto
Santa Cruz

West
Falkland

Río Gallegos

Puerto
Natales

Archipiélago
de la Reina
Adelaida

Punta Arenas

Estrecho de Magallanes

Bahía San Sebastián

Isla Grande
de Tierra
del Fuego

Río Grande

Port
Stephens

Stanley
East
Falkland

I. Santa
Inés

Mte Darwin
2488 m ▲

Ushuaia

I. de los
Estados

Cabo de Hornos
(Cape Horn)

The 2 metre (7 foot) long giant anteater
lives in Central and South America.

0   200   400 kilometres

0   200   miles

Scale 1:15,000,000

FACT FILE

Record holder
- The deepest known part of the Atlantic is the Milwaukee Deep, 8,648 metres (28,326 feet) below the surface; it is part of the Puerto Rico Trench
- The first people to explore the Atlantic were Phoenician traders in the 700s BC
- The first person to cross the Atlantic was Christopher Columbus, in 1492
- The Sargasso Sea, west of the Canary Islands, is an elliptical-shaped area thick with seaweed and characterised by weak currents and light winds
- The Gulf Stream, a warm current carrying waters from the tropics north along the coast of east North America towards Europe, is responsible for milder temperatures in countries such as Ireland and Denmark
- The Grand Banks, in the North Atlantic off Newfoundland, is the world's richest fishing ground
- Bermuda has one of the highest per capita incomes in the world
- Bermuda is the most northerly group of coral islands in the world
- Greenland is the biggest island in the world

CAPE VERDE

Capital Praia
Population 405,748
Official language Portuguese
Main religions Roman Catholic and indigenous beliefs, often in combination, 98%; Protestant 2%
Currency Cape Verdean escudo
Form of government Republic

The waters of the South Atlantic are among the winter breeding grounds of the southern right whale.

A vast ocean

The Atlantic covers about one-third of the world's surface. Many leading industrial nations border its shores and its waters are important to commerce as a highway for their manufactured goods. Beneath the waves, the Mid-Atlantic Ridge, a vast underwater volcanic mountain chain, curves in a nearly continuous long 'S' from Iceland south to Antarctica. Islands on the ridge, such as the Azores, are volcanic peaks. Along the line of the Ridge, two sets of the great plates that make up the hard crust of the Earth are slowly moving apart, causing earthquakes and volcanoes which release molten rock that solidifies into new seabed. Because of this activity, the Atlantic is widening at the rate of about 2.5 centimetres (1 inch) a year. *[SEE THE WORLD'S OCEANS].*

Cape Verde is a group of exposed
volcanic peaks. The islands were discovered, uninhabited, by Portuguese navigators in 1456. For several centuries they were used by slave-traders as a depot for assembling slaves and provisioning ships. Descendants of these slaves now make up more than 70 per cent of the population. Most of Cape Verde's people live on the coastal plain of São Tiago, in the southern group. A chronic lack of water makes agriculture difficult and droughts regularly devastate the

Ice floes dot the water around the town of Narsaq in Greenland.

crops of maize, beans and sweet potatoes. About 90 per cent of food is imported and Cape Verde is heavily dependent on foreign aid.

The Azores, **Canary Islands** and **Madeira** are autonomous regions of Portugal. The Azores were discovered by the Portuguese navigator Gonzalo Cabral in 1431. The islands produce fruit and vegetables. The subtropical climate and fertile soils of the Canary Islands support farming and fruit-growing; fishing is also important. The islands are a major tourist destination all year round. Madeira, also a group of volcanic peaks, produces wine (madeira), sugar and bananas.

Ascension, **Bermuda**, **St Helena**, **South Georgia** and **Sandwich Islands** are dependencies of the United Kingdom. In the North Atlantic, Bermuda's low-lying coral islands have grown on top of ancient submarine volcanoes. Its financial services, offering tax-haven advantages, is the major income earner. The balmy climate and lush vegetation draw many tourists. Its people are mainly descendants of former African slaves or British or Portuguese settlers. In the South Atlantic, St Helena, together with Ascension and Tristan da Cunha is a British crown colony. St Helena was Napoleon's place of exile from 1815 to 1821; today the island's main activities are fishing, livestock-raising and the sale of handicrafts. South Georgia, also in the South Atlantic, consists of the exposed barren peaks of the South

A village in Madeira, looking out at the vast Atlantic Ocean.

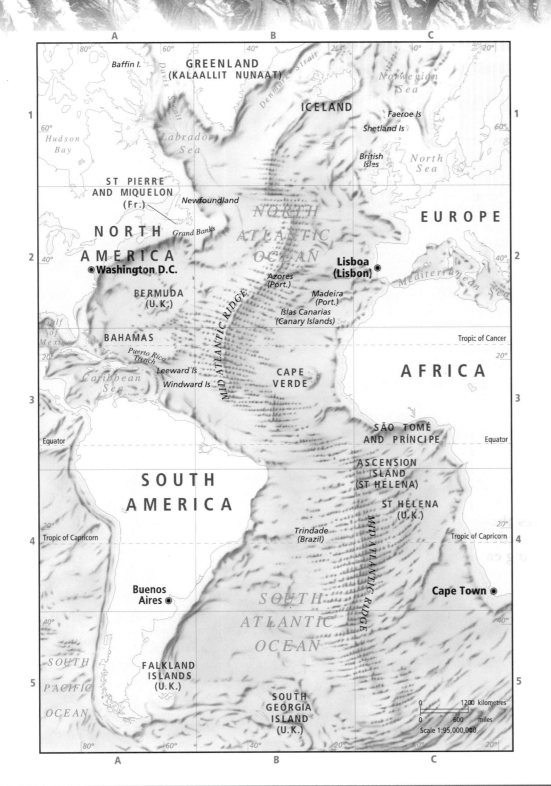

A colony of king penguins on Golden Harbour in South Georgia.

Georgia Ridge, which runs east from the tip of South America. Annexed for the British by the explorer James Cook in 1775, South Georgia was long used as a whaling base. Today it has a military base and biological station only, and no permanent population. The Sandwich Islands are six uninhabited volcanic cones.

The **Faeroe Islands** and **Greenland** are self-governing overseas administrative divisions of Denmark. The Faeroe Islands are formed from volcanic lava. The group has been administered solely by Denmark since 1709, but has a high degree of autonomy, with its own parliament elected every four years. Sheep-raising and fishing are the main income earners, and the Faeroese continue to hunt whales, despite international criticism. Greenland is nearly fifty times the size of its 'mother country', but has only 1 per cent of its population. Most Greenlanders are of mixed Inuit and Danish descent. Fishing and fish-processing makes up 95 per cent of all exports.

St Pierre and Miquelon, a group of two islands south of Newfoundland, is a territorial collectivity of France. Surrounded by the rich fishing grounds of the Grand Banks, the islands were settled by French fishermen in the 1600s.

Looking over the islands of the Great Sounds from Gibbs Hill, Bermuda.

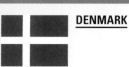

DENMARK

Capital Copenhagen
Population 5,356,845
Official language Danish
Main religion Lutheran 91%
Currency Danish krone
Form of government Constitutional monarchy

FINLAND

Capital Helsinki
Population 5,158,372
Official language Finnish
Main religion Lutheran 98%
Currency Markka
Form of government Republic

ICELAND

Capital Reykjavík
Population 272,512
Official language Icelandic
Main religion Lutheran 96%
Currency Króna
Form of government Republic

NORWAY

Capital Oslo
Population 4,438,547
Official language Norwegian
Main religion Evangelical Lutheran 94%
Currency Norwegian krone
Form of government Constitutional monarchy
Record holder Norway produces more oil and gas than any other European country

SWEDEN

Capital Stockholm
Population 8,911,296
Official language Swedish
Main religion Lutheran 94%
Currency Swedish krona
Form of government Constitutional monarchy

Scandinavia

Viking heritage

Culturally, geographically and geologically, the countries of Scandinavia and the island country of Iceland, have much in common. All have, at various times in their history, been ruled by one of the other states, and today's boundaries only date from the early 1900s. Apart from Finland, all have closely related languages and a common religion— Lutheran Protestantism. Despite a harsh climate, all have maintained successful agricultural and fishing industries, and since industrialisation and more recent technological advances, they have achieved some of the highest standards of living in Europe. All have well-developed social security systems and high rates of education and literacy.

In medieval times, seafaring Vikings from Scandinavia reached Britain, Ireland, Russia, Germany, France, Spain and Italy. Although their initial purpose was to raid, they later set up trading centres. In the AD 900s Norse Viking ships carried settlers to Iceland and Greenland. In about AD 1000 Norse Viking explorer, Leif Ericson, landed in North America and founded a short-lived colony on the island of Newfoundland. Swedish Vikings settled in eastern Europe.

[See Traders & travellers]

High plateau country, dotted with tiny lakes, in Norway. More than 100,000 lakes, legacy of past glacial activity, are scattered across the Scandinavian region.

mostly low-lying, its surface covered in many places by rocky glacial debris. Fishing and agriculture provide the raw materials for food processing industries.

Finland's forests of pine, birch and spruce cover more than half of its surface, and timber-related industries such as wood processing, pulp and papermaking are important revenue-earners. Less than one-tenth of the land is suitable for agriculture, and in summer months, when the country is not snowbound, cereals, potatoes and sugar beet are grown.

Iceland's spectacularly rugged and volcanic landscape includes hot springs, sulfur beds, geysers, deep canyons and plummeting waterfalls. It has more than 200 volcanoes, many of them active, and earth tremors are frequent. Following its settlement by Norwegian Vikings, Iceland came under Danish rule when the Norwegian and Danish monarchies were combined. Iceland became independent in 1918, and became a republic in 1944.

Norway's coastline is indented with many deep fjords (long, narrow coastal inlets). Fishing and fish farming are major industries. Most of the country consists of mountains with deep valleys formed by ancient glaciers. More than one-quarter of the land is forested and pulp and paper manufacturing are major industries. Like the Swedes and the Danes, modern Norwegians are descendants of the Vikings.

Sweden is the fourth largest country in Europe. Its mountains, shaped by ancient glaciers, are heavily forested. Numerous rivers

Sleds pulled by reindeer are a traditional but widely used form of winter transport in Finland.

Denmark is now the smallest and most southerly of the Scandinavian countries, but for many centuries it ruled over what is now Norway and Sweden. Denmark still controls Greenland whose inhabitants are Danish citizens. Unlike the other Scandinavian countries, Denmark is

ICELAND

Ísafjörður · Ólafsfjörður · Húsavík
Blönduós · Akureyri
Stykkishólmur · Seyðisfjörður
Borgarnes · Djúpivogur
Hafnarfjörður · Reykjavik
Hvannadalshnúkur 2119 m ▲
Vík

Arctic Circle

ARCTIC OCEAN

Nordkapp
Honningsvåg
Hammerfest
Rustefjelbmá · Vardø
Varangerhalvøya · Vadsø
Poluostrov Rybachiy
Kirkenes

Sandbukta
Alta · Lakselv · Utsjoki
Karasjok
Tromsø

Andenes
Finnsnes · Haiti 1328 m · Kautokeino
Kaaresuvanto · Inari
Narvik · Ivalo
Svolvær · Kebnekaise 2111 m · Kiruna · Vuotso
1115 m Gora Ebruchorr
Mørsvik · Vittangi · Kittilä · Muonio · Savukoski
Bodø · Sodankylä · Saija
Fauske · Porjus · Gällivare · Pajala · Pello
Storjord · Kvikkjokk · Kemijärvi
Mo i Rana · Jokkmokk · Kåbdalis · Övertorneå · Ylitornio · Kuusamo
Rovaniemi

NORWEGIAN SEA

Vega · Västansjö · Boden · Haparanda · Kemi · Taivalkoski · Suomussalmi
Mosjøen · Sorsele · Arvidsjaur · Luleå · Pudasjärvi
Rørvik · Storuman · Piteå · Jörn · Oulu · Muhos · Hyrynsalmi
Namsos · Vilhelmina · Skellefteå · Raahe · Rantsila · Kajaani · Kuhmo
Smøla · Hitra · Dorotea · Åsele · Umeå · Kalajoki · Ylivieska · Maanselkä
Kristiansund · Steinkjer · Strömsund · Kokkola · Haapajärvi · Silinjärvi · Ahmovaara
Molde · Levanger · Åre · Brëcke · Lunde · Örnsköldsvik · Pietarsaari · Pihtipudas · Iisalmi · Lieksa
Ålesund · Trondheim · Støren · Östersund · Sollefteå · Vaasa · Veteli · Kuopio · Joensuu
Stranda · Oppdal · Hede · Härnösand · Laihia · Lapua · Kyyjärvi · Saarijärvi · Varkaus
Måløy · Dombås · Tynset · Røros · Sveg · Ramsjö · Sundsvall · Kurikka · Seinäjoki · Jyväskylä · Pieksämäki · Savonlinna
Florø · Otta · Koppang · Särna · Ljusdal · Kauhajoki · Parkano · Kankaanpää · Jämsä · Mikkeli
Førde · Hermansverk · Øye · Rena · Hudiksvall · Pori · Tampere · Heinola · Imatra · Ladozhskoye Ozero
Høyanger · Galdhøpiggen 2469 m ▲ · Lillehammer · Åsen · Bollnäs · Söderhamn · Rauma · Hämeenlinna · Lahti · Lappeenranta
Voss · Gjøvik · Hamar · Mora · Gävle · Ahvenanmaa (Åland) · Forssa · Mäntsälä · Hamina
Bergen · Odda · Hønefoss · Kongsvinger · Malung · Falun · Turku · Salo · Porvoo
Leirvik · Rjukan · Ludvika · Avesta · Naantali · Karjaa · Hanko
Sauda · Kongsberg · Drammen · Sala · Uppsala · Espoo · Helsinki
Haugesund · Bykle · Oslo · Arvika · Karlstad · Västerås · Stockholm · Tallinn
Stavanger · Sandnes · Moss · Tønsberg · Örebro · Katrineholm
Egersund · Bygland · Skien · Åmål · Nyköping · Hiiumaa
Evje · Larvik · Mariestad · Norrköping · **ESTONIA**
Flekkefjord · Arendal · Uddevalla · Vänersborg · Falköping · Linköping · Saaremaa
Kristiansand · Grimstad · Tranås · Västervik · Visby
Göteborg (Gothenburg) · Alingsås · Eksjö · Vetlanda · Oskarshamn · Gotland · Gulf of Riga
Thisted · Hjørring · Jönköping · Kungsbacka · Värnamo · Öland · Riga · **LATVIA**
Ålborg · Varberg · Falkenberg · Växjö · Nybro · Kalmar
Skive · Viborg · Halmstad · Ljungby · Öland
Holstebro · Herning · Ängelholm · Karlskrona · **BALTIC SEA**
DENMARK · Århus · Helsingborg · Kristianstad
NORTH SEA · Varde · København (Copenhagen) · Malmö · Simrishamn
Esbjerg · Vejle · Odense · Køge · Ystad
Tønder · Svendborg · Bornholm
Rødby · Nyköbing
LITHUANIA · **BELARUS**

Scale 1:8,000,000
0 — 100 — 200 kilometres
0 — 50 — 100 miles

provide hydroelectricity for Sweden's many
manufacturing industries. These include cars,
aircraft, chemicals, telecommunications and
electrical equipment. Sweden is rich in mineral
resources; it has large reserves of uranium. The
reindeer-herding Saami people (Lapps), who live
in the far north, differ in appearance, language
and way of life from most other Swedes.

*Cafés along the harbour front in Copenhagen, Denmark. For much of its
history, Denmark was the dominant country on the Scandinavian peninsula.*

IRELAND

Capital Dublin
Population 3,632,944
Official languages Irish Gaelic, English
Main religions Roman Catholic 93%, Anglican 3%
Currency Irish pound
Form of government Republic

UNITED KINGDOM

Capital London
Population 57,832,824
Official language English
Main religions Anglican 63%, Roman Catholic 14%, Presbyterian 4%, Methodist 3%, Muslim 3%
Currency Pound sterling
Form of government Constitutional monarchy
Record holder Ben Nevis, at 1,343 metres (4,406 feet), in western Scotland, is the highest mountain in the British Isles; Thames River, 346 kilometres (215 miles), is the longest river in the British Isles

Dependencies & Territories

GUERNSEY

Capital St Peter Port
Population 65,386
Currency Guernsey pound
Form of government British crown dependency

ISLE OF MAN

Capital Douglas
Population 75,686
Currency Manx pound
Form of government British crown dependency

JERSEY

Capital St Helier
Population 89,721
Currency Jersey pound
Form of government British crown dependency

THE
British Isles & Ireland

Island nations and far-flung empires

The British Isles and Ireland are unique in Europe in that they have escaped invasion for almost 1,000 years. This is due to both the natural protection offered by the surrounding waters, as well as British maritime supremacy during certain periods of history. Before the last conquest, by William, Duke of Normandy, in 1066, Britain had been invaded and occupied by many different peoples, including the Celts, Romans, Anglo-Saxons and Vikings. The population reflects this diversity of ethnic origin and the language shows a mixture of influences over many centuries. In more recent years post-war migration from former colonies and dependencies in the Caribbean, Africa and the Indian subcontinent have continued the ongoing change to the racial mix.

Moated Scotney Castle, Kent, dates from the 1300s. When the Normans began to rule in Britain, they built castles to protect the occupants from attack and to help control the conquered Anglo-Saxons.

Ireland's Celtic traditions date from about 400 BC. Christianity is said to have arrived in AD 432, with St Patrick. From 1846 to 1851, famine following the failure of successive potato crops resulted in a massive loss of population. More than a million people died, and of those who survived, about half left Ireland, emigrating to other parts of the world, mainly to the United States. In 1916, long-felt resentment after five centuries of British rule erupted in the Easter Rebellion, which led to the granting of home rule to most of Ireland in 1921. The Republic of Ireland was declared in 1949; the troubled northeast corner of the island, Northern Ireland, remains a part of the United Kingdom.

The **United Kingdom** (or Great Britain) consists of England, which occupies the greatest part of the main island, Scotland, Wales, Northern Ireland and some smaller island dependencies. The Romans arrived in AD 55. Over the next 350 years they built a network of roads stretching north and west from London, established a number of towns with drainage systems and paved streets, and introduced Christianity. They withdrew in the early AD 400s as the Roman Empire declined. By the time of Elizabeth I, in the late 1500s, Britain had become a leading power in the world,

despite its small size. In the following centuries its supremacy at sea helped it build an empire which extended throughout much of the world, including India, Australia, New Zealand, parts of North America and large parts of Africa. General prosperity greatly increased during the Industrial Revolution in the 1800s when rapidly expanding industrial cities in the Midlands, such as Birmingham, Manchester and Liverpool, produced manufactured goods for export to the world.

Guernsey is one of the Channel Islands. Its picturesque scenery, gentle climate and relaxed lifestyle make it a popular tourist destination. Market gardening is also important, and the island is famed for its distinctive fawn and white dairy cattle.

The **Isle of Man** has its own legal and taxation system and, although English is the main language, many of its inhabitants speak the local Gaelic, known as Manx. In recent years financial and business services and tourism have replaced the traditional activities of fishing and farming as main sources of income.

Jersey, the largest of the Channel Islands, is said to be the sunniest part of the British Isles and is noted for its fine beaches. It has its own taxation system. Financial services, tourism and flower growing are major income earners. Jersey is also known for its dairy cattle, which produce milk with a high butterfat content.

The Shetland Islands are administered by an island council authority as part of Scotland; before the development in the 1970s of the oil industry, the island group was best known for its distinctive knitwear and its hardy ponies.

A patchwork of fields on one of the Aran Islands, Galway Bay, on the west coast of Ireland. The islands are limestone, with no naturally occurring topsoil. Islanders make soil from seaweed, sand and manure in which they grow oats and potatoes. Cattle raising and fishing are the other major activities. The Aran Islands are also known for their distinctive knitwear.

BELGIUM

Capital Brussels
Population 10,182,034
Official languages French, Dutch, German
Main religions Roman Catholic 75%, Protestant or other 25%
Currency Belgian franc
Form of government Federal constitutional monarchy
Record holder One of the most densely populated countries in the world

GERMANY

Capital Berlin
Population 82,087,361
Official language German
Main religions Protestant 45%, Roman Catholic 37%, unaffiliated and other 18%
Currency Mark
Form of government Federal republic
Record holder World's third largest producer of cars; Germany is one of the world's largest importers of agricultural goods, importing about one third of its food; Highest point in the region is Zugspitze, 2,962 metres (9,718 feet) high, in the Bavarian Alps

LUXEMBOURG

Capital Luxembourg
Population 429,080
Official languages French, German
Main religion Roman Catholic 97%
Currency Luxembourg franc
Form of government Constitutional monarchy
Record holder One of the most affluent countries in Europe

NETHERLANDS

Capital Amsterdam (The Hague is the seat of government)
Population 15,807,641
Official language Dutch
Main religions Roman Catholic 34%, Protestant 25%, Muslim 3%, other 2%, unaffiliated 36%
Currency Netherlands guilder
Form of government Constitutional monarchy
Record holder Lowest point in the region is Prins Alexander Polder, 6.7 metres (22 feet) below sea level; In the 1600s the Netherlands was the world's major sea power

WESTERN
Europe
Quest for territory

The modern-day borders of this region are the result of centuries of conflict. From Roman times to the Austro-Hungarian Empire, and from the Spanish campaigns in the 1500s to the ambitions of the French under Napoleon in the late 1700s, the boundaries of Western Europe have constantly been pushed back and forth as countries and empires rose and fell.

Belgium's
central location between the powerful nations of France, Germany and the Netherlands has, over the centuries, made it an important hub of trade and industry. It has also, in times of conflict between its neighbours, turned Belgium's flat lands into bloody battle-fields. The country today is the site of the headquarters of international organisations such as NATO (the North Atlantic Treaty Organization) and the European Union. Belgium is named after the Belgae people who occupied the area when invading Roman armies arrived in the 50s BC. Since then the region has been dominated by a succession of foreign powers, which explains why several languages are still

A tiny village nestled at the foot of the Alps in southern Germany.

spoken in the country. From the 1700s, Belgium was ruled by Austria, France, then by the Netherlands. Today there are two main groups of people in the country: the Flemings, who live in the north and speak Flemish, a language similar to Dutch; and the French-speaking minority, the Walloons, who live in the south.

Most Belgians live in cities or towns. Belgium is heavily industrialised, with petroleum refining, machinery manufacture and plastics industries

Neuschwanstein Castle, a fairytale-like structure built by 'Mad' King Ludwig II in the late 1800s in Bavaria, southern Germany. The castle became the model used by the Disneyland theme parks.

concentrated in the north and contributing significantly to Belgium's export earnings. But the country pays the price of acid rain from air pollution caused by this industry ▼ *[SEE POLLUTION]*. Apart from coal, Belgium is poor in natural resources and relies mainly on imported raw materials. For centuries the manufacture of textiles, lace in particular, has been based around the historic northern towns of Ghent and Bruges. Agriculture is centred on the rich northern plain where the rearing of cattle and pigs is the most important activity, followed by crop-growing: sugar beet, potatoes, wheat and barley.

Germany's
boundaries today are roughly the same as defined in the AD 900s when Duke Conrad became king of the German-speaking part of the Frankish Empire. In the 1,000 years since, its territory has been fought over and the country divided in many different ways. Austria, France, Poland and Russia have all at different times ruled parts of what is now Germany. Following the Franco-Prussian War (1870 to 1871) northern and southern Germany were united for the first time as one German Empire; but Germany's plans to expand its territory under Kaiser Wilhelm came to an end with its defeat in World War I. In World War II, under Adolf Hitler's Nazi Party, Germany invaded France, Belgium, the Netherlands, Poland and Russia, but its territorial expansion was again ultimately unsuccessful.

In the post-war period the country was again divided, this time into East and West, finally being reunited in 1990. The former East Germany is still far behind the former West Germany in economic development. But as a whole Germany now has a sound economy. Manufacturing is centred on the steel mills of the Ruhr Valley and in large cities such as Frankfurt, Stuttgart, Munich and Berlin. About one-third of German land is cultivated; cereal crops are widely grown, as are hops for the German beers that are famous throughout the world. Vineyards are most widespread in the Rhine and Mosel river valleys. Livestock raising, mainly pigs and cattle, is concentrated on the northern plain.

Luxembourg became an independent

duchy in 1351. There were hundreds of such states in medieval Europe but Luxembourg is the only one to survive as an independent nation today, despite having been ruled at various times by Austria, Spain, France and the Netherlands. Germany occupied Luxembourg in both world wars. The country has forested mountains in the north and rich farming land in the south. More than 5 million cattle and 6 million pigs are raised here and crops such as potatoes, wheat and barley are grown. Increasingly, however, the country's wealth is created by service industries, particularly banking.

About half of the **Netherlands** lies below sea level. The country is protected from floods by a complex series of coastal dikes, canals and sand dunes. The Dutch have over many years reclaimed large amounts of land from the sea; these flat, fertile areas, called 'polders', have the country's most productive farmlands. The Netherlands, too, have come under the successive control of French, Austrian and Spanish rulers.

Today, the people of the Netherlands enjoy a high standard of living. The country has natural gas in the north and a strong agricultural sector in the northwest where dairy farming is centred. Most of the population lives in a series of densely populated urban areas along the southwest coast, including the cities of Amsterdam, the capital, and Rotterdam, one of the world's biggest and busiest ports.

These houseboats are moored at the edge of one of the more than 150 canals that wind between tall, narrow terraces in Amsterdam, capital of the Netherlands.

The flat lands of Belgium, Luxembourg and the Netherlands are known as the Low Countries. Flowers, especially tulips and other bulb plants, are grown on small farming plots and transform the countryside in spring into a patchwork of bright blooms. Tulip bulbs from here are exported worldwide.

ANDORRA

Capital Andorra la Vella
Population 65,939
Official language Catalan
Main religion Roman Catholic
Currency French franc, Spanish peseta
Form of government Co-principality

FRANCE

Capital Paris
Population 58,978,172
Official language French
Main religions Roman Catholic 90%,
Protestant 2%
Currency French franc
Form of government Republic
Record holder The largest country in
Western Europe; France produces more
cheeses than any other country

MONACO

Capital Monaco
Population 32,149
Official language French
Main religion Roman Catholic 95%
Currency French franc
Form of government Constitutional
monarchy
Record holder The world's smallest
independent nation after the Vatican,
1.9 square kilometres (0.7 square mile)

France

The Left Bank, Paris, has long been associated with artists, literary figures and philosophers. Café de Flore is one of its most famous haunts.

Crossroads of Europe

People and ideas have converged on this region over many centuries from both northern and southern Europe. The Vikings and Franks invaded from the north and east, and the Greeks and Romans travelled north and west to occupy ancient Gaul. A country roughly equivalent to modern-day France was first established in AD 843. Strong traditions arose in art, literature and education, which were to make it one of the world's great cultural centres. The region has also been at the centre of Europe's most bloody conflicts—in the trench warfare of World War I almost a million and a half French lives were lost and the northeast of the country was devastated.

Andorra, located high in the Pyrenees mountains, is a tiny principality which was for centuries governed jointly by France and Spain. Today it has a democratically elected council but France and Spain are still responsible for its defence. Its main source of income is the 12 million tourists per year who visit it to ski and to buy duty-free goods. Only about one in five of the population are citizens

of Andorra, the rest are foreign residents, mainly French and Spanish. Almost two-thirds of the population live in the capital and two other cities. Many village dwellers are small farmers who grow tobacco, fruit and vegetables and graze cattle and sheep in upland meadows during the summer months.

France's rich artistic heritage dates from the prehistoric cave paintings of Lascaux (about 15,000 years old), continuing with the religious and artistic fervour of the Renaissance through to the flourishing of the arts under the royal patronage of King Louis XIV in the 1700s. Later, the art movements of the nineteenth and early twentieth centuries such as the Impressionism of Manet, Degas and Monet, and the Cubism of Picasso, Braque and Duchamp established France, and in particular its capital Paris, as the artistic centre of Europe.

Much of the country is a low-lying basin, drained by great rivers that were once the country's main transportation routes. A vast plateau, the Massif Central, covers the centre and south; it includes rugged uplands characterised by granite outcrops. France is often thought to be dominated by rural industries due to its important exports of food and wine, and although 75 per cent of the country is farmland, only 25 per cent of the population now lives in

France produces more than 750 different types of cheese. They vary from the small soft, fresh cheeses from the warm valleys and plains of the south, made to be eaten immediately, to the huge hard cheese wheels of the mountains of the north and east, which traditionally were matured for months in caves.

The Formula 1 Grand Prix race, held each May, is one of the great tourist attractions in Monaco.

rural areas. France is one of Europe's leading industrialised nations. Chemical factories, car manufacturing and textiles are concentrated in Paris, Lille, Nantes and other northern cities, while high-technology industries such as computers and aerospace are centred on the cities of Lyon and Toulouse further south.

Monaco has been governed by members of the Grimaldi family since 1297, unbroken for almost 500 years till 1792. It was then declared a republic, but the Grimaldis were returned to power in 1861. It has some light industry but its major sources of income are tourism and the state-run casino, from which Monaco residents are banned. The Formula 1 Grand Prix is held through the streets of Monaco each year, and is a major tourist attraction. The people of Monaco pay no income tax.

A village in the foothills of the Pyrenees, southwest France. This region has many cultural links with Spain, which lies on the other side of the forbidding slopes.

PORTUGAL

Capital Lisbon
Population 9,918,040
Official language Portuguese
Main religion Roman Catholic 97%
Currency Escudo
Form of government Republic
Record holder Portugal produces more cork than the rest of the world combined; Portugal is the westernmost country of continental Europe

SPAIN

Capital Madrid
Population 39,167,744
Official language Spanish (Castillian)
Main religion Roman Catholic 99%
Currency Peseta
Form of government Constitutional monarchy
Record holder Madrid is the highest capital city in Europe at 646 metres (2,120 feet) above sea level

Dependencies & Territories

GIBRALTAR

Capital Gibraltar
Population 29,165
Currency Gibraltar pound
Form of government Self-governing dependent territory of the United Kingdom

Storks are common in Spain and are often seen roosting on rooftops in untidy nests of twigs.

Iberian Peninsula

Exploration and conquest

Spain and Portugal share the Iberian Peninsula, a region bounded in the north by the mighty Pyrenees and with a long history of human habitation. In northern Spain the Altamira cave shelters an astonishing 12,000 year-old gallery of prehistoric art. The peninsula was part of the Roman empire and aqueducts built by the Romans still cross the dry lands. In the south, Africa is less than 15 kilometres (9 miles) away across the Strait of Gibraltar, and in the 700s Spain was invaded by Muslim Moors from northern Africa. In the 1500s both Spain and Portugal were powerful seafaring nations, sending ships out into unknown waters in their quest for colonies to supply precious minerals and spices.

Farm buildings at the foot of Mount Giestoso, in rugged northern Portugal. Most Portuguese live in rural villages, with the smaller farms in the north growing crops and raising livestock in traditional ways.

Portugal was once the heart of a worldwide empire, with colonies in Africa, South America, India and Southeast Asia. Portuguese navigator Bartolomeu Dias was the first European to sail around Africa's Cape of Good Hope and his countryman Vasco da Gama was the first European to reach India, opening the sea route to the East. Portugal's power declined following its invasion by Spain in 1581. Today it is one of the poorer countries in Europe. Much of the country's workforce is employed in the agricultural and fishing sectors. It is best known for its port wine and cork production and as a winter tourist destination.

Spain is dominated by the huge, dry plateau of the Meseta, which occupies more than half its land area. Here natural resources are scarce and poor soil restricts agriculture; sheep and goats are raised. Productive land is found in the north, and wine is produced in the south and east. Islamic influence in the south, such as

Energetic performances of the flamenco, bolero, fandango and other regional dances are accompanied by guitars and tambourines.

Grenada's Alhambra palace, is a legacy of more than six centuries of Moorish rule which ended in 1492. Then, unified under Catholic rule, Spain began a century of exploration and conquest. Starting with the voyage of Christopher Columbus, it acquired colonies in Central and South America as well as the Philippines in Southeast Asia. Spain's decline as a world power dates from the 1588 defeat of the great Armada of 130 ships it sent to invade Britain. By 1714 Spain had lost all its European possessions and by 1826, it had surrendered all its American colonies except Cuba and Puerto Rico. From 1936 to 1939 Spain was torn apart by a bitter civil war.

The Balearic Islands, a province of Spain, are a popular tourist resort. The three provinces that are home to Spain's Basque people became a self-governing region within Spain in 1980.

Gibraltar guards the entrance to the Mediterranean Sea. Spain's capture in 1462 of this strategic prize ended seven centuries of Moorish rule. By 1713 it was under British control, and despite several attempts by Spain to regain it, has remained in British hands ever since. Known as 'The Rock', it consists of a high rocky mountain joined to the Spanish mainland by a sand spit.

Barcelona's tree-lined street called The Ramblas curves like a river all the way down to the waterfront. Barcelona is Spain's most important manufacturing and trading city.

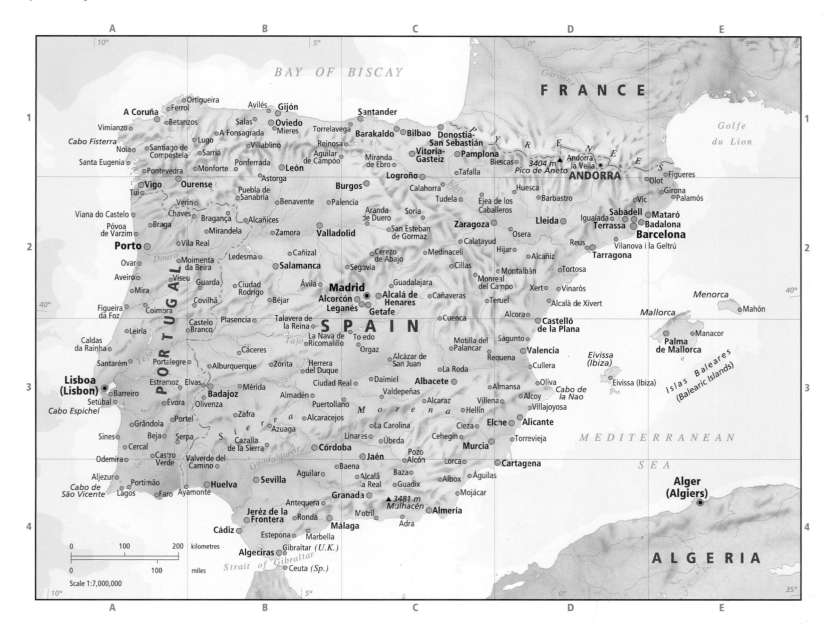

Capital Vienna
Population 8,139,299
Official language German
Main religions Roman Catholic 85%, Protestant 6%
Currency Schilling
Form of government Federal republic

ITALY

Capital Rome
Population 56,735,130
Official language Italian
Main religion Roman Catholic 98%
Currency Lira
Form of government Republic
Record holder Mont Blanc, at 4,807 metres (15,771 feet), is the highest point in Western Europe; Italy produces more wine than any other country

LIECHTENSTEIN

Capital Vaduz
Population 32,057
Official language German
Main religions Roman Catholic 87%, Protestant 8%
Currency Swiss franc
Form of government Constitutional monarchy

MALTA

Capital Valletta
Population 381,603
Official languages Maltese, English
Main religion Roman Catholic 98%
Currency Maltese lira
Form of government Republic
Record holder The most densely populated country in Europe

SAN MARINO

Capital San Marino
Population 25,061
Official language Italian
Main religion Roman Catholic 95%
Currency Italian lira
Form of government Republic
Record holder A republic since the AD 300s, making it the world's oldest surviving republic

CENTRAL SOUTHERN
Europe

Mediterranean might

For nearly 800 years, from about 400 BC, Rome was the hub of a mighty empire that stretched from the British Isles to the Persian Gulf. It included all the countries of the Mediterranean and, north of the natural barrier of the Alps, the lands now known as Switzerland and Austria. In the 1500s, 1,000 years after the empire's decline, the powerful Italian city states of Florence, Venice, Pisa and Genoa led the great cultural revival known as the Renaissance. Italy in the Middle Ages was also a centre of world trade.

Austria's present borders date only from the 1919 Treaty of Versailles, after the defeat in World War I of the Austro-Hungarian (Hapsburg) Empire. Roman conquest in ancient times of most of present-day Austria was followed by invasions by Germanic and Celtic tribes, then in the 700s, by the Franks under Charlemagne. In 1278 Rudolf of Hapsburg won control of the country, named himself Archduke, and declared the title hereditary. By the 1500s Austria's Hapsburg Empire dominated much of Europe. Almost all Austria's agricultural land is in the

St Peter's Square in Vatican City, seen from the roof of St Peter's Basilica. Pilgrims visit the Basilica in vast numbers throughout the year, but particularly at Easter and Christmas, when crowds fill the square.

northeast; potatoes, cereal crops, wine-making and cattle- and pig-raising are the main activities. Iron and steel manufacture and aluminium, chemicals and food processing are the main export earners.

Italy as a modern, independent country dates only from 1861, when it was united as a monarchy headed by King Victor Emmanuel II of Sardinia. Most of the country is mountainous. In the south are the active volcanoes of Mount Vesuvius and Mount Etna. Most of Italy's people live in the north, on the fertile Plain of Lombardy. Two-fifths of the country's crops are grown here, including potatoes, wheat, maize, olives and other vegetables, and a wide range of citrus and stone fruits. The north is also heavily industrialised, with the building of cars and aircraft, and the manufacture of chemicals, tools and textiles. There is a sharp contrast in the living standards of the affluent north—cities such as Milan (Italy's banking and fashion centre), Turin (the home of Fiat cars) and Genoa (a major seaport)—and the largely undeveloped south, especially Calabria, where unemployment is high. The rugged island of Sardinia is sparsely populated.

The rooftops of Florence, Italy, dominated by the dome of its cathedral. In the 1500s Florence was the centre of the Renaissance, a period of great blossoming of artistic, musical, literary and scientific activity.

A | B | C | D | E

5° · 10° · Donau (Danube) · 15° · 20°

SLOVAKIA
▲1458 m

GERMANY
Donau

AUSTRIA
•Wien (Vienna) ·Bratislava

Bodensee
Basel Zürich Winterthur
Biel Vaduz **LIECHTEN-STEIN**
Bern Luzern
Davos
Merano
Bolzano
Großglockner ▲3797 m

•Budapest

HUNGARY
Balaton

SWITZERLAND
Lausanne
Saint Moritz
Rhône Sion Sierre A Bellinzona Male Edolo
4807 m▲ 4478 m Domodossola Sondrio
Mont Blanc Matterhorn Aosta
Biella Varese Riva del Garda Trento Belluno Udine
FRANCE Torino Novara Monza Rovereto Conegliano
(Turin) **Milano** Brescia **Verona Vicenza Mestre** Trieste
Pinerolo (Milan) Piacenza Mantova **Padova Venezia (Venice)** Chioggia
Carmagnola Po Rovigo
Fossano Acqui Alessandria **Parma Modena Ferrara** Porto Tolle
Cuneo Terme **Reggio Bologna** Ravenna
Savona **Genova** nell'Emilia
Loano (Genoa) Carrara Forli Cesenatico
Imperia Rapallo Barga **Rimini**
San **La Spezia** Lucca **Prato SAN** San Marino
Remo Pisa **Firenze MARINO** Fano
Livorno (Florence) Urbino
Cecina Volterra Arezzo Jesi
LIGURIAN Siena Macerata **Ancona**
SEA Piombino Follonica **Perugia** Fermo
Isola Grosseto Foligno San Benedetto
d'Elba Orvieto Spoleto del Tronto
Orbetello Viterbo Terni Giul anova
Corse ▲2710 m Rieti Pescara
(Corsica) Mte Cinto Civitavecchia L'Aquila Vasto
(France) Cerveteri Sulmona Termoli
Ajaccio Citta del Vaticano **Roma** Vieste
VATICAN CITY (Rome) Sora Agnone Manfredonia
Velletri Campobasso **Foggia**
Anzio Lat na Cassino Benevento Andria Molfetta
Terracina Caserta Altamura **Bari**
Tempio **Napoli** Vesuvio Avigliano Matera Monopoli
Pausania Olbia (Naples) ▲1281 m **Salerno** Potenza Fasano
Sassari Torre del Greco Pisticci Brindisi
Alghero Ozieri Sorrento Capaccio **Taranto** Manduria
Sardegna Nuoro Moliterno Lauria Lecce
(Sardinia) Mti del **TYRRHENIAN** Palinuro Golfo Gallipoli
Oristano Gennargentu di Ugento Tricase
Sanluri ▲1834 m **SEA** Castrovillari Taranto
Carbonia Iglesias **Cagliari** Paola **Cosenza** Rossano
Sant'Antioco Nicastro Rogliano Crotone **IONIAN**
Capo Vibo Valentia **Catanzaro** **SEA**
Teulada Gioia Tauro
MEDITERRANEAN Palmi Locri
Messina
Trapani **Palermo** Milazzo **Reggio**
Alcamo Cefalù di Calabria
Marsala Corleone Taormina
Castelvetrano Nicosia ▲3323 m
Sciacca Monte Etna Sicilia
Agrigento Caltanissetta **Catania** (Sicily)
Licata Gela **Siracusa**
Ragusa Modica
Tunis Pachino

ADRIATIC SEA

SLOVENIA
·Ljubljana
CROATIA
•Zagreb
BOSNIA AND HERZEGOVINA
Cincar ▲2006 m ·Sarajevo
2396 m▲ Maglic

ALGERIA **TUNISIA**

MALTA
•Valletta

0 — 100 — 200 kilometres
0 — 50 — 100 miles
Scale 1:6,000,000

Liechtenstein was

created as a principality in 1713 and takes its name from the Austrian family who became its rulers. In 1868 Liechtenstein's army was abolished and the country declared itself permanently neutral. Pig-, cattle-, and sheep-raising are the main forms of agriculture. Postage stamps are a major source of revenue.

More than half of Switzerland is covered by the peaks and glaciers of the Alps and only about one-tenth of the land is suitable for agriculture. The country produces less than half of its food needs. Wheat, potatoes and sugar beet are the main crops, and dairy farming the principal agricultural activity.

SWITZERLAND

Capital Bern
Population 7,275,467
Official languages German, French, Italian
Main religions Roman Catholic 48%, Protestant 44%
Currency Swiss franc
Form of government Federal republic
Record holder Europe's most mountainous country; A world leader in the production of precision instruments; One of the world's most stable and prosperous countries

VATICAN CITY

Capital Vatican City
Population 1,000
Official languages Italian, Latin
Main religion Roman Catholic
Currency Vatican lira
Form of government Monarchical-sacerdotal state
Record holder World's smallest state

Central Southern Europe continued...

The Italian city of Venice covers about 120 small islands linked by bridges and with more than 150 canals taking the place of streets. Motorboats have now largely replaced the pole-powered gondolas.

Malta's strategic location in the centre of the Mediterranean and the value of its many sheltered harbours have been recognised by traders and empire builders since the days of the Phoenicians in the 800s BC. It has since been occupied by the Greeks, Romans, Arabs and Spanish. In 1530 the Spanish king gave the island to the Knights of St John, a religious order who had fought against the Muslims since the time of the First Crusade in the 1090s. The island was seized by Napoleon in 1798, then held by the British from 1800 until 1947. It gained full independence in 1964. Malta has little natural vegetation and no forests or major rivers. Tourism, based on its rugged scenery and historic towns, provides the main source of revenue.

San Marino, entirely surrounded by

Italian territory, was one of the many mini-states that once crowded the Italian peninsula. Although in 1861 it declined to join the newly unified Italy, it today shares its currency and enjoys a roughly similar standard of living. Postage stamps account for 10 per cent of its total revenue.

This megalithic temple in Malta was built more than 5,000 years ago.

Austria's alpine region is characterised by snowfields, glaciers and snowy peaks. Winter in the town of Zel am Zeere.

Switzerland was a province of the Roman empire called Helvetia. The modern country dates from the late 1200s, when three German cantons (districts) combined to form a federation. Other cantons joined, and in 1815, once more independent after the defeat of Napoleon who had seized the country, Switzerland declared itself permanently neutral. Industries include precision instruments such as clocks and watches, heavy engineering, textile manufacture, clothing and food processing, such as chocolate. Banking is a key industry, attracting almost half the world's foreign investment capital.

Vatican City is all that remains of the former Papal States, which once covered an area of 45,000 square kilometres (17,000 square miles). Surrounded by medieval walls, it occupies a hill in the city of Rome and consists of St Peter's Basilica, the Papal Palace, Government Palace and parklands. It has its own radio station, newspaper, stamps and coins. The Pope is the head of state.

Capital Minsk
Population 10,401,784
Official language Belarusian
Main religions Eastern Orthodox 60%, other (including Roman Catholic and small Muslim and Jewish communities) 40%
Currency Belarusian rouble
Form of government Republic

ESTONIA

Capital Tallinn
Population 1,408,523
Official language Estonian
Main religion Evangelical Lutheran 96%
Currency Kroon
Form of government Republic
Record holder Lake Peipus is the largest lake in the region and forms most of Estonia's border with Russia

LATVIA

Capital Riga
Population 2,353,874
Official language Lettish
Main religions Mainly Lutheran with Russian Orthodox and Roman Catholic minorities
Currency Lats
Form of government Republic

LITHUANIA

Capital Vilnius
Population 3,584,966
Official language Lithuanian
Main religions Roman Catholic 90%, Russian Orthodox, Muslim and Protestant minorities 10%
Currency Litas
Form of government Republic

Baltic States

A common history

Estonia, Latvia and Lithuania are known collectively as the Baltic States. Although physically similar, they have distinct ethnic and linguistic identities and diverse earlier histories. The cultures of Estonia and Latvia show strong German influence—many people, for example, are Lutherans. The Baltic States gained independence in 1991. The region also includes an isolated portion of the Russian Federation (see Russian Federation).

Rooftops in a town in Latvia. More than two-thirds of the people in Latvia are urban dwellers.

Belarus (meaning 'White Russia') was settled by Slavic tribes in the AD 500s. Controlled and influenced by Ukrainian Kiev, Lithuania, Poland and Russia, Belarus finally gained independence in 1991. It remains economically dependent on its huge and powerful eastern neighbour. Almost half the land is devoted to agriculture, and dairying and pig farming are also important. The drained southern swamps, formerly richly cultivated, are still contaminated after the nuclear spill at Chernobyl in 1986 [SEE GLOBAL NUCLEAR INDUSTRY]. Belarus has significant quantities of peat and rock salt, and small reserves of coal.

Estonia—the mainland and more than 800 islands in the Baltic Sea and the Gulf of Finland—is a stony landscape left by ancient glaciers, dotted with more than 1,500 lakes. It has infertile black soil and is about two-fifths tree covered. Timber products and textile manufacture are important export earners. Estonia's extensive deposits of oil shale produce gas and chemicals. The scarce arable land is mainly used for dairy cattle and raising livestock, especially pigs. The Roman historian, Tacitus (circa AD 55–120) mentioned the Estonians in his *Germania*. Before independence, Germans, Swedes and Russians variously controlled the country.

Latvia has large areas of bogs and swamps; trees cover about 40 per cent of the land. Forestry and fishing are currently reviving industries. Small farms raise dairy and beef cattle and grow grain and vegetables. Latvia imports the raw materials for its industries, which include manufacturing electrical goods, shipbuilding and vehicle making. Air and water pollution from industrial wastes causes concern [SEE POLLUTION]. Before gaining independence, Latvians were successively ruled by Germans, Poles, Swedes and Russians for more than 1,000 years.

A city square in the medieval city of Tallinn. The capital of Estonia, Tallinn is also its cultural heart. It has an opera house, several theatres, and is known for its song festivals.

Map labels

FINLAND
Helsinki

Tallinn, Narva, Kohtla-Järve, Tapa, Rakvere, Kauksi, Paide, Haapsalu, Põltsamaa, **ESTONIA**, Tartu, Pärnu, Viljandi, Kilingi-Nõmme, Võru, Kuressaare, Saaremaa, Sääre, Ainaži, Valka, Valga, Kolka, Valmiera, Alüksne, Roja, Saulkrasti, Cēsis, Gulbene, Balvi, Ugāle, Talsi, Inčukalns, **LATVIA**, Madona, Kārsava, Kuldīga, Tukums, **Rīga**, Ogre, Rēzekne, Ludza, Skrunda, Saldus, Jelgava, Jēkabpils, Malta, **Liepāja**, Dobele, Bauska, Viesīte, Daugava

Hurki, Mažeikiai, Joniškis, Biržai, Špoģi, Krāslava, Navapolatsk, Haradok, Plungė, Telšiai, **Šiauliai**, Pumpėnai, Rokiškis, **Daugavpils**, Dzisna, Polatsk, Shumilina, Falanga, Gargždai, **Panevėžys**, Utena, Yody, Prazaroki, **Vitsyebsk**, **Klaipėda**, Kelmė, Ukmergė, Pastavy, Hlybokaye, Byeshankovichy, Skaudvilė, Raseiniai, Svir, Lyepyel', Chashniki, **Kaunas**, Jonava, **Vilnius**, Dawhinava, **Orsha**, Talachyn, Horki, Silutė, Jurbarkas, Vilyeyka, Shklow, Mstsislaw, **LITHUANIA**, Sovetsk, Tauragė, Pašiūnai, Maladzyechna, **Barysaw**, Zhodzina, **Mahilyow**, Zelenogradsk, Marijampolė, **R. F.**, Chernyakhovsk, Merkinė, Byerazino, Krychaw, Klimavichy, Svetlyy, Gusev, **Kaliningrad**, Alytus, Valozhyn, **Minsk**, Bykhaw, Slawharad, Baltiysk, Bagrationovsk, Kalvarija, **BELARUS**, Klichaw, Lida, Dzyarzhynsk, Navahrudak, Asipovichy, Dowsk, **Hrodna**, **Babruysk**, Chachersk, Masty, Slutsk, Zhlobin, Vawkavysk, Slonim, **Baranavichy**, Lyuban', **Salihorsk**, **Homyel'**, Dobrush, Ivatsevichy, **Rechytsa**, Pruzhany, Byaroza, Luninyets, **Mazyr**, Kalinkavichy, **POLAND**, Kobryn, **Pinsk**, Stolin, Yel'sk, Narowlya, **Warszawa (Warsaw)**, **Brest**, Malaryta, **UKRAINE**, **Kyyiv (Kiev)**

RUSSIAN FEDERATION

Gotland, **BALTIC SEA**, Kuršskiy Zaliv, R. F.

Scale 1:5,000,000

Lithuania

Lithuania, in the AD 1400s, was a major European power with boundaries extending further than they do today. In the AD 1500s it merged with Poland for more than 200 years. More recently it has been under Russian control. Most of Lithuania is a relatively fertile, well-watered plain with extensive forests and marshes. Dairy and beef cattle and pig raising are the predominate forms of agriculture. Cereals and vegetables are grown on reclaimed marshland. Key industries, a cause of soil and groundwater pollution [SEE POLLUTION], include machine manufacturing, petroleum refining, shipbuilding and food processing. Oil and most raw materials are imported from Russia.

The Svislach River in Minsk, Belarus, runs through the centre of the Janki Kupaly Park.

CZECH REPUBLIC

Capital Prague
Population 10,280,513
Official language Czech
Main religions Roman Catholic 39.2%,
Protestant 4.6%, Orthodox 3%,
non-denominational 39%
Currency Koruna
Form of government Republic
Record holder Bohemian glass is
famous worldwide

HUNGARY

Capital Budapest
Population 10,186,372
Official language Hungarian
Main religions Roman Catholic 67.5%,
Calvinist 20%, Lutheran 5%
Currency Forint
Form of government Republic

POLAND

Capital Warsaw
Population 38,608,929
Official language Polish
Main religion Roman Catholic 95%
Currency Zloty
Form of government Republic

SLOVAKIA

Capital Bratislava
Population 5,396,193
Official language Slovak
Main religions Roman Catholic 60.3%,
Protestant 8.4%, Orthodox 4.1%,
other 27.2%
Currency Koruna
Form of government Republic

CENTRAL Europe

World wars and shifting boundaries

The collapse of the Austro-Hungarian Empire after World War I reshaped this region. In 1918, Czechs and Slovaks merged to become one nation: Czechoslovakia. In 1918, Hungary also became a nation but lost one-third of its land and almost 60 per cent of its population to surrounding states. After World War II, Poland's borders expanded westwards, but the Soviet Union (Russia) gained control of substantial areas to the east, resulting in an overall loss of Polish territory and population.

The Danube River runs through Budapest, the capital city of Hungary.

The **Czech Republic**, part of the former Czechoslovakia, was peacefully established in 1993 when the 'western' Czechs were divided from 'eastern' Slovaks. The Czech Republic consists mainly of the ancient provinces of Bohemia and Moravia and a small part of Silesia. The gentle Bohemian hills and plateaus are separated from hillier Moravia by the Moravian Heights. Wheat, barley and potatoes are grown and transported along the

The city of Strambeck in the hills of Moravia, an ancient province in eastern Czech Republic.

river systems. Although not rich in natural resources, sufficient black coal and iron ore reserves have allowed important iron and steelmaking industries to develop. Glass, clothing and car manufacturing also contribute to the country's revenue.

Hungary was settled by the Magyars, nomads from the central Volga, in the AD 700s. The Great Hungarian Plain, traversed by the Danube and Tisza Rivers, and the Little Hungarian Plain, provide fertile agricultural country, some dry sandy expanses and marshlands beloved by waterbirds. Maize, wheat, sugar beet and sunflowers are the most important crops; pigs and poultry are also extensively farmed. Lignite, a low-quality coal, fuels most of the country's power stations. Raw materials are imported for iron and steel production and other industries, which include the manufacture of fertilisers, pharmaceuticals and cement. Aluminium, using local bauxite, is also produced. Air, soil and water pollution is a serious problem.

Poland, despite comparatively recent communist governments, has maintained its strong Catholic faith since the king of the Polanie (plain-dwellers) was converted to Christianity in the AD 900s. Most of this low-lying country is fertile and almost self-sufficient in a range of cereal and vegetable crops. Farmers also raise cattle, pigs and other livestock. Rich coal reserves, natural gas, iron ore and salt all help to make Poland successful as a producer of chemicals. Shipbuilding and steel and cement manufacture were established after World War II. Coal-generated electricity, used by half the country, has resulted in polluted air and acid rain [SEE POLLUTION]. At various times Poland has been controlled by foreign powers. Entirely free elections were held for the first time in 1991.

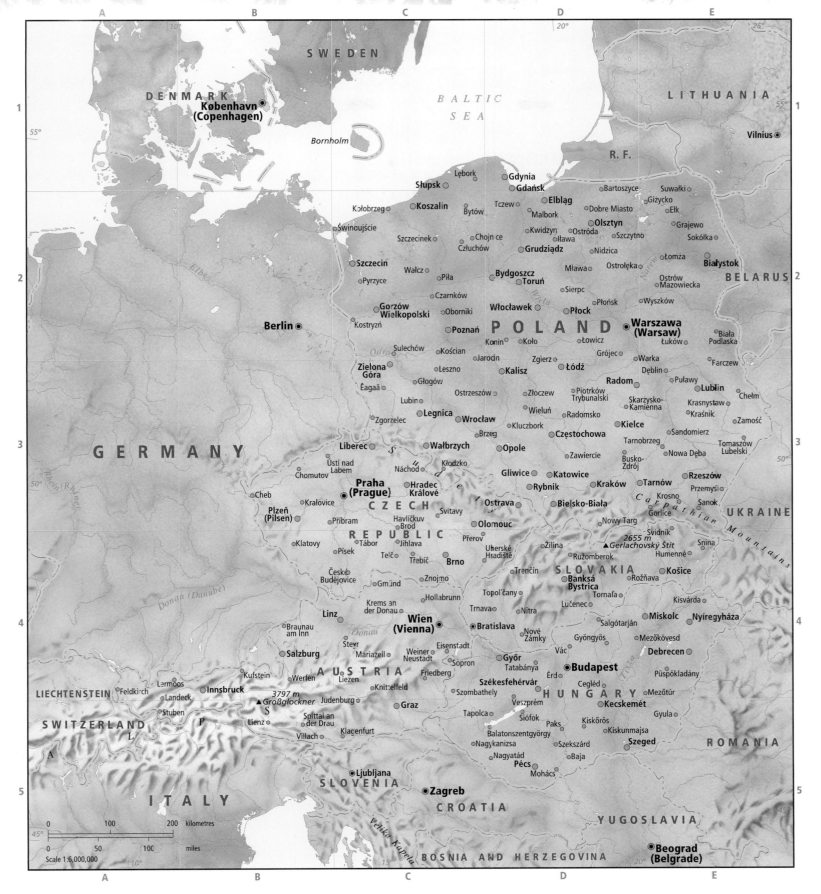

Map labels

SWEDEN

DENMARK
København
(Copenhagen)

BALTIC
SEA

LITHUANIA

Bornholm

R.F.

Vilnius

BELARUS

Lębork · Gdynia
Słupsk · Gdańsk · Elbląg
Kołobrzeg · Koszalin · Bytów · Tczew · Malbork · Dobre Miasto · Gizycko
Świnoujście · Szczecinek · Chojnice · Kwidzyn · Ostróda · Szczytno · Grajewo
Człuchów · Grudziądz · Nidzica · Sokółka
Szczecin · Wałcz · Piła · Bydgoszcz · Mława · Ostrołęka · Łomża · Białystok
Pyrzyce · Czarnków · Toruń · Sierpc · Ostrów Mazowiecka
Gorzów Wielkopolski · Oborniki · Włocławek · Płock · Płońsk · Wyszków
Berlin · Kostrzyń · Poznań · POLAND · Warszawa (Warsaw) · Biała Podlaska
Sulechów · Kościan · Konin · Koło · Łowicz · Grójec · Warka · Łuków · Farczew
Zielona Góra · Leszno · Jarocin · Zgierz · Łódź · Dęblin · Puławy · Lublin
Głogów · Ostrzeszów · Złoczew · Piotrków Trybunalski · Skarżysko-Kamienna · Krasnystaw · Chełm
Lubin · Wieluń · Radomsko · Radom · Kraśnik
Zgorzelec · Legnica · Wrocław · Kluczbork · Kielce · Sandomierz · Zamość
Liberec · Wałbrzych · Brzeg · Opole · Częstochowa · Zawiercie · Tarnobrzeg · Nowa Dęba · Tomaszów Lubelski
Ústí nad Labem · Náchod · Kłodzko · Gliwice · Katowice · Busko-Zdrój · Rzeszów
Chomutov · Hradec Králové · Rybnik · Kraków · Tarnów · Krosno · Przemyśl
Cheb · Praha (Prague) · Svitavy · Ostrava · Bielsko-Biała · Gorlice · Sanok
Kralovice · Příbram · Havlíčkuv Brod · Olomouc · Nowy Targ · Svidník · UKRAINE
Plzeň (Pilsen) · Přerov · Uherské Hradiště · Žilina · 2655 m Gerlachovský Štit · Humenné · Snina
Klatovy · Tábor · Jihlava · Trenčín · SLOVAKIA · Košice
Písek · Telč · Třebíč · Brno · Banská Bystrica · Rožňava · Kisvárda
České Budějovice · Znojmo · Topoľčany · Lučenec · Tornaľa
Gmünd · Hollabrunn · Trnava · Nitra · Salgótarján · Miskolc · Nyíregyháza
Linz · Krems an der Donau · Bratislava · Nové Zámky · Gyöngyös · Mezőkövesd · Debrecen
Braunau am Inn · Wien (Vienna) · Vác · Tatabánya · Győr · Budapest · Püspökladány
Salzburg · Steyr · Mariazell · Eisenstadt · Sopron · Érd · Cegléd · HUNGARY · Mezőtúr
Lermoos · Kufstein · Werfen · Wiener Neustadt · Friedberg · Szombathely · Székesfehérvár · Kecskemét · Gyula
Feldkirch · Landeck · Innsbruck · 3797 m Großglockner · Judenburg · Knittelfeld · Veszprém · Kiskőrös · Kiskunmajsa
LIECHTENSTEIN · Stuben · Lienz · Spittal an der Drau · Graz · Tapolca · Siófok · Paks · Szekszárd · Szeged
SWITZERLAND · Klagenfurt · Villach · Balatonszentgyörgy · Nagykanizsa · Baja · ROMANIA
AUSTRIA · Nagyatád · Pécs · Mohács
ITALY · Ljubljana · SLOVENIA · Zagreb · CROATIA · YUGOSLAVIA
Beograd (Belgrade)
BOSNIA AND HERZEGOVINA

GERMANY

CZECH REPUBLIC

Donau (Danube)

Carpathian Mountains

0 100 200 kilometres
0 50 100 miles
Scale 1:6,000,000

Slovakia

Slovakia is ruggedly mountainous and forested, except in the south and southeast. It is the smaller, less populous and less industrially developed part of the former state of Czechoslovakia. Ski resorts in the Tatra Mountains attract many tourists. The Danube, forming part of the border with Hungary, waters an extensive fertile plain. Slovakia's principal crops are wheat and potatoes; sheep, cattle and pigs are widely raised. Industries, such as iron and steelmaking, and car and clothing manufacture. employ a third of the workers and are concentrated around Bratislava and Kosice.

Gdansk is one of northern Poland's major ports. It is also the birthplace of the trade union Solidarity.

ALBANIA

Capital Tiranë
Population 3,364,571
Official language Albanian
Main religions Muslim 70%, Albanian Orthodox 20%, Roman Catholic 10%
Currency Lek
Form of government Republic

BOSNIA AND HERZEGOVINA

Capital Sarajevo
Population 3,482,495
Official languages Serbian, Croatian
Main religions Muslim 40%, Orthodox 31%, Catholic 15%, Protestant 4%
Currency Dinar
Form of government Federal republic
Record holder On 28 June 1914, a Bosnian Serb assassinated the Austrian heir apparent, Archduke Francis Ferdinand, and his wife, this event precipitated World War I

BULGARIA

Capital Sofia
Population 8,194,772
Official language Bulgarian
Main religions Bulgarian Orthodox 35%, Muslim 13%
Currency Lev
Form of government Republic
Record holder Mt Musala, at 2,925 metres (9,596 feet), is the highest point on the Balkan Peninsula

CROATIA

Capital Zagreb
Population 4,676,865
Official language Croatian
Main religions Catholic 76.5%, Orthodox 11.1%
Currency Kuna
Form of government Republic

SOUTHEAST
Europe

Europe's powder keg

The countries occupying the Balkan peninsula, including Moldova (see Eastern Europe), are collectively called the Balkans. Recently, however, the name has been used more specifically for members of the former Yugoslavian Federal Republic. The Balkans' present troubles originated with the Turkish Empire's decline in the 1800s when newly formed nation-states disregarded the ethnic, religious and linguistic mix of the population. All Balkan countries suffered terribly in World War II. Afterwards, strong communist leadership held Yugoslavia together until 1980, but then Eastern Europe's collapsing communist regimes encouraged its disintegration. Civil wars followed. United Nations involvement and an uneasy truce in 1995 have not prevented violence erupting again in Kosovo.

 *[SEE Global guardians]*

Albania, part of the Turkish Ottoman

Empire for 500 years, became independent in 1912. Many Albanians are Muslims, an isolating factor in the region. In 1992, Albania was the last European country to abandon communist government. Its rugged terrain discourages inland rail links; there are no railway lines to neighbouring countries; and marshes restrict coastal access. In most areas, Albanians travel by horse- or mule-drawn vehicles. Where farming is

The town of Gjirokastra in Albania boasts a citadel dating from the fourteenth century.

possible, corn, wheat, barley and fruit are grown. Despite abundant resources of petroleum, mineral ores and natural gas, Albania is underdeveloped and remains prey to poverty and food shortages, made worse by Muslim refugees flooding in from Yugoslavia.

Bosnia and Herzegovina,

formerly part of the Kingdom of Serbs, Croats and Slovenes (later renamed Yugoslavia), was formed in 1994 when Bosnian Croats and Muslims agreed reluctantly to joint control of the region. For a further eighteen months, Bosnian Serbs fought to have a portion of the country incorporated into the Yugoslavian province of Serbia. Forestry products were a major source of earnings before the economy collapsed. War has seriously affected the small farms, which grow fruit and cereals and raise sheep, and disrupted health and education services. Industry is virtually at a standstill and Bosnia-Herzegovina relies on imported food and United Nations aid.

This old stone bridge spanning a river in Montenegro, Yugoslavia, suggests nothing of the havoc wreaked elsewhere in the country by the savagery of civil war.

Map Labels

AUSTRIA

Budapest

HUNGARY

Maribor
Ptuj
Kranj
Ljubljana
Celje
Brežice
SLOVENIA
Postojna
Kočevje
Karlovac
Opatija
Rijeka
Pula
Senj
Velika Kapela
CROATIA
Zagreb
Vara din
Virovitica
Subotica
Sombor
Kikinda
Bečej
MOLDOVA
Chişinău (Kishinev)

ROMANIA

CARPAȚII MERIDIONALI

Carpathian Mts

Mures

Tisza

Osijek
Đakovo
Sisak
Bosanska Dubica
Slavonski Brod
Novi Sad
Zrenjanin
Vršac
Prijedor
B hać
Modriča
Banja Luka
Doboj
Brčko
BOSNIA
Tuzla
Šabac
Beograd (Belgrade)
Požarevac
Ruma
Velika Plana
Bucureşti (Bucharest)
AND
Zenica
Valjevo
YUGOSLAVIA
Gospić
Gračac
Ključ
Jajce
Zadar
Knin
Cincar 2006 m
HERZEGOVINA
Sarajevo
Čačak
Kragujevac
Zaječar
Kraljevo
Šibenik
Sinj
Livno
Konjic
Priboj
Kruševac
Trogir
Jablanica
Foča
Pljevlja
Ušće
Prokuplje
Niš
Split
Omiš
Mostar 2396 m Maglić
Stolac
Bajovo Polje
Bijelo Polje
Novi Pazar
Leskovac
Pirot
Drvenik
Metković
Bileća
Nikšić
Rožaj
Kosovska Mitrovica
STARA
Dubrovnik
Podgorica
Peć
Priština
Vranje
Sofiya (Sofia)
PLANINA
BULGARIA
Cetinje
Prizren
ADRIATIC
Koplik
Shkodër
Kukës
Kumanovo
Skopje
Bar
Lezhë
Tetovo
Veles
Štip
SEA
Tiranë (Tirana)
Kičevo
MACEDONIA
Durrës
Ohrid
Gevgelija
Kavajë
Elbasan
Bitola
Serres
Drama
Xanthi
Komotiní
▲1281 m Vesuvio
Berat
Edessa
Kilkis
Kavala
Alexandroupoli
ITALY
ALBANIA
Korçë
Veroia
Thessaloniki (Salonica)
Thasos
Vlorë
Kastoria
Agri
Ersekë
Kozani
Katerini
Sikea
Limnos
Gjirokastër
2917 m Oros Olympos (Mt Olympus)
Konitsa
TURKEY
▲3323 m Monte Etna
Ioannina
Tyrnavos
Mytilini
Kerkyra (Corfu)
Igoumenitsa
Trikala
Larisa
Lesvos (Lesbos)
Sicilia (Sicily)
Karditsa
Volos
AEGEAN
Arta
Chios
Preveza
Domokos
Lamia
Samos
GREECE
Agrinio
SEA
Mesolongi
Levadeia
Thiva
Chalkida
IONIAN
Aigio
Patra
Korinthos (Corinth)
Athina (Athens)
Ermoupoli
Kyklades (Cyclades)
Amaliada
Argos
Peiraias (Piraeus)
SEA
Pyrgos
Zacharo
Tripoli
Naxos
Kalamata
Sparti (Sparta)
Gytheio
Rodos (Rhodes)
Akra Tainaro
Kriti (Crete)
Karpathos
Chania
Rethymno
Irakleio (Iraklion)
Siteia

Scale 1:6,000,000

0   100   200 kilometres
0   50   100 miles

The Temple of Poseidon on Cape Soúnio is one of the many reminders of the glory of ancient Greece.

Bulgaria's people are descendants of the Bulgars from north of the Danube who, in the late AD 600s, established dominance over the Slavic races that had settled the area around AD 400. Christianity arrived in the AD 800s. Bulgaria sided with the losers in the two world wars, and each time suffered changes of boundaries. The fertile Danube Valley supports cereal crops; vineyards around the Maritsa River produce some of Southern Europe's finest wines. Bulgaria's economy, far from robust, is buoyed by tourism and by machinery and other manufacturing industries.

GREECE

Capital Athens
Population 10,707,135
Official language Greek
Main religion Greek Orthodox 98%
Currency Drachma
Form of government Republic
Record holder The first athletic contests were held in Greece some 3,500 years ago (later the Olympic Games held at O ympia, upon which the modern Olympics a e based, became famous throughout the ancient Greek world); The world's narrowest navigable straits are those between the Aegean island of Euboea and the Greek mainland. The gap is only 40 metres (130 feet) wide at Khalkis

MACEDONIA

Capital Skopje
Population 2,022,604
Official language Macedonian
Main religions Eastern Orthodox 67%, Muslim 30%
Currency Denar
Form of government Republic

ROMANIA

Capital Bucharest
Population 22,334,312
Official language Romanian
Main religions Romanian Orthocox 87%, Roman Catholic 5%, Protestant 5%
Currency Leu
Form of government Republic

SLOVENIA

Capital Ljubljana
Population 1,970,570
Official language Slovenian
Main religion Roman Catholic 96%
Currency Tolar
Form of government Republic

YUGOSLAVIA

Capital Belgrade
Population 10,526,478
Official language Serbian
Main religions Eastern Orthodox 65%, Muslim 19%, Roman Catholic 4%, Protestant 1%
Currency Yugoslav dinar
Form of government Federal republic

Dubrovnik's Old Town is built on the very edge of the Adriatic Sea. The Croatians are working to restore historic buildings damaged by shelling in the conflict of the 1990s and the picturesque walled port to its former tourist appeal.

Southeast Europe continued...

Croatia emerged in the AD 800s, peopled by Slavic immigrants from present-day Ukraine. In 1918, declaring its independence from the Austro-Hungarian Empire, Croatia joined the Kingdom of Serbs, Croats and Slovenes. Serbian domination of the new country provoked agitation by Croatian separatists; in 1939 Croatia became a self-governing region within Yugoslavia. After independence was declared in 1991, civil war broke out, hostilities continuing until 1995. The Croatians grow cereal crops, fruit and tobacco, and raise sheep. Timber is a significant resource, and minerals, coal and iron ore are mined.

Greece consists of the mainland and more than 1,500 islands, about one-tenth inhabited, scattered across the Aegean and Ionian Seas. Greek civilisation began with the Minoans on the island of Crete about 3500 BC. Athens became the centre of Greek culture in the BC 500s. Modern Greece emerged in AD 1832 when the country established a monarchy after almost 400 years of Turkish domination. Despite generally poor soils and rugged terrain, Greece is almost self-sufficient; olives are a major export. Most industries, such as food and chemical processing and textile manufacture, are centred on Athens. The warm climate, unspoilt beaches and ancient historical sites attract more than 10 million tourists a year.

Macedonia, once the heart of the Greek Empire, then a Roman province, was weakened by repeated invasions from AD 300. Now the least developed of the former Yugoslav republics, it has a declining standard of living, partly as a result of the trade embargoes imposed by Greece since independence in 1991. Nevertheless, it is self-sufficient in food, growing cereals, fruit, vegetables and cotton, and raising sheep and cattle. One-quarter of the land is used for agriculture; cereals, fruits, vegetables and cotton are grown. Coal reserves supply power.

Romania's boundaries, like many others in this region, have shifted through the centuries. Much land was lost during World War II when Romania, which sided with Nazi Germany, came under Soviet control. From 1967 onwards, Romania distanced itself from the Soviets. The Carpathian Mountains separate the timbered uplands of Transylvania from the fertile Danube Plain where maize, wheat, vegetables and wine grapes are grown. Sheep and pigs are the main livestock. Romania, which has a relatively low standard of living, is rich in coal, natural gas, iron ore and petroleum. Chemical and metal processing and machine manufacturing have caused widespread pollution. Lumbering has depleted the country's forests.

Slovenia was first settled by Slavic peoples in the AD 500s. In the AD 1000s Austria gained control, and much later Slovenia was absorbed into the Austro-Hungarian Empire. Slovenia declared its independence from Yugoslavia in 1991. Dairy farming and pig-raising are the main agricultural activities. Almost half the workforce is employed in mining and manufacturing. Nuclear power supplies one-third of the country's electricity. The once thriving tourist industry, based on alpine scenery and beaches, has suffered from the many conflicts in the region.

Yugoslavia, 'Land of the South Slavs', shares borders with seven countries. Today it comprises the republics of Montenegro and Serbia, the latter containing the province of Kosovo. Bosnia and Herzegovina, Croatia, Macedonia and Slovenia joined with them from 1918 until 1991, when independence sparked four years of bitter ethnic-based conflict with Serbia, ending in a shaky peace. Ethnic Albanians, predominantly Muslims, made up 90 per cent of Kosovo's population. In 1999 the Serbians forced most of them to leave. The conflict still simmers despite intervention from the United States, the United Kingdom, United Nations and others. Yugoslavia's northern plain farmers continue to grow wheat, maize and vegetables, and to raise livestock and poultry. Montenegro's farmers keep sheep and goats. Mining and heavy machine manufacture are major contributors to the country's economy. Though self-sufficient in fuel, industries and trade links are seriously destabilised by war.

Intense blues and spotless whites are the predominant colours in many Greek buildings, such as the restaurant in this alleyway in Mykonos.

The Church of Sveti Jovan Bogoslov Kaneo on the shores of Ohrid Lake, Macedonia.

Capital Yerevan
Population 3,409,234
Official language Armenian
Main religion Armenian Orthodox 94%
Currency Dram
Form of government Republic
Record holder Armenia claims to be the resting place of Noah's Ark—its capital was supposedly founded by Noah himself (Mt Ararat itself is in Turkey); First country in the world to make Christianity its state religion

AZERBAIJAN

Capital Baki (Baku)
Population 7,908,224
Official language Azerbaijani
Main religions Mulim 93.5%, Russian Orthodox 2.5%, Armenian Orthodox 2%
Currency Manat
Form of government Federal republic

CYPRUS

Capital Lefkosia (Nicosia)
Population 768,895
Official languages Greek, Turkish
Main religions Greek Orthodox 78%, Muslim 18%
Currency Cypriot pound, Turkish lira
Form of government Two de facto republics

GEORGIA

Capital T'bilisi
Population 5,066,499
Official language Georgian
Main religions Christian Orthodox 75% (Georgian Orthodox 65%, Russian Orthodox 10%), Muslim 11%, Armenian Apostolic 8%
Currency Lari
Form of government Republic
Record holder The town of Gori is the birthplace of Georgia's most famous son, Josef Stalin, general secretary of the Soviet Communist Party from 1922 to 1953

EASTERN
Europe
Edging two continents

Moldova, the Ukraine and a small part of Turkey are in Europe; to the east, the rest of Turkey, Armenia, Azerbaijan and Georgia lie in Asia. The island of Cyprus, which is physically Asian, politically straddles both continents. Greek Cypriots are firmly separated from Turkish Cypriots, their divisions rooted in religion. The region's rich legendary associations were established long before its modern boundaries. The birthplace of Aphrodite, ancient Greek goddess of love, is located off the coast of Cyprus. The fabled city of Troy stood on the Aegean shore in what is now Turkey. Georgia's Plain of Kolchida was the Greek mythological land of the Golden Fleece.

Aphrodite, the ancient Greek goddess of love, is said to have been born in the waves of this beach off the coast of Cyprus.

Armenia

Armenia has been fought over by Romans, Persians and Monguls. It had been a distinct country for 1,000 years before becoming Christian in the AD 300s. A Soviet republic from 1922 until gaining independence in 1991, Armenia developed industrially, supplying manufactured goods to other republics in exchange for raw materials and energy. Fruit and cereals are major crops; exports include quality brandies and wines. Armenia lies in an active seismic area—1988's devastating earthquake killed around 25,000 people *[SEE NATURAL DISASTERS].* In the same year, conflict began over its claim to Nagorno-Karabakh, an internal Azerbaijani area largely populated by Christian Armenians.

Turkish and Azerbaijani blockades of pipeline and railroad traffic into the country have harmed Armenia's economy. Recovery is unlikely before this dispute is settled.

Azerbaijan

Azerbaijan was once known as 'the land of eternal fire' for the burning natural gas that flamed out of the ground here. Oil was being collected from the Caspian Sea near Baku at least 1,000 years ago. Today oil is the mainstay of Azerbaijan's economy, although production has declined in recent years. This Azeri state, independent from at least the 400s BC, later came under the control of Persia and then Turkic-speaking people. Part of the Soviet Union from 1936, Azerbaijan was one of the first Soviet republics to declare independence in 1991. The territorial dispute with Armenia over the Nagorno-Karabakh region is a serious ongoing problem. Azerbaijan's limited arable land produces cotton, tobacco, grapes and other fruit. Oil production and overuse of toxic defoliants have damaged the environment. Serious water pollution has affected sturgeon from the Caspian Sea, once an important source of Azerbaijan's caviar industry *[SEE POLLUTION].* The Abseron Peninsula is one of the most ecologically devasted areas in the world.

Along a buffer zone that separates the two regions of Cyprus, and divides Nicosia itself, some 2,000 UN troops costing more than US$100,000,000 per year continue to supervise an uneasy peace.

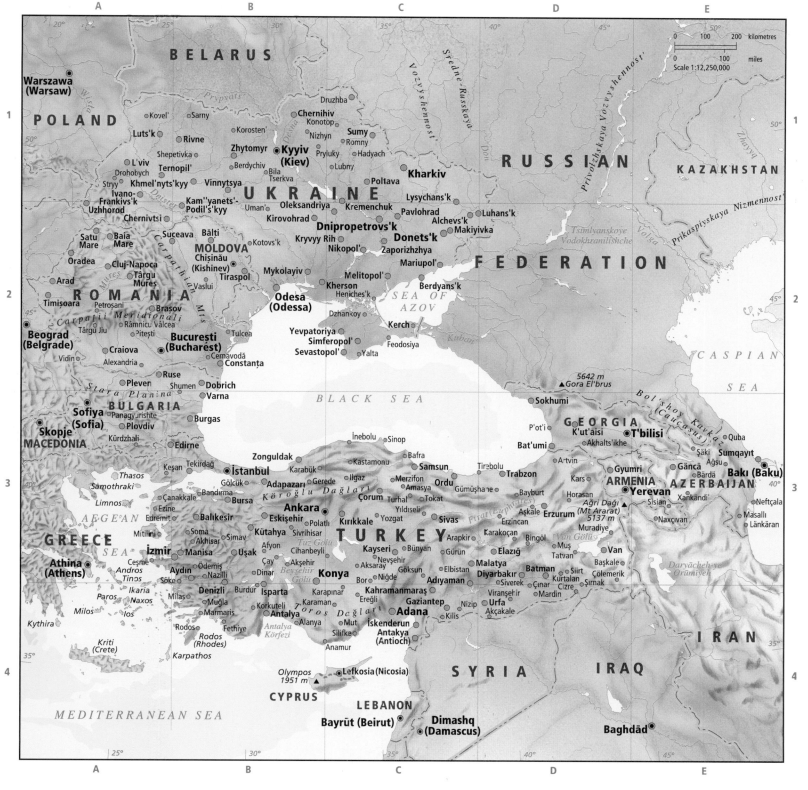

Cyprus (from *kypros* meaning copper in Greek) still exports copper, first extracted there 3,500 years ago. Occupied successively by Phoenicians, Greeks and Romans, by the Turks from 1571 and the British from 1878, civil war between the Greek majority and the Turkish minority broke out after independence in 1960. In 1974 Turkey invaded and occupied 40 per cent of the land in the north, expelling 200,000 Greek Cypriots to the south. The 'Turkish Republic of Northern Cyprus', declared in 1982 and recognised only by Turkey, now operates autonomously. Reunification talks are deadlocked; United Nations troops maintain a buffer zone between the deeply divided regions. Economically, the Greek sector is the more prosperous, gaining income from tourism, military installations and manufacturing, as well as from growing potatoes, grapes, citrus fruits and cereals. The Turkish sector depends almost entirely on agriculture.

Gypsy girls wearing traditional Turkish clothing of loose pantaloons dance in front of the tents and wagons of the family camp.

MOLDOVA

Capital Chisinau
Population 4,460,838
Official language Moldovan
Main religion Eastern Orthodox 98.5%
Currency Leu
Form of government Republic

TURKEY

Capital Ankara
Population 65,597,383
Official language Turkish
Main religions Muslim 99.8%
(mostly Sunni)
Currency Turkish lira
Form of government Republic
Record holder Mt Ararat, 5,166 metres
(16,949 feet) and the highest point in the
region, is said to be Noah's Ark's
resting place

UKRAINE

Capital Kiev
Population 49, 811,174
Official language Ukrainian
Main religions Predominantly Christian
(Ukrainian Orthodox, Ukrainian Autocephalus
Orthodox, Roman Catholic), small Protestant,
Jewish and Muslim minorities
Currency Hryvna
Form of government Republic

Eastern Europe continued...

The golden dome of the refectory church of St Anthony and Theodosius, Monastry of Caves, in Kiev, Georgia. Below the church is a network of medieval catacombs.

Georgia

Georgia is protected against cold air from the north by the high peaks of the Caucacus Mountains, a barrier that allows the Black Sea to warm the region. Nearly 40 per cent of the country is forested; the rest is difficult to farm. Georgia produces citrus fruits, tea (the main crop), grapes, tobacco, wheat, barley and vegetables. Food processing and wine production are major industries. Other factories, mostly powered by hydroelectricity, produce machinery, chemicals and textiles, including silk from the Imeretia district. Manganese, copper, cobalt and vanadium are mined. Georgia's long national history included conquests by Romans, Persians, Arabs, Tartars and Turks before it fell to the Russians around 1800. Tourism, once important, has suffered from the effects of civil strife in Abkhazia and South Ossetia since independence from the Soviet Union in 1991.

Moldova

Moldova is low-lying but hilly steppe country, with numerous deep river valleys and gorges. Black fertile soil ensures high-yield crops, principally vegetables, sunflower seeds, tobacco, cereals and wine grapes. Cattle and pigs also thrive. Moldova and Romania are ethnically and linguistically linked, but when Moldova became a Soviet republic after World War II, many Romanians living there were forcibly moved to other Soviet countries. Violent clashes between the Russian population and ethnic Romanians followed independence in 1991. These tensions persist, despite the efforts of a Russian-Moldovan peacekeeping force, set up in 1992. Moldova imports oil, coal and gas from Russia. Electricity, too, is imported, and power shortages are quite frequent.

Turkey

Turkey encompasses Asia Minor's large mountainous plateau and a much smaller region in Europe across the narrow straits of the Bosphorus. Ethnically and culturally distinct groups have inhabited this region since early prehistoric times. Ancient sites, such as Ephesus, attract visitors. The Turkish republic was founded in 1923 after the fall of the Ottoman Empire. Its leader attempted to create a modern Islamic state that could be part of Europe. Full integration with Europe seems remote. The Turkish Kurds' demand for an independent homeland and Turkey's claim to northern Cyprus (not recognised internationally) remain unresolved problems. The Turkish economy combines modern industry with village agriculture and crafts. Tobacco, figs and cotton are grown; chrome, copper, oil, gold and coal are mined; and abundant hydroelectricity supplements other sources of power.

Ukraine

Ukraine has been independent of the Soviet Union since 1991 but still retains close ties with Russia. A Viking tribe established a centre at Kiev in the AD 800s. Later Mongols and Poles took control before Russia absorbed the country into their empire. Formerly called 'the granary of the Soviet Union', most of the country is covered by fertile black-soil plains that support cereal grains, vegetables, fruit and fodder crops. Agricultural output is still badly affected by the widespread contamination caused by the nuclear accident at Chernobyl in 1986 [*SEE GLOBAL NUCLEAR INDUSTRY*]. Coal is Ukraine's most abundant resource; its industries include steel production, machine building, engineering and chemical processing.

Hieropolis Theatre, Panukkale, Turkey. Known in ancient times as Anatolia, the region was colonised more than 2,500 years ago by the Greeks and was later part of the empire of Alexander the Great, the Roman Empire and the Byzantine Empire.

Floor mosaic at Curium, Cyprus. This form of wall and floor decoration was widespread throughout the eastern Mediterranean from the 300s BC.

BAHRAIN

Capital   Al Manāmah (Manama)
Population   629,090
Official language   Arabic
Main religions   Shi'a Muslim 75%,
Sunni Muslim 25%
Currency   Bahraini dinar
Form of government   Traditional
monarchy

IRAN

Capital   Tehrān
Population   70,351,549
Official language   Farsi (Persian)
Main religions   Shi'a Muslim 89%,
Sunni Muslim 10%
Currency   Rial
Form of government   Theocratic republic
Record holder   Home of the world's
largest theocracy (a form of government in
which the established church has political
power); Qolleh-ye Damāvand 5,671 metres
(18,605 feet) is the highest point in
the region

IRAQ

Capital   Baghdād
Population   23,871,623
Official languages   Arabic, Kurdish
Main religion   Muslim 97% (Shi'a
60%–65%, Sunni 32–37%)
Currency   Iraqi dinar
Form of government   Republic

JORDAN

Capital   'Ammān
Population   4,561,147
Official language   Arabic
Main religions   Sunni Muslim 92%,
Christian 8%
Currency   Jordanian dinar
Form of government   Constitutional
monarchy
Record holder   The Dead Sea is the
lowest point on the Earth's surface, at
400 metres (1,312 feet) below sea level

KUWAIT

Capital   Al Kuwayt (Kuwait)
Population   1,991,115
Official language   Arabic
Main religions   Muslim 85% (Sunni 45%,
Shi'a 30%, other 10%), other (including
Christian, Hindu, Parsi) 15%
Currency   Kuwaiti dinar
Form of government   Constitutional
monarchy

THE
Middle East

Oil, water and antiquity

Much of this region is oil rich and water poor. In Bahrain, for example, there is no natural surface fresh water; supplies come from underground springs and desalinated seawater. Qatar has occasional winter showers, but is also dependent on desalinisation and groundwater supplies. Notwithstanding, people have lived in the better-watered parts since ancient times.

Bahrain, consisting of 35 small, low-lying islands that were once the heart of the ancient Dilmun civilisation, has been a focus of trade for more than 4,000 years. Today it is the major banking centre of the Arab world. A 25 kilometre (16 mile) causeway, which links the main island with Saudi Arabia, brings in many weekend visitors from the Gulf States. Oil spills and oil tanker discharges have damaged coastlines, coral reefs and sea life. Fruit and vegetables are grown in small, fertile areas of imported soil.

Hadrian's Arch in Jerash, Jordan. Jordan was a Roman city and major trading centre in ancient times.

Iran's most productive and densely populated areas lie around its edges. Some 8 per cent of the land is cultivated; 11 per cent of it is forested. In the north are fisheries, tea gardens and rice fields. To the south are sugar plantations and oilfields. Wheatfields lie to the west, and fruit groves grow in the east. After 1945, Iran's economy depended almost entirely on oil. The invasion by Iraq in 1980 and the subsequent eight-year war caused living standards to decline. There is ongoing conflict between Iran's strict religious leaders and reformist politicians over the country's modernisation.

This massive rock relief sculpture at Naqsh-e-Rostam, southwest Iran, dates from the Persian Empire, around 500 BC. Nearby Persepolis, founded by Darius I, was ancient Persia's greatest city.

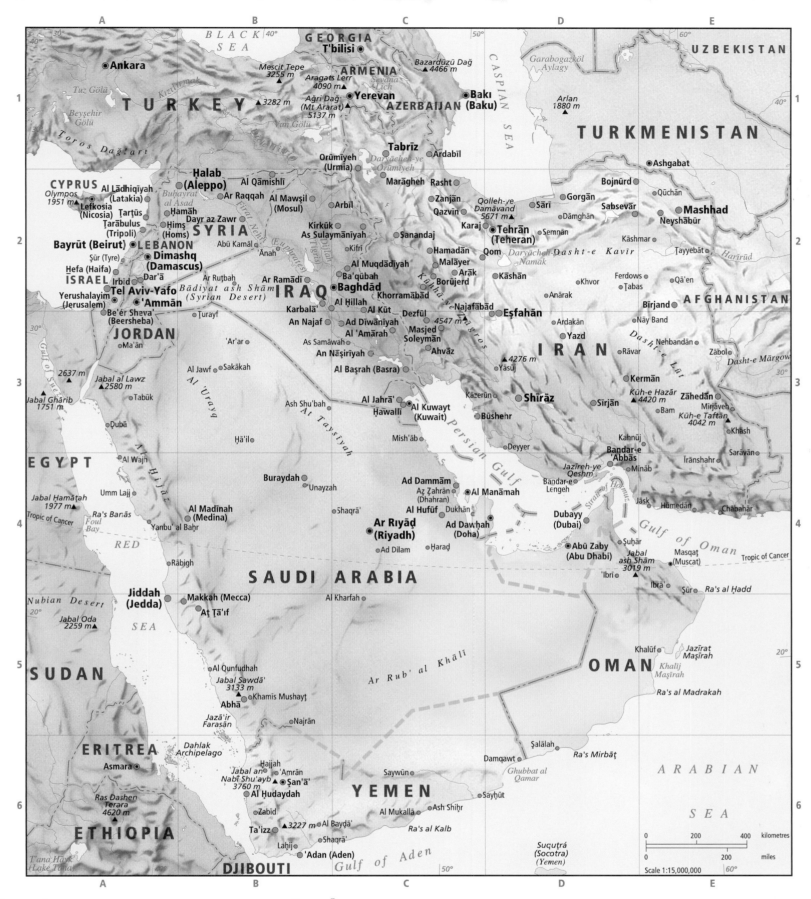

Iraq's first city-states date from 3500 BC. The land once called Mesopotamia lies between the Tigris and Euphrates Rivers, and lays claim to being the cradle of Western civilisation. Later, the Muslim world centred on Baghdad. One-third of the farms in the Tigris–Euphrates basin are irrigated, producing vegetables, cereals and dates. The economy suffered from the war between Iraq and Iran during the 1980s, and the invasion of Kuwait in 1990–91. International embargoes caused a sharp fall in oil exports, previously the country's major revenue-earner. Living standards have fallen in recent years, a situation made worse by excessive government spending on defence.

Jordan has poor water and coal supplies and is not well endowed with oil. Although 80 per cent of its area is desert, irrigation makes it possible to grow vegetables, olives and fruit in some places. In 1967 the West Bank, containing both Jerusalem and much of Jordan's best land, was lost to Israel. Now poverty, debt and unemployment are continuing problems. Historical sites and the spas and thermal springs along the Dead Sea attract tourists.

Kuwait was settled by Arab peoples in the AD 1700s. A British protectorate from 1914, it became independent in 1961, and was then claimed by Iraq. Despite having received large loans from Kuwait during the Iran–Iraq War (1980 to 1988), Iraq invaded Kuwait in 1990, destroying the capital and oil wells, and deliberately spilling oil into the Persian Gulf [SEE POLLUTION]. Kuwait's economy still depends on petroleum products. The shortage of water limits industrial activities and almost all food, except fish, needs to be imported.

OMAN

Capital Muscat
Population 2,446,645
Official language Arabic
Main religions Ibadhi Muslim 75%,
Sunni Muslim, Shi'a Muslim and Hindu 25%
Currency Omani rial
Form of government Monarchy

QATAR

Capital Ad Dawhah (Doha)
Population 723,542
Official language Arabic
Main religion Muslim 95%
Currency Qatari rial
Form of government Monarchy

SAUDI ARABIA

Capital Ar Riyad (Riyadh)
Population 21,504,613
Official language Arabic
Main religions Sunni Muslim 85%,
Shi'a Muslim 15%
Currency Saudi riyal
Form of government Monarchy

SYRIA

Capital Damascus (Dimashq)
Population 17,213,871
Official language Arabic
Main religions Sunni Muslim 74%, other
Muslim sects 16%, Christian 10%, tiny
Jewish communities
Currency Syrian pound
Form of government Republic

UNITED
ARAB EMIRATES

Capital Abu Dhabi
Population 2,344,402
Official language Arabic
Main religion Muslim 96% (Shi'a 16%)
Currency Emirian dirham
Form of government Federation of
Emirates

YEMEN

Capital San'a'
Population 16,942,230
Official language Arabic
Main religions Muslim: predominantly
Sunni in the south, Shi'ite majority in the
north
Currency Yemeni rial
Form of government Republic

The Middle East continued...

Oman's rural dwellers, assisted by irrigation, grow dates, limes, bananas, alfalfa and vegetables, and keep camels, cattle, sheep and goats. Townspeople, including many guest workers, live on imported food. The nation's wealth depends on oil; huge additional reserves were found in 1991. In the past, trading dhows travelled from Muscat, the capital, to India and down Africa's coast to Zanzibar. Oman is the second largest country in the Arabian peninsula.

Qatar, once home to Bedouin nomadic herders, was completely changed by the discovery of oil in 1949. Guest workers arrived from the Indian subcontinent, Iran and northern Africa. Now, 90 per cent of the people live in Doha and its suburbs. Although there is a shortage of fresh water, a few farmers cultivate vegetables where groundwater can be tapped. Qatar chose not to join the United Arab Emirates when they became independent in 1971.

Saudi Arabia covers an area about the size of western Europe. The country is 95 per cent arid or semi-arid; only the Asir Highlands in the southwestern corner, terraced for grain crops and fruit trees, have reliable rainfall. Desert dwellers had to abandon their traditional life when oil was found near Riyadh in 1937. Foreign workers poured in, and soon Saudi Arabia was supplying oil to several major industrial nations. Saudi Arabia contains Islam's most holy places: Mecca, the birthplace of Muhammad (circa AD 570), and Medina, where Islam began. Two million pilgrims each year contribute to the national income. In 1990–91, Saudi Arabia fought Iraq with the help of 500,000 Western troops.

Syria has been invaded by ancient Egyptians, Hittites, Persians, Greeks and Romans. Arabs introduced the Muslim faith in AD 634; Crusaders seized power in the 1100s but were ousted by the Kurds. Under French control from 1920, Syria became independent in 1946. It is intensively farmed on its Mediterranean coast where water is abundant. Exports include oil, textiles, cotton and agricultural produce. Most industry is controlled by the government. The main industries are textiles, food processing, tobacco, petroleum and cement. Syria has a youthful population and unemployment is rising.

A village in the mountains of Oman, surrounded by terraced cultivation. Every piece of land suitable for agriculture is put to good use.

This Bahrain spice seller's shop is typical of the way goods are displayed in markets throughout the region.

The **United Arab Emirates** (UAE), a collection of seven small principalities, are covered with sparse and scrubby vegetation. Less than 1.2 per cent of the land is suitable for cultivation and much food is imported. However, recent irrigation works have assisted farmers. The UAE has close links with Britain and the United States; among Arab countries it acts a force for moderation in world affairs. Oil and gas production will sustain the economy for some years to come. Water will always be in short supply.

Yemen is arid along the Red Sea coastal plain, where cotton growing predominates, and from the coast of the Gulf of Aden to the rugged Yemen Plateau. The comparatively fertile interior supports vines and other fruit crops. Divided into North and South Yemen until 1990, the country is currently weak economically despite its oil and gas reserves. It must support returning Yemeni workers who were expelled from Saudi Arabia and Kuwait after the Gulf War of 1990–91 when Yemen supported Iraq.

Women in traditional dress herd goats on the outskirts of a small village near Dhamar, in the hot and dry Central Highlands of Yemen.

Capital Al Qāhirah (Cairo)
Population 67,273,906
Official language Arabic
Main religion Muslim (mostly Sunni) 94%
Currency Egyptian pound
Form of government Republic
Record holder The Nile, 6,670 kilometres (4,140 miles), is the longest river in the world; The world's first national government was created in ancient Egypt about 5,000 years ago; The ancient Egyptians had the world's first paper (made from the stems of a reed called papyrus) and invented a form of picture writing called hieroglyphics; The Great Pyramid of Cheops (Khufu) is the largest stone building in the world, built about 4,500 years ago, it stands 146 metres (479 feet) high and contains nearly 2.5 million blocks of limestone (it is estimated it took 100,000 men 20 years to build it); Al Qāhirah (Cairo) is the largest city in Africa

ISRAEL

Capital Jerusalem
Population 5,749,760
Official languages Hebrew, Arabic
Main religions Jewish 82%, Muslim 14%, Druze 2%, Christian 2%
Currency Shekel
Form of government Republic
Record holder The Dead Sea is the saltiest body of water in the world

LEBANON

Capital Beirut
Population 3,562,699
Official languages Arabic, French
Main religions Muslim 70%, Christian 30%
Currency Lebanese pound
Form of government Republic

LIBYA

Capital Tarābulus (Tripoli)
Population 5,903,128
Official language Arabic
Main religion Sunni Muslim 97%
Currency Libyan dinar
Form of government Republic
Record holder Libya has neither lakes nor permanent rivers; The highest recorded temperature in the world, 58°C (136°F) in the shade, was recorded in Libya in September 1922

Ancient civilisations and modern conflicts

For many thousands of years the extremely fertile black silt spread by the annual flooding of the Nile has provided the people living there with plants and animals for food. On either side of the valley there is spreading desert. The civilisation of ancient Egypt began in the Nile valley more than 5,000 years ago and flourished for more than 2,000 years.

In the eastern Mediterranean, the modern state of Israel (comprising the Holy Land of the Bible) was the birthplace of the major religions of Judaism and Christianity. Recent decades have seen religious divisions between Muslims and Christians and bitter territorial disputes involving Israel.

Egypt's own ancient civilisation was followed by a series of rulers and conquerors—the Persians, Alexander the Great and the Romans. The region converted to Islam after the arrival of Muslims in the AD 600s. Following

The Church of the Holy Sepulchre in Jerusalem is just one of the many houses of worship in Israel.

A statue among the ruins at Luxor. Ancient Egypt's art, architecture, pyramids and tombs are among the treasures of civilisation.

the construction of the Suez canal in 1869, Egypt came under French and British influence, with Britain declaring it a protectorate in 1914; the country became an independent republic in 1953. Useable land is confined to the Nile valley and delta, only about 3 per cent of the country's total area. More than 99 per cent of its people live along this narrow strip, more than half of them in overcrowded cities and towns. The rest farm small plots or tend livestock. Cotton is the main crop; citrus fruits, rice and sugar cane are also grown. Scattered across the desert are isolated fertile oases where date palms grow. It is hoped that agricultural production of these oases will increase with the use of deep artesian bores.

Israel was created in 1948 as a homeland for Jewish people from all parts of the world. It involves three of the world's great religions [SEE World religions]. Since 1948 there has been continual territorial conflict between the new state and its Arab neighbours. The building of Israeli settlements on the disputed west bank of the Jordan River is particularly resented by that area's mainly Palestinian Arab inhabitants. Israel has the most industrialised economy in the region, with iron ore smelting and chemical manufacture at Haifa and steel factories at Acre. Cut diamonds, high-technology equipment and agricultural products are the main exports.

Lebanon consists of the region known in ancient times as the Levant. In its long history it has been settled by Phoenician traders and seen the armies of Alexander the Great and the

The people of Beirut are no strangers to conflict—the sight of a tank in the main street barely rates a second glance.

Roman Empire. From the 1200s to the 1400s, in the conflict known as the Crusades, it was invaded by Western Christians trying to take control of the nearby Holy Land from the Muslims. From the 1970s to 1990s the modern country was torn by civil war between Muslim and non-Muslim groups which left the economy in ruins. Banking and financial services, which have been the country's main source of income since the 1820s, are slowly recovering from the severe disruption caused by the recent conflict. Agriculture is also important, with apples, citrus fruits, grapes, tomatoes and olives the main crops. Lebanon depends heavily on foreign aid.

Libya in ancient times was settled by the Greeks, was part of the empire of Alexander the Great and was later ruled by the Romans. In AD 642 the region was conquered by the Arabs, and later still became part of the Ottoman Empire. The country is 93 per cent desert, with cereals the main crop grown in the narrow fertile strip along the coast. Oil provides almost all export earnings. The revenue earned from oil finances large-scale tree planting and the Great Manmade River Project, one of the world's largest water development projects, which will bring water from reserves under the Sahara to coastal cities. Most of the industrial sector is controlled by the state.

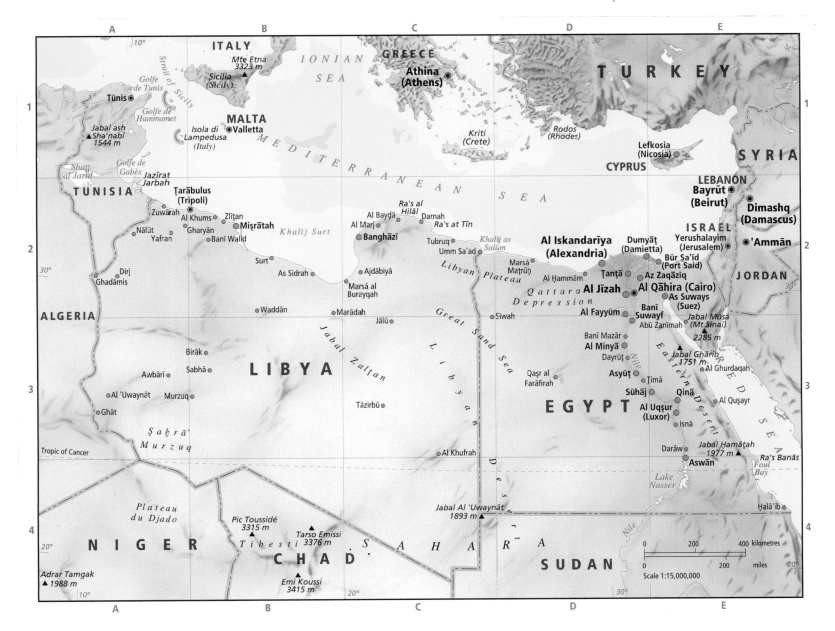

ALGERIA

Capital Alger (Algiers)
Population 31,133,486
Official language Arabic
Main religion Sunni Muslim 99%
Currency Algerian dinar
Form of government Republic
Record holder Largest state in the north of Africa

MOROCCO

Capital Rabat
Population 29, 661, 636
Official language Arabic
Main religion Muslim 99%
Currency Moroccan dirham
Form of government Constitutional monarchy

TUNISIA

Capital Tūnis
Population 9,513,603
Official language Arabic
Main religion Muslim 98%
Currency Dinar
Form of government Republic
Record holder Extends further north than any other country in Africa

Dependencies & Territories

WESTERN SAHARA

Capital None
Population 239, 333
Official language Arabic
Main religion Muslim 99%
Currency Moroccan dirham
Form of government Territory disputed by Morocco and Polisario Front independence movement
Record holder World's largest known deposits of phosphate rock

NORTHWEST
Africa

Traders and pirates

The world's largest desert, the Sahara, stretches across northern Africa from the Atlantic Ocean to the Red Sea. Along the Mediterranean coast is a narrow fringe of fertile land where the winters are cool and wet and the summers hot and dry. This strip is home to most of the region's people. About 5,000 years ago the nomadic Berber peoples arrived here. Two thousand years later, the seafaring Phoenicians from the eastern Mediterranean set up trading colonies along the coast. Next, in the AD 600s, came the Arabs, bringing with them Islam. From the 1500s to the 1800s, the strip was known as the Barbary Coast, and the seas were controlled by Muslim pirates (called corsairs), who raided passing ships and also traded slaves.

A gold-seller in Morocco, a region long known for its fine metalware.

Algeria has been home to nomadic Berber peoples since early times. The country has seen empires come and go. It was once a province of the Roman Empire known as Numidia. In the 1500s it was taken into the Islamic Ottoman Empire; and from 1848 until its independence in 1962, it was a colony of France. Inland, desert covers 85 per cent of the country, and over the centuries, a number of oasis towns have grown up around precious watering holes along trading routes. Beneath the sands are rich deposits of oil and natural gas, which today are Algeria's main revenue earners. Olives, grapes, barley, oats and vegetables for the European market are grown in the farming regions of the coastal strip.

Morocco's name comes from the Arabic *Maghreh-el-aksal*, meaning 'the furthest west'. The Arab majority live in the lowlands, while the Berber-speaking minority, which make up about 35 per cent of Morocco's people, live in the Atlas Mountains as peasant farmers and nomadic herders. Agriculture, mainly cereals, citrus fruit and vegetables, is the main export earner. Dates are grown in desert oases. Morocco's wildlife includes Cuvier's gazelle, the Barbary macaque, and the mouflon (a wild sheep). Desert animals such as the fennec fox can be found in the south of the country.

City workers in Tunisia wearing a mixture of traditional and Western-style clothing.

Tunisia has had strong links with people and ideas from Europe since the founding of colonies here by the Phoenicians 3,000 years ago. The wealthy trading centre of Carthage, which stood near modern-day Tūnis, was one of the greatest cities in the ancient world until its destruction by the Romans in 146 BC. In modern times Tunisia was a French protectorate until independence in 1956. Mineral and petroleum exports, agriculture and tourism (Tunisia has a good climate and many Roman remains) are the main revenue earners. Tourism employs around 200,000 people. However, the activities of Islamic militants have discouraged some tourists from visiting Tunisia.

....

Western Sahara, a former Spanish possession, has been occupied and administered by Morocco since 1975. Moroccan sovereignty over these phosphate-rich desert lands is disputed by the Polisario Front (Popular Front for the Liberation of the Saguia el Hamra and Rio di Oro), which is fighting for independence on behalf of the country's indigenous Berber and Arab population, the Sahrawis. Many thousands of Sahrawi refugees have fled Western Sahara and are living in camps in Algeria.

Ghardaïa, the most famous of Algeria's oasis towns, lies between hills of bare rock on the northern edge of the Sahara Desert. Date palms cluster on its outskirts and rising above blue and beige buildings are the minarets of its mosques.

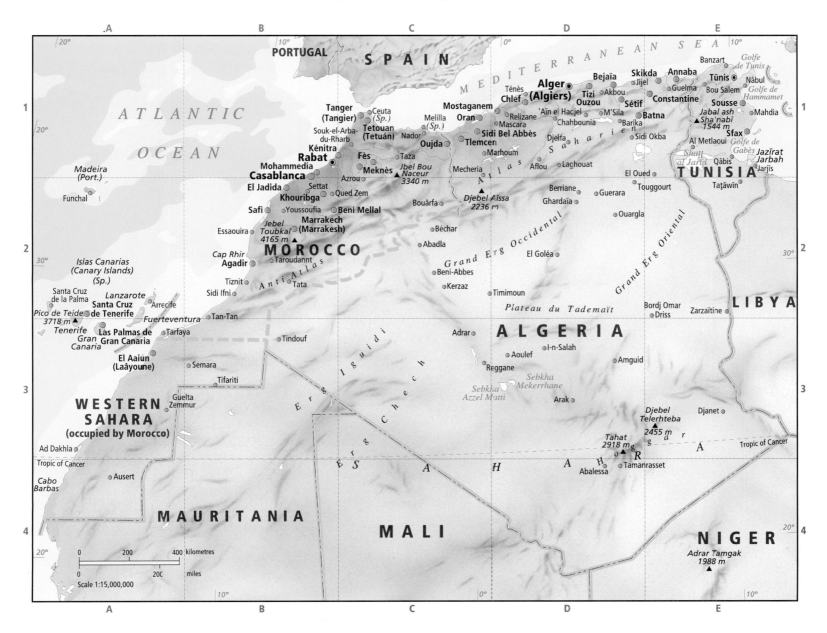

Capital Porto-Novo
Population 6,305,567
Official language French
Main religions Indigenous beliefs 70%, Muslim 15%, Christian 15%,
Currency CFA (Communauté Financière Africaine) franc
Form of government Republic

BURKINA FASO

Capital Ouagadougou
Population 11,575,898
Official language French
Main religions Muslim 50%, indigenous beliefs 40%, Roman Catholic 8%
Currency CFA (Communauté Financière Africaine) franc
Form of government Republic

CÔTE D'IVOIRE

Capital Yamoussoukro
Population 15,818,068
Official language French
Main religions Indigenous beliefs 63%, Muslim 25%, Christian 12%
Currency CFA (Communauté Financière Africaine) franc
Form of government Republic

GAMBIA

Capital Banjul
Population 1,336,320
Official language English
Main religions Muslim 90%, Christian 9%
Currency Dalasi
Form of government Republic
Record holder Africa's smallest independent state

GHANA

Capital Accra
Population 18,887,626
Official language English
Main religions Indigenous beliefs 38%, Muslim 30%, Christian 24%
Currency Cedi
Form of government Republic

WEST
Africa

Slave trade

From the 1500s onwards, West Africa was overrun by colonial powers, including France, Britain, Portugal and Germany. Over the next three centuries about 12 million men and women were shipped from here as slaves to work on plantations in the Americas. The current borders of the nations of Africa were determined during colonial times, and often cut across tribal areas, separating members of the same ethnic groups while bringing together tribes that were antagonistic towards one another. Most of the coastal strip is swampy, with few natural harbours. Inland, dry stony plateaus stretch east to the Sahara. As in most of Africa, the 'winds of change' that swept the continent in the early 1960s saw the nations in this region gain independence.

Gambia's subtropical climate and sunny dry season have led to a recent growth in tourism. However, tourist life has conflicted with the main religion, Islam.

Benin
was a major slave-trading post. From the 1600s to the 1800s several million slaves, bound mainly for Brazil, were shipped from here. In 1850 the country came under French control. It became independent in 1960.

Burkina Faso
means 'land of the honest people'. The Mossi, the dominant tribal group and traditional rulers of the area, live near the capital city of Ougadougou, where they grow sorghum and millet. Drought has caused acute agricultural difficulties and the country depends heavily on foreign aid.

Only about 10 per cent of the dry plateau of Burkina Faso is arable. These grass huts in a small village store precious grain.

Côte d'Ivoire's Vridi Canal, built by the colonial French, cuts through the sandbars to Abīdjan, providing the country with a valuable deepwater port. Côte d'Ivoire has varied mineral resources—petroleum, diamonds, manganese, bauxite and copper—and is one of the world's main producers of coffee, cocoa beans and palm oil. Côte d'Ivoire's three major national parks are home to such wildlife as elephant and pygmy hippopotamus.

Gambia was once a part of the Mali Empire. It became a British colony in 1816 and has been independent since 1965. Gambia consists mostly of swamps and river plains. Large ships are able to travel some 200 kilometres (125 miles) up the Gambia River and its estuary, to Georgetown. Gambia's main export is peanuts, grown on the higher ground.

Ghana, a former British colony, was once known as the Gold Coast, for the gold mined there. In the 1600s the local Ashanti people sold slaves to Portuguese, British, Dutch and Danish traders. In 1956, Ghana became the first tropical African colony to win independence. Soon after, it became a Soviet-style one-party state. Ghana is well-supplied with natural resources, but is not self-sufficient in food.

Children from Burkina Faso. More than 80 per cent of the people of Burkina Faso work on the land.

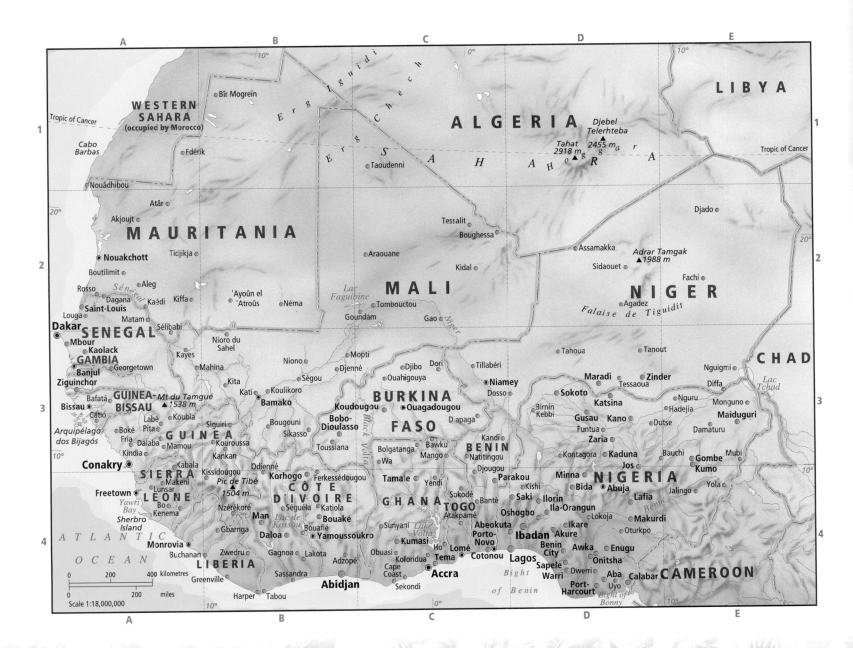

FACT FILE

GUINEA

Capital Conakry
Population 7,538,953
Official language French
Main religions Muslim 85%, Christian 8%, indigenous beliefs 7%
Currency Guinean franc
Form of government Republic

GUINEA-BISSAU

Capital Bissau
Population 1,234,555
Official language Portuguese
Main religions Indigenous beliefs 65%, Muslim 30%, Christian 5%
Currency CFA (Communauté Financière Africaine) franc
Form of government Republic

LIBERIA

Capital Monrovia
Population 2,923,725
Official language English
Main religions Indigenous beliefs 70%, Muslim 20%, Christian 10%
Currency Liberian dollar
Form of government Republic

MALI

Capital Bamako
Population 10,429,124
Official language French
Main religions Muslim 90%, indigenous beliefs 9%, Christian 1%
Currency CFA (Communauté Financière Africaine) franc
Form of government Republic

MAURITANIA

Capital Nouakchott
Population 2,581,738
Official languages French, Hasaniya Arabic
Main religion Muslim 99%
Currency Ouguiya
Form of government Republic

NIGER

Capital Niamey
Population 9,962,242
Official language French
Main religions Muslim 80%, Christian and indigenous beliefs 20%
Currency CFA (Communauté Financière Africaine) franc
Form of government Republic
Record holder One of the pcorest nations in Africa

NIGERIA

Capital Abuja
Population 113,828,587
Official language English
Main religions Muslim 50%, Christian 40%, indigenous beliefs 10%
Currency Naira
Form of government Military regime
Record holder Nation with the largest population in Africa

SENEGAL

Capital Dakar
Population 9,051,930
Official language French
Main religions Muslim 92%, indigenous beliefs 6%, Christian 2%
Currency CFA (Communauté Financière Africaine) franc
Form of government Republic
Record holder Includes the westernmost point of Africa

SIERRA LEONE

Capital Freetown
Population 5,296,651
Official language English
Main religions Muslim 60%, indigenous beliefs 30%, Christian 10%
Currency Leone
Form of government Republic

TOGO

Capital Lomé
Population 5,081,413
Official languages French
Main religion Indigenous beliefs 70%, Christian 20%, Muslim 10%
Currency CFA (Communauté Financière Africaine) franc
Form of government Republic

West Africa continued...

Guinea, one of the earliest slave-trading centres, was a French colony from 1890 until 1958. Then followed a 25-year Marxist dictatorship. The country has extensive but largely undeveloped high-grade bauxite deposits.

Guinea-Bissau was used by both the British
and French as a slave-trading station in the 1600s and 1700s. It then became a Portuguese colony. Rice is grown on the floodplains and in the swamps, but not enough to make the country self-sufficient in food. Ninety per cent of the workforce is employed in fishing and agriculture.

Liberia was settled by freed slaves from America from
the 1820s on. The ex-slaves, with Christian religion and a colonial American lifestyle, became the ruling elite over the long-established tribal peoples of the interior. Until the outbreak of civil war in 1990, Liberia was a producer and exporter of iron ore, rubber, timber and coffee. Following the collapse of the economy at the end of the 1990s, many people reverted to subsistence farming.

Mali is named after the Malinke or Mandingo people
whose empire flourished here between the 900s and 1500s. In the late 1800s it became a French colony. Mali's flat landscape is mostly plains and sandstone plateaus. Its people live by farming and fishing. Mali is a very poor country and is heavily reliant on foreign aid.

Mauritania stretches east into the wastes of the
Sahara. Islam here dates from the 1300s. Most of the population are Arabic-speaking 'white' Moors (*Maure* in French means Moor, hence the country's name). There is deep tension between the white Moors and the black Africans (the 'black' Moors) of the south.

Niger, although named after a great river, is two-thirds
desert, with stony basins and plains of drifting sands. The region was part of French West Africa from 1922 to 1960.

Devastating droughts in the 1970s and 1980s virtually destroyed the livelihood of Niger's nomadic herders. Here women draw water from a deep well.

On Benin's coastal strip there are many lagoons. Villagers often build huts on stilts along the banks of lagoons and rivers. To the northeast lie the plains of the Niger, part of the boundary with the state of Niger being formed by the Niger River itself.

In the 1970s, when prices were high, uranium became the main source of revenue, and it is still the country's most valuable export.

Nigeria is one of the most populous
nations in Africa. Its people belong to more than 200 different ethnic groups, each with its own language. There is also a major religious division, with the north largely Islamic. There is much tension between the main tribal groups. Nigeria is rich in natural resources, with oil providing about 90 per cent of exports.

Senegal was a major slave-trading base in
the 1600s and 1700s. It later became a French colony, with Dakar the administrative centre of the huge region of French West Africa. Peanuts have long been the basis of Senegal's economy, and are grown on half the cultivated land.

Siérra Leone was settled by freed
slaves from 1787, hence the name of its capital, Freetown. As in Liberia, the freed slaves became a ruling class over the Africans already living in the country. Unlike most of West Africa, Sierra Leone is mountainous near the sea. Since 1992 civil war has raged in the east and the south. Subsistence farming dominates the agricultural sector, which employs about two-thirds of the population.

Togo was colonised by Germany in 1884 and
later became French Togoland. Most people live on the coast and adjacent plains and depend on subsistence agriculture. There is deep division between the ruling Kabye people of the north, and the majority Ewe of the south. Most people live on the coast and adjacent plains.

Seen here after a dust storm, Mali's legendary Tombouctou (formerly Timbuktu) was a wealthy centre of trade and Islamic scholarship in the 1300s.

CAMEROON

Capital Yaoundé
Population 15,456,092
Official languages French, English
Main religions Indigenous beliefs 51%,
Christian 33%, Muslim 16%
Currency CFA (Communauté Financière
Africaine) franc
Form of government Republic

CENTRAL
AFRICAN REPUBLIC

Capital Bangui
Population 3,444,951
Official language French
Main religions Protestant 25%, Roman
Catholic 25%, indigenous beliefs 24%,
Muslim 15%
Currency CFA (Communauté Financière
Africaine) franc
Form of government Republic

CHAD

Capital Ndjamena
Population 7,557,436
Official languages French, Arabic
Main religions Muslim 50%,
Christian 25%, indigenous beliefs 25%
Currency CFA (Communauté Financière
Africaine) franc
Form of government Republic

CONGO

Capital Brazzaville
Population 2,716,814
Official language French
Main religions Christian 50%,
indigenous beliefs 48%, Muslim 2%
Currency CFA (Communauté Financière
Africaine) franc
Form of government Republic

DEMOCRATIC
REPUBLIC OF CONGO

Capital Kinshasa
Population 50,481,305
Official language French
Main religions Roman Catholic 50%,
Protestant 20%, Kimbanguist 10%,
Muslim 10%, other indigenous beliefs 10%
Currency New zaire
Form of government Presidential rule

EQUATORIAL
GUINEA

Capital Malabo
Population 465,746
Official language Spanish
Main religions Roman Catholic 85%,
indigenous beliefs 15%
Currency CFA (Communauté Financière
Africaine) franc
Form of government Republic

GABON

Capital Libreville
Population 1,225,853
Official language French
Main religion Christian 94%
Currency CFA (Communauté Financière
Africaine) franc
Form of government Republic
Record holder Possesses one-quarter of the
world's known reserves of manganese

SÃO TOMÉ AND
PRÍNCIPE

Capital São Tomé
Population 154,878
Official language Portuguese
Main religions Roman Catholic 80%,
Protestant and other 20%
Currency Dobra
Form of government Republic

*The mountainous interior of São Tomé,
where 70 per cent of the steep volcanic
slopes are covered with dense rainforest
and streams drain swiftly to the sea.*

CENTRAL
Africa

Post-colonial development

The countries of Central Africa have won their
freedom from European colonial administration
comparatively recently. In general, this has meant
facing poverty while indigenous governments
struggle to assert themselves and cope with civil
unrest. Difficulties of modernisation, changing
export prices for crops and mineral resources,
and natural disasters all add pressure.

Cameroon has been variously ruled by the Portuguese,
Germans, British and French. It became independent in 1960.
An oil boom between 1970 and 1985 bolstered Cameroon's
prosperity. Although still self-sufficient in food, Cameroon's
economy has become leaner because of falling prices since then
for its major exports: coffee, cocoa and petroleum.

The **Central African Republic** (CAR)
contains dense rainforest in the south and southeast that is
one of the last refuges for lowland gorillas. Subsistence crops
include manioc, yams, millet, maize and bananas; cotton, coffee
and tobacco are grown for cash. Most export revenue comes
from diamond mining, but limited resources, unskilled
workers, inadequate roads and telecommunications, and
serious diseases keep the country poor.

Chad, mainly semi-desert and thinly populated, is one of
the world's poorest and least developed countries. The harsh
climate, continuing government corruption since gaining
independence from the French in 1960, and civil war in the
1980s all contribute to Chad's poverty. Foreign aid shores up
the country's economy. Oil production could provide a future
source of income.

Congo has mortgaged a large part of its oil earnings, the
principal export, to set up expensive development projects. A
spectacular French-built railway line takes freight around the
River Congo's many cataracts below Brazzaville. The people
grow cassava, rice, maize and vegetables for themselves; coffee
and cocoa are exported.

The **Democratic Republic of Congo**
(DRC), the third largest country in Africa, was freed from
Belgian control in 1960. It contains the immense basin of the
Congo River, one of the world's most navigable waterways. Rare
animals such as okapi inhabit its rainforest. The DRC could be a
rich country, but is currently extremely poor, hampered by
government mismanagement and corruption, and inadequate
roads and telecommunications systems. Refugees flooding in
from neighbouring countries add to the DRC's problems.

Equatorial Guinea's largest island, Bioco, was
once a Portuguese slave depot. The Spanish took over in 1778.
Economic and political upheaval followed independence in
1968, causing some 100,000 people to flee. Most of the
remainder subsistence farm. Timber, cocoa and coffee are
exported; mineral resources are undeveloped but recent oil
exploration has been successful.

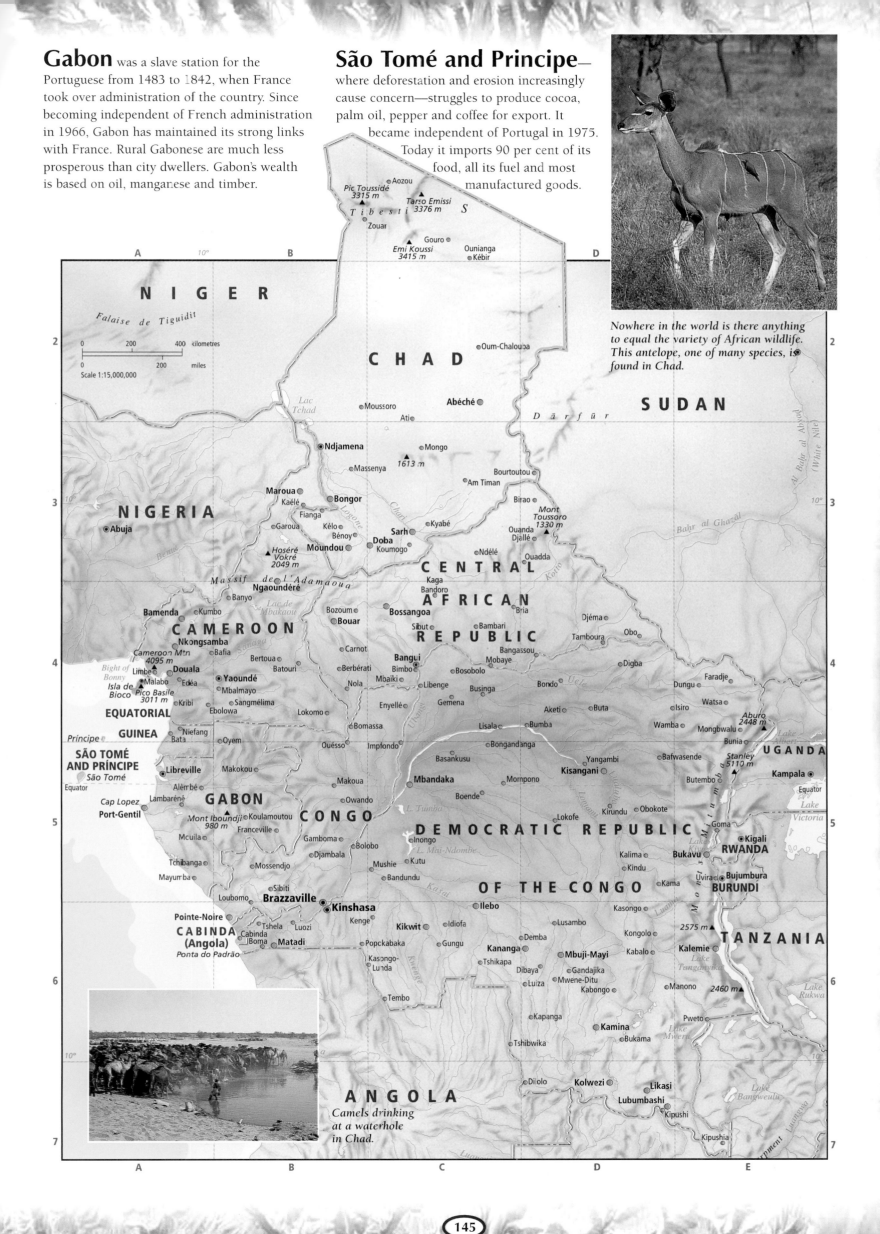

Gabon was a slave station for the Portuguese from 1483 to 1842, when France took over administration of the country. Since becoming independent of French administration in 1966, Gabon has maintained its strong links with France. Rural Gabonese are much less prosperous than city dwellers. Gabon's wealth is based on oil, manganese and timber.

São Tomé and Principe— where deforestation and erosion increasingly cause concern—struggles to produce cocoa, palm oil, pepper and coffee for export. It became independent of Portugal in 1975. Today it imports 90 per cent of its food, all its fuel and most manufactured goods.

Nowhere in the world is there anything to equal the variety of African wildlife. This antelope, one of many species, is found in Chad.

Camels drinking at a waterhole in Chad.

Scale 1:15,000,000

NIGER
CHAD
SUDAN
NIGERIA
CAMEROON
CENTRAL AFRICAN REPUBLIC
EQUATORIAL GUINEA
SÃO TOMÉ AND PRÍNCIPE
GABON
CONGO
DEMOCRATIC REPUBLIC OF THE CONGO
CABINDA (Angola)
ANGOLA
UGANDA
RWANDA
BURUNDI
TANZANIA

EAST
Africa

Giraffe and zebra roam Tanzania's vast grasslands. Visible above the cloud in the background is the snow-capped Mount Kilimanjaro.

BURUNDI

Capital   Bujumbura
Population   5,735,937
Official languages   Kirundi, French
Main religions   Roman Catholic 62%, indigenous beliefs 32%, Protestant 5%, Muslim 1%
Currency   Burundi franc
Form of government   Republic

DJIBOUTI

Capital   Djibouti
Population   447,439
Official languages   Arabic, French
Main religions   Muslim 94%, Christian 6%
Currency   Djiboutian franc
Form of government   Republic

ERITREA

Capital   Asmara
Population   3,984,723
Official languages   Tigrinya, Arabic
Main religions   Muslim 50%, Christian 50%
Currency   Ethiopian birr
Form of government   Transitional government
Record holder   The Danakil Desert, in places 116 metres (380 feet) below sea level, is one of the hottest places in the world

ETHIOPIA

Capital   Adis Abeba (Addis Ababa)
Population   59,690,383
Official language   Amharic
Main religions   Ethiopian Orthodox 51%, Muslim 35% , animist 12%
Currency   Birr
Form of government   Federal republic
Record holder   The famous 'Lucy' skeleton, 3.2 million years old, a short, upright, human-like creature, was found at Hadar

KENYA

Capital   Nairobi
Population   28,808,658
Official languages   English, Swahili
Main religions   Protestant 38%, Roman Catholic 28%, indigenous beliefs 26%, other 8%
Currency   Kenya shilling
Form of government   Republic
Record holder   Kenya has one of the highest population growths in the world

RWANDA

Capital   Kigali
Population   8,154,933
Official languages   French, Kinyarwanda
Main religions   Roman Catholic 65%, Protestant 9%, Muslim 1%, indigenous beliefs and other 25%
Currency   Rwandan franc
Form of government   Republic
Record holder   Rwanda is the most densely populated country in Africa

SOMALIA

Capital   Muqdisho (Mogadishu)
Population   7,140,643
Official language   Somali
Main religions   Sunni Muslim with tiny Christian minority
Currency   Somali shilling
Form of government   Republic
Record holder   Somalia is the only country in Africa where the population feel 'one people', without ethnic divisions

SUDAN

Capital   Al Khartūm (Khartoum)
Population   34,475,690
Official language   Arabic
Main religions   Sunni Muslim 70%, indigenous beliefs 25%, Christian 5%
Currency   Sudanese pound
Form of government   Military regime
Record holder   Sudan is the largest country in Africa

TANZANIA

Capital   Dodoma
Population   31,270,820
Official languages   Swahili, English
Main religions   Mainland: Christian 45%, Muslim 35%, indigenous beliefs 20%; Zanzibar: Muslim 99%
Currency   Tanzanian shilling
Form of government   Republic
Record holder   Mount Kilimanjaro, at 5,895 metres (19,340 feet), is the highest mountain in Africa; Footprints in hardened volcanic ash from 3.5 million years ago at Laetoli are the earliest evidence of a human-like creature walking

UGANDA

Capital   Kampala
Population   21,470,864
Official language   English
Main religions   Roman Catholic 33%, Protestant 33%, indigenous beliefs 18%, Muslim 16%
Currency   Ugandan shilling
Form of government   Republic
Record holder   Lake Victoria is the largest body of water in Africa; The Ruwenzoris (the Mountains of the Moon) is Africa's tallest mountain range

Traders at the goat and donkey market in Lalibela, northern Ethiopia.

Out of Africa

The earliest known fossils of modern humans were found in this region, at Olduvai Gorge, in the Great Rift Valley. Scientists believe a movement of people from here out of Africa eventually took humans to all parts of the world. Running through Ethiopia, Kenya and Tanzania, the Great Rift Valley—a series of dramatic, steep-walled valleys—is the result of the spreading apart of two of the rigid plates that make up the Earth's crust. Deep lakes and active and extinct volcanoes (including Mount Kilimanjaro) are found along its line.

Burundi, with neighbouring Rwanda, is in a state of civil war between its Tutsi and Hutu peoples. About 90 per cent of the population are farmers, living off their crops and cattle herds. Cash crops include coffee, tea and cotton.

Djibouti has few natural resources. Its strategic position at the entrance to the Suez Canal brings revenue from refuelling services to shipping and a port to landlocked Somalia and Ethiopia.

Eritrea, forced to join Ethiopia in 1962, fought a 30-year war of independence, winning separate nationhood in 1993. The hot dry desert strip along the Red Sea shore is dominated by rugged mountains in the north. Its people struggle to survive by farming; 75 per cent rely on food aid.

Ethiopia, like Eritrea, has been hard-hit by thirty years of conflict and famine. The country is now destitute. The Ancient Egyptians called this region Punt.

Kenya became independent of Britain in 1963. Most people live on the coast and are farmers; coffee and tea are the main cash crops. The country also produces plastics, furniture, textiles and soap. Kenya's national parks are a major destination for overseas tourists [SEE GLOBAL TOURISM]. Kenya is home to the Masai, who live traditionally as herders.

Rwanda's Mufumbiro Range is one of the last refuges of the endangered mountain gorilla [*SEE Endangered species*]. Farming land in Rwanda is intensively cultivated; coffee and tea are the main cash crops. In recent years the country has been torn by civil turmoil between the Tutsi and the Hutu; in 1994 half a million Tutsi were massacred by Hutu.

Somalia, despite its ethnic homogeneity, has been torn by civil unrest since it gained independence in 1960. In 1992, when an estimated 2,000 people a day were dying from war and starvation, the United Nations intervened but was unable to stop the fighting. Somalia is now largely lawless.

Sudan has at various times been under Muslim, Egyptian and British rule. With more than 100 languages and some 570 distinct ethnic groups, it has been difficult to form Sudan into a unified modern state. Most of the population lives along the Nile or one of its tributaries.

Tanzania is famed for its spectacular scenery, diverse wildlife and important archaeological sites. From the AD 700s on, this region came under the Islamic influence of Arab traders, who made a base on the island of Zanzibar (since 1964 a part of Tanzania). Most Tanzanians live by farming.

Uganda's lake system is the source of the Nile River. Most Ugandans are farmers; tobacco, cotton and coffee are grown as cash crops. Since independence in 1962 the country has suffered civil turmoil and much bloodshed. Order and prosperity are now returning.

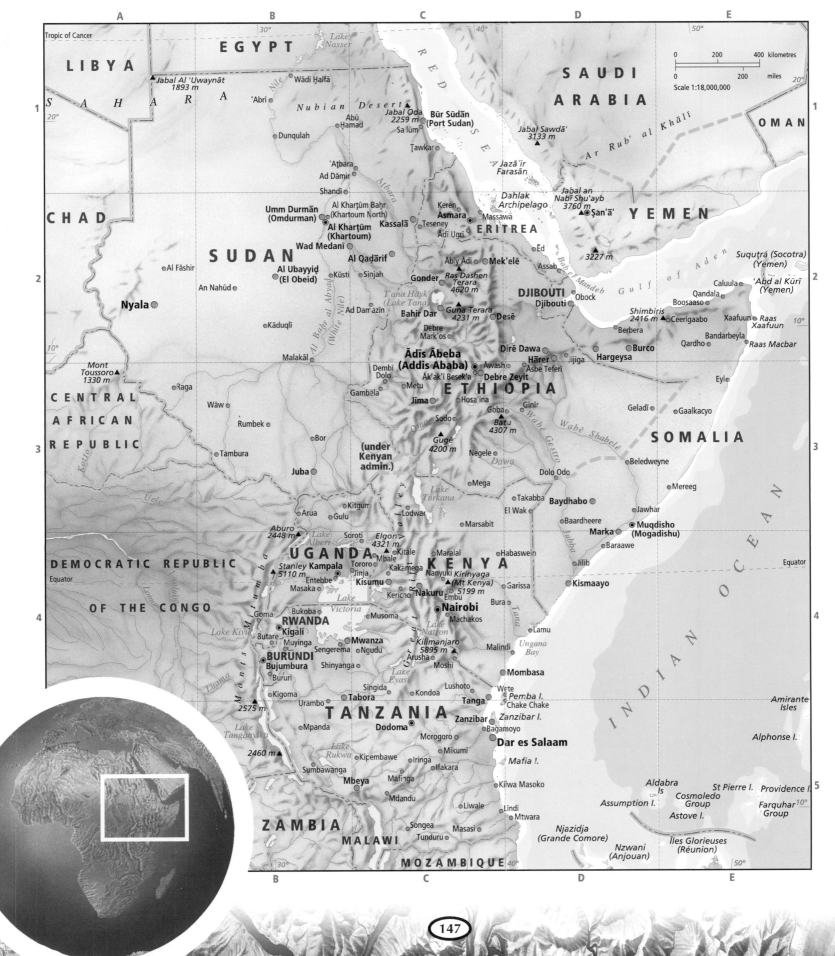

ANGOLA

Capital Porto-Novo
Population 6,305,567
Official language French
Main religions Indigenous beliefs 70%, Muslim 15%, Christian 15%
Currency CFA (Communauté Financière Africaine) franc
Form of government Republic

BOTSWANA

Capital Gaborone
Population 1,464,167
Official language English
Main religions Indigenous beliefs 50%, Christian 50%
Currency Pula
Form of government Republic

LESOTHO

Capital Maseru
Population 2,128,950
Official languages Sesotho, English
Main religions Christian 80%, indigenous beliefs 20%
Currency Loti
Form of government Constitutional monarchy
Record holder Only country in the world where all the land is higher than 1,000 metres (3,300 feet)

MALAWI

Capital Lilongwe
Population 9,888,601
Official languages Chichewa, English
Main religions Protestant 55%, Roman Catholic 20%, Muslim 20%, indigenous beliefs 5%
Currency Kwacha
Form of government Republic

MOZAMBIQUE

Capital Maputo
Population 19,124,335
Official language Portuguese
Main religions Indigenous beliefs 55%, Christian 30%, Muslim 15%
Currency Metical
Form of government Republic

NAMIBIA

Capital Windhoek
Population 1,648,270
Official language English
Main religions Christian 85% (Lutheran at least 50%), indigenous beliefs 15%
Currency Namibian dollar
Form of government Republic
Record holder World's second largest producer of lead

SOUTH AFRICA

Capital Pretoria (administrative), Cape Town (legislative), Bloemfontein (judicial)
Population 43,426,386
Official languages Afrikaans, English, Ndebele, Pedi, Sotho, Swazi, Tsonga, Tswana, Venda, Xhosa, Zulu
Main religions Christian 68%, Hindu 2%, Muslim 2%, indigenous beliefs 28%
Currency Rand
Form of government Republic
Record holder World's largest producer of manganese, platinum and chromium

SWAZILAND

Capital Mbabane
Population 985,335
Official languages English, Swazi
Main religions Christian 60%, indigenous beliefs 40%
Currency Lilangeni
Form of government Monarchy

ZAMBIA

Capital Lusaka
Population 9,663,535
Official language English
Main religions Christian 72%, indigenous beliefs 27%
Currency Kwacha
Form of government Republic

ZIMBABWE

Capital Harare
Population 11,163,160
Official language English
Main religions Mixed Christian-indigenous beliefs 50%, Christian 25%, indigenous beliefs 24%, Muslim and other 1%
Currency Zimbabwean dollar
Form of government Republic

This dancer from Malawi in traditional costume performs at funerals and also at more cheerful festivities.

SOUTHERN
Africa

Saving the wildlife

The future of Africa's varied wildlife is of major international concern. Throughout the continent, particularly in Southern Africa, areas are set aside to protect of species in their own habitat. Kruger National Park is the oldest and best known reserve; careful management in other South African parks has saved the white rhinoceros from extinction.

[See Endangered species; Global tourism]

Angola became a Portuguese colony in the 1500s, thereafter supplying around 3 million slaves to Brazil and other places. Although rich in mineral reserves, forests, fisheries and arable land, civil war since 1975 has impeded self-sufficiency.

Botswana is a dry country where widely scattered Bantu herders graze their cattle on savanna grassland. After gold was discovered in the 1800s, British and Boers fought for supremacy. The British Bechuanaland Protectorate, established in 1885, became Botswana in 1966.

Lesotho's higher mountains often bear snow in winter; water is the main natural resource. Sheep and goats thrive on the treeless high plateau, providing wool and mohair for a cottage industry making woven rugs. About 60 per cent of Lesotho's male wage earners work in South Africa.

Malawi's Lake Malawi supports a sizeable fishing industry, but crops are often drought afflicted and diseased, and forests are continually depleted for fuelwood. The country relies heavily on foreign aid. David Livingstone and other British missionaries brought Christianity to the area from the 1860s.

Mozambique is divided by the Zambezi River physically, politically and socially. Visited by Vasco da Gama in 1498 and colonised by Portuguese gold hunters, it remained a slave-trading centre until the 1850s. Devastating floods in 2000 resulted in great loss of life and property.

Namibia became independent in 1990; previously it had been a German protectorate and then came under South African control. Its indigenous peoples work poor soils in a generally dry climate. Livestock farmers produce beef and mutton. Almost half the country's food is imported, mainly from South Africa.

South Africa, the economic powerhouse of Southern Africa, passed apartheid (apartness) laws separating white from black people in 1948. These racial policies produced internal unrest and international isolation. After these policies were dropped in 1994, South Africa renewed trading relations with the rest of the world. Both the Bantu and the first Europeans to colonise South Africa were farmers. Gold and diamonds attracted new settlers in the 1800s; gold and precious stones still contribute hugely to South Africa's wealth.

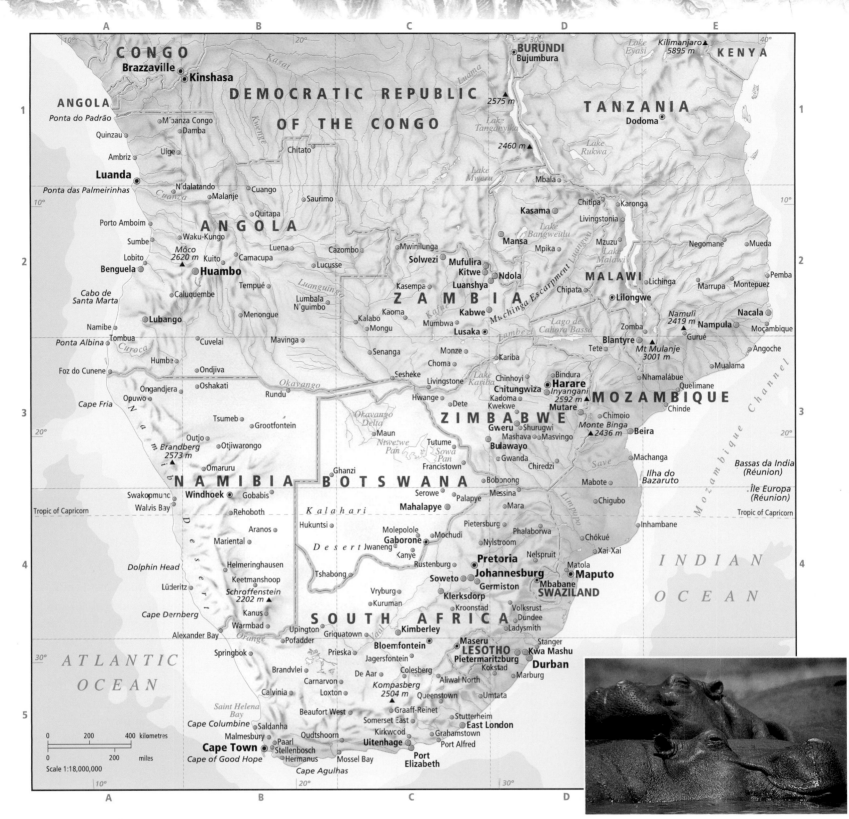

Map labels

CONGO
Brazzaville
Kinshasa
ANGOLA
Ponta do Padrão
Quinzau
M'banza Congo
Damba
Uíge
Ambriz
Luanda
Ponta das Palmeirinhas
N'dalatando
Malanje
Cuango
Saurimo
Chitato

DEMOCRATIC REPUBLIC
OF THE CONGO
2575 m
Lake Tanganyika
2460 m
Lake Mweru

BURUNDI
Bujumbura
Lake Eyasi
Kilimanjaro 5895 m
KENYA

TANZANIA
Dodoma
Lake Rukwa
Mbala
Chitipa
Karonga
Kasama
Livingstonia
Mzuzu
Lake Malawi
Negomane
Mueda

Porto Amboim
Sumbe
Waku-Kungo
Moço 2620 m
Kuito
Camacupa
Cazombo
Mwinilunga
Solwezi
Mufulira
Kitwe
Ndola
Luanshya
Mansa
Lake Bangweulu
Mpika
Lichinga
Marrupa
Montepuez
Pemba

Lobito
Benguela
Cabo de Santa Marta
Lubango
Namibe
Ponta Albina
Tombua
Foz do Cunene
Humbe
Caluquembe
Tempué
Luena
Lucusse
Lumbala N'guimbo
Kalabo
Kaoma
Mumbwa
Kabwe
Lusaka
Senanga
Monze
Choma
Kariba
Kasempa
Mongu
ZAMBIA
Muchinga Escarpment
Chipata
MALAWI
Lilongwe
Zomba
Blantyre
Mt Mulanje 3001 m
Tete
Lago de Cahora Bassa
Namuli 2419 m
Nampula
Nacala
Moçambique
Gurué
Angoche

Ongandjera
Cuvelai
Mavinga
Sesheke
Livingstone
Hwange
Chinhoyi
Chitungwiza
Harare
Kadoma
Kwekwe
Inyangani 2592 m
Mutare
Chimoio
Monte Binga 2436 m
Beira
MOZAMBIQUE
Chinde
Nhamalábue
Quelimane
Mualama

Cape Fria
Opuwo
Oshakati
Rundu
Okavango
Okavango Delta
Maun
Ntwetwe Pan
Tutume
Sowa Pan
ZIMBABWE
Gweru
Shurugwi
Mashava
Masvingo
Gwanda
Chiredzi
Machanga
Mabote
Ilha do Bazaruto
Bassas da India (Réunion)
Île Europa (Réunion)

Tsumeb
Grootfontein
Brandberg 2573 m
Outjo
Otjiwarongo
Omaruru
Ghanzi
Francistown
Bobonong
Messina
Chigubo
Inhambane
Tropic of Capricorn

NAMIBIA
Swakopmund
Windhoek
Gobabis
BOTSWANA
Serowe
Palapye
Mara
Pietersburg
Phalaborwa
Chókué

Walvis Bay
Rehoboth
Kalahari
Mahalapye
Desert
Molepolole
Mochudi
Nylstroom
Xai-Xai

Dolphin Head
Helmeringhausen
Keetmanshoop
Schroffenstein 2202 m
Aranos
Mariental
Hukuntsi
Tshabong
Jwaneng
Gaborone
Kanye
Rustenburg
Pretoria
Johannesburg
Soweto
Germiston
Klerksdorp
Nelspruit
Matola
Mbabane
Maputo
SWAZILAND
INDIAN OCEAN

Lüderitz
Kanus
Warmbad
Upington
Vryburg
Kuruman
SOUTH AFRICA
Volksrust
Kroonstad
Dundee
Ladysmith

Cape Dernberg
Alexander Bay
Orange
Pofadder
Griquatown
Prieska
Kimberley
Bloemfontein
Maseru
LESOTHO
Pietermaritzburg
Kokstad
Kwa Mashu
Durban

Springbok
Calvinia
Brandvlei
Carnarvon
Loxton
Jagersfontein
De Aar
Colesberg
Aliwal North
Kompasberg 2504 m
Queenstown
Umtata
Marburg

ATLANTIC OCEAN
Saint Helena Bay
Cape Columbine
Saldanha
Malmesbury
Beaufort West
Graaff-Reinet
Somerset East
Stutterheim
East London

Cape Town
Stellenbosch
Paarl
Hermanus
Mossel Bay
Oudtshoorn
Kirkwood
Uitenhage
Grahamstown
Port Alfred
Port Elizabeth
Cape of Good Hope
Cape Agulhas

0 200 400 kilometres
0 200 miles
Scale 1:18,000,000

Swaziland

Swaziland, a former British protectorate, gained full independence in 1968. Swazi farmers still measure their traditional wealth in cattle. European-run estates produce sugar, citrus fruits, tobacco and wood pulp. Mining industries are declining; manufacturing industries employ about one-tenth of the workforce.

Zambia's

Zambia's Tonga people first arrived in the area in the AD 700s. Once a British colony, known as Northern Rhodesia, Zambia became independent in 1964. Export earnings largely depend on copper; drought and a drop in world copper prices are among the difficulties affecting the country.

Zimbabwe

Zimbabwe means 'house of the chief', referring to the stone citadel in the south probably built in the AD 800s. Agricultural exports include tobacco, cotton and sugarcane. Small-scale farms produce most of the country's food.

The hippopotamus, the world's largest even-toed hoofed mammal, is among Africa's unique wildlife.

In Lesotho most of the population live in small villages, with buildings grouped in family communes such as this.

COMOROS

Capital Moroni
Population 562,723
Official languages Arabic, French
Main religions Sunni Muslim 86%, Roman Catholic 14%
Currency Cormoron franc
Form of government Federal republic

MADAGASCAR

Capital Antananarivo
Population 14,873,387
Official languages Malagasy, French
Main religions Indigenous beliefs 52%, Christian 41%, Muslim 7%
Currency Malagasy franc
Form of government Republic
Record holder Half of the world's species of chameleon live on Madagascar; Seventy-five per cent of the flora and fauna on Madagascar is found nowhere else in the world

MALDIVES

Capital Male
Population 300,220
Official language Divehi
Main religion Predominantly Sunni Muslim
Currency Rufiyaa
Form of government Republic

MAURITIUS

Capital Port Louis
Population 1,182,212
Official language English
Main religions Hindu 52%, Roman Catholic 26%, Protestant 2.3%, Muslim 16.6%
Currency Mauritian rupee
Form of government Republic
Record holder Mauritius was the exclusive home of the dodo, a large flightless bird related to the pigeon which became extinct in the late 1600s

SEYCHELLES

Capital Victoria
Population 79,164
Official languages English, French, Creole
Main religions Roman Catholic 90%, Anglican 8%
Currency Seychelles rupee
Form of government Republic
Record holder Ninetyeast Ridge, 4,506 kilometres (2,800 miles) long, is the world's longest and straightest ocean ridge; The Java Trench, stretching more than 2,574 kilometres (1,600 miles), is the world's second longest ocean trench; Sunda Deep in the Java Trench is the deepest point in the Indian Ocean, at 7,450 metres (24,442 feet)

Indian Ocean

Ocean trade routes

As early as 2300 BC, ancient Egyptian dhows skimmed along the edge of the Indian Ocean to the 'land of Punt' (Ethiopia/Somalia). From around AD 800 Arab and Persian navigators began detailing routes and ports from Sofala in Mozambique to China. Sailing ships relied upon the monsoon winds. Modern shipping needs no such assistance to cross this watery expanse, which accounts for about one-fifth of the surface area of the world's oceans [SEE THE WORLD'S OCEANS].

Comoros, off the coast of Mozambique, consists of three large volcanic islands and smaller coral islets. For centuries, Indian and Arab traders stopped here. Areas of porous soil and erosion limit agriculture, so much food is imported. Vanilla, cloves, perfume oil and copra earn revenue, but Comoros depends heavily on foreign aid. Mayotte, a fourth volcanic island in the group, is not part of the Republic of Comoros. It is a territorial collectivity of France and produces coconuts, cocoa and spices.

Madagascar, the world's fourth largest island, features swift streams, steep faulting, volcanic outcrops, deep-cut valleys and thick forest. Unique wildlife species have evolved here. Rice is grown in the central highlands, cassava and maize elsewhere. Exports include coffee, sugar and spices. Madagascar is extremely poor, and suffers from food shortages and political instability.

The **Maldives** is an archipelago of nearly 2,000 islands and coral atolls. Just 202 islands are inhabited; if the sea level rises, some atolls may be submerged. [SEE CLIMATE CHANGE]. The Maldives' first visitors were probably Dravidians

The warm waters of the Indian Ocean are home to beautiful flora, such as this seawhip.

from southern India around 400 BC. Now tourism provides the major income, and fishing is a leading export. Manufacturing includes clothing, boats and handicrafts. Little land is suitable for farming and most food staples must be imported.

Mauritius was uninhabited until after 1715 when French settlers brought African slaves to work on sugar plantations; the British later introduced Indian labourers. These colonial origins produced two distinct communities who compete for influence and power, but despite occasional unrest, Mauritius prospers. Sugar is still the predominant crop. Textile and garment manufacture and the rapidly growing tourist trade also earn revenue. Rodrigues, an island dependency of Mauritius, depends mainly on farming and fishing. Onions and chillies are exported.

The **Seychelles**, four large, 36 small granite islands and about 65 coralline islands lying outside the cyclone belt, were uninhabited until the French arrived in 1742. Vanilla, tobacco, tea, cinnamon and copra are exported. Mindful of over-dependence on the booming tourist industry, the government is encouraging farming, fishing and small-scale manufacturing.

A typical street scene in Toliara, a town in the southwest of Madagascar.

Fish are plentiful in the crystal clear waters of the Maldives. Bonito and tuna are among the main exports.

Island dependencies and territories

Andaman and Nicobar Islands, a group of mostly uninhabited islands in the Bay of Bengal, form a union territory of India; rice, coconuts and sugarcane are grown.

The **Chagos Islands** are British Indian Ocean Territory. Diego Gracia was developed as a major United States–United Kingdom air and naval refuelling and support station in the 1960 and 1970s. In 1973 the copra plantations were closed and the population was relocated to Mauritius.

Christmas Island and the **Cocos (Keeling) Islands** are external territories of Australia. Christmas Island's phosphate deposits have been mined since the 1890s; its casino complex, built in 1993, draws visitors mainly from Southeast Asia. The Cocos (Keeling) Islands, uninhabited when discovered by William Keeling in 1609, were settled in 1827. Coconuts are the sole cash crop.

Réunion, a French overseas département, is France's main military base in the area. Tourism is growing and the island exports vanilla, perfume oils and tea.

Socotra, meaning 'island abode of bliss' in Sanskrit, is the largest island in a group belonging to Yemen. The inhabitants engage in fishing, pearl diving and small-scale agriculture. Ghee (clarified butter), fish and frankincense are exported.

Carrying their work tools on their heads, these women walk past a huge sugarcane field. In Mauritius, as in many parts of the world, women do the majority of the agricultural work.

Capital Moscow
Population 146,393,569
Official language Russian
Main religions Russian Orthodox 27%; Muslim, Jewish, Roman Catholic and other minorities 73%
Currency Ruble
Form of government Federal republic
Record holder The world's largest country, at 17,075,200 square kilometres (6,592,735 square miles); Lake Baikal in Siberia, 1,620 metres (5,335 feet) deep, is the deepest lake in the world; The Caspian Sea is the world's largest inland body of water; Lake Ladoga, near St Petersburg, is the largest lake entirely within Europe; The Volga River is the longest river in Europe; The Lena River is the longest river in Russia; The Trans-Siberian is the world's longest railway line

Russian Federation

Vast lands, past glories

Russia is so big that it covers eleven time zones and stretches across almost two-thirds of Asia and one-third of Europe. It has the sixth largest population in the world. The history of Russia has seen the rise and fall of several mighty empires. Different political systems have flourished, then crumbled, defeated by the difficulties of bringing political stability and economic development to such a vast area.

Food shortages are a way of life for many Russians. Here, a woman stocks up on freshly baked bread.

Russia traces its history from the growth of Viking trading posts around the Baltic Sea in the AD 800s. Its name probably comes 'Kievan Rus' the name given by Slavic groups to the Kiev region in present-day Ukraine (see Eastern Europe). From the 1200s to the 1500s, this region was part of the Mongol Empire until the invaders were expelled by Moscow-based Duke Ivan III (grandfather of Ivan 'the Terrible') who declared himself 'Tsar of all the Russians'; under his rule the country expanded eastward to Siberia. Tsar Peter the Great (1682–1725) moved the capital north to St Petersburg and acquired territories along the Baltic Sea. In the 1800s and 1900s, Russia again extended its borders—this time south and east into Asia.

The Russian Revolution, in 1917, followed growing civil unrest. The Tsar was overthrown and the All-Russian Communist party took power with V. I. Lenin as leader. In 1922, Russia, with Moscow as capital, became the dominant power in the newly formed Union of Soviet Socialist Republics (USSR) having seized Georgia, Armenia and Azerbaijan. At the end of World War II, regions of Eastern Europe occupied by Soviet forces also came under Soviet

Russia's second largest city, St Petersburg, is the most Western European in appearance, with palaces, squares and boulevards resembling those of London and Paris. Founded in 1703 by Peter the Great, the city has known three names—the original St Petersburg, now restored to use, Petrograd (1914–24) and Leningrad (1924–91).

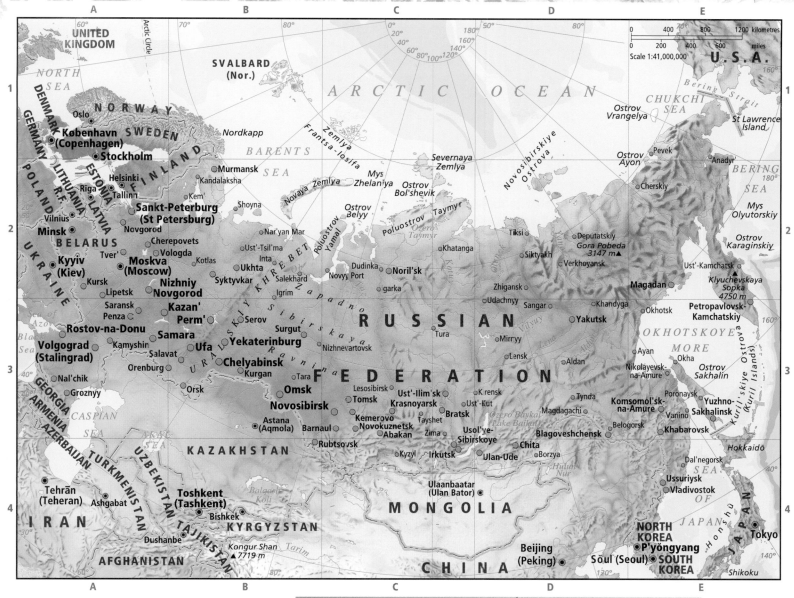

Map of the Russian Federation and surrounding regions (Scale 1:41,000,000)

Selected labels visible on the map:

UNITED KINGDOM · NORTH SEA · SVALBARD (Nor.) · ARCTIC OCEAN · U.S.A. · CHUKCHI SEA · Ostrov Vrangelya · Bering Strait · St Lawrence Island · Pevek · Ostrov Ayon · Anadyr' · BERING SEA · Mys Olyutorskiy · Ostrov Karaginskiy · Ust'-Kamchatsk · Klyuchevskaya Sopka 4750 m · Petropavlovsk-Kamchatskiy

DENMARK · NORWAY · SWEDEN · Oslo · København (Copenhagen) · Stockholm · Nordkapp · Murmansk · Kandalaksha · BARENTS SEA · Novaya Zemlya · Zemlya Frantsa-Iosifa · Severnaya Zemlya · Ostrov Bol'shevik · Novosibirskiye Ostrova · Cherskiy

GERMANY · POLAND · LITHUANIA · Vilnius · ESTONIA · LATVIA · Riga · Tallinn · Helsinki · FINLAND · Sankt-Peterburg (St Petersburg) · Novgorod · Shoyna · Ust'-Tsil'ma · Inta · Nar'yan Mar · Ostrov Belyy · Poluostrov Yamal · Mys Zhelaniya · Ostrov Belyy · Poluostrov Taymyr · Ozero Taymyr · Tiksi · Khatanga · Deputatskiy · Gora Pobeda 3147 m · Verkhoyansk · Magadan · OKHOTSKOYE MORE

Minsk · BELARUS · Cherepovets · Vologda · Tver' · Kotlas · Ukhta · Syktyvkar · Salekhard · Dudinka · Novyy Port · Noril'sk · Zhigansk · Udachnyy · Sangar · Khandyga · Okhotsk · Ayan · Okha · Ostrov Sakhalin

UKRAINE · Kyyiv (Kiev) · Kursk · Moskva (Moscow) · Nizhniy Novgorod · Lipetsk · Saransk · Penza · Kazan' · Perm' · Serov · Igrim · Zapadno Sibirskaya Ravnina · Tura · Mirnyy · Lensk · Aldan · Nikolayevsk-na-Amure · Poronaysk · Ostrov Sakhalin · Kuril'skiye Ostrova (Kuril Islands)

Sea of Azov · Rostov-na-Donu · Samara · Ufa · Yekaterinburg · Nizhnevartovsk · RUSSIAN FEDERATION · Yakutsk · Vilyuy · Lena

Volgograd (Stalingrad) · Kamyshin · Salavat · Chelyabinsk · Kurgan · URAL'SKIY KHREBET · Nal'chik · Orenburg · Orsk · Omsk · Tara · Lesosibirsk · Tomsk · Ust'-Ilimsk · K rensk · Tynda · Magdagachi · Komsomol'sk-na-Amure · Belogorsk · Khabarovsk · Yuzhno-Sakhalinsk · Vanino

GEORGIA · ARMENIA · Groznyy · CASPIAN SEA · Astana (Aqmola) · Barnaul · Novosibirsk · Kemerovo · Novokuznetsk · Abakan · Zima · Krasnoyarsk · Tayshet · Bratsk · Ust'-Kut · Usol'ye-Sibirskoye · Ozero Baykal (Lake Baikal) · Blagoveshchensk · Dal'negorsk · Hokkaidō

AZERBAIJAN · TURKMENISTAN · UZBEKISTAN · Rubtsovsk · Kyzyl · Irkutsk · Ulan-Ude · Chita · Borzya · Ussuriysk · Vladivostok · SEA OF JAPAN

Tehrān (Teheran) · Ashgabat · KAZAKHSTAN · Balqash Köli · Toshkent (Tashkent) · Bishkek · Ulaanbaatar (Ulan Bator) · MONGOLIA · Hulun Nur · Honshū · Tokyo

IRAN · TAJIKISTAN · Dushanbe · KYRGYZSTAN · Konyur Shan 7719 m · Tarim · NORTH KOREA · P'yŏngyang · SOUTH KOREA · Sŏul (Seoul) · JAPAN · Shikoku

AFGHANISTAN · Beijing (Peking) · CHINA

---

domination. However, growing social unrest and a resurgence of nationalism eventually created such immense strains that the Soviet Union was officially dissolved in 1991.

The fertile European Plain, stretching from the Arctic Ocean in the north to Kazakhstan in the south, is where most Russians live and where most industry and agriculture is located. Agriculture is concentrated in the south; cereals are the main crop. In most years only half the grain the nation needs is produced; the rest is imported. Cattle and dairy farming are based in the west of the plain. Most industries, such as steelmaking, manufacturing agricultural machinery, chemicals, textiles and food processing are centred on the cities Moscow, St Petersburg, Novgorod and Volgograd.

Northern Russia is mainly Arctic tundra— a sparsely populated, treeless expanse which remains frozen throughout the year. Despite the harsh climate, some of its mineral wealth, such as natural gas, nickel and platinum, is exploited.

Siberia begins east of the Ural Mountains at the largely desolate, flat and treeless Siberian Plain; further east a series of high plateaus and mountain ranges border Mongolia and China. Siberia's rich mineral resources include coal, petroleum, natural gas, iron ore, bauxite, copper, lead and zinc. The Kamchatka Peninsula and the Kuril Islands form part of the Pacific 'Rim of Fire' with about thirty active volcanoes.

The colourful spires and domes of St Basil's Cathedral, Moscow. Dating from the early 1600s, St Basil's is now part of the State Historical Museum.

AFGHANISTAN

Capital   Kābol (Kabul)
Population   25,824,882
Official languages   Dari (Afghan Persian), Pashto
Main religions   Sunni Muslim 84%, Shi'a Muslim 15%
Currency   Afghani
Form of government   Transitional government

KAZAKHSTAN

Capital   Aqmola (Astana)
Population   16,824,825
Official language   Kazakh
Main religions   Muslim 47%, Russian Orthodox 44%, Protestant 2%
Currency   Tenge
Form of government   Republic

KYRGYZSTAN

Capital   Bishkek
Population   4,546,055
Official language   Kyrghiz
Main religions   Sunni Muslim 70%, Christian (predominantly Russian Orthodox) 30%
Currency   Som
Form of government   Republic

TAJIKISTAN

Capital   Dushanbe
Population   6,102,854
Official language   Tajik
Main religions   Sunni Muslim 80%, Shi'a Muslim 5%, other (including Russian Orthodox) 15%
Currency   Tajik ruble
Form of government   Republic
Record holder   Highest point is Pik imeni Ismail Samani at 7,495 metres (24,590 feet)

TURKMENISTAN

Capital   Ashgabat
Population   4,366,383
Official language   Turkmen
Main religions   Muslim 87%, Eastern Orthodox 11%
Currency   Manat
Form of government   Republic

UZBEKISTAN

Capital   Toshkent (Tashkent)
Population   24,102,473
Official language   Uzbek
Main religions   Muslim 88% (mostly Sunnis), Eastern Orthodox 9%
Currency   Som
Form of government   Republic
Record holder   The most populous country in Central Asia; One of the world's largest goldmines at Murantau

CENTRAL
Asia

East meets West

With the exception of Afghanistan, these Central Asian countries are all former republics of the Union of Soviet Socialist Republics. Since becoming independent in 1991, they have been torn by ethnic tensions *[SEE GLOBAL GUARDIANS]*. Their borders are a legacy of the Soviet years, and reflect attempts to divide and control, rather than ethnic or geographical boundaries. In ancient times the southern area was part of the empire of Alexander the Great, and came under the influence of Greek ideas. From around 100 BC, traders from China carrying silk and other luxury goods began travelling east along the Silk Road, a major trading route that passed through this region. The Silk Road was also a two-way channel for ideas and religions, such as Islam, which in the 600s spread west along it and into Central Asia.

Afghanistan ranges from scorching

deserts to snowy peaks. In ancient times it was a part of the Persian empire and was later conquered by Alexander the Great. Today more than 70 per cent of its people live in rural areas, and the country depends on wheat farming and the raising of sheep and goats.

Nomadic herders of Central Asia live in collapsible cone-shaped dwellings called yurts, which are carried between pastures on horseback or small wagons. This yurt is pitched on summer pastures in the high plateau of the Pamir region of Tajikistan, 'the roof of the world'.

Kazakhstan grows wheat (planted

under Soviet rule on the steppes traditionally used by nomadic herders), fruits and vegetables. It supplies surrounding countries with meat and is a producer of high quality wool. Cotton growing, a major agricultural activity both here and in neighbouring countries, is responsible for serious environmental damage due to the overuse of pesticides *[SEE POLLUTION]*. In addition, the diversion of rivers flowing into the Aral Sea for irrigation schemes has reduced the size of the inland water body by 70 per cent and caused salination problems. In Soviet times, Kazakhstan was used for testing nuclear weapons *[SEE GLOBAL NUCLEAR INDUSTRY]*.

Kyrgyzstan is separated from China by

the massive and permanently snow-capped peaks of the Tian Shan Range. Nomadic Muslim Kyrgyz pastoralists tend herds of sheep, cattle, goats, horses and yaks in lowland pastures. Fruit and vegetables are also grown and the country is self-sufficient in food. The main agricultural products for export are cotton, wool and meat. Most of the population lives in rural areas. Ethnic tensions between the Kyrgyz majority and the Uzbeks is a feature of everyday life.

Tajikistan's Tajik people, who make up

some 60 per cent of its population, are of Persian-Iranian origin, and not Turkic-Mongol, like most of the peoples in Central Asia. Today the country has the fastest growing population and one of the lowest standards of living of the former USSR republics. The country no longer receives Soviet aid and a state of near civil war that has existed since independence in 1991 has weakened the economy.

Women at the market in the town of Osh, Kyrgyzstan.

Turkmenistan's deserts (which cover about 90 per cent of its land) hold valuable, but as yet largely untouched, reserves of oil and natural gas. The country's main revenue-earners are Astrakhan rugs and cotton. Industry is largely confined to the mining of sulfur and salt.

Uzbekistan's main ethnic group, the Uzbeks, seem to have taken their name from the Mongol leader Öz Beg Khan (AD 1313–40), who may also have converted them to Islam. Bukhoro, a major Muslim religious centre on a par with Mecca, is in Uzbekistan. Most of Uzbekistan's people live in rural areas and are farmers, although grain needs to be imported to meet the country's needs. The country is the world's fourth largest producer of cotton.

Melon sellers at a market in Turkmenistan.

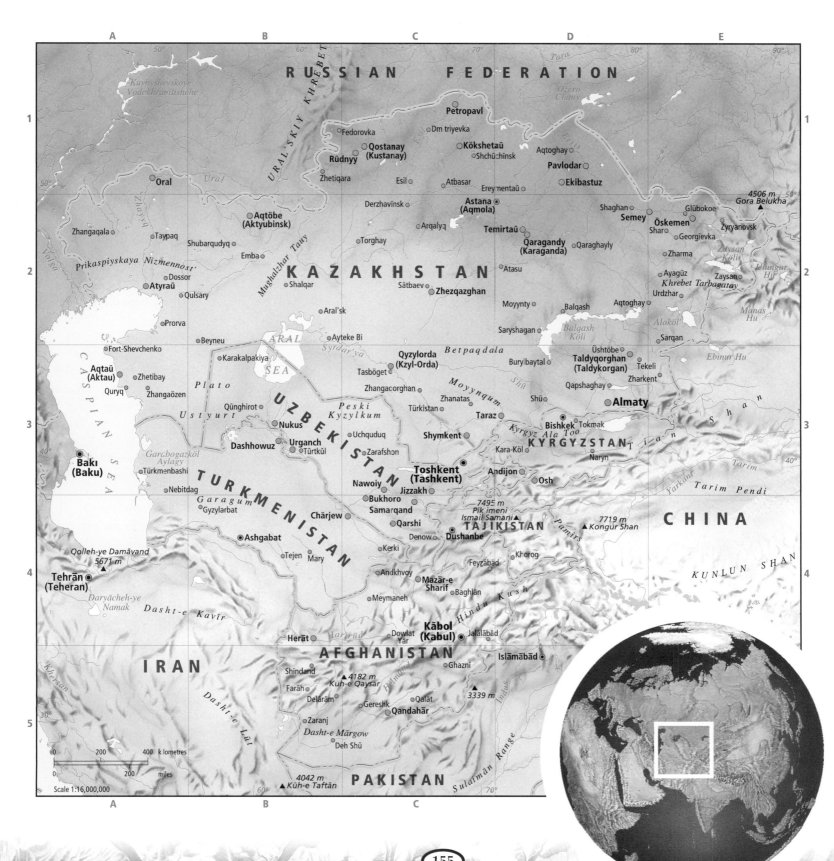

BANGLADESH

Capital Dhaka (Dacca)
Population 129,859,779
Official language Bangla
Main religions Muslim 83%, Hindu 16%
Currency Taka
Form of government Republic
Record holder The world's longest beach, 120 kilometres (75 miles) in length at Cox's Bazar; The confluence of the Ganges, Brahmaputra and Megna Rivers forms the biggest delta in the world; The world's largest supplier of high quality jute

BHUTAN

Capital Thimphu
Population 1,951,965
Official language Dzongkha
Main religions Lamaistic Buddhism 75%, Hinduism 25%
Currency Ngultrum
Form of government Monarchy
Record holder World's most 'rural' country with fewer than 6 per cent of its population living in towns

INDIA

Capital New Delhi
Population 999,826,804
Official languages Hindi, Bengali, Telugu, Marathi, Tamil, Urdu, Gujurati, Malayalam, Kannada, Oriya, Punjabi, Assamese, Kashmiri, Sindhi, Sanskrit, English
Main religions Hindu 80%, Muslim 14%, Christian 2.4%, Sikh 2%, Buddhist 0.7%
Currency Indian rupee
Form of government Federal republic
Record holder World's largest democracy

With its hood spread to make it look more fearsome, a cobra rises to the music of a snake charmer.

Indian Subcontinent

An overcrowded region

Asia contains some 60 per cent of the world's population, mostly crowded into the monsoon belt. In Bangladesh more than 900 people occupy a square kilometre (2,335 per square mile). In contrast, Bhutan's population density is 42 to the square kilometre (108 per square mile). In India, the world's second most populous country, millions live in desperate poverty, many suffering from malnutrition. Sri Lanka, which is almost as densely populated as India, has the longest average life expectancy in South Asia—69 years for men and 73 years for women. In Bangladesh, male and female life expectancy is only about 56 years. Nepal and Pakistan have population densities of around 170 per square kilometre (approximately 445 per square mile). *[SEE POPULATION EXPLOSION]*

On sale at this vegetable market in Jaisalmer, Rajasthan, northern India, are many of the fresh ingredients needed for a traditional curry.

Bangladesh is known as 'the land of the Bengalis'. Formerly East Pakistan, Bangladesh did not become an independent state until 1971. Since then, it has been troubled by political and civil unrest, as well as by natural disasters. In 1991 a cyclone killed more than 140,000 people *[SEE NATURAL DISASTERS]*. Indian Nobel prize-winning poet, Rabindranath Tagore (1861–1941), wrote about the beautiful Bengali countryside; his song, 'Our Golden Bengal', became Bangladesh's national anthem. The landscape is predominantly flat; during monsoons, floodwaters from the Ganges, Brahmaputra and Meghna Rivers submerge two-thirds of it, threatening life and property and depositing fertile silt. Rice, tea, sugarcane and jute are staple crops. Raw jute and jute processed as hessian, sacking and carpet backing are exported. Other industries include garment manufacturing. Bangladesh receives much foreign aid.

Bhutan, ruled by the hereditary 'Dragon King', restricts tourists to 4,000 per year. In 1960, a trip from Phuntsholing on the Indian border to Thimphu took six days by mule; nowadays cars travel the 190 kilometre (120 mile) winding mountain road in six hours. Nearly three-quarters forested, Bhutan contains Great Himalayan high peaks; fertile Lesser Himalayan slopes and river valleys; and the Duars Plain rolling away from the foothills. Timber is exported to India. More than 90 per cent of the people live by agriculture, mainly growing maize, wheat, barley and potatoes. Bhutan's huge hydropower potential remains undeveloped. Most of the country's manufacturing is on a cottage-industry scale.

India—together with Bangladesh and most of Pakistan—forms a well-defined subcontinent divided from the rest of Asia by the Himalayas in the north and lesser adjoining mountain ranges to the west and east. India itself has three main regions: the Himalayas ('home of snows') and their foothills, the Indo-Gangetic Plain, and the Deccan Plateau, which contains some of the world's oldest rocks. Farming is diverse. Herders graze sheep in the western highlands;

Map labels

TURKMENISTAN
Ashgabat
Dushanbe
UZBEKISTAN
KYRGYZSTAN
TAJIKISTAN
7719 m
Kongur Shan
Yarkant
Tarim Pendi
SHAN
Muztag
7723 m
Bayan Har Shan
KUNLUN
100°
CHINA
Hindu Kush
Gilgit
Karakoram Range
K2
8611 m
Tielongtan
Kâbol
(Kabul)
8126 m
Nanga Parbat
Peshâwar
Srinagar
Leh
7315 m
QINGZANG GAOYUAN
(PLATEAU OF TIBET)
Kuh-e
Qaysar
4182 m
Râwalpindi
Islâmâbâd
3339 m
AFGHANISTAN
Harirud
Gujrât
Sargodha
Zhob
Lahore
Amritsar
Shimla
Nanda Devi
7817 m
Nyainqêntanglha
Feng
7114 m
Dîbrugarh
Faisalâbâd
Ludhiâna
Chandigarh
Muzaffarpur
Tinsukia
PAKISTAN
Sâhiwâl
Haridwâr
BHUTAN
Thimphu
Itânagar
Multân
Gangânagar
Karnâl
NEPAL
HIMALAYA
Dhaulagiri
8167 m
Pokhara
Mt Everest
8848 m
Kula Kangri
7554 m
Quetta
Bahâwalpur
Pânipat
Meerut
Kathmandu
Nok Kundi
Rahîmyâr
Khân
Bîkâner
Sîkar
Delhi
New
Delhi
Rampur
Shâhjahânpur
Birâtnagar
Shilîguri
Guwâhâti
Rangpur
Shillong
Dispur
Imphâl
4042 m
Kuh-e Taftân
Shikârpur
Jaisalmer
Jaipur
Alwar
Lucknow
Muzaffarpur
Pûrnia
Bâlurghât
Mymensingh
Sylhet
IRAN
Lârkâna
Sukkur
Phalodi
Pokaran
Âgra
Yamuna
Kanpur
Patna
Godda
Rajshahi
Pâbna
Aizawl
Jodhpur
Ajmer
Gwalior
Allahâbad
Vârânasi
(Benares)
Dhanbâd
Dhaka
(Dacca)
Tropic of Cancer
Nawâbshâh
Ajmer
Beâwar
Jhânsi
Mirzâpur
Rewa
Garwa
Rânchî
Bânkura
Khulna
MYANMAR
(BURMA)
Gwâdar
Turbat
Ormâra
Central Makrân Range
Gândhîdhâm
Pâtan
Bhîlwâra
Kota
Guna
Sâgar
Murwâra
Jamshedpur
Bâleshwar
Chittagong
Hyderâbâd
Mîrpur
Khâs
Jâmnagar
Râjkot
Ahmadâbâd
Ânand
Indore
Bhopâl
Jabalpur
Bilâspur
Korba
Raurkela
3053 m
Mt Victoria
Karâchi
Porbandar
Bhâvnagar
Jûnâgadh
Vadodara
Bharûch
Khandwa
Chhindawâra
Sambalpur
Bâlângir
Palmyras Pt
Kodinar
Gulf of
Kachchh
Surat
Dhule
Burhânpur
Nâgpur
Raipur
Bhubaneshwar
Dâman
Mâlegaon
INDIA
Chandrapur
Kânker
Puri
Nâsik
Aurangâbad
Jâlna
Jagdalpur
Brahmapur
Mumbai
(Bombay)
Ahmadnagar
Parbhani
Godavari
Pimpri-Chinchwad
Pune
Lâtûr
Nizâmâbad
Warangal
Vizianagaram
Vishâkhapatnam
Sâtâra
Solâpur
Hyderâbad
Kâkinâda
Ratnâgiri
Sângli
Bijâpur
Krishna
Vijayawâda
Bay
Kolhâpur
Ichalkaranji
Kurnool
Tenâli
Cape Chirâla
of
Panaji
Belgaum
Âdoni
Cuddapah
Bengal
ARABIAN
Hubli
Anantapur
Nellore
Dâvangere
Shimoga
Bangalore
Vellore
Chennai
(Madras)
SEA
Mangalore
Mysore
Pondicherry
Cannanore
Mâhe
Salem
Cuddalore
Lakshadweep Is
(Laccadive Is)
Kozhikode
(Calicut)
Coimbatore
Tiruchchirâppalli
Andaman and Nicobar Islands
(India)
North
Andaman
Middle
Andaman
South
Andaman
Little
Andaman
Kochi
(Cochin)
Alleppey
Kâraikkudi
Madurai
Jaffna
Nicobar Is
(India)
Thiruvananthapuram
(Trivandrum)
Nâgercoil
Tuticorin
Trincomalee
SRI
LANKA
Cape Comorin
Kurunegala
Kandy
Pidurutalagata
2524 m
MALDIVES
Colombo
Sri Jayawardanapura-Kotte
Dehiwala-Mount Lavinia
Matara
Hambantota
Dondra Head
INDIAN OCEAN
Male
0 200 400 kilometres
0 200 miles
Scale 1:18,000,000

rice, buckwheat and barley grow on the terraced
slopes of the eastern highlands. In different parts
of the plains country, farmers grow winter wheat,
summer rice, cotton and sugarcane, sorghum,
millet and jute. Millet and pulses grow on the
plateau; beyond its western edge defined by the
mountain chain of the Western Ghats, the coastal
plain supports coconut groves, fishing villages,
ricefields and tapioca plantations.

Bengali women in colourful saris
carting earth away.

NEPAL

Capital Kathmandu
Population 24,302,653
Official language Nepali
Main religions Hindu 90%, Buddhist 5%, Muslim 3%
Currency Nepalese rupee
Form of government Constitutional monarchy
Record holder Mount Everest, on the border between Nepal and China, is the highest point on Earth

PAKISTAN

Capital Sri Jayawardenapura
Population 138,123,359
Official languages Urdu, English
Main religions Muslim 97% (Sunni 77%, Shi'a 20%), other (Christian, Hindu) 3%
Currency Pakistani rupee
Form of government Republic

SRI LANKA

Capital Colombo
Population 19,144,875
Official language Sinhala
Main religions Buddhist 69%, Hindu 15%, Christian 8%, Muslim 8%
Currency Sri Lankan rupee
Form of government Republic
Record holder World's leading producer of high-grade graphite

The Taksang monastery, like many other places in Bhutan, is difficult to reach.

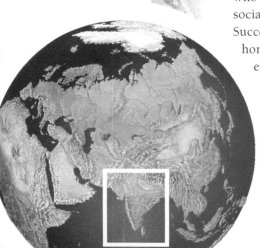

The Ganges, sacred to people of the Hindu faith, is a wide and sluggish stream for most of its course through India and Bangladesh. It is an important source of water for both irrigation and washing.

Indian subcontinent continued...

The Indus Civilisation dominated the Indus Valley about 2600 BC and the Ganges Valley around 1500 BC. It is thought that this civilisation was overtaken by Sanskrit-speaking Aryan peoples who introduced the caste system, a scheme of social division that still underpins Indian life. Successive waves of colonisation made India home to many castes and tribes. British control, effectively beginning in 1805 and ending in 1947, introduced the civil service and code of law of modern India. Since 1991 production, trade and investment reforms have provided new industry and business opportunities. Despite this, India lacks social services, good roads and adequate port facilities and telecommunications. Defence spending on the continuing conflict with Pakistan is high.

Nepal, clinging to the southern slopes of the Himalayas, has been influenced by Tibetan Buddhist/Mongol and by Hindu/Indian culture. Nepal is said to be the birthplace of the Buddha. In 1769 the Gurkhas conquered the Nepal Valley, moved the capital to Kathmandu, and founded modern Nepal. The uplands, home to most of the population, produces rice and fruit. Wheat, maize, sugarcane and jute are other staple crops. About 90 per cent of Nepalis are subsistence farmers. More than 40 per cent of them are undernourished. Industries include processing jute, sugarcane, tobacco and grain, textile and carpet production, and tourism. Environmental concerns have so far prevented development of the country's limitless hydropower resources. Although tourism has contributed to the national income, Nepal remains very poor.

Pakistan shares India's history of early civilisations, migrations and invasions. Independent since 1947, the ongoing dispute over ownership of Kashmir poisons relations with India. Ethnic differences within Pakistan's complex mixture of indigenous peoples cause internal conflict.

Irrigation agriculture combined with new plant varieties introduced during the 'green revolution' of the 1970s produces abundant cotton, wheat, rice and sugarcane; fruit and vegetables are also widely grown [SEE THE AGRICULTURAL FRONTIER]. The country has large reserves of copper, bauxite, phosphates and manganese. Pakistan manufactures textiles, petroleum products, construction materials, foodstuffs and paper products. Much of the nation's revenue funds defence spending on items such as nuclear weaponry and the army.

Wearing a mixture of traditional and Western-style clothing, these Pakistani boys are on their way to school.

Sri Lanka

Sri Lanka, known as Ceylon until 1972, has a mountainous centre and a string of coral islets called 'Adam's Bridge' linking it to India in the northwest. Its cultural heritage dates back to the BC 300s. Sri Lankans grow rice, the people's staple; fruit, vegetables, spices, tea, coconuts and rubber are exported. Mining includes precious and semi-precious stones, graphite, mineral sands and phosphates. The Portuguese arrived in 1505, followed by Dutch and English colonists. Sri Lanka became independent in 1948. Its ethnic composition is as varied as its physical and cultural landscapes: violence, principally caused by Tamil Tiger guerillas (who seek an independent Tamil state) and Sinhalese extremists, discourages tourists and foreign investment.

Mount Everest, the highest point on Earth, and surrounding peaks in Nepal.

CHINA

Capital Beijing

Population 1,246,871,951

Official language Mandarin Chinese

Main religions Officially atheist; traditionally Confucian, Taoist, Buddhist; small Muslim and Christian minorities

Currency Yuan

Form of government Communist republic

Record holder Most populous country in the world; Third largest country in the world; China's Great Wall is the only built structure on Earth that can be seen from space; The giant panda, an endangered species, is found only in the forests of west-central China where it feeds mainly on bamboo

China

Ancient dynasties and religions

The first Chinese kingdom for which there is definite historical material is the Shang Dynasty, which originated in the Huang Valley around 1700 BC and lasted until 1122 BC. It was a culture with a calendar and a form of writing, skilled in working bronze and using the wheel. During the following Zhou Dynasty, iron casting, metal coinage and silk were introduced. The philosopher-teacher Confucius (551–479 BC) outlined a pattern of orderly behaviour for families and government officials that influenced society for centuries to come. The Qin Dynasty (221–206 BC) saw the unification of China as a nation. In 206 BC, 400 years of Han Dynasty began. During this time Buddhism reached China from India; and the Chinese invented paper and the seismograph, were the first to make steel, and pushed their boundaries to almost the present limits.

A Mongolian musician playing a fiddle strung with horsehair.

China has large deposits of coal and iron ore and is a major producer of tungsten. Its main exports are textiles, oil and oil products, chemicals, light industrial goods and military weapons. Its problems include air pollution, water pollution, nationwide water shortages and untreated sewage. In 1979 a 'one-child families' policy was introduced to curb population growth.

There are three major regions in China. The mountains to the west include the vast Plateau of Tibet, the highest region in the world. The series of deserts and desert basins start in the northwest with the Tarim Basin and the Taklimakan Desert and reach across the Nei Mongol Plateau to Manchuria in the northeast. And last, the largely low-lying eastern region consists of the valleys and floodplains of the Yangtze (Chang Jiang) and Yellow (Huang) Rivers, and extend to the coastal plains including the Pearl River in the south.

Part of the Great Wall of China. The Wall was built during the Ming Dynasty (AD 1368–1644) to fortify China's northern boundary. The brick-faced wall was intended to keep out Mongolian invaders.

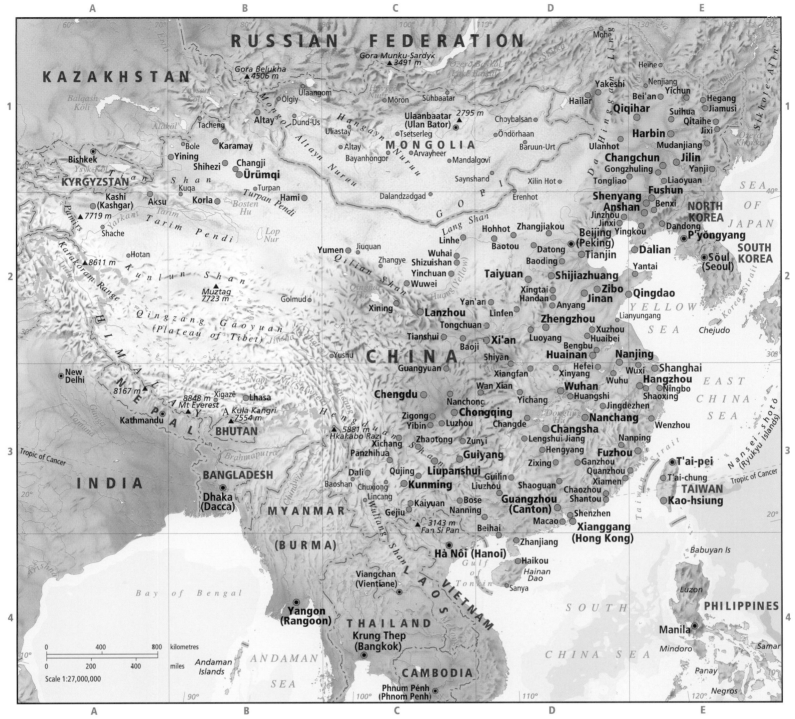

China's mountainous western region contains Tibet. The majority of Tibetans had the same ethnic origin, spoke the same language and practised Tibetan Buddhism. From 1950 to 1959 China tried to modernise the country by weakening religious authority, and by building roads, bridges, hospitals and schools. Before this, travellers to isolated Tibet went on foot, rode pack animals and crossed the larger rivers in small boats. In 1959, the Tibetans rose unsuccessfully against the Chinese. For the next 25 years or so China forcibly attempted to remake Tibetan society, forbidding the public practice of Buddhism. China is unlikely to restore Tibet's independence because of its strategic position as a defensive barrier. Tibet's rich mineral resources remain undeveloped. The people grow barley, wheat, millet, buckwheat, beans, hemp and mustard and supplement their diet with garden produce and dairy products from the yak. Stored grain will keep safely for fifty to sixty years in the cool, dry air.

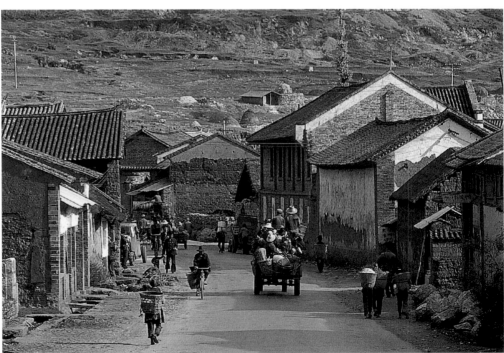

As few families in rural China own motor vehicles, transport of people and produce is by tractor-drawn cart or bicycle. Goods are also carried on the back in traditional woven panniers. Mud-brick buildings line the village street.

MONGOLIA

Capital Ulaanbaatar

Population 2,617,379

Official language Khalka Mongol

Main religions Predominantly Tibetan Buddhist with small Muslim minority

Currency Tugrik

Form of government Republic

Record holder World's largest and most thinly populated landlocked country; Highest number of livestock per capita in the world; World's third largest producer of fluorspar (a mineral that is the main source of fluorine)

TAIWAN

Capital T'ai-pei (Taipei)

Population 22,113,250

Official language Mandarin Chinese

Main religions Buddhist, Confucian and Taoist 93%; Christian 4.5%

Currency New Taiwan dollar

Form of government Republic

China continued...

China's northwest desert region is mostly too cold for agriculture and is inhabited by pastoralists who keep herds of sheep, goats and horses. Oasis crops grow round the rim of the Taklimakan Desert and there are small farming settlements in the Gansu corridor to the north of the Qilian Mountains. Coarse grains and soya beans are cultivated on the Manchurian Plains; in Northern Manchuria only 90 days a year are frost free.

China's eastern region, where two-thirds of the country's people now live, was the cradle of Chinese civilisation. The Yellow (Huang) River, known as 'China's sorrow' for its frequent flooding that destroys life and property, waters the North China Plain and is constrained today by modern flood-control schemes. The Yangtze (Chang Jiang), also capable of devastating flooding, is China's largest and most important river and navigable for much of its length by boats of varying sizes. In the 'Red Basin' of Sichuan, rice fields terrace the hillsides. Crops grown in the south include sugar, bananas and tropical fruits.

A fertile valley in the cold highlands of Tibet. Surrounded by towering alps, Tibet is one of the most isolated regions in the world.

Hong Kong developed under British administration from 1841. It is a centre of international trade with an excellent natural harbour and a population nearly 97 per cent Chinese. China repossessed Hong Kong in 1997. **Macao**, formerly a Portuguese territory, is now under Chinese control.

Wheat flour dough, formed into either buns or noodles, is an integral part of the diet in northern China. Here, a bowl of steaming noodles makes a warming winter meal. In the south, the staple is rice.

The distinctive limestone hills of southern China, where dramatic wooded spires and pinnacles rise above small, intensively cultivated plains. Sinkholes, caverns and underground streams are common.

Mongolia, partly mountainous and

partly arid desert, is home to nomadic pastoralists who raise herds of goats, sheep, yaks, camels and horses in time-honoured ways. More present-day Mongolians, however, live in towns than in the country and modern methods of textile manufacturing and food processing have been established. Deposits of copper, molybdenum, fluorspar and coking coal are mined, but foreign aid has not been forthcoming to allow development of the considerable oil and gas reserves. In the days of Genghis Ghan (1162–1227), Mongolia's impressive empire stretched from eastern Europe to the Pacific and into northern India. The Mongol Empire collapsed in 1368 and China then controlled Mongolia. Following the Russian Civil War (1918–22) the Chinese were expelled and Mongolia adopted the Soviet system. Today, the country is trying to remake itself in a more democratic mould.

Taiwan is a large island off the coast of

China. It was under China's control from the AD 1600s until the Japanese took it over in 1895. In 1945 it reverted to China. In 1949, after being driven from mainland China by the communists, the Nationalist Kuomintang took refuge on the island, turning it into a political, military and economic fortress. China now wants Taiwan to rejoin the mainland and political relations between the two countries are cool. The mountainous interior of Taiwan is lushly vegetated but much of the timber is unsuitable for commercial use. Rice is grown on the well-watered western coastal plain together with sugarcane, sweet potatoes, tea, bananas, pineapples and peanuts. Agriculture, however, is less important than the thriving industrial sector. Many of the highly educated workforce have been trained in the United States. Taiwan exports electrical machinery, electronic products, textiles, footwear, foodstuffs, and plywood and wood products.

Native to the cold Tibetan plateau, the yak, or Asian wild ox, has been bred over the centuries into a sturdy pack animal able to carry heavy loads over mountain trails. It also provides rich milk, and its long, soft hair can be woven into cloth.

JAPAN

Capital Tokyo
Population 126,182,077
Official language Japanese
Main religion Shinto and Buddhist 84%
Currency Yen
Form of government Constitutional monarchy
Record holder Fuji-san (Mount Fuji) at 3,776 metres (12,388 feet), is the highest mountain in the region; Tokyo is the biggest urban area in the world; *Genji monogatari (The Tale of Genji)* by Murasaki Shikibu, a Japanese court lady in the late AD 900s, is considered the world's first important novel; Japan has a lower population growth and higher life expectancy than other parts of Asia.

NORTH KOREA

Capital P'yongyang
Population 22,337,878
Official language Korean
Main religions Buddhist and Confucian 51%, traditional beliefs 45%, Christian 4%
Currency Won
Form of government Communist state
Record holder Paektu-san (Paektu Mountain) 2,744 metres (10,033 feet) is the highest on the Korean peninsula

SOUTH KOREA

Capital Seoul
Population 46,884,800
Official language Korean
Main religions Christianity 21%, Buddhism 24%, Confucianism 1.5%, no religion 52.5%
Currency Won
Form of government Republic

Japan & Korea

High-tech industries and rural rice fields

Japan and South Korea are among the most highly industrialised nations in Asia. Industries are privately owned, and heavily dependent on imported raw materials and fuel; exports of manufactured goods, such as cars and electronic equipment are major revenue earners. The standard of living in both countries is among the highest in the Asian region. Industry is also important in communist North Korea. There, state-owned industry produces 95 per cent of all manufactured goods, including military weapons, chemicals and food products. The greater part of the Korean Peninsula and the islands of Japan are mountainous and forested. All suitable land is intensively farmed, with traditional rural scenes a stark contrast to the high-tech cities; rice is the main crop and the basic food throughout the region.

Japan consists of a chain of four main islands, connected by bridges and a tunnel, and more than 4,000 smaller islands. It occupies a highly unstable area on the Earth's crust and is subject to earthquakes, volcanic eruptions, typhoons and tsunamis *[SEE NATURAL DISASTERS].*

A Japanese worker enjoys a quick snack from a wayside food stall. Buckwheat noodles, skewers of grilled chicken and grilled slices of beancurd are favourite snacks commonly sold by street vendors.

People have lived in Japan for more than 6,000 years. By AD 400 Japan was controlled by a number of rival clans. In 1542 Portuguese missionaries became the first Europeans to reach Japan. Soon after, in 1603, the country came under the strong rule of the Tokugawa family, who stopped trade and contact between Japan and the outside world. This situation continued until the arrival of Commodore Perry of the United States Navy in 1865. Over the next fifty years Japan adopted many western ways and rapidly industrialised.

The nation's expanding territorial claims led to its involvement in World War II. In 1945 Japan became the first and only country in the world to suffer attack by nuclear weapons when two fission bombs were dropped by the United States, one each on the cities of Hiroshima and Nagasaki *[SEE GLOBAL NUCLEAR INDUSTRY].*

Less than one-tenth of Japan is suitable for agriculture, yet it produces most of its food and is self-sufficient in rice.

North Korea is a communist state with both industrial and agricultural production controlled by the government. Rice is the main crop, with millet, fruit, vegetables, oilseed rape, flax and cotton also grown. In 1995, when floods destroyed the harvest, the country came close to famine. Industries in North Korea include the production of military weapons, chemicals and minerals.

In 1950 communist North Korea invaded South Korea, sparking the bitter Korean War, which continued until 1953. The present border is the ceasefire line, which roughly follows the 38th parallel, dividing the Korean Peninsula into two countries. North Korea continues to fall behind South Korea in both development and living standards.

South Korea followed Japan in developing a highly industrialised economy, and there is little at the high-tech end of modern industry that it does not manufacture and sell. Textiles and clothing are also important exports. Besides rice, South Korea also grows barley, apples, grapes and stone fruits, and is one of the world's leading fishing countries.

Heavily cultivated river plains, South Korea. The Korean Peninsula was unified as a kingdom in 1392 and, despite attempted invasions by both China and Japan, remained independent until 1910, when Japan took control.

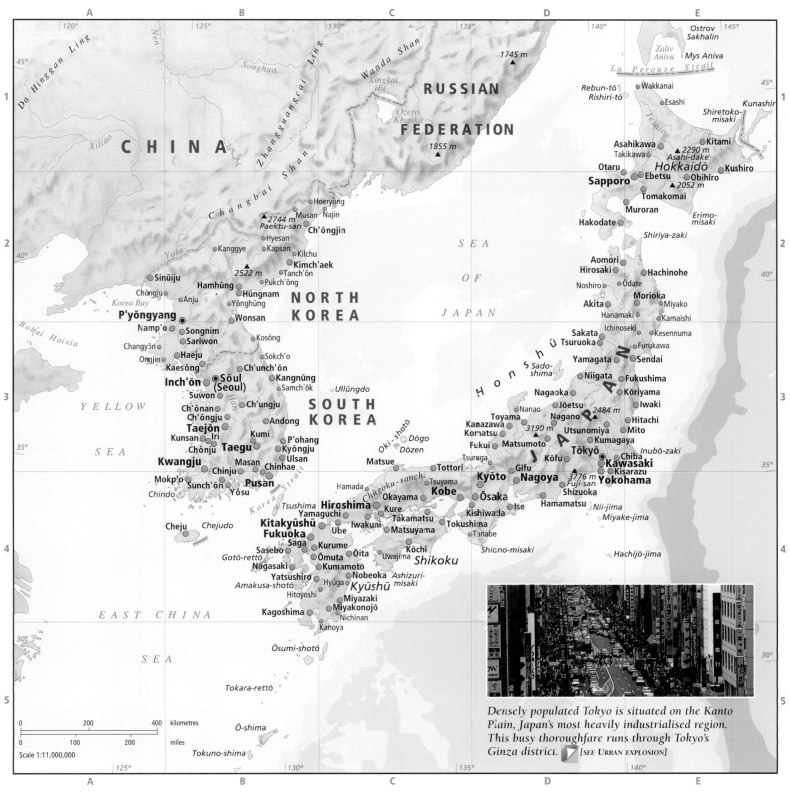

Densely populated Tokyo is situated on the Kanto Plain, Japan's most heavily industrialised region. This busy thoroughfare runs through Tokyo's Ginza district. [SEE URBAN EXPLOSION]

Asia

CAMBODIA

Capital Phnom Penh

Population 11,780,285

Official language Khmer

Main religion Theravada Buddhism 95%

Currency Riel

Form of government Constitutional monarchy

Record holder World's largest group of religious buildings at Angkor Wat and Angkor Thom

LAOS

Capital Vientiane

Population 5,407,453

Official language Lao

Main religions Buddhist 60%, animist and other 40%

Currency Kip

Form of government Communist state

MYANMAR (BURMA)

Capital Yangon (Rangoon)

Population 48,081,302

Official language Burmese

Main religions Buddhist 89%, Christian 4%, Muslim 4%

Currency Kyat

Form of government Military regime

Record holder World's largest producer of opium poppies

The mighty Mekong

The Mekong—4,350 kilometres (2,700 miles) long—is the longest river in Southeast Asia. It forms part of the borders between Myanmar and Laos and between Laos and Thailand, and flows through southern Laos, Cambodia and Vietnam before reaching the South China Sea. About one-third of the combined population of Cambodia, Laos, Thailand and Vietnam live on the Lower Mekong River basin. Laos and Cambodia's capital cities stand on the river's banks. Its waters, which rise and fall with the seasonal rainfall brought by the monsoon winds, contribute to agriculture, the most important activity in all five countries. Rice is the basin's chief crop and Vietnam has become the world's third largest exporter of rice.

Cambodia, once known as the 'gentle

kingdom', dominated Southeast Asia from the 1100s. Yet by the 1400s Khmer rulers were frequently at war with Vietnam and Siam (Thailand) and often had to answer to one or the other. French rule was established in 1863 and lasted until 1954 when Cambodia became independent. The Khmer Rouge seized power from 1975 to 1978 and tried to create an immediate, classless, rural society. They exterminated the professional classes and forced

From the early centuries of the first millennium AD, Buddhist kingdoms were beginning to appear throughout mainland Southeast Asia. Even in the communist countries of Vietnam and Laos, Buddhism is today's dominant religion. These young boys are novices in a Laotian monastery.

townspeople into the country. Half a million refugees fled to Thailand. Cambodia is now classified as one of the poorest countries in the world but is struggling to reconstruct its economy. Fishing and rice growing sustain the people. Logging, strip mining and destroying mangrove swamps have all taken their toll on the environment [SEE HABITAT DESTRUCTION; RESOURCE DEPLETION].

Laos is a mountainous country with more

than 90 per cent of its land more than 180 metres (600 feet) above sea level. Despite defoliant damage during the Vietnam War, deforestation and erosion, 55 per cent of Laos is still forested. Most Laotians are subsistence farmers using the limited area suitable to grow maize, vegetables, tobacco, coffee and cotton in addition to rice, and the illegal cultivation of opium poppies and cannabis. Although garment manufacturing and motorcycle assembly have

A Vietnamese fisherman casts his net from a basket boat. Opportunities to raise livestock in Southeast Asia are limited and fish are an important source of protein.

been established to boost the economy, lack of railroads and inadequate roads and telecommunications continue to hamper economic growth. From the 1300s to the early 1700s the powerful Laotian Buddhist kingdom of Lang Xang (the Million Elephant Kingdom) flourished. After that, the country's fortunes declined and Laos is now one of the poorest countries in the world, and is heavily dependent on overseas aid.

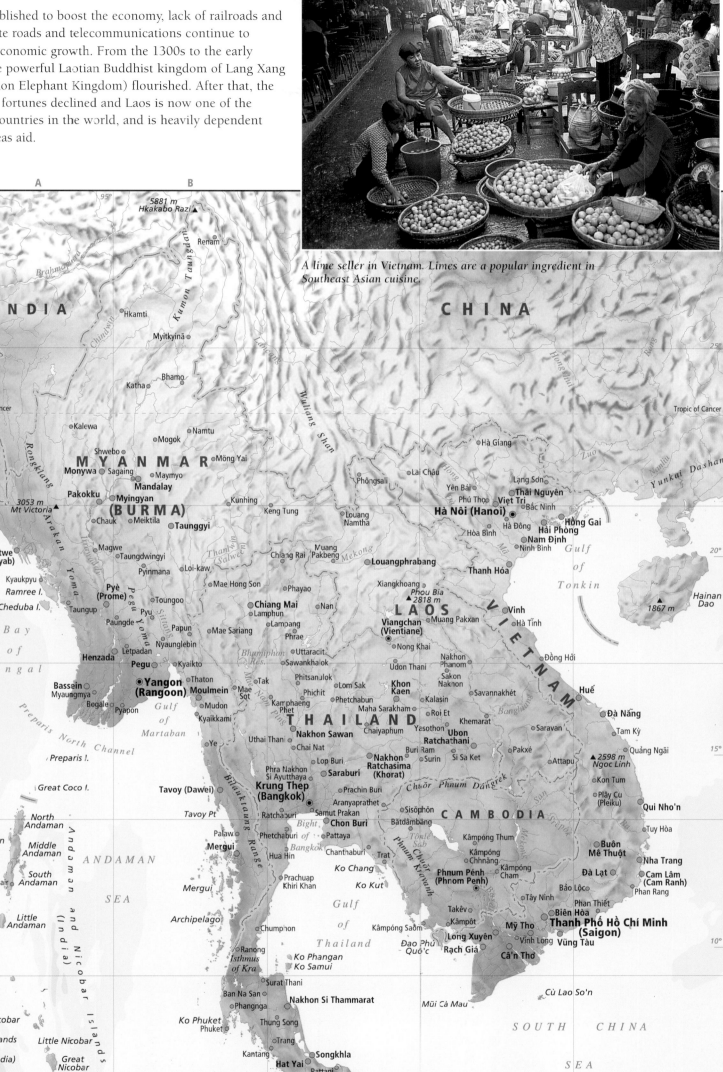

A lime seller in Vietnam. Limes are a popular ingredient in Southeast Asian cuisine.

INDIA

CHINA

5881 m
Hkakabo Razi ▲

Renam

Hkamti

Myitkyinā

Tropic of Cancer

Kalewa

Bhamo

Katha

Namtu

Mogok

MYANMAR

Shwebo

Mōng Yai

Hà Giang

Monywa

Sagaing

Maymyo

Phôngsali

Lai Châu

Lang Sơn

Pakokku

Mandalay

Myingyan

Kunhing

Keng Tung

Yên Bái

Phú Thọ

Thái Nguyên

Việt Tri

Bắc Ninh

(BURMA)

Chauk

Meiktila

Taunggyi

Muang
Pakbeng

Louang
Namtha

Hà Nội (Hanoi)

Hà Đông

Hải Phòng

Hòa Bình

Nam Định

Ninh Bình

Gulf

Mt Victoria ▲
3053 m

Magwe

Taungdwingyi

Chiang Rai

Louangphrabang

Thanh Hóa

of

Sittwe
(Akyab)

Pyinmana

Loi-kaw

Phayao

Nan

Xiangkhoang

Tonkin

Kyaukpyu

Pyè
(Prome)

Toungoo

Mae Hong Son

Chiang Mai

Lamphun

Phou Bia ▲
2818 m

Ramree I.

Taungup

Pyu

Lampang

LAOS

Vinh

1867 m ▲

Cheduba I.

Paungde

Papun

Mae Sariang

Phrae

Viangchan
(Vientiane)

Muang Pakxan

Hà Tĩnh

Hainan
Dao

Bay

Nyaunglebin

Letpadan

Uttaracit

Nong Khai

Đồng Hới

of

Henzada

Pegu

Kyaikto

Bhumiphon
Res.

Sawankhalok

Udon Thani

Nakhon
Phanom

Bengal

Myaungmya

Thaton

Phitsanulok

Lom Sak

Khon
Kaen

Sakon
Nakhon

Savannakhét

Huế

Bassein

Yangon
(Rangoon)

Moulmein

Tak

Phichit

Phetchabun

Kalasin

Đà Nẵng

Bogale

Mudon

Mae
Sot

Kamphaeng
Phet

Maha Sarakham

Roi Et

Khemarat

Pyapon

Kyaikkami

THAILAND

Chaiyaphum

Yasothon

Ubon
Ratchathani

Saravan

Tam Kỳ

Gulf
of
Martaban

Ye

Uthai Thani

Nakhon Sawan

Buri Ram

Surin

Si Sa Ket

Pakxé

Attapu

Quảng Ngãi

Chai Nat

2598 m ▲
Ngoc Linh

Lop Buri

Nakhon
Ratchasima
(Khorat)

Kon Tum

Preparis
North Channel

Preparis I.

Phra Nakhon
Si Ayutthaya

Saraburi

Prachin Buri

Chŏr Phnum Dângrek

Plây Cu
(Pleiku)

Great Coco I.

Tavoy (Dawei)

Krung Thep
(Bangkok)

Samut Prakan

Sisôphôn

Bătdâmbâng

CAMBODIA

Qui Nho'n

North
Andaman

Ratchaburi

Phetchaburi

Bight
of
Bangkok

Chon Buri

Pattaya

Phnum
Krâvanh

Tuy Hòa

Andaman
Islands

Middle
Andaman

Palaw

Hua Hin

Chanthaburi

Trat

Tônlé
Sab

Kâmpóng Thum

Buôn
Mê Thuột

Nha Trang

South
Andaman

Mergui

Prachuap
Khiri Khan

Ko Chang

Phnum Krâvanh

Kâmpóng
Chhnăng

Kâmpóng
Cham

Đà Lạt

Port Blair

Ko Kut

Phnum Pénh
(Phnom Penh)

Cam Lâm
(Cam Ranh)

Mergui

Chumphon

Gulf
of
Thailand

Takêv

Bảo Lộc

Phan Rang

Little
Andaman

Archipelago

Kâmpóng Saôm

Tây Ninh

Biên Hòa

Phan Thiết

Kâmpôt

Mỹ Tho

Thanh Phố Hồ Chí Minh
(Saigon)

Ranong

Ko Phangan

Long Xuyên

Vũng Tàu

Nicobar

Isthmus
of Kra

Ko Samui

Đao Phủ
Quố'c

Rạch Giá

Vĩnh Long

Cản Tho

Islands

Little Nicobar

Surat Thani

Cù Lao So'n

(India)

Great
Nicobar

Ban Na San

Nakhon Si Thammarat

Mũi Cà Mau

Phangnga

SOUTH CHINA

Ko Phuket

Thung Song

Phuket

Trang

SEA

Kantang

Songkhla

Hat Yai

Pattani

P. Langkawi

Yala

Narathiwat

P. Redang

0   200   400 kilometres
0   100   200 miles
Scale 1:7,000,000

Tg Jambuair

MALAYSIA

Brahmaputra

Chindwin

Kumon Taungdan

Rongklang

Arakan Yoma

Pegu Yoma

Irrawaddy

Sittang

Salween

Thanlwin (Salween)

Mae Nam Ping

Bhumhong

Mekong

Waliang Shan

Hong (Red)

Mã

Bangfai

Sẽ Kong

Sẽ San

Mekong

Chŏr Phnum Krâvanh

ANDAMAN

SEA

Andaman and Nicobar Islands (India)

Bilauktaung Range

Tavoy Pt

Bay
of
Bengal

Yunkai Dashan

Nanliu

Zuo

Rang

Hong (Red)

THAILAND

Capital Bangkok
Population 60,609,046
Official language Thai
Main religion Buddhist 95%
Currency Baht
Form of government Constitutional monarchy
Record holder World's second largest producer of tungsten; World's third largest producer of tin

VIETNAM

Capital Hanoi
Population 77,311,210
Official language Vietnamese
Main religions Buddhist 60%, Roman Catholic 7%, Taoist, Islam and indigenous beliefs 33%
Currency Dong
Form of government Communist state

Mainland Southeast Asia continued...

Myanmar (Burma), one of Asia's least densely populated countries, is a land of villages. Fewer than a quarter of its people live in urban areas. The country has been variously ruled by the Tibeto-Burman kings in AD 1100 to 1200, by the Mongols under Kublai Khan (1289), and by the British as part of its Indian Empire from 1886. Myanmar's literary tradition and style of script dates back to the Mon civilisation 2,300 years ago. Upon gaining independence in 1948, the government abolished private enterprise and trade, a policy that rapidly produced poverty. Today's government is faced with quelling rebellions led by various ethnic groups, who cultivate opium poppies to fund their resistance. Myanmar has fertile soils where rice, sugarcane, cotton and jute are grown; good fisheries; reserves of natural gas and oil; and plentiful monsoon forests, which yield teak and other hardwoods. High-quality jade is mined in the northern mountains.

gypsum and gemstones. Recent years have seen the development of high-technology goods for export. Tourism is the largest source of foreign exchange, especially from the resorts on the coast of the Andaman Sea.

Vietnam grows rice to feed its people and for export, together with sweet potatoes and cassava. Tea, coffee and rubber plantations cover the slopes of the Annam Highlands. Crude oil is the country's largest single export item; coal, the principal energy source, is also exported. For more than a thousand years, Vietnam was under

The colourful garb of these traditional dancers from Thailand is a reflection of that country's Buddhist culture.

Thailand, called Siam until 1939, has largely escaped the destructive effects of war. Stability prevailed from AD 1300 to 1700 during the period of the Buddhist kingdom of Ayutthaya. Siam remained free of European colonisation and between 1800 and 1910 signed treaties with the West, abolished slavery and encouraged study abroad. The military currently plays an important part in political and industrial life. Thailand's hills produce tin ore and plantation rubber; its forests supply teak and other valuable timbers; the fertile valleys of the Rivers Ping, Yom, Wang and Nan support intensive crops; and the central plains are Thailand's rice bowl. Most people are employed in the agricultural sector. Besides tin, mineral resources include tungsten, lead, lignite,

Chinese domination, achieving a degree of independence in AD 939. Christian missionaries arrived between 1600 and 1700; and Vietnam became a French colony in 1883. A communist-led resistance movement fought the Japanese during World War II, and later fought the returning French, defeating them in 1954. In that year, the country was divided, south of the 17th parallel, into a communist-governed, Soviet-supported northern half and a United States-supported southern half. The north declared war on the south in 1955. The war dragged on for twenty years and the Socialist Republic of Vietnam then came into being. Recently, Vietnam has improved relations with some Asian and Western nations and shown strong growth in the tourism industry, as well as industrial output.

The forested slopes of the Himalayas extend into the northern region of Thailand and are inhabited by hill tribes who live by the shifting cultivation of dry rice and opium poppies.

Angkor Wat, dating from between AD 1100 and 1200, and intended as Hindu King Suryavarman II's last resting place, is the largest of many temples built by the Khmer people in Cambodia. It was taken over by Theravada Buddhist monks.

MARITIME SOUTHEAST Asia

FACT FILE

BRUNEI

Capital Bandar Seri Begawan
Population 322,982
Official languages English, Malay
Main religions Muslim 63%, Buddhism 14%, Christian 8%, indigenous beliefs and other 15%
Currency Bruneian dollar
Form of government Sultanate
Record holder The biggest palace in the world—1,788 rooms at Bandar Seri Begawan spread over 20 hectares (50 acres)

EAST TIMOR

Capital Dili
Population Unconfirmed
Official language Undecided
Main religion Roman Catholic (percentage unconfirmed)
Currency Unconfirmed
Form of government Undecided

INDONESIA

Capital Jakarta
Population 216,108,345
Official language Bahasa Indonesia
Main religions Muslim 87%, Protestant 6%, Roman Catholic 3%, Hindu 2%, Buddhist 1%
Currency Rupiah
Form of government Republic
Record holder The world's largest Buddhist monument at Borobudur on Java; World's largest archipelago

Tiger sharks are found in tropical and subtropical waters, and can be found in the seas of Southeast Asia where the warm temperatures suit them.

Scale 1:15,000,000

The Spice Islands

The Indonesian islands of Maluku (Moluccas) were once the only place where cloves and nutmeg grew. These precious spices first lured Indian and Chinese traders to this region. The Islamic trade network stretched from Arabia to Southeast Asia long before European ships ventured this far.

These scattered islands, many of which are uninhabited, once formed an ancient land bridge linking Asia and Australia. Indigenous people have been island hopping since prehistoric times between mainland and island Malaysia, Singapore and its offshore islets, and the archipelagoes of Indonesia (13,677 islands) and the Philippines (7,107 islands).

The cavity in the tree trunk makes a perfect home for this rock carving in Indonesia.

MALAYSIA

Capital Kuala Lumpur
Population 21,376,066
Official language Malay (Bahasa Malaysia)
Main religions Muslim 53%, Buddhist 17.5%, Confucian and Taoist 11.5%, Christian 8.5%, Hindu 7%
Currency Ringgit (Malaysian dollar)
Form of government Federal constitutional monarchy
Record holder World's biggest producer of disk drives; World's biggest producer of palm oil; World's biggest producer of tin; Exports more tropical timber than any other country

PHILIPPINES

Capital Manila
Population 79,345,812
Official languages Filipino, English
Main religions Roman Catholic 83%, Protestant 9%, Muslim 5%, Buddhist and other 3%
Currency Philippine peso
Form of government Republic
Record holder World's biggest supplier of refractory chrome

SINGAPORE

Capital Singapore
Population 3,531,600
Official languages Malay, Chinese, Tamil, English
Main religions Buddhist and Taoist 56%, Christian 19%, Muslim 15%, Hindu 5%
Currency Singapore dollar
Form of government Republic

Mt Pinatubo in the Philippines erupted in 1991 causing widespread damage and devastating mud slides, which swamped a large area including the town of Lahar.

Maritime Southeast Asia continued…

A traditional fishing village on the eastern Malay peninsula. Between November and March, this palm-fringed coast is drenched by flooding rain, as monsoon winds carry in moisture-laden air from the South China Sea.

Brunei is a small country made rich by exports of oil and natural gas. Its territorial boundaries have shrunk since the Portuguese explorer, Ferdinand Magellan, anchored his ships off its coast in 1521. The arable land, less than 2 per cent, is farmed effectively to produce rice, fruit and vegetables. However, the country is unable to achieve self-sufficiency and imports about 80 per cent of its food. Lately, the government Forestry Department has been developing activities such as furniture production. Brunei is firmly controlled by the sultan. The people pay no personal income tax, food and housing are subsidised by the government, and medical care is free.

East Timor, mainly

Roman Catholic after 300 years of Portuguese rule, was forcibly incorporated into Indonesia in 1975. In August 1999, the people voted for independence, sparking violent clashes. In September 1999 a United Nations peacekeeping force entered East Timor. The territory will remain under United Nations protection until the people choose a form of government. This interim period is expected to last for 2 to 3 years.

Indonesia's main islands are mountainous and forested. Sumatra, Java and the Lesser Sunda Islands (Nusa Tenggara) form an arc containing 200 volcanoes, some of which are still active.

Traders brought Buddhism, Hinduism and Islam to Indonesia. Christianity arrived in the 1500s with Portuguese (Roman Catholic) and then Dutch (Protestant) colonists. Despite natural resources including oil, natural gas, timber, metals and coal, this heavily populated country is relatively poor. Most people live by growing staple crops: rice, maize, cassava and sweet potatoes. Plantations of rubber, palm oil, sugarcane, coffee and tea earn export income. Old agricultural methods and traditional customs exist side by side with modern practices and technology. Political unrest since 1998 has interrupted 30 years of industrial progress and had a negative effect on the country's world standing. Bali, a well-established tourist destination, and other islands attract visitors.

Malaysia has, at times, been Buddhist Sumatran and Hindu Javanese. The part of the country known as the Kingdom of Malacca once controlled local sea routes. In 1414 its ruler converted to Islam, and this remained the dominant religion. In 1511 the Portuguese made Malacca the base of their spice trade; the Dutch ousted them in 1641. The British captured Malacca in 1795 and it remained in British hands until independence was achieved in 1948. Some government policies favour the more numerous and poorer Malays over the Chinese and Indians. Rice, rubber and palm oil are staple crops. The peninsula's main industries are rubber and palm oil processing, light industry, electronics, tin mining and smelting, and logging and timber processing. The main activities in Sabah and Sarawak are logging, petroleum production and processing agricultural products. Malaysia's 'national car', the Proton, is now being exported.

The **Philippines** consists of the Luzon and Visayan groups of islands, and the Mindanao and Sulu Islands. The archipelago is generally mountainous with narrow coastal plains; isolated volcanoes occur in southeastern Luzon. Typhoons frequently strike the more northerly eastern coast and earthquakes are common. Mindanao was Muslim long before Ferdinand Magellan named the islands for Philip II of Spain. Nearly 400 years of Spanish colonisation established Roman Catholicism and left a Latin American flavour. The US presence after the Spanish-American War of 1898 introduced American influences. The Philippines is rich in mineral resources and refines and processes nickel, tin, copper, zinc and lead. The economy also depends on agriculture, light industry and tourism. Filipinos grow rice, much of it on irrigated hillside terraces, and maize as staple crops; coconuts, sugarcane, bananas and pineapples earn export income. There are at least 800 species of native orchid.

Colourful religious festivals are a feature of Balinese life. Here, bowls of food are laid out before the temple as part of the Galungan festival. The central dish of the festive meal is made from the meat of sacrificed pigs.

Singapore

Singapore is a low-lying, undulating island. A causeway across the Johore Strait links Singapore with mainland Malaysia. The scarce arable land, about 4 per cent of Singapore's total area, is some of the world's most productive cropland. Poultry production almost meets local demand but most other foodstuffs must be imported. Singapore was a trading centre until the Javanese destroyed it in the 1300s. In 1819, Sir Stamford Raffles began reviving the city as a free-trading port for the British East India Company. It became a strategic British base, attracted many Chinese immigrants, imported raw materials and became wealthy on the export of manufactured goods. Most Singaporeans are urban dwellers. Singapore achieved self-government in 1959. The government limits political debate and personal freedom—for example, chewing gum is forbidden, and vandalism is punished by caning

Borobudur, a mountain of Buddhist sculptures, was built in Java between AD 778 and 850. Soon afterwards it was buried beneath volcanic ash and vegetation and remained so until 1814. Restored in 1973, the site now attracts many tourists.

AUSTRALIA

Capital Canberra
Population 18,783,551
Official language English
Main religions Roman Catholic 27%, Anglican 22%, other Christian 22%
Currency Australian dollar
Form of government Federal constitutional monarchy
Record holder Australia is the world's smallest continental landmass; The Great Barrier Reef, off the northeast coast, stretches some 2,500 kilometres (1,550 miles) and is the world's biggest coral reef complex; The highest point is Mount Kosciuszko, 2,229 metres (7,313 feet); Fraser Island, Queensland, is the largest sand island in the world

PAPUA NEW GUINEA

Capital Port Moresby
Population 4,705,126
Official languages English, Pidgin, Motu
Main religions Protestant 44%, indigenous beliefs 34%, Roman Catholic 22%
Currency Kina
Form of government Constitutional monarchy
Record holder Papua New Guinea has more than 750 different languages, more than any other people in the world

The Tasmanian devil was once a common sight on mainland Australia. Unfortunately, it is now found only in certain parts of Tasmania.

Australia
& Papua New Guinea

Great southern land

The generally flat landscape of Australia reflects the continent's great age—it is a result of erosion that has taken place over thousands of millions of years. This is one of the most geologically stable regions on Earth. None of the plates that make up the Earth's crust come together in the Australian landmass, so mountain ranges are not forced up, nor are deep-seated earthquakes caused. By contrast the high, young landforms of the island of New Guinea result from the collision of two major plates. Australia was the last continent to be settled—the ancestors of the Australian Aborigines arrived here less than 70,000 years ago, and the first known European visitors (Dutch explorers) touched here briefly less than 500 years ago. The continent shares some of its unique plants and animals with Papua New Guinea, to which it was once joined by a land bridge.

Australia's western edge contains some of the most ancient rocks on the surface of the planet, including the mineral-rich Pilbara region (today ores from here are a major export earner). In northwestern and northern Australia, huge cattle holdings spread across the Kimberley and Arnhem Land. The arid centre alternates between time-worn ranges and stretching deserts. Further east, bores tapping into the enormous reserves of the Great Artesian Basin make sheep and cattle raising possible in the

The Devils Marbles in Australia's Northern Territory. Aboriginal legend tells us these huge boulders are the eggs laid by the Rainbow Serpent.

semi-arid lands of inland Queensland and northwestern New South Wales. The Eastern Highlands (commonly called the Great Dividing Range) run roughly parallel to the eastern coast from rainforest slopes in the north to the Southern Alps, snow-covered in winter.

The narrow eastern coastal plain has the heaviest rainfall, the most abundant vegetation and the densest human settlement. Tasmania has spectacular mountain wilderness areas, with more than 30 per cent of the island protected in World Heritage areas, national parks and reserves. Most Australian native animals are marsupials (animals that keep and feed their young in a pouch) and include kangaroos, koalas, wombats and possums. Australia is also home to two monotremes (egg-laying mammals)—the platypus and the echidna. Once heavily dependent on wool and wheat exports, Australia's economy has diversified with tourism, minerals and manufactured goods now major income earners.

Papua New Guinea

consists of the eastern half of the large island of New Guinea and also includes the island of Bougainville (currently working towards independence) as well as 600 or so smaller islands. The largely rural

Two great icons of Sydney, Australia— the Opera House and Harbour Bridge.

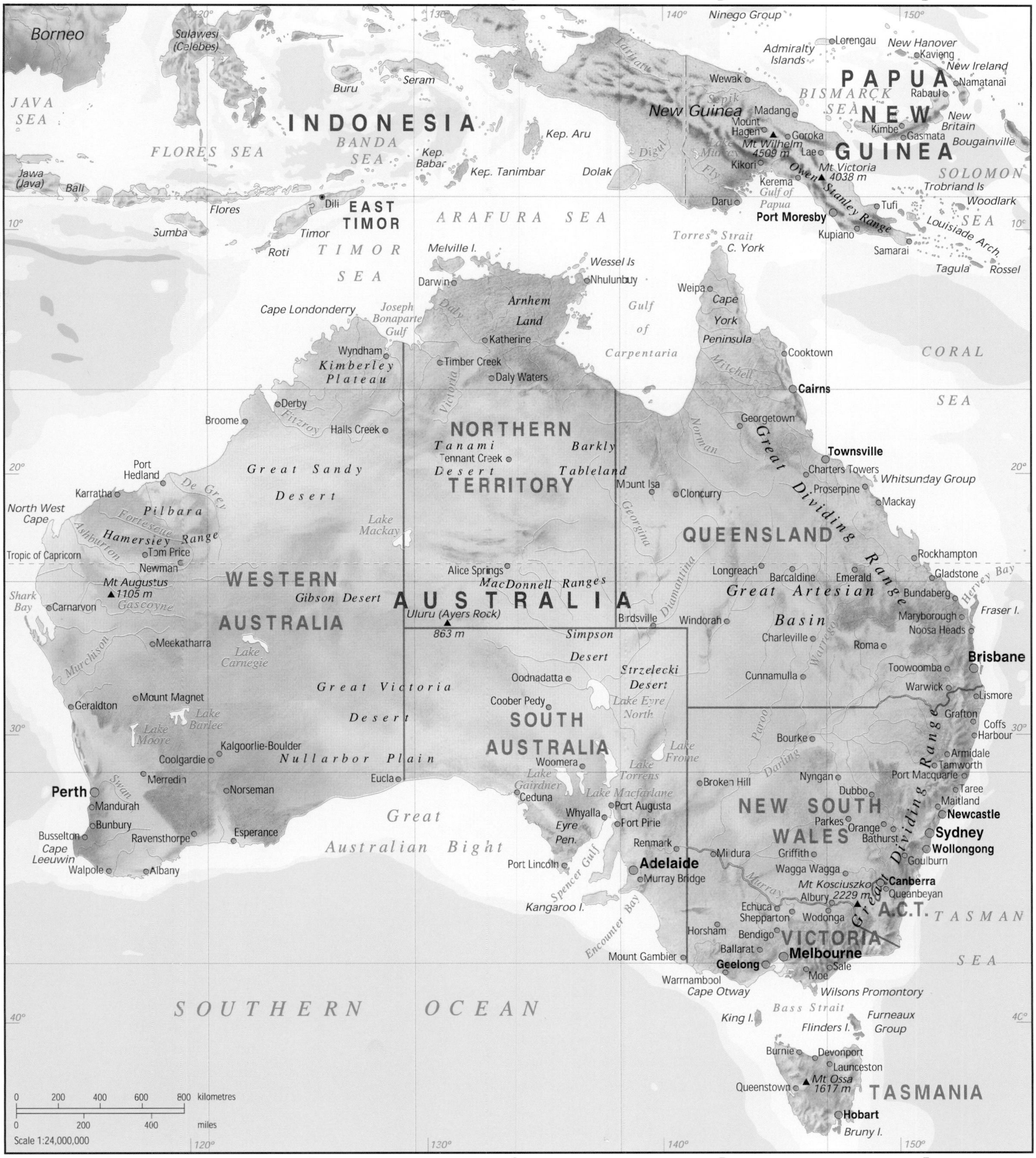
A
B
C
D
E
1
2
3
4
5
6
Borneo
Sulawesi (Celebes)
JAVA SEA
INDONESIA
Buru
Seram
BANDA SEA
FLORES SEA
Jawa (Java)
Bali
Flores
Sumba
Timor
Roti
Dili
EAST TIMOR
TIMOR SEA
Kep. Aru
Kep. Babar
Kep. Tanimbar
Dolak
ARAFURA SEA
Ninego Group
Admiralty Islands
Lorengau
New Hanover
Kavieng
New Ireland
Namatanai
Wewak
BISMARCK SEA
Rabaul
PAPUA NEW GUINEA
New Guinea
Madang
Mount Hagen
Goroka
Mt Wilhelm 4509 m
Lae
Kimbe
Gasmata
New Britain
Bougainville
Kikori
Mt Victoria 4038 m
Kerema
Gulf of Papua
Owen Stanley Range
SOLOMON SEA
Trobriand Is
Woodlark
Daru
Port Moresby
Tufi
Kupiano
Samarai
Louisiade Arch.
Tagula
Rossel
Torres Strait
C. York
Melville I.
Wessel Is
Nhulunbuy
Darwin
Arnhem Land
Weipa
Cape York Peninsula
Gulf of Carpentaria
Cape Londonderry
Joseph Bonaparte Gulf
Wyndham
Katherine
Kimberley Plateau
Timber Creek
Daly Waters
Cooktown
CORAL SEA
Cairns
Derby
Broome
Fitzroy
Halls Creek
NORTHERN TERRITORY
Tanami Desert
Tennant Creek
Barkly Tableland
Georgetown
Great Dividing Range
Townsville
Charters Towers
Whitsunday Group
Proserpine
Mackay
Port Hedland
Great Sandy Desert
De Grey
Mount Isa
Cloncurry
Karratha
North West Cape
Pilbara
Hamersley Range
Tom Price
Newman
Lake Mackay
Georgina
QUEENSLAND
Tropic of Capricorn
Rockhampton
Gladstone
Hervey Bay
Longreach
Barcaldine
Emerald
Alice Springs
MacDonnell Ranges
WESTERN AUSTRALIA
Mt Augustus 1105 m
Gascoyne
Shark Bay
Carnarvon
Gibson Desert
AUSTRALIA
Uluru (Ayers Rock) 863 m
Great Artesian Basin
Bundaberg
Fraser I.
Maryborough
Noosa Heads
Birdsville
Windorah
Charleville
Simpson Desert
Diamantina
Meekatharra
Lake Carnegie
Roma
Brisbane
Toowoomba
Strzelecki Desert
Oodnadatta
Cunnamulla
Warwick
Lismore
Murchison
Great Victoria Desert
Geraldton
Mount Magnet
Coober Pedy
Lake Eyre North
SOUTH AUSTRALIA
Grafton
Coffs Harbour
Lake Barlee
Lake Moore
Bourke
Kalgoorlie-Boulder
Coolgardie
Nullarbor Plain
Woomera
Lake Frome
Lake Torrens
Armidale
Tamworth
Port Macquarie
Perth
Merredin
Norseman
Eucla
Lake Gairdner
Broken Hill
Nyngan
Darling
Dubbo
Taree
Maitland
Newcastle
Mandurah
Swan
Ceduna
Lake Macfarlane
Port Augusta
Whyalla
Fort Pirie
Eyre Pen.
NEW SOUTH WALES
Parkes
Orange
Bathurst
Sydney
Wollongong
Bunbury
Great Australian Bight
Busselton
Cape Leeuwin
Ravensthorpe
Esperance
Renmark
Mildura
Griffith
Goulburn
Walpole
Albany
Port Lincoln
Adelaide
Murray Bridge
Wagga Wagga
Canberra
Queanbeyan
Mt Kosciuszko 2229 m
Albury
A.C.T.
Spencer Gulf
Kangaroo I.
Encounter Bay
Echuca
Shepparton
Wodonga
TASMAN SEA
Horsham
Bendigo
VICTORIA
Ballarat
Melbourne
Geelong
Mount Gambier
Sale
Moe
Warrnambool
Cape Otway
Wilsons Promontory
SOUTHERN OCEAN
Bass Strait
King I.
Flinders I.
Furneaux Group
Burnie
Devonport
Launceston
Mt Ossa 1617 m
Queenstown
TASMANIA
Hobart
Bruny I.
0 200 400 600 800 kilometres
0 200 400 miles
Scale 1:24,000,000
120°
130°
140°
150°
10°
20°
30°
40°

population of the 'mainland' is made up of hundreds of distinct tribal groups, broadly divided into the lowlanders of the coast and the highlanders of the mountainous and densely forested interior. Most of the population lives by farming. Exports of copper and gold are the main revenue earners; coffee, cocoa, coconuts, palm kernels, tea, rubber and timber are also important. Papua New Guinea became fully independent in 1975. The western half of the island of New Guinea, Irian Jaya (West Papua), is part of Indonesia.

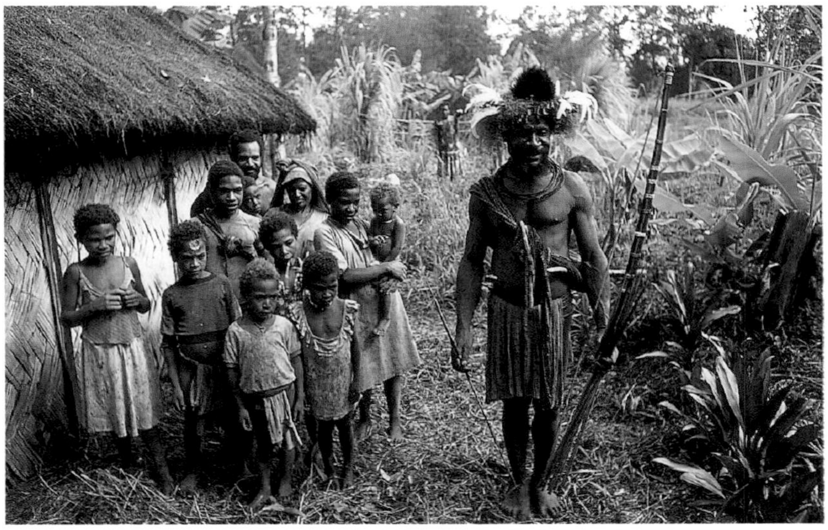

A Huli man from Papua New Guinea proudly displays his weapons and adornments—and his family.

NEW ZEALAND

Capital   Wellington
Population   3,662,265
Official language   English
Main religions   Anglican 18%,
Roman Catholic 13%, Presbyterian 13%,
other Christian 17%
Currency   New Zealand dollar
Form of government   Monarchy
Record holder   New Zealand is the
biggest of the island groups of Oceania;
Lake Taupo, New Zealand's largest natural
lake, occupies an ancient crater; Mount
Cook, at 3,764 metres (12,349 feet), is the
highest point in the country; the Waikato
River, 425 kilometres (264 miles), on the
North Island, is the longest river; New
Zealand is one of the world's main
exporters of wool, cheese, butter and meat;
There are 20 sheep for every New
Zealander; In 1893 New Zealand became
the first country in the world to give
women the vote

New Zealand

A young land

Geologically, New Zealand is a young country. It lies within the collision zone of two of the rigid plates that make up the surface of the planet. Movement of these plates thrust up the Southern Alps of the South Island around 5 million years ago and more recently, 1 to 4 million years ago, caused the volcanic activity that shaped much of the North Island, where the central plateau, covered with a layer of lava, has two active volcanoes, and geysers and hot mud springs. White Island, in the Bay of Plenty, is New Zealand's most active volcano.

The kiwi, one of the many flightless birds in the country, is an enduring symbol of New Zealand.

New Zealand ranges from subtropical in the northern part of the North Island to glaciers and snowy winters in the southern extremity. The islands were separated from other landmasses long before the appearance of mammals. When the Polynesian ancestors of the Maori, the first people to reach New Zealand, arrived around 1,000 years ago, flightless, slow-moving birds, such as the kiwi and now extinct moa (which grazed on grasslands), occupied the ecological niches normally taken by mammals. The Maori brought with them the dog and rat, the only mammals, apart from two species of bat, present at the time of European contact. All other mammals have been introduced over a period of little more than 200 years. New Zealand has no snakes, but has the tuatara, a prehistoric form of reptile. In 1642 Dutch explorer Abel Tasman was probably the first European to sight the islands; in 1769 British navigator James Cook was the first European to land and European settlement dates from the arrival of whalers and sealers in the 1790s.

Today, New Zealand exports meat and dairy products, wool, and fresh fruit, such as kiwifruit and apples. It has a burgeoning wine industry, and tourism is also important.

The North Island is home to about 75 per cent of New Zealand's people. The population today is made up of descendants of British settlers, Pacific Islanders and immigrants from Asia; and about 15 per cent of New Zealanders have Maori ancestry.

The South Island is dominated by the Southern Alps, a massive, ice-capped mountain range, with towering Mount Cook at its centre. Grain-growing is important on the Canterbury Plains in the northeast. Sheep-raising is the dominant industry in the southeast. In the far southwest, the rugged coastline, deeply indented with fiords, makes up Fiordland, the country's largest national park.

Offshore to the south is Stewart Island, where the population of about 500 live by fishing, and 800 kilometres (500 miles) to the east are the Chatham Islands, where the 750 or so people live mainly by sheep-farming and fishing.

The spectacular landscape of Fiordland, in New Zealand's South Island, and the country's alpine snowfields, such as Coronet Peak and the Remarkables, attract large numbers of tourists.

Fossilised gastropods and other marine life found at Hawkes Bay on the North Island.

TASMAN SEA

North Island

NEW ZEALAND

South Island

SOUTH PACIFIC

OCEAN

Cape Reinga
North Cape
Cape Maria van Diemen
Great Exhibition Bay
Doubtless Bay
Tauroa Peninsula
Kerikeri
Bay of Islands
Cape Brett
Kaikohe
Whakapara
Hokianga Harbour
Dargaville
Bream Bay
Wellsford
Great Barrier I. (Aotea I.)
Kaipara Harbour
Helensville
Hauraki Gulf
Mercury Bay
Waitakere
Howick
Auckland
Manukau
Tuakau
Rangiriri
Waihi
White Island
Cape Runaway
Ngaruawahia
Tauranga
East Cape
Hamilton
Bay of Plenty
Matata
Putaruru
Raukumara Range
Marau Point
Tirua Point
Te Kuiti
Rotorua
Mangakino
Murupara
Mahoenui
Taupo
Tuai
New Plymouth
Manunui
Putorino
Wairoa
Mt Egmont (Taranaki) 2518 m
Whangamomona
Mt Ruapehu 2797 m
Mahia Pen.
Opunake
Ohakune
Hawke Bay
Hawera
Taradale
Napier
Tainape
Hastings
Cape Kidnappers
Waitotara
Wanganui
Feilding
Hatuma
Cape Farewell
Palmerston North
Farewell Spit
Foxton
Cape Turnagain
Whanganui Inlet
Golden
Otaki
Tararua Ra.
Tasman Bay
Masterton
Motueka
Porirua
Karamea
Nelson
Lower Hutt
Upper Hutt
Richmond
Picton
Wellington
Karamea Bight
Richmond Ra.
Blenheim
Tuturumuri
Cape Foulwind
Saint Arnaud
Palliser Bay
Cape Palliser
Westport
Cape Campbell
Reefton
Seaward Kaikoura Ra.
Tapuae-o-Uenuku 2885 m
Springs Junction
Greymouth
Kaikoura
Hokitika
Rotomanu
Waiau
Hurunui
Motunau Beach
Pegasus Bay
Kaiapoi
Staveley
Christchurch
3764 m Mt Cook
Akaroa
Banks Peninsula
Cascade Point
Haast
Ashburton
Akaroa Harbour
Jackson Bay
Lake Tekapo
Canterbury Bight
Big Bay
Twizel
Temuka
Milford Sound
Mt Aspiring 3027 m
Timaru
Milford Sound
Wanaka
Waimate
Caswell Sound
Queenstown
Cromwell
Ranfurly
Oamaru
Secretary I.
Treble Cone 2324 m
Alexandra
Doubtful Sound
Te Anau
Cheerless Cove
Resolution I.
Lumsden
Dunedin
Dusky Sound
Winton
Balclutha
Clarksville
Colac Bay
Invercargill
Bluff
Ruapuke I.
Doughboy Bay
Halfmoon Bay
Stewart Island
South Cape

SOUTHERN ALPS

0   100   200 kilometres

0   100   miles

Scale 1:6,000,000

FIJI

Capital Suva
Population 812,918
Official language English
Main religions Christian 52%
(Methodists 37%, Roman Catholic 9%),
Hindu 38%,Muslim 8%
Currency Fiji dollar
Form of government Republic

KIRIBATI

Capital Bairiki
Population 85,501
Official language English
Main religions Roman Catholic 52%,
Protestant 41%
Currency Australian dollar
Form of government Republic

MARSHALL ISLANDS

Capital Dalap-Uliga-Darrit
Population 65,507
Official language English
Main religions Protestant 90%,
Roman Catholic 9%
Currency US dollar
Form of government Republic

MICRONESIA

Capital Palikir
Population 131,500
Official language English
Main religions Roman Catholic 50%,
Protestant 47%
Currency US dollar
Form of government Federal republic

NAURU

Capital None; government offices
in Yaren
Population 10,605
Official language Nauruan
Main religions Protestant 67%,
Roman Catholic 33%
Currency Australian dollar
Form of government Republic

PALAU

Capital Koror
Population 17,797
Official languages Palauan, English
Main religions Roman Catholic 40%,
indigenous Modekngei religion 27%,
Protestant 25%
Currency US dollar
Form of government Republic

SAMOA

Capital Apia
Population 229,979
Official languages Samoan, English
Main religion Christian 98%
Currency Tala
Form of government Constitutional
monarchy

Pacific Ocean

The vibrantly coloured soft coral gardens of Fiji are home to a great diversity of fish.

Oceania: rich pickings

Scattered across the vast waters of the Pacific, the world's largest ocean, are thousands of islands, collectively called Oceania. Most lie in the southern hemisphere and vary from mountainous peaks to low coral atolls vulnerable to rising sea levels. There are three main regions: Micronesia (meaning 'small islands'), to the east of the Philippines; Melanesia ('black islands', a reference to the skin colour of the people), to the east of Indonesia and Australia; and Polynesia ('many islands'), in the centre of the Pacific. By the end of the 1800s Britain, France, Spain, Germany and the United States had taken control of most of Oceania.

Fiji's main islands are of volcanic origin. When the British assumed control in the 1870s they imported labour from India to work on the sugar plantations. By the time of Fijian independence in 1970, people of Indian descent outnumbered ethnic Fijians (who are Melanesian); racial tension is a continuing source of instability. Sugar exports and tourism are major revenue earners.

Kiribati (pronounced 'Kiribass') consists of thirty-three coral atolls. It was the site of the first British nuclear tests in the Pacific in 1957. As its rich phosphate deposits were exhausted by

the 1970s, the main export revenues now come from copra, seaweed and fish.

The **Marshall Islands** includes Bikini and Enewetak atolls, where the United States carried out their nuclear bomb tests; cleanup work to remove residual radiation continues *[SEE GLOBAL NUCLEAR INDUSTRY]*. Tourism from Japan and the United States is the main source of revenue.

Micronesia's 607 islands, formerly known as the Caroline Islands, include Chuuk, a major Japanese base during World War II which now attracts tourists who scuba dive among the numerous wartime wrecks.

Nauru's rich phosphate deposits (the result of many centuries of seabird droppings) reward it with one of the highest per capita incomes in the region, although this situation will change when the phosphate runs out in 2006. More than ninety years of mining has left the island with a lunar-like landscape.

Palau was settled by Southeast Asian peoples from about 1000 BC. Natural resources include timber, gold and marine products. Tourism and the export of handicrafts are main revenue earners.

Samoa's larger islands are volcanic, densely forested and cut by fast-flowing streams; coral reefs lie offshore. Timber, fish and tropical fruits and vegetables are the main exports. Rank

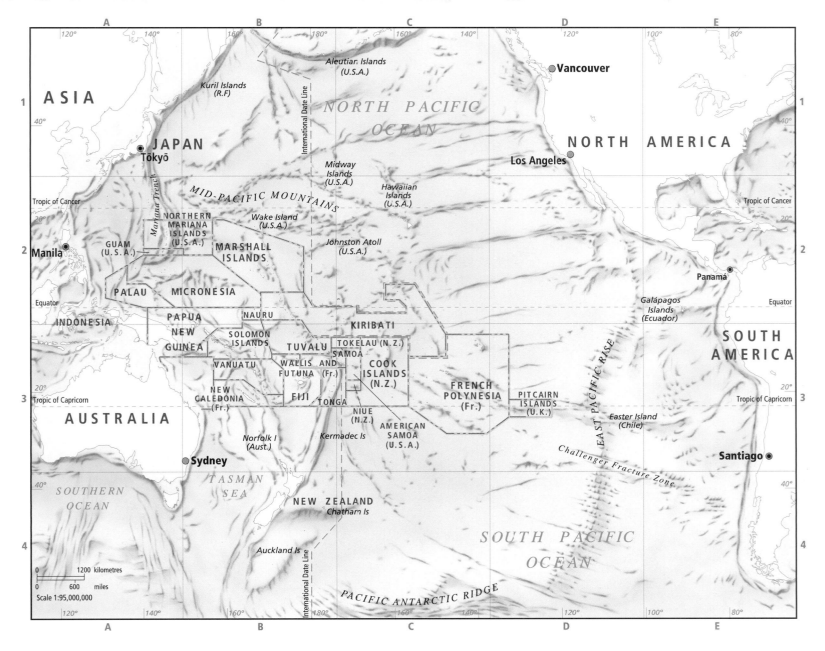

plays an important part in Samoan society with matai (men who head extended families) having much more power than commoners.

The **Solomon Islands** have been inhabited by Melanesian people for about 3,000 years. The chain was named in 1568 by Spanish navigator Alvaro de Mendana, who thought he had found 'the riches of Solomon'. During World War II, the islands were invaded by the Japanese and were the scene of several fierce battles between Japanese and United States forces. The six main islands of the group are mountainous, densely forested and of volcanic origin; most of the population lives by farming on the narrow coastal fringes.

This young girl from the Solomon Islands is paddling in a canoe made from a hollowed tree trunk.

SOLOMON ISLANDS

Capital Honiara
Population 455,429
Official language English
Main religions Protestant 77%, Roman Catholic 19%, indigenous beliefs 4%
Currency Solomon Islands dollar
Form of government Constitutional monarchy

TONGA

Capital Nuku'alofa
Population 109,082
Official languages Tongan, English
Main religions Protestant 60%, Roman Catholic 16%, Mormon 12%
Currency Pa'anga
Form of government Constitutional monarchy

TUVALU

Capital Funafuti
Population 10,588
Official languages Tuvaluan, English
Main religion Church of Tuvalu (Congregationalist) 97%
Currency Tuvaluan dollar, Australian dollar
Form of government Constitutional monarchy

VANUATU

Capital Port Vila
Population 189,036
Official languages English, French
Main religions Presbyterian 37%, Anglican 15%, Catholic 15%, indigenous beliefs 8%, Seventh-Day Adventist 6%, Church of Christ 4%
Currency Vatu
Form of government Republic

Record holder

- Covering some 170 million square kilometres (66 million square miles), the Pacific is the world's largest body of water
- The Mariana Trench, near Guam, includes the Challenger Deep, which at 11,033 metres (3,798 feet) is the deepest point in the world's oceans
- Nauru is the world's smallest republic
- Niue is one of the world's largest coral atolls
- There are three great phosphate islands in the Pacific—Banaba (in Kiribati), Makatea (French Polynesia) and Nauru
- The islands of French Polynesia are scattered over an area as large as Europe
- Pitcairn Island is the United Kingdom's most isolated dependency
- New Caledonia is France's largest overseas territory
- Mount Tabwemasana in Vanuatu, at 1,879 metres (6,158 feet), is the highest point of the Pacific Islands
- Tuvalu is the lowest-lying Pacific country, with no part of it more than 5 metres (15 feet) above sea level
- The inhabitants of Norfolk Island speak a mixture of 1800s English, Gaelic and Old Tahitian
- Vanuatu, with 105 distinct languages, has the world's highest per capita density of language forms

Pacific Ocean continued...

Tonga—named the 'Friendly Isles' by British navigator James Cook—was never fully colonised, and its people see themselves and their royal family as unique in the Pacific. Most Tongans live by farming. Coconuts, bananas and vanilla beans are the main exports.

Tuvalu, formerly known as the Ellice Islands, was populated by Polynesian peoples from Samoa and Tonga in the 1300s. In the 1800s many islanders, through either trickery or abduction, were shipped to Fiji and Australia to work on sugar plantations. Known as 'blackbirding', this labour trade abuse also took place in Vanuatu.

Vanuatu is populated almost entirely by ethnic Melanesians who live mainly by farming. Copra and tourism are the main revenue earners. Formerly known as the New Hebrides, Vanuatu was jointly administered by France and Britain from 1887 until independence in 1980.

Dependencies and territories in the South Pacific include **Ashmore and Cartier Islands, Coral Sea Islands** and **Norfolk Island,** which are external territories of Australia; and the **Cook Islands, Niue** and **Tokelau,** which are territories of New Zealand. **French Polynesia,** which includes Tahiti in the Society Islands and the nuclear test site of Mururoa, **New Caledonia** and the **Wallis and Futuna Islands** are all overseas territories of France. **Pitcairn Islands,** used as a refuge by the mutineers from HMS *Bounty*, is a dependent territory of the United Kingdom.

Islands off the coast of the Americas include **Easter Island,** known for the more than 600 huge, carved stone statues (called moai), which is governed by Chile. The **Galapagos Islands** belong to Ecuador and are named for their giant tortoises (*galápagos* is the Spanish word for 'tortoise'). In the northern Pacific, the **Hawaiian Islands** are a state of the United States, **American Samoa** and **Northern Mariana Islands** are both territories of the United States and **Guam, Midway Island, Wake Island** and several smaller coral islets and atolls are all unincorporated territories of the United States.

This Samoan dancer performs with knives and fire—an exciting but dangerous combination.

The wreck of this Japanese tank from World War II is in waters off the island of Chuuk in Micronesia.

An aerial view of some of the islands of Palau.

Polar regions

Polar extremes

The polar regions lie between 66° latitude and the North and South Poles. Permanently covered in ice and snow, they are the coldest and windiest places on the planet. During the winter months there is little or no sunlight. In the south is the continent of Antarctica, separated from all other major landmasses by the wild and stormy waters of the Southern Ocean, the only continuous water body to circle the Earth. It was one of the last regions on Earth to be explored. In the north is the Arctic Ocean, a huge region of frozen sea surrounded by the northern fringes of the Eurasian and North American landmasses.

The **Arctic**, in contrast to uninhabited Antarctica, has been home for thousands of years to indigenous groups such as the Inuit in Canada, the Saami in Scandinavia and the Nanets and Yakuts of Russia. All move with the seasons and, apart from the Saami who herd reindeer, traditionally lived by hunting. Coastal waters yield such fish as cod, trout and salmon, which are an integral part of the diet of the people living in the Arctic. In the summer there are many species of whales and fish in the sea, seals on the ice floes and foxes, wolves, bears, caribou and reindeer on land. Many birds also migrate north in the warmer months, including the puffin, petrel, eider duck and species of gulls.

The Arctic is rich in mineral resources, including natural gas and oil, coal, tin, zinc and iron ore.

A lone polar bear in Arctic Siberia.

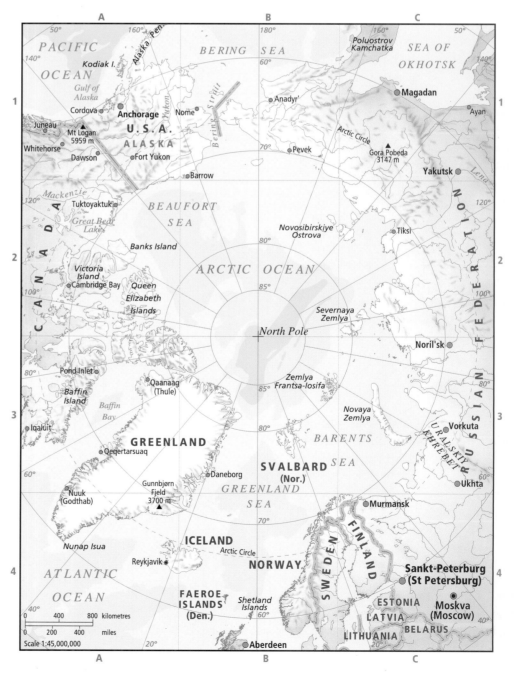

Fishing through the ice is a popular pastime in Arctic regions, such as Siberia.

Orcas, or killer whales, swim in Antarctic waters where there are rich sources of food. Here they are inspecting their prey. Orcas hunt in packs and eat seals, penguins, fish and other whales.

Antarctica

Antarctica is the world's fifth largest continent and consists of a vast foundation of rock, covered by a massive ice cap. The first humans to winter on the continent were members of Norwegian explorer Carsten Borchgrevink's expedition in 1899. In December 1911 fellow Norwegian Roald Amundsen's party became the first to reach the South Pole. The British team, led by Robert Falcon Scott, reached the Pole a month later, in January 1912, but died tragically as they tried to return—exhausted, frozen and out of food. No nation owns Antarctica, but scientists from many nations are based there, conducting oceanographic, geological, glaciological and biological research programs. Animal life in Antarctica depends on the tiny phytoplankton and shrimp-like krill, which form part of an elaborate food chain that includes crustaceans, molluscs, fish, whales, dolphins and seals. There are 43 species of bird, the best known being the penguin. The Emperor penguin is the only warm-blooded animal to remain on the continent during the bitter winter months. Plant life on the continent consists almost entirely of mosses, lichens and algae.

Several island dependencies lie north of Antarctica. **Bouvet Island** and **Peter I Island** are dependent territories of Norway. Both are cold, windy, largely covered with snow and ice and uninhabited except for occasional visiting meteorologists. **French Southern and Antarctic Lands** are an overseas territory of France in the southern Indian Ocean. They are wet and stormy, with snowfields in the centre and in summer breeding colonies of penguins and seals. **Heard and MacDonald Islands,** external territories of Australia, are classed as subantarctic islands. They have ice caps, glaciers and furious gales; seals and penguins breed ashore in summer.

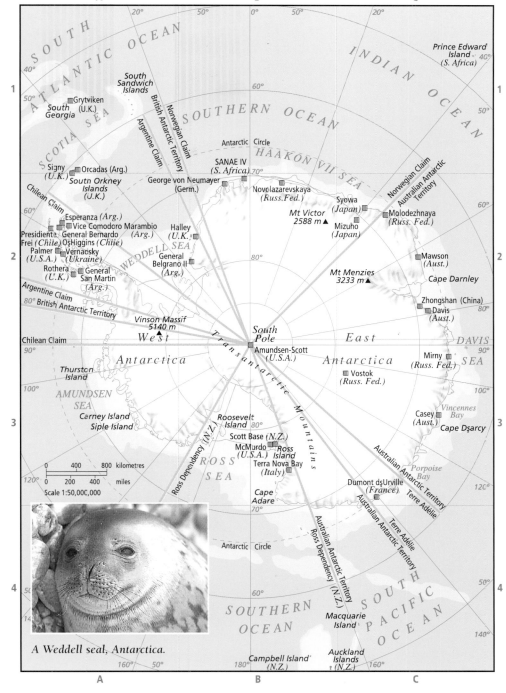

A Weddell seal, Antarctica.

Adélie penguins skilfully negotiate the ice at Cape Bird, Antarctica.

Gazetteer

- In the code given to locate a place, the number in **bold** type refers to the page on which the map is to be found, and the letter-number combination refers to the grid square.
- Where a name appears on more than one map, the gazetteer generally lists the map that accompanies the relevant text.
- Names that have a symbol (town or mountain peak) are given an area reference according to the location of the symbol. Names without a symbol are entered in the gazetteer according to the first letter of the name.
- Words in *italic* type describe features in the gazetteer, for example, *island, point* and *mountain peak*.
- All entries include the country or area in which the name is located. In the United States and Canada, the state or province name is also given.

A Coruña, Spain, **115** A1
A.C.T., *state,* Australia, **115** E5
A Fonsagrada, Spain, **115** B1
Aachen, Germany, **111** B3
Aalen, Germany, **111** C4
Aba, Nigeria, **141** D4
Abaco, *island,* Bahamas **93** B1
Abadla, Algeria **141** C2
Abakan, Russian Federation **153** C3
Abalessa, Algeria **141** D4
Abancay, Peru, **101** B4
Abbeville, France **113** C1
Abd al Kūrī, *island,* Yemen **147** E2
Abéché, Chad, **145** C2
Abeokuta, Nigeria, **141** D4
Aberdeen, Scotland, **109** D3
Abergavenny, Wales, **109** D6
Aberystwyth, Wales, **109** C6
Abhā, Saudi Arabia, **133** B5
Abidjan, Côte d'Ivoire, **141** B4
Abilene, *Texas*, U.S.A. **85** B6
Ābīy Ādī, Ethiopia, **147** C2
Abrī, Sudan, **147** B1
Abū Ḩamad, Sudan, **147** B1
Abū Kamāl, Syria, **133** B2
Abū Zaby (Abu Dhabi), United Arab Emirates, **133** D4
Abū Zanīmah, Egypt, **137** E3
Abuja, Nigeria, **141** D4
Aburo, *mountain,* Democratic Republic of the Congo, **145** E4
Acaponeta, Mexico, **89** B3
Acapulco, Mexico, **89** C4
Accra, Ghana, **141** C4
Acklins Island, Bahamas, **93** B2
Acqui Terme, Italy, **117** B2
Ad Dakhla, Western Sahara/Morocco, **141** A3
Ad Damazīn, Sudan, **147** C2
Ad Dāmir, Sudan,**147** C1
Ad Dammām, Saudi Arabia, **133** C4
Ad Dawḩah (Doha), Qatar, **133** D4
Ad Dilam, Saudi Arabia, **133** C4
Ad Dīwānīyah, Iraq, **133** C3
Adıyaman, Turkey, **129** C4
Ada, *Oklahoma*, U.S.A., **85** C5
'Adan (Aden), Yemen, **133** B6
Adana, Turkey, **129** C4
Adapazarı, Turkey, **129** B3
Adaut, Indonesia, **171** H7
Adelaide, Australia, **175** D5
Ādī Ugrī, Eritrea, **147** C2
Ādīs Ābeba (Addis Ababa), Ethiopia, **147** C3
Admiralty Islands, Papua New Guinea, **175** D1
Ādoni, India, **157** C5
Adra, Spain, **115** C4
Adrar, Algeria, **141** C3
Adrar Tamgak, *mountain,* Niger, **141** D2
Adzopé, Côte d'Ivoire, **141** B4
Afghanistan, *country,* **155** B5
Aflou, Algeria, **141** D1
Afognak Island, *Alaska,* U.S.A., **79** B2
Afyon, Turkey, **129** B4
Agadez, Niger, **141** D2
Agadir, Morocco, **141** B2
Agen, France, **113** B4
Agnone, Italy, **117** D4
Āgra, India, **157** C3
Agri, *river,* Italy, **117** D4
Ağri Daği (Mt Ararat), *mountain,* Armenia, **129** D3
Agrigento, Italy, **117** C6
Agrinio, Greece, **125** C5
Ağsu, Azerbaijan, **129** E3
Aguascalientes, Mexico, **89** C3
Aguilar, Spain, **115** B4
Aguilar de Campóo, Spain **115** B1
Águilas, Spain, **115** C
Ahmadābād, India, **157** B3
Ahmadnagar, India, **157** B4
Ahmovaara, Finland, **107** E4
Ahvāz, Iran, **133** C3
Ahvenanmaa (Åland), *island,* Finland, **107** C4
Aigio, Greece, **125** C5
'Aïn el Hadjel, Algeria, **141** D1
Ainaži, Latvia, **121** B2
Airbangis, Indonesia, **170** B5
Aix-en-Provence, France, **113** D4
Āīzawl, India, **157** E3
Ajaccio, France, **113** E5
Ajdābiyā, Libya, **137** C2
Ajmer, India, **157** B3
Ajo, *Arizona*, U.S.A., **83** C6
Āk'ak'ī Besek'a, Ethiopia, **147** C3
Akşehir, Turkey, **129** B4
Akaroa, New Zealand, **177**, C5
Akaroa Harbour, *gulf,* New Zealand, **177** C5
Akbou, Algeria, **141** D1
Akçakale, Turkey, **129** D4
Aketi, Democratic Republic of the Congo, **145** D4
Akhalts'ikhe, Georgia, **129**, D3
Akhisar, Turkey, **129** B4
Akimiski Island, *Ontario*, Canada, **81** B2
Akita, Japan, **165** D2
Akjoujt, Mauritania, **141** A2
Aklavik, *Northwest Territories*, Canada, **79** D2
Akra Tainaro, *point*, Greece, **125** C6
Akron, *Ohio*, U.S.A., **87** C3
Aksaray, Turkey, **129** C4
Aksu, China, **161** A3
Akure, Nigeria, **141** D4
Akureyri, Iceland, **107** A1
Al 'Amārah, Iraq, **133** C3
Al Baḩr al Abyaḑ (White Nile), *river*, Sudan, **147**, B2
Al Başrah (Basra), Iraq, **133** C3
Al Bayḑā', Yemen, **133** B6
Al Bayḑā', Libya, **137** C2
Al Fāshir, Sudan, **147** A2
Al Fayyūm, Egypt, **137** D2
Al Ghurdaqah, Egypt, **137** E3
Al Ḩammām, Egypt, **137** D2
Al Ḩijāz, *desert,* Saudi Arabia, **133** A3
Al Ḩillah, Iraq, **133** B2
Al Ḩudaydah, Yemen, **133**, B6
Al Hufūf, Saudi Arabia, **133** , C4
Al Iskandarīya (Alexandria), Egypt, **137** D2
Al Jīzah, Egypt, **137** D2
Al Jahrā', Kuwait, **133** C3
Al Jawf, Saudi Arabia, **133**, B3
Al Kūt, Iraq, **133** C2
Al Kharţūm (Khartoum), Sudan, **147** B2
Al Kharţūm Baḩr (Khartoum North), Sudan, **147** B2
Al Kharfah, Saudi Arabia, **133** C5
Al Khufrah, Libya, **137** C3
Al Khums, Libya, **137** B2
Al Kuwayt (Kuwait), Kuwait, **133** C3
Al Lādhiqīyah (Latakia), Syria, **133** A2
Al Madīnah (Medina), Saudi Arabia, **133** B4
Al Manāmah, Bahrain, **133**, C4
Al Marj, Libya, **137** C2
Al Mawşil (Mosul), Iraq, **133** B2
Al Metlaoui, Tunisia, **141** E1
Al Minyā, Egypt, **137** D3
Andes, *mountain range*, Peru, **101** B3
Andes, *mountain range*, Chile, **103** B4
Andijon, Uzbekistan, **155** D3
Andkhvoy, Afghanistan, **155** C4
Andong, South Korea, **165** B3
Andorra, *country,* **113** B5
Andorra la Vella, Andorra, **113** C5
Andover, England, **109** D6
Andrews, *Texas*, U.S.A., **85**, B6
Andria, Italy, **117** D4
Andros, *island*, Greece, **129** A4
Andros Island, Bahamas, **93** B1
Angara, *river*, Russian Federation, **161** C1
Ängelholm, Sweden, **107** B6
Angers, France, **113** B3
Angoche, Mozambique, **149**, E3
Angol, Chile, **103** B4
Angola, *country,* **149** B2
Angoulême, France, **113** B3
Anguilla, U.K. Dependency, **93** E3
Anju, North Korea, **165** B2
Ankara, Turkey, **129** B3
Anklam, Germany, **111** E2
Annaba, Algeria, **141** E1
Annan, Scotland, **109** C4
Annecy, France, **113** D3
Ansbach, Germany, **111** D4
Anshan, China, **161** E3
Antakya (Antioch), Turkey, **129** C4
Antalya, Turkey, **129** B4
Antalya Körfezi, *gulf,* Turkey, **129** B4
Antequera, Spain, **115** B4
Anti Atlas, *mountain*, Morocco, **141** B2
Antigo, *Wisconsin*, U.S.A., **85** E2
Antigua and Barbuda, *country,* **93** E3
Antofagasta, Chile, **103** B2
Antwerpen (Antwerp), Belgium, **111** B3
Anyang, China, **161** D3
Anzio, Italy, **117** C4
Aomori, Japan, **165** D2
Aosta, Italy, **117** A2
Aoulef, Algeria, **141** D3
Aozou, Chad, **145** C1
Apalachee Bay, *gulf,* U.S.A., **87** B6
Apata, New Zealand, **177** D3
Apolo, Bolivia, **101** C4
Appalachian Mountains, *mountain range, Pennsylvania*, U.S.A., **87** D3
Appennino, *mountain*, Italy, **117** B3
Appleton, *Wisconsin*, U.S.A., **85** E3
Aqtaū (Aktau), Kazakhstan, **155** A3
Aqtöbe (Aktyubinsk), Russian Federation, **155** B2
Aqtoghay, Kazakhstan, **155**, D1
Ar Rıyāḑ (Riyadh), Saudi Arabia, **133** C4
Ar Ramādī, Iraq, **133** B2
Ar Raqqah, Syria, **133** B2
Ar Ruţbah, Iraq, **133** B2
Ar Rub' al Khālī, *desert*, Saudi Arabia, **133** C5
Arāk Iran, **133** C2
Aracaju, Brazil, **97** E3
Aracati, Brazil, **97** E2
Araçatuba, Brazil, **97** C4
Arad, Romania, **129** A2
Aragats Lerr, *mountain*, Armenia, **133** C1
Araguacema, Brazil, **97** D2
Araguaia, *river*, Brazil, **97** C3
Araguari, Brazil, **97** D4
Araguatins, Brazil, **97** D2
Arak, Algeria, **141** D3
Arakan Yoma, *mountain*, Myanmar (Burma), **167** A3
Aral'sk, Kazakhstan, **155** B2
Aranda de Duero, Spain, **115** C2
Aranos, Namibia, **149** B4
Aranyaprathet, Thailand, **167** C4
Araouane, Mali, **141** C2
Arapiraca, Brazil, **97** E3
Arapkir, Turkey, **129** C4
'Ar'ar, Saudi Arabia, **133** B3
Arbīl, Iraq, **133** C2
Arcadia, *Florida*, U.S.A., **87**, C7
Archipiélago de la Reina Adelaida, *island,* Chile, **103** A7
Archipiélago de los Chonos, *island*, Chile, **103** A5
Ardabīl, Iran, **133** C1
Ardakān, Iran, **133** D3
Åre, Sweden, **107** B3
Arendal, Norway, **107** A5
Arequipa, Peru, **101** C4
Arezzo, Italy, **117** C3
Argentina, *country,* **103** B4
Argos, Greece, **125** C5
Århus, Denmark, **107** B6
Arica, Colombia, **97** B4
Arica, Chile, **103** B1
Aripuanã, *river,* Brazil, **99**, B2
Arisaig, Scotland, **109** C3
Arizona, *state,* U.S.A., **83** C6
Arkadelphia, *Arkansas*, U.S.A., **85** D5
Arkansas, *river, Colorado*, U.S.A., **83** E4
Arkansas, *river, Kansas*, U.S.A., **85** B4
Arkansas, *state*, U.S.A., **85** D5
Arkansas City, *Kansas,* U.S.A., **85** C4
Arklow, Ireland, **109** B5
Arlan, *mountain,* Turkmenistan, **133** D1
Arles, France, **113** D4
Arlon, Belgium, **111** B4
Armenia, Colombia, **97** A3
Armenia, *country,* **129** D3
Armidale, Australia, **175** E4
Arnhem, Netherlands, **111** B2
Arqalyq, Kazakhstan, **155** C2
Arquipélago dos Bijagós, *island,* Guinea-Bissau, **141**, A3
Arrecife, Islas Canarias/Spain, **141** A2
Arta, Greece, **125** C4
Artesia, *New Mexico,* U.S.A., **83** E6
Artvin, Turkey, **129** D3
Arua, Uganda, **147** B3
Aruba, Netherlands Autonomous Region, **93** C4
Arusha, Tanzania, **147** C4
Arvayheer, Mongolia, **161** C2
Arviat, *Nunavut*, Canada, **79** F4
Arvidsjaur, Sweden, **107** C3
Arvika, Sweden, **107** B5
As Samāwah, Iraq, **133** C3
As Sidrah, Libya, **137** B2
As Sulaymānīyah, Iraq, **133**, C2
As Suways (Suez), Egypt, **137** E2
Asahi-dake, *mountain,* Japan, **165** E1
Asahikawa, Japan, **165** E1
Āsbe Teferī, Ethiopia, **147** D3
Ascension Island, St Helena Dependency, **105** C3
Åsele, Sweden, **107** C3
Åsen, Sweden, **107** B4
Ash Shiḩr, Yemen, **133** C6
Ash Shu'bah, Saudi Arabia, **133** B3
Ashburton, *river,* Australia, **175** A3
Ashburton, New Zealand, **177** C5
Asheville, *North Carolina*, U.S.A., **87** C5
Ashford, England, **109** E6
Ashgabat, Turkmenistan, **155** B4
Ashizuri-misaki, *point,* Japan, **165** C4
Ashland, *Wisconsin*, U.S.A., **85** D2
Asipovichy, Belarus, **121** D4
Aşkale, Turkey, **129** D3
Asmara, Eritrea, **147** C2
Aspen, *Colorado*, U.S.A., **83** D4
Assab, Eritrea, **147** D2
Assamakka, Niger, **141** D2
Assen, Netherlands, **111** B2
Assumption Island, Seychelles, **147** D5
Astana (Aqmola), Kazakhstan, **155** D2
Asti, Italy, **117** B2
Astorga, Spain, **115** B1
Astove Island, Seychelles, **147** E5
Asunción, Paraguay, **103** D2
Aswān, Egypt, **137** E4
Asyūţ, Egypt, **137** D3
Aţ Ţā'if, Saudi Arabia, **133** B5
At Taysīyah, *desert,* Saudi Arabia, **133** B3
Atakpamé, Togo, **141** C4
Atambua, Indonesia, **171** G7
Atâr, Mauritania, **141** A2
Atasu, Kazakhstan, **155** D2
'Aţbara, Sudan, **147** C1
'Aţbara, *river,* Sudan, **147** C1
Atbasar, Kazakhstan, **155** C1
Athina (Athens), Greece, **125** D5
Athlone, Ireland, **109** B5
Ati, Chad, **145** C2
Atkri, Indonesia, **171** H5
Atlanta, *Georgia*, U.S.A., **87** B5
Atlas Saharien, *mountain,* Algeria, **141** C2
Attapu, Laos, **167** D4
Attawapiskat, *Ontario,* Canada, **81** B2
Atyraū, Kazakhstan, **155** A2
Aubusson, France, **113** C3
Auch, France, **113** B4
Auckland, New Zealand, **177** D2
Auckland Islands, New Zealand, **183** B4
Aue, Germany, **111** D3
Augsburg, Germany, **111** D5
Augusta, *Georgia*, U.S.A., **87** C5
Augusta, *Maine*, U.S.A., **87** E2
Aurangābād, India, **157** B4
Aurillac, France, **113** C4
Aurora, *Colorado*, U.S.A., **83** E4
Ausert, Western Sahara/Morocco, **141** A4
Austin, *Minnesota*, U.S.A., **85** D3
Austin, *Nevada,* U.S.A., **83** B4
Austin, *Texas*, U.S.A., **85** C6
Australia, *country,* **175** C4
Austria, *country,* **117** C1
Autun, France, **113** C3
Auxerre, France, **113** C2
Aveiro, Portugal, **115** A2
Avesta, Sweden, **107** C5
Aviemore, Scotland, **109** C3
Avigliano, Italy, **117** D4
Avignon, France, **113** D4
Ávila, Spain, **115** B2
Avilés, Spain, **115** B1
Āwash, Ethiopia, **147** D3
Awbārī, Libya, **137** A3
Awka, Nigeria, **141** D4
Axel Heiberg Island, *Nunavut,* Canada, **79** F1
Ayacucho, Peru, **101** B3
Ayagūz, Kazakhstan, **155** E2
Ayamonte, Spain, **115** A4
Ayan, Russian Federation, **153** E3
Ayaviri, Peru, **101** C4
Aydın, Turkey, **129** B4
Aylesbury, England, **109** D6
'Ayoûn el 'Atroûs, Mauritania, **141** B2
Ayr, Scotland, **109** C4
Ayteke Bi, Kazakhstan, **155** B2
Aẓ Ẓahrān (Dhahran), Saudi Arabia, **133** C4
Az Żaqāzīq, Egypt, **137** D2
Azerbaijan, *country,* **129** E3
Azores, *island,* Portugal, **105** B2
Azrou, Morocco, **141** C2
Azuaga, Spain, **115** B3

Ba, *river,* Vietnam, **167** E5
Baardheere, Somalia, **147** D3
Bab el Mandeb, *gulf,* Yemen, **147** D2
Babruysk, Belarus, **121** D4
Babuyan Island, Philippines, **171** F1
Bắc Ninh, Vietnam, **167** D3
Bacabal, Brazil, **97** D2
Bacarra, Philippines, **171** F1
Back, *river, Nunavut,* Canada, **79** F3
Bacolod, Philippines, **171** F3
Bad Kreuznach, Germany, **111** C4
Bad Mergentheim, Germany, **111** C4
Bad Neustadt an der Saale, Germany, **111** D4
Badajoz, Spain, **115** B3
Badalona, Spain, **115** D2
Bādıyat ash Shām (Syrian Desert), Jordan, **133** B2
Baena, Spain, **115** B4
Bafatá, Guinea-Bissau, **141**, A3
Baffin Bay, *gulf,* Canada, **79** G2
Baffin Island, Canada, **79** G2
Bafia, Cameroon, **145** A4
Bafra, Turkey, **129** C3
Bafwasende, Democratic Republic of the Congo, **145** D5
Bagamoyo, Tanzania, **147** C5
Baganga, Philippines, **171** G3
Bagé, Brazil, **97** C5
Baghdād, Iraq, **133** C2
Baghlān, Afghanistan, **155**, C4
Bago, Philippines, **171** F3
Bagrationovsk, Russian Federation, **121** A4
Bagua Grande, Peru, **101** A2
Baguio, Philippines, **171** F1
Bahāwalpur, Pakistan, **157**, B2
Bahamas, *country,* **93** B1
Baharampur, India, **157** D3
Bahía Blanca, Argentina, **103** C4
Bahia de Campeche, *gulf,* Mexico, **89** D3
Bahía Grande, *gulf,* South America, **103** B6
Bahía Salada, *gulf,* Chile, **103** A2
Bahía San Sebastián, *gulf,* Argentina, **103** C7
Bahir Dar, Ethiopia, **147** C2
Baḩr al Ghazāl, *river*, Sudan, **145** E3
Baia Mare, Romania, **129** A2
Baie-Comeau, *Québec,* Canada, **81** C3
Baja, Hungary, **123** D5
Baja California, *point,* Mexico, **89** A1
Bajovo Polje, Yugoslavia, **125** B3
Bakı (Baku), Azerbaijan, **129** E3
Baker City, *Oregon*, U.S.A., **83** B2
Baker Lake, *Nunavut*, Canada, **79** F3
Bakersfield, *California*, U.S.A., **83** B5
Balabac, Philippines, **170** E3
Balabac Island, Philippines, **170** E3
Balāngīr, India, **157** D4
Balaton, *lake*, Hungary, **117** E2
Balatonszentgyörgy, Hungary, **123** D5
Balclutha, New Zealand, **177** B6
Baldy Pk, *mountain, Arizona*, U.S.A., **83** D6
Bāleshwar, India, **157** D4
Bali, *island,* Indonesia, **170** E7
Balıkesir, Turkey, **129** B4
Balikpapan, Indonesia, **170**, E5
Balimbing, Indonesia, **170**, C6
Balingen, Germany, **111** C5
Ballaghaderreen, Ireland, **109** B5
Ballantrae, Scotland, **109** C4
Ballarat, Australia, **175** D5
Ballater, Scotland, **109** D3
Ballinasloe, Ireland, **109** B5
Ballymena, Northern Ireland, **109** B4
Ballyshannon, Ireland, **109**, B4
Balqash, Kazakhstan, **155**, D2
Balqash Köli, *lake*, Kazakhstan, **155** D2
Balsas, *river*, Mexico, **89** C4
Balsas, Brazil, **97** D2
Bălţi, Moldova, **129** B2
Baltimore, *Maryland*, U.S.A., **87** D4
Baltiysk, Russian Federation, **121** A3
Bālurghāt, India, **157** D3
Balvi, Latvia, **121** C2
Bam, Iran, **133** E3
Bamako, Mali, **141** B3
Bambari, Central African Republic, **145** C4
Bamberg, Germany, **111** D4
Bamenda, Cameroon, **145** A4
Ban Na San, Thailand, **167** B6
Banbury, England, **109** D6
Bandırma, Turkey, **129** B3
Banda Aceh, Indonesia, **170** A4
Bandar Seri Begawan, Brunei, **170** E4
Bandarbeyla, Somalia, **147**, E2
Bandar-e 'Abbās, Iran, **133**, D4
Bandar-e Lengeh, Iran, **133**, D4
Bandon, Ireland, **109** A6
Bandundu, Democratic Republic of the Congo, **145** C5
Bandung, Indonesia, **170** C6
Banff, *Alberta*, Canada, **79** D5
Banff, Scotland, **109** D2
Bangalore, India, **157** C5
Bangassou, Central African Republic, **145** D4
Banghāzī, Libya, **137** C2
Banghiang, *river*, Laos, **167**, D4
Bangladesh, *country,* **157** D3
Bangor, *Maine*, U.S.A., **87**, E2
Bangor, Northern Ireland, **109** C4
Bangor, Wales, **109** C5
Bangui, Central African Republic, **145** C4
Banī Mazār, Egypt, **137** D3
Banī Suwayf, Egypt, **137** D3
Banī Walīd, Libya, **137** B2
Banja Luka, Bosnia and Herzegovina, **125** B2
Banjarmasin, Indonesia, **170** E6
Banjul, Gambia, **141** A3
Banks Island, *Northwest Territories*, Canada, **79** E2
Banks Peninsula, *point*, New Zealand, **177** C5
Banksá Bystrica, Slovakia, **123** D4
Bānkura, India, **157** D3
Bantè, Benin, **141** C4
Bantry, Ireland, **109** A6
Banyo, Cameroon, **145** B4
Banzart, Tunisia, **141** E1
Bảo Lộc, Vietnam, **167** E5
Baoding, China, **161** D3
Baoji, China, **161** C3
Baoshan, China, **161** C4
Baotou, China, **161** D3
Başqūbah, Iraq, **133** C2
Bar, Yugoslavia, **125** B3
Baraawe, Somalia, **147** D4
Barahona, Dominican Republic, **93** C3
Barakaldo, Spain, **115** C1
Baramanni, Guyana, **97** D2
Baranavichy, Belarus, **121**, C4
Barbacena, Brazil, **97** D4
Barbados, *country,* **93** E4
Barbastro, Spain, **115** D2
Barcaldine, Australia, **175**, D3
Barcelona, Venezuela, **97** C2
Barcelona, Spain, **115** D2
Barcelos, Brazil, **97** B1
Bärdä, Azerbaijan, **129** E3
Barga, Italy, **117** B3
Bari, Italy, **117** D4
Barika, Algeria, **141** D1
Barinas, Venezuela, **97** B2
Barito, *river*, Indonesia, **170** E5
Barkly Tableland, *mountain*, Australia, **175** C3
Bārmer, India, **157** B3
Barnaul, Russian Federation, **153** C3
Barnstaple, England, **109** C6
Barquisimeto, Venezuela, **97** B2
Barra, Brazil, **97** D3
Barra, *island*, Scotland, **109** B3
Barrancabermeja, Colombia, **97** A2
Barranquilla, Colombia, **97**, A1
Barras, Brazil, **97** D2
Barreiras, Brazil, **97** D3
Barreiro, Portugal, **115** A3
Barrow, U.S.A., **182** B1
Barrow-in-Furness, England, **109** C5
Barstow, *California*, U.S.A., , **83** B5
Bartoszyce, Poland, **123** D1
Baru, Maluka, Indonesia, **171** G5
Baru, Irian Jaya, Indonesia, **171** H5
Baruun-Urt, Mongolia, **161**, D2
Barysaw, Belarus, **121** D3
Bąsăk, *river*, Cambodia, **167** D5
Basankusu, Democratic Republic of the Congo, **145** C5
Basel, Switzerland, **117** A1
Basilan Island, Philippines, **171** F4
Basingstoke, England, **109**, D6
Başkale, Turkey, **129** D4
Bass Strait, *gulf,* Australia, **175** D6
Bassas da India, *island*, France, **149** E3
Bassein, Myanmar (Burma), **167** A4
Basseterre, St Kitts and Nevis, **93** E3
Basse-Terre, France, **93** E3
Bastia, France, **113** E5
Bastogne, Belgium, **111** B4
Bata, Equatorial Guinea, **145** A4
Batakan, Indonesia, **170** E6
Batangas, Philippines, **171**, F2
Bătdâmbâng, Cambodia, **167** C5
Bath, England, **109** D6
Bathurst, *New Brunswick*, Canada, **81** D3
Bathurst, Australia, **175** E5
Bathust Island, Australia, **171** H7
Batman, Turkey, **129** D4
Batna, Algeria, **141** D1
Baton Rouge, *Louisiana*, U.S.A., **85** D6
Batouri, Cameroon, **145** B4
Batu, *mountain*, Ethiopia, **147** C3
Batu Niah, Malaysia, **170** E4
Batui, Indonesia, **171** F5
Batşumi, Georgia, **129** D3
Bauchi, Nigeria, **141** D3
Bauru, Brazil, **97** D4
Bauska, Latvia, **121** B3
Bautzen, Germany, **111** E3
Bawku, Ghana, **141** C3
Bay City, *Texas*, U.S.A., **85**, C7
Bay of Bengal, *gulf,* India, **157** D4
Bay of Biscay, *gulf,* France, **113** A3
Bay of Fundy, *gulf,* U.S.A., **81** D4
Bay of Islands, *island*, New Zealand, **177** D2
Bay of Plenty, *gulf,* New Zealand, **177** D3
Bayamo, Cuba, **93** B2
Bayan Har Shan, *mountain*, China, **157** E1
Bayanhongor, Mongolia, **161** C2
Bayburt, Turkey, **129** D3
Baydhabo, Somalia, **147** D3
Bayonne, France, **113** B4
Bayovar, Peru, **101** A2
Bayrūt (Beirut), Lebanon, **137** E2
Baza, Spain, **115** C4
Bazardüzü Dağ, *mountain*, Azerbaijan, **133** C1
Beāwar, India, **157** B3
Bečej, Yugoslavia, **125** C2
Beatrice, *Nebraska*, U.S.A., **85** C4
Beaufort West, South Africa, **149** C5
Beaumont, *Texas*, U.S.A., **85** C6
Beauvais, France, **113** C2
Béchar, Algeria, **141** C2
Be'ér Sheva' (Beersheba), Israel, **133** A3
Bei'an, China, **161** E2
Beihai, China, **161** D5
Beijing (Peking), China, **161** D2
Beira, Mozambique, **149** D3
Beja, Portugal, **115** A3
Bejaïa, Algeria, **141** D1
Béjar, Spain, **115** B2
Belarus, *country,* **121** D4
Belcher Island, *Québec*, Canada, **79** G4
Beledweyne, Somalia, **147**, D3
Belém, Brazil, **97** D2
Belen, *New Mexico*, U.S.A., **83** D5
Belfast, Northern Ireland, **109** C4
Belgaum, India, **157** B5
Belgium, *country,* **111** A3
Belize, Belize, **91** A2
Belize, *country,* **91** A2
Bella Unión, Uruguay, **103** D3
Bellingham, *Washington*, U.S.A., **83** A1
Bellinzona, Switzerland, **117** B2
Bello, Colombia, **97** A2
Belluno, Italy, **117** C2
Belmopan, Belize, **91** A2
Belogorsk, Russian Federation, **153** D3
Ben Macdui, *mountain*, Scotland, **109** C3
Ben Nevis, *mountain*, Scotland, **109** C3
Benavente, Spain, **115** B2
Bend, *Oregon*, U.S.A., **83** A2
Bendigo, Australia, **175** D5
Benevento, Italy, **117** D4
Bengbu, China, **161** D3
Bengkulu, Indonesia, **170** B6
Benguela, Angola, **149** A2
Beni, *river*, Bolivia, **101** C3
Beni Mellal, Morocco, **141** B2
Beni-Abbes, Algeria, **141** C2
Benin, *country,* **141** C3
Benin City, Nigeria, **141** D4
Benjamin Constant, Brazil, **97** A2
Bénoy, Chad, **145** B3
Benue, *river*, Nigeria, **141** D4
Benwee Head, *point*, Ireland, **109** A4
Benxi, China, **161** E3
Beograd (Belgrade), Yugoslavia, **125** C2
Berat, Albania, **125** B4
Berbera, Somalia, **147** D2
Berbérati, Central African Republic, **145** B4
Berck, France, **113** C1
Berdyans'k, Ukraine, **129** C2
Berdychiv, Ukraine, **129** B1
Bergamo, Italy, **117** B2
Bergen, Norway, **107** A4
Bergerac, France, **113** B4
Bering Strait, *gulf,* U.S.A., **182** B1
Berlin, Germany, **111** E2
Bermuda, U.K. Dependency, **105** A2
Bern, Switzerland, **117** A1
Bernburg, Germany, **111** D3
Berriane, Algeria, **141** D2
Bertoua, Cameroon, **145** B4
Berwick-upon-Tweed, England, **109** D4
Besançon, France, **113** D3
Betanzos, Spain, **115** A1
Bethel, *Alaska*, U.S.A., **79** B2
Betpaqdala, *mountain*, Kazakhstan, **155** C3
Beyşehir Gölü, *lake*, Turkey, **129** B3
Beyneu, Kazakhstan, **155** B2
Béziers, France, **113** C5
Bhamo, Myanmar (Burma), **167** B2
Bharūch, India, **157** B4
Bhāvnagar, India, **157** B4
Bhīlwāra, India, **157** B3
Bhopāl, India, **157** C3
Bhubaneshwar, India, **157**, D4
Bhumiphon Reservoir, *lake*, Thailand, **167** B3
Bhutan, *country,* **157** D3
Biała Podlaska, Poland, **123** E2
Białystok, Poland, **123** E2
Biarritz, France, **113** B4
Bida, Nigeria, **141** D4
Biel, Switzerland, **117** A1
Bielefeld, Germany, **111** C3
Biella, Italy, **117** B2
Bielsko-Biała, Poland, **123**, D3
Biên Hòa, Vietnam, **167** D5
Biescas, Spain, **115** D1
Big Bay, *gulf,* New Zealand, **177** A6
Big Snow Mt, *mountain, Montana*, U.S.A., **83** D2
Bighorn, *river, Wyoming*, U.S.A., **83** D2
Bight of Bangkok, *gulf,* Thailand, **167** C5
Bight of Benin, *gulf,* Ghana, **141** C4
Bight of Bonny, *gulf,* Nigeria, **141** D4
Bihać, Bosnia and Herzegovina, **125** A2
Bijāpur, India, **157** C4
Bijelo Polje, Yugoslavia, **125** B3
Bikāner, India, **157** B3
Bilāspur, India, **157** C4
Bila Tserkva, Ukraine, **129** B1
Bilauktaung Range, *mountain,* Myanmar (Burma), **167** B4
Bilbao, Spain, **115** C1
Bileča, Bosnia and Herzegovina, **125** B3
Billings, *Montana*, U.S.A., **83** D2
Biloku, Guyana, **97** D3
Biloxi, *Mississippi*, U.S.A., **85** E6
Bimbo, Central African Republic, **145** C4
Bindura, Zimbabwe, **149** D3
Bingöl, Turkey, **129** D4
Bintulu, Malaysia, **170** D4
Bîr Mogreïn, Mauritania, **141** B1
Birāk, Libya, **137** B3
Birātnagar, Nepal, **157** D3
Bīrjand, Iran, **133** E2
Birao, Central African Republic, **145** D3
Birdsville, Australia, **175** D4
Birmingham, *Alabama*, U.S.A., **87** B5
Birmingham, England, **109** D6
Birnin Kebbi, Nigeria, **141** D3
Biržai, Lithuania, **121** C3
Bishkek, Kyrgyzstan, **155** D3
Bishops Stortford, England, **109** E6
Bislig, Philippines, **171** G3
Bismarck, *North Dakota*, U.S.A., **85** B2
Bissau, Guinea-Bissau, **141** A3
Bitola, Macedonia, **125** C4
Bjelovar, Croatia, **125** B1
Black Volta, *river*, Burkina Faso, **141** C3
Blackburn, England, **109** D5
Blackfoot, *Idaho*, U.S.A., **83** C3
Blackpool, England, **109** D5
Blagoveshchensk, Russian Federation, **153** D3
Blantyre, Malawi, **149** D3
Blenheim, New Zealand, **177** C4
Bloemfontein, South Africa, **149** C5
Blois, France, **113** C3
Blönduós, Iceland, **107** A1
Bloomington, *Illinois*, U.S.A., **85** E4
Bloomington, *Indiana*, U.S.A., **85** E4
Bluefield, *West Virginia*, U.S.A., **87** C4
Bluefields, Nicaragua, **91** B3
Bluff, New Zealand, **177** B7
Blumenau, Brazil, **97** C5
Bo, Sierra Leone, **141** A4
Boa Vista, Brazil, **97** B1
Bobo-Dioulasso, Burkina Faso, **141** B3
Bobonong, Botswana, **149** C3
Bôca do Acre, Brazil, **97** A2
Boden, Sweden, **107** D3
Bodensee, *lake*, Germany, **117** B1
Bodø, Norway, **107** C2
Boende, Democratic Republic of the Congo, **145** C5
Bogale, Myanmar (Burma), **167** A4
Bogor, Indonesia, **170** C6
Bogotá, Colombia, **97** A3
Bohai Haixia, *gulf,* China, **165** A3
Bohol, *island*, Philippines, **171** G3
Boise, *Idaho*, U.S.A**83** B3
Bojnūrd, Iran, **133** D2
Boké, Guinea, **141** A3
Bole, China, **161** B2
Bolgatanga, Ghana, **141** C3
Bolivia, *country,* **101** D4
Bollnäs, Sweden, **107** C4
Bolobo, Democratic Republic of the Congo, **145** B5
Bologna, Italy, **117** C3
Bolsshoy Kavkaz (Caucasus), *mountain*, Russian Federation, **129** E3
Bolton, England, **109** D5
Bolzano, Italy, **117** C2
Boma, Democratic Republic of the Congo, **145** B6
Bomassa, Congo, **145** B4
Bonaire, *island*, Netherlands, **93** D4
Bondo, Democratic Republic of the Congo, **145** D4
Bongabong, Philippines, **171** F2
Bongandanga, Democratic Republic of the Congo, **145** C5
Bongor, Chad, **145** B3
Bonn, Germany, **111** B3
Boosaaso, Somalia, **147** E2
Boothia Peninsula, *point, Nunavut*, Canada, **79** F2
Bor, Turkey, **129** C4
Bor, Sudan, **147** B3
Borba, Brazil, **97** B2
Bordeaux, France, **113** B4
Bordj Omar Driss, Algeria, **141** E2
Borgarnes, Iceland, **107** A1
Borger, *Texas*, U.S.A., **85** B5
Borna, Germany, **111** D3
Borneo, *island*, Indonesia, **170** E5
Bornholm, *island*, Denmark, **107** B6
Borūjerd, Iran, **133** C2
Borzya, Russian Federation, **153** D4
Bosanska Dubica, Bosnia and Herzegovina, **125** B2
Bose, China, **161** C4
Bosnia and Herzegovina, *country,* **125** B2
Bosobolo, Democratic Republic of the Congo, **145**, C4
Bossangoa, Central African Republic, **145** C4
Bosten Hu, *lake*, China, **161** B3
Boston, *Massachusetts*, U.S.A., **87** E3
Botswana, *country,* **149** B3
Bou Salem, Tunisia, **141** E1
Bouaflé, Côte d'Ivoire, **141** B4
Bouaké, Côte d'Ivoire, **141** B4
Bouar, Central African Republic, **145** B4
Bouârfa, Morocco, **141** C2
Bougainville, *island*, Papua New Guinea, **175** E1
Boughessa, Mali, **141** C2
Bougouni, Mali, **141** B3
Boulder, *Colorado*, U.S.A., **83** E4
Boulder City, *Nevada*, U.S.A**83** C5
Boulogne-Billancourt, France, **113** C2
Boulogne-sur-Mer, France, **113** C1
Bourges, France, **113** C3

Ḩawallī, Kuwait, **133** C3
Hawera, New Zealand, **177** C4
Hawick, Scotland, **109** D4
Hawke Bay, *gulf*, New Zealand, **177** E3
Hawthorne, *Nevada*, U.S.A., **83** B4
Hay River, *Northwest Territories* Canada, **79** E4
Hayden, *Colorado*, U.S.A., **83** D4
Hays, *Kansas*, U.S.A., **85** B4
Heard & McDonald Islands, Australian Territory, **151** B4
Hearst, *Ontario*, Canada, **81** B3
Hede, Sweden, **107** B4
Heerenveen, Netherlands, **111** B2
Ḩefa (Haifa), Israel, **133** A2
Hefei, China, **161** D4
Hegang, China, **161** E2
Heidelberg, Germany, **111** C4
Heihe, China, **161** E2
Heilbronn, Germany, **111** C4
Heinola, Finland, **107** D4
Helena, *Montana*, U.S.A., **83** C2
Helensville, New Zealand, **177** D2
Hellín, Spain, **115** C3
Helmand, *river*, Afghanistan, **155** C5
Helmeringhausen, Namibia, **149** B4
Helmsdale, Scotland, **109** C2
Helsingborg, Sweden, **107** B6
Helsinki, Finland, **107** D5
Henderson, *Nevada*, U.S.A., **83** C5
Hengduan Shan, *mountain*, China, **161** B4
Hengyang, China, **161** D4
Henichesk, Ukraine, **129** C2
Henzada, Myanmar (Burma), **167** B3
Herāt, Afghanistan, **155** B4
Hereford, *Texas*, U.S.A., **85** B5
Hereford, England, **109** D6
Hermansverk, Norway, **107** A4
Hermanus, South Africa, **149** B5
Hermiston, *Oregon*, U.S.A., **83** B2
Hermosillo, Mexico, **89** B2
Herning, Denmark, **107** A6
Herrera del Duque, Spain, **115** B3
Hervey Bay, *gulf*, Australia, **175** E4
Hialeah, *Florida*, U.S.A., **87** C7
Hidalgo del Parral, Mexico, **89** B2
Hiiumaa, *island*, Estonia, **121** B1
Híjar, Spain, **115** D2
Himalaya, *mountain range*, China, **161** A3
Himalaya, *mountain range*, Bhutan, **161** A3
Himalaya, *mountain range*, Nepal, **161** A3
Himalaya, *mountain range*, India, **161** A3
Ḩimş (Homs), Syria, **133** A2
Hindu Kush, *mountain*, Pakistan, **155** C4
Hindu Kush, *mountain*, Afganistan, **157** B1
Hinoba-an, Philippines, **171** F3
Hirosaki, Japan, **165** D2
Hiroshima, Japan, **165** C4
Hispaniola, *island*, Haiti/Dominican Republic, **93** C3
Hitachi, Japan, **165** E3
Hitoyoshi, Japan, **165** C4
Hitra, *island*, Norway, **107** B3
Hjørring, Denmark, **107** B5
Hkakabo Razi, *mountain peak*, Myanmar (Burma), **167** B1
Hkamti, Myanmar (Burma), **167** B1
Hlybokaye, Belarus, **121** D3
Ho, Ghana, **141** C4
Hà Tĩnh, Vietnam, **167** D3
Hòa Bình, Vietnam, **167** D3
Hobart, Australia, **175** E6
Hobbs, *New Mexico*, U.S.A., **85** A5
Hoeryŏng, North Korea, **165** B2
Hof, Germany, **111** D4
Hoggar, *mountain range*, Algeria, **139** D3
Hohhot, China, **161** D3
Hokianga Harbour, *gulf*, New Zealand, **177**, C2
Hokitika, New Zealand, **177** B5
Hokkaidō, *island*, Japan, **165** E1
Holbrook, *Arizona*, U.S.A., **83** D5
Holguín, Cuba, **93** B2
Hollabrunn, Austria, **123** C4
Hollywood, *Florida*, U.S.A., **87** C7
Holstebro, Denmark, **107** A6
Holyhead, Wales, **109** C5
Homer, *Alaska*, U.S.A., **79** C2
Homyeĺs, Belarus, **121** E4
Honduras, *country*, **91** A2
Hønefoss, Norway, **107** B4
Hộng, *river*, Vietnam, **167** D2
Hồng Gai, Vietnam, **167** D3
Hongshui, *river*, China, **167** D2
Honningsvåg, Norway, **107** D1
Honshū, *island*, Japan, **165** D3
Hoorn, Netherlands, **111** B2
Hopedale, *Newfoundland*, Canada, **81** D2
Horasan, Turkey, **129** D3
Horki, Belarus, **121** E3
Horoshiri-dake, *mountain*, Japan, **165** E2
Horsham, Australia, **175** D5
Hosa'ina, Ethiopia, **147** C3
Hosséré Vokré, *mountain*, Cameroon, **145** B3
Hot Springs, *South Dakota*, U.S.A., **85** B3
Hot Springs, *Arkansas*, U.S.A., **85** D5
Hotan, China, **161** A3
Houghton, *Michigan*, U.S.A., **87** B2
Houlton, *Maine*, U.S.A., **87** E2
Houma, *Louisiana*, U.S.A., **85** D6
Houston, *Texas*, U.S.A., **85** C6
Hövsgöl Nuur, *lake*, Mongolia, **161** C2
Howick, New Zealand, **177** D2
Hoy, *island*, Scotland, **109** C2
Høyanger, Norway, **107** A4
Hoyerswerda, Germany, **111** E3
Hradec Králové, Czech Republic, **123** C3
Hrodna, Belarus, **121** B4
Huế, Vietnam, **167** E4
Hua Hin, Thailand, **167** C5
Huacho, Peru, **101** B3
Huaibei, China, **161** D3
Huainan, China, **161** D3
Huambo, Angola, **149** B2
Huancayo, Peru, **101** B3
Huang (Yellow), *river*, China, **161** C3
Huangshi, China, **161** D4
Huánuco, Peru, **101** B3
Huarmey, Peru, **101** A3
Hubli, India, **157** B5
Hudiksvall, Sweden, **107** C4
Hudson Bay, *gulf*, Canada, **81** A1
Hudson Strait, *gulf*, Canada, **81** C1
Huelva, Spain, **115** B4
Huesca, Spain, **115** D2
Hukuntsi, Botswana, **149** B4
Hulun Nur, *lake*, China, **153** D4
Humaitá, Brazil, **97** B2
Humbe, Angola, **149** A3
Hūmedān, Iran, **133** E4
Humboldt, *river*, *Nevada*, U.S.A., **83** B3
Humenné, Slovakia, **123** E4
Humphreys Pk, *mountain*, *Arizona* U.S.A., **83** C5
Hungary, *country*, **123** D4
Hŭngnam, North Korea, **165** B2
Huntingdon, England, **109** E6
Huntington, *West Virginia*, U.S.A., **87** C4
Huntly, Scotland, **109** D3
Huntsville, *Ontario*, Canada, **81** B4
Huntsville, *Alabama*, U.S.A., **87** B5
Hurki, Belarus, **121** D3
Hurunui, *river*, New Zealand, **177** C5
Húsavík, Iceland, **107** A1
Husum, Germany, **111** C1
Hutchinson, *Kansas*, U.S.A., **85** C4
Hvannadalschnúkur, *mountain* Iceland, **107**, A1
Hwange, Zimbabwe, **149** C3
Hyūga, Japan, **165** C4
Hyderābād, Pakistan, **157** B3
Hyderābād, India, **157** C4
Hyesan, North Korea, **165** B2
Hyrynsalmi, Finland, **107** E3

Ibadan, Nigeria, **141** D4
Ibagué, Colombia, **97** A3
Ibarra, Ecuador, **101** A1
Ibrā', Oman, **133** E4
'Ibrī, Oman, **133** D4
Ica, Peru, **101** B4
Iceland, *country*, **107** A1
Ichalkaranji, India, **157** B4
Ichinoseki, Japan, **165** E3
Idabel, *Oklahoma*, U.S.A., **85** C5
Idaho, *state*, U.S.A., **83** C3
Idaho Falls, *Idaho*, U.S.A., **83** C3
Idiofa, Democratic Republic of the Congo, **145** C6
Ieper (Ypres), Belgium, **111** A3
Ifakara, Tanzania, **147** C5
Igarka, Russian Federation, **153** C2
Iglesias, Italy, **117** B5
Igoumenitsa, Greece, **125** C4
Igrim, Russian Federation, **153** B2
Igualada, Spain, **115** D2
Iguatu, Brazil, **97** E2
Iisalmi, Finland, **107** E3
IJsselmeer, *gulf*, Netherlands, **111** B2
Ikare, Nigeria, **141** D4
Ikaria, *island*, Greece, **129** A4
Ilagan, Philippines, **171** F1
Ila-Orangun, Nigeria, **141** D4
Iława, Poland, **123** D2
Île Amsterdam, *island*, France, **151** B3
Île Europa, *island*, France, **149** E4
Ilebo, Democratic Republic of the Congo, **145** C6
Îles de Crozet, *island*, France, **151** A4
Îles de Kerguélen, *island*, France, **151** B4
Îles Glorieuses, *island*, France, **147** E5
Ilgaz, Turkey, **129** C3
Ilha do Bazaruto, *island*, Mozambique, **149** E3
Ilhéus, Brazil, **97** E3
Iliamna Lake, *Alaska*, U.S.A., **79** B2
Iligan, Philippines, **171** G3
Illinois, *river*, Illinois U.S.A., **85** D4
Illinois, *state*, U.S.A., **85** D4
Ilo, Peru, **101** C4
Iloilo, Philippines, **171** F3
Ilorin, Nigeria, **141** D4
Imatra, Finland, **107** E4
Imperia, Italy, **117** A3
Impfondo, Congo, **145** C5
Imphāl, India, **157** E3
Inari, Finland, **107** D2
Inarijärvi, *lake*, Finland, **107** D2
Inchŏn, South Korea, **165** B3
Inčukalns, Latvia, **121** B2
India, *country*, **157** C4
Indiana, *state*, U.S.A., **87** B4
Indianapolis, *Indiana*, U.S.A., **87** B4
Indonesia, *country*, **170** D6
Indore, India, **157** C3
Indus, *river*, Pakistan, **157** B2
Indus, *river*, India, **161** A3
İnebolu, Turkey, **129** C3
Ingolstadt, Germany, **111** D4
Inhambane, Mozambique, **149** D4
Inner Hebrides, *island*, Scotland, **109** B3
Innsbruck, Austria, **123** B4
Inongo, Democratic Republic of the Congo, **145** C5
I-n-Salah, Algeria, **141** D3
Inta, Russian Federation, **153** B2
Inubō-zaki, *point*, Japan, **165** E3
Inukjuak, *Québec*, Canada, **81** B2
Inuvik, *Northwest Territories* Canada, **79** D2
Invercargill, New Zealand, **177** B7
Inverness, Scotland, **109** C3
Inverurie, Scotland, **109** D3
Inyangani, *mountain*, Zimbabwe, **149** D3
Ioannina, Greece, **125** C4
Ios, *island*, Greece, **129** A4
Iowa, *state*, U.S.A., **85** D3
Iowa City, *Iowa*, U.S.A., **85** D3
Ipiaú, Brazil, **97** E3
Ipoh, Malaysia, **170** B4
Ipswich, England, **109** E6
Iqaluit, *Québec*, Canada, **81** C1
Iquique, Chile, **103** B1
Iquitos, Peru, **101** B2
Irakleio (Iraklion), Greece, **125** D6
Iran, *country*, **133** D3
Īrānshahr, Iran, **133** E4
Irapuato, Mexico, **89** C3
Iraq, *country*, **133** B2
Irbid, Jordan, **133** A2
Ireland, *country*, **109** B5
Iri, South Korea, **165** B3
Iringa, Tanzania, **147** C5
Iriri, *river*, Brazil, **99** C2
Irkutsk, Russian Federation, **153** C4
Irrawaddy, *river*, Myanmar (Burma), **167** A3
Irtysh, *river*, Russian Federation, **161** A1
Irvine, Scotland, **109** C4
Ísafjörður, Iceland, **107** A1
Ise, Japan, **165** D4
Isiro, Democratic Republic of the Congo, **145** D4
İskenderun, Turkey, **129** C4
Islāmābād, Pakistan, **157** B2
Isla Cozumel, *island*, Mexico, **89** E3
Isla de Bioco, *island*, Equatorial Guinea, **145** A4
Isla de Coiba, *island*, Panama, **91** B4
Isla de la Juventud, *island*, Cuba, **93** A2
Isla de los Estados, *island*, Argentina, **103**, C7
Isla de Margarita, *island*, Venezuela, **93** D4
Isla del Rey, *island*, Panama, **91** C4
Isla Grande de Chiloé, *island* Chile, **103** A5
Isla Grande de Tierra del Fuego, *island* Chile, **103** B7
Isla Santa Inés, *island*, Chile, **103** B7
Isla Baleares, *mountain*, Spain, **115** E3
Islas Canarias (Canary Islands), *island* Spain, **105** B2
Islas Tres Marías, *island*, Mexico, **89** B3
Isle of Lewis, Scotland, **109** B2
Isle of Man U.K. Crown Dependency, **109** C4
Isle of Wight, England, **109** D7
Isnā, Egypt, **137** E3
Isola d'Elba, *island*, Italy, **117** B3
Isola di Lampedusa, *island*, Italy, **137** B1
Isparta, Turkey, **129** B4
Israel, *country*, **133** E2
İstanbul, Turkey, **129** B3
Itānagar, India, **157** E3
Itabuna, Brazil, **97** E3
Italy, *country*, **117** C3
Ithaca, *New York*, U.S.A., **87** D3
Itzehoe, Germany, **111** C1
Ivalo, Finland, **107** D2
Ivano-Frankivs'k, Ukraine, **129** A1
Ivatsevichy, Belarus, **121** C4
Iwaki, Japan, **165** E3
Iwakuni, Japan, **165** C4
İzmir, Turkey, **129** B4

Jabal al Lawz, *mountain*, Saudi Arabia, **133** A3
Jabal Al 'Uwaynāt, *mountain* Sudan, **147** A1
Jabal an Nabī Shu'ayb, *mountain peak* Yemen, **133** B6
Jabal ash Shām, *mountain*, Oman, **133** D4
Jabal ash Shaşnabī, *mountain peak* Tunisia, **139** E1
Jabal Ghārib, *mountain peak*, Egypt, **137** E3
Jabal Ḩamāţah, *mountain*, Egypt, **137** E3
Jabal Ḩamātah, *mountain*, Egypt, **133** A4
Jabal Mūsá (Mt Sinai), *mountain* Egypt, **137** E3
Jabal Oda, *mountain peak*, Sudan, **147** C1
Jabal Sawdā', *mountain peak* Saudi Arabia, **133** B5
Jabal Zalţan, *mountain*, Libya, **137** B3
Jabalpur, India, **157** C3
Jablanica, Bosnia and Herzegovina, **125** B2
Jackson, *Mississippi*, U.S.A., **85** D6
Jackson Bay, *gulf*, New Zealand, **177** B5
Jacksonville, *Florida*, U.S.A., **87** C6
Jacksonville, *North Carolina*, *U.S.A.*, **87** D5
Jacmel, Haiti, **93** C3
Jacobina, Brazil, **97** E3
Jaén, Spain, **115** C3
Jaffna, Sri Lanka, **157** C6
Jagdalpur, India, **157** C4
Jagersfontein, South Africa, **149** C5
Jaguarão, Brazil, **97** C5
Jaipur, India, **157** C3
Jaisalmer, India, **157** B3
Jajce, Bosnia and Herzegovina, **125** B2
Jakarta, Indonesia, **170** C6
Jalālābād, Afghanistan, **155** C4
Jalingo, Nigeria, **141** E4
Jālna, India, **157** C4
Jālū, Libya, **137** C3
Jamaica, *country*, **93** A3
Jambi, Indonesia, **170** B5
James, *river*, *South Dakota*, U.S.A., **85** C2
James Bay, *gulf*, Canada, **81** B2
Jamestown, *North Dakota*, U.S.A., **85** C2
Jāmnagar, India, **157** B4
Jämsä, Finland, **107** D4
Jamshedpur, India, **157** D3
Jangeru, Indonesia, **170** E5
Januária, Brazil, **97** D3
Japan, *country*, **165** D3
Japurá, *river*, Brazil, **99** A2
Jarjis, Tunisia, **141** E1
Jarocin, Poland, **123** C2
Jašiūnai, Lithuania, **121** C3
Jāsk, Iran, **133** E4
Jawa (Java), *island*, Indonesia, **170** C7
Jawhar, Somalia **147** D3
Jayapura, Indonesia, **171** K, 5
Jazā'ir Farasān, *island*, Saudi Arabia, **133** B5
Jazīrat Jarbah, *island*, Tunisia, **139** E1
Jazīrat Ma'īrah, *island*, Oman, **133** E5
Jazīreh-ye Qeshm, *island*, Iran, **133** D4
Jbel Bou Naceur *mountain*, Morocco, **141** C1
Jebel Toubkal, *mountain*, Morocco, **141** B2
Jedburgh, Scotland, **109** D4
Jefferson City, *Missouri*, U.S.A., **85** D4
Jēkabpils, Latvia, **121** C2
Jelgava, Latvia, **121** B2
Jena, Germany, **111** D3
Jequié, Brazil, **97** E3
Jeremoabo, Brazil, **97** E3
Jerez de la Frontera, Spain, **115** B4
Jesi, Italy, **117** C3
Jhānsi, India, **157** C3
Jiamusi, China, **161** E2
Jiddah (Jedda), Saudi Arabia, **133** A5
Jihlava, Czech Republic, **123** C4
Jijel, Algeria, **141** D1
Jijiga, Ethiopia, **147** D2
Jilib, Somalia, **147** D4
Jilin, China, **161** E2
Jīma, Ethiopia, **147** C3
Jimulco, *mountain*, Mexico, **89** C2
Jinan, China, **161** D3
Jingdezhen, China, **161** D4
Jinja, Uganda, **147** C4
Jinsha (Yangtze), *river*, China, **161** B3
Jinzi, China, **161** D3
Jinzhou, China, **161** D3
Jiuquan, China, **161** C3
Jixi, China, **161** E2
Jizzakh, Uzbekistan, **155** C3
João Pessoa, Brazil, **97** E2
Jochpur, India, **157** B3
Joensuu, Finland, **107** E4
Jōetsu, Japan, **165** D3
Johannesburg, South Africa, **149** C4
Johnston Atoll, *island*, U.S.A., **179** B2
Johor Bahru, Malaysia, **170** C5
Joinville, Brazil, **97** C5
Jokkmokk, Sweden, **107** C2
Joliette, *Québec*, Canada, **81** C4
Jolo Island, Philippines, **171** F4
Jonava, Lithuania, **121** B3
Jonesboro, *Arkansas*, U.S.A., **85** D5
Joniškis, Lithuania, **121** B3
Jönköping, Sweden, **107** B5
Joplin, *Missouri*, U.S.A., **85** D4
Jordan, *country*, **133** A3
Jörn, Sweden, **107** C3
Jos, Nigeria, **141** D4
Joseph Bonaparte Gulf, *gulf*, Australia, **175** B2
Juazeiro, Brazil, **97** E3
Juba, Sudan, **147** B3
Jubba, *river*, Somalia, **147** D3
Judenburg, Austria, **123** C5
Juiz de Fora, Brazil, **97** D4
Juliaca, Peru, **101** C4
Jūnāgadh, India, **157** B4
Juneau, *Alaska*, U.S.A., **79** C3
Junsele, Sweden, **107** C3
Jurbarkas, Lithuania, **121** B3
Juruá, *river*, Brazil, **99** A2
Juruena, *river*, Brazil, **99** B3
Jwaneng, Botswana, **149** C4
Jyväskylä, Finland, **107** D4

Kaaresuvanto, Finland, **107** D2
Kabala, Sierra Leone, **141** A3
Kabalo, Democratic Republic of the Congo, **145** D6
Kådalis, Sweden, **107** C3
Kābol (Kabul), Afghanistan, **155** C4
Kabongo, Democratic Republic of the Congo, **145** D6
Kabwe, Zambia, **149** C2
Kadoma, Zimbabwe, **149** D3
Kaduna, Nigeria, **141** D3
Kāduqlī, Sudan, **147** B2
Kaédi, Mauritania, **141** A2
Kaélé, Cameroon, **145** B3
Kaesŏng, North Korea, **165** B3
Kafue, *river*, Zambia, **149** C2
Kaga Bandoro, Central African Republic, **145** C4
Kagoshima, Japan, **165** C4
Kahnūj, Iran, **133** E3
Kahramanmaraş, Turkey, **129** C4
Kaiapoi, New Zealand, **177** C5
Kaikohe, New Zealand, **177** C2
Kaikoura, New Zealand, **177** C5
Kaimana, Indonesia, **171** J6
Kaipara Harbour, *gulf*, New Zealand, **177** C2
Kaiyuan, China, **161** C4
Kajaani, Finland, **107** E3
Kakamega, Kenya, **147** C4
Kākināda, India, **157** C4
Kalabo, Zambia, **149** C2
Kalajoki, Finland, **107** D3
Kalamata, Greece, **125** C5
Kalamazoo, *Michigan*, U.S.A., **87** B3
Kalasin, Thailand, **167** D4
Kalemie, Democratic Republic of the Congo, **145** E6
Kalewa, Myanmar (Burma), **167** A2
Kalgoorlie-Boulder, Australia, **175** B4
Kalibo, Philippines, **171** F2
Kalima, Democratic Republic of the Congo, **145** D5
Kaliningrad, Russian Federation, **121** A3
Kalinkavichy, Belarus, **121** D4
Kalispell, *Montana*, U.S.A., **83** C1
Kalisz, Poland, **123** D3
Kalmar, Sweden, **107** C6
Kalvarija, Lithuania, **121** B4
Kama, Democratic Republic of the Congo, **145** D5
Kamaishi, Japan, **165** E2
Kamina, Democratic Republic of the Congo, **145** D6
Kamloops, *British Columbia*, Canada, **79** D5
Kampala, Uganda, **147** B4
Kampar, Malaysia, **170** B4
Kamphaeng Phet, Thailand, **167** C4
Kâmpóng Cham, Cambodia, **167** D5
Kâmpóng Chhnăng, Cambodia, **167** D5
Kâmpóng Saôm, Cambodia, **167** D5
Kâmpóng Thum, Cambodia, **167** D5
Kâmpôt, Cambodia, **167** D5
Kam''yanets'-Podil's'kyy, Ukraine, **129** B2
Kamyshin, Russian Federation, **153** A3
Kananga, Democratic Republic of the Congo, **145** D6
Kanazawa, Japan, **165** D3
Kandalaksha, Russian Federation, **153** B2
Kandi, Benin, **141** C3
Kandy, Sri Lanka, **157** C6
Kangar, Malaysia, **170** B4
Kangaroo Island, Australia, **175** C5
Kanggye, North Korea, **165** B2
Kangnŭng, South Korea, **165** B3
Kankaanpää, Finland, **107** D4
Kankan, Guinea, **141** B3
Kanker, India, **157** C4
Kano, Nigeria, **141** D3
Kanoya, Japan, **165** C4
Kanpur, India, **157** C3
Kansas, *state*, U.S.A., **85** B4
Kansas, *river*, *Kansas*, U.S.A., **85** C4
Kansas City, *Missouri*, U.S.A., **85** D4
Kantang, Thailand, **167** C6
Kanus, Namibia, **149** B4
Kanye, Botswana, **149** C4
Kao-hsiung, Taiwan, **161** E4
Kaolack, Senegal, **141** A3
Kaoma, Zambia, **149** C2
Kapanga, Democratic Republic of the Congo, **145** D6
Kapsan, North Korea, **165** B2
Kapuas, *river*, Indonesia, **170** D5
Karāchi, Pakistan, **157** A3
Karabük, Turkey, **129** B3
Kāraikkudi, India, **157** C6
Karaj, Iran, **133** C2
Karakalpakiya, Uzbekistan, **155** B3
Karakoçan, Turkey, **129** D4
Kara-Köl, Kyrgyzstan, **155** D3
Karakoram Range, *mountain range*, Pakistan, **155** D4
Karakoram Range, *mountain range* India, **157** B1
Karaman, Turkey, **129** C4
Karamay, China, **161** B2
Karamea, New Zealand, **177** C4
Karamea Bight, *gulf*, New Zealand, **177** B4
Karapınar, Turkey, **129** C4
Karasjok, Norway, **107** D1
Karbalā', Iraq, **133** B2
Karditsa, Greece, **125** C4
Kŭrdzhali, Bulgaria, **129** A3
Kariba, Zimbabwe, **149** D3
Karjaa, Finland, **107** D5
Karlovac, Croatia, **125** A2
Karlskrona, Sweden, **107** C6
Karlsruhe, Germany, **111** C4
Karlstad, Sweden, **107** B5
Karnāl, India, **157** C2
Karonga, Malawi, **149** D2
Karpathos, *island*, Greece, **125** E6
Karratha, Australia, **175** A3
Kars, Turkey, **129** D3
Kārsava, Latvia, **121** C2
Kasai, *river*, Zaire, **145** C5
Kasai, *river*, Zaire, **149** B1
Kasama, Zambia, **149** D2
Kasempa, Zambia, **149** C2
Kāshān, Iran, **133** D2
Kashi (Kashgar), China, **161** A3
Kāshmar, Iran, **133** E2
Kasongo, Democratic Republic of the Congo, **145** D6
Kasongo-Lunda, Democratic Republic of the Congo, **145** C6
Kassalā, Sudan, **147** C2
Kassel, Germany, **111** C3
Kastamonu, Turkey, **129** C3
Kastoria, Greece, **125** C4
Katerini, Greece, **125** C4
Katha, Myanmar (Burma), **167** B2
Katherine, Australia, **175** C2
Kathmandu, Nepal, **157** D3
Kati, Mali, **141** B3
Katiola, Côte d'Ivoire, **141** B4
Katowice, Poland, **123** D3
Katrineholm, Sweden, **107** C5
Katsina, Nigeria, **141** D3
Kattegat, *gulf*, Denmark, **107** B6
Kauhajoki, Finland, **107** D4
Kauksi, Estonia, **121** C1
Kaunas, Lithuania, **121** B3
Kautokeino, Norway, **107** D2
Kavajë, Albania, **125** B4
Kavala, Greece, **125** D4
Kavieng, Papua New Guinea, **175** E1
Kawasaki, Japan, **165** D3
Kayes, Mali, **141** A3
Kayseri, Turkey, **129** C4
Kazakhstan, *country*, **155** B2
Kazan', Russian Federation, **153** A3
Kāzerūn, Iran, **133** D3
Keşan, Turkey, **129** A3
Kearney, *Nebraska*, U.S.A., **85** C3
Kebnekaise, *mountain*, Sweden, **107** C2
Kecskemét, Hungary, **123** D5
Kediri, Indonesia, **170** D7
Keele Peak, *mountain*, *Northwest Territories* Canada, **79** D3
Keetmanshoop, Namibia, **149** B4
Kelang, Malaysia, **170** B4
Kelmė, Lithuania, **121** B3
Kélo, Chad, **145** B3
Kelso, *Washington*, U.S.A., **83** A2
Kemş, Russian Federation, **153** B2
Kemerovo, Russian Federation, **153** C3
Kemi, Finland, **107** D3
Kemijärvi, Finland, **107** E2
Kemijoki, *river*, Finland, **107** D3
Kenai, *Alaska*, U.S.A., **79** C2
Kendal, England, **109** D4
Kendari, Indonesia, **171** F6
Kendawangan, Indonesia, **170** D5
Kenema, Sierra Leone, **141** A4
Keng Tung, Myanmar (Burma), **167** C3
Kenge, Democratic Republic of the Congo, **145** C6
Kénitra, Morocco, **141** C1
Kennet, *river*, England, **113** B1
Kennett, *Missouri*, U.S.A., **85** D5
Kenora, *Ontario*, Canada, **79** F5
Kentucky, *state*, U.S.A., **87** B4
Kentucky Lake, Tennessee, U.S.A., **87** B4
Kenya, *country*, **147** C4
Kep. Alor, *island*, Indonesia, **171** G7
Kep. Anambas, *island*, Indonesia, **170** C4
Kep. Aru, *island*, Indonesia, **171** J6
Kep. Babar, *island*, Indonesia, **171** H6
Kep. Banggai, *island*, Indonesia, **171** F5
Kep. Batu, *island*, Indonesia, **170** A5
Kep. Kai, *island*, Indonesia, **171** H6
Kep. Kangean, *island*, Indonesia, **170** E6
Kep. Talaud, *island*, Indonesia, **171** G4
Kep. Tanimbar, *island*, Indonesia, **171** H6
Kerch, Ukraine, **129** C2
Kerema, Papua New Guinea, **175** D1
Keren, Eritrea, **147** C2
Kericho, Kenya, **147** C4
Kerikeri, New Zealand, **177** C2
Kerki, Turkmenistan, **155** C4
Kerkyra, Greece, **125** B4
Kerkyra (Corfu), *island*, Greece, **125** B4
Kermān, Iran, **133** D3
Kermadec Island, New Zealand, **179** B3
Kermit, *Texas*, U.S.A., **85** A6
Kerrville, *Texas*, U.S.A., **85** B6
Kerzaz, Algeria, **141** C2
Kesennuma, Japan, **165** E3
Ketaun, Indonesia, **170** B6
Ketchikan, *Alaska*, U.S.A., **79** C4
Key Largo, *Florida*, U.S.A., **87** C7
Key West, *Florida*, U.S.A., **87** C7
Khārān, Pakistan, **157** A2
Khāsh, Iran, **133** E3
Khabarovsk, Russian Federation, **153** E3
Khalīj as Salūm, *gulf*, Egypt, **137** C2
Khalīj Maşīrah, *gulf*, Oman, **133** E5
Khalīj Surt, *gulf*, Libya, **137** B2
Khalūf, Oman, **133** E5
Khamīs Mushayţ, Saudi Arabia, **133** B5
Khandwa, India, **157** C4
Khandyga, Russian Federation, **153** D3
Kharkiv, Ukraine, **129** C1
Khatanga, Russian Federation, **153** C2
Khemarat, Thailand, **167** D4
Kherson, *river*, Iran, **155** A5
Kherson, Ukraine, **129** B2
Khmel'nyts'kyy, Ukraine, **129** B1
Khon Kaen, Thailand, **167** C4
Khorog, Tadzhikistan, **155** D4
Khorramābād, Iran, **133** C2
Khouribga, Morocco, **141** B2
Khrebet Tarbagatay, *mountain* Kazakhstan, **155** E2
Khulna, Bangladesh, **157** D3
Khvor, Iran, **133** D2
Kičevo, Macedonia, **125** C3
Kiamba, Philippines, **171** G4
Kidal, Mali, **141** C2
Kiel, Germany, **111** D1
Kielce, Poland, **123** D3
Kiffa, Mauritania, **141** A2
Kifrī, Iraq, **133** C2
Kigali, Rwanda, **147** B4
Kigoma, Tanzania, **147** B4
Kikinda, Yugoslavia, **125** C1
Kikori, Papua New Guinea, **175** D1
Kikwit, Democratic Republic of the Congo, **145** C6
Kilchu, North Korea, **165** B2
Kilimanjaro, *mountain peak*, Tanzania, **147** C4
Kilingi-Nõmme, Estonia, **121** B2
Kilis, Turkey, **129** C4
Kilkeel, Northern Ireland, **109** B5
Kilkenny, Ireland, **109** B5
Kilkis, Greece, **125** C4
Killarney, Ireland, **109** A6
Killeen, *Texas*, U.S.A., **85** C6
Kilmarnock, Scotland, **109**, C4
Kilrush, Ireland, **109**, A5
Kilwa Masoko, Tanzania, **147**, C5
Kimbe, Papua New Guinea, **175**, E1
Kimberley, South Africa, **149**, C4
Kimberley Flateau, *mountain* Australia, **175**, B2
Kimch'aek, North Korea, **165**, B2
Kindia, Guinea, **141**, A3
Kindu, Democratic Republic of the Congo, **145** D5
King Island, Australia, **175** D6
King's Lynn, England, **109** E5
Kings Pk, *mountain*, *Utah*, U.S.A., **83** D4
Kingston, Jamaica, **93** B3
Kingston upon Hull, England, **109** D5
Kingstown, St Vincent and the Grenadines, **93** E4
Kingsville, *Texas*, U.S.A., **85** C7
Kinsale, Ireland, **109** A6
Kinshasa, Democratic Republic of the Congo, **145** B6
Kipembawe, Tanzania, **147** C5
Kipushi, Democratic Republic of the Congo, **145** D7
Kipushia, Democratic Republic of the Congo, **145** E7
Kirensk, Russian Federation, **153** D3
Kiribati, *country*, **179** C3
Kırıkkale, Turkey, **129** C4
Kirinyaga (Mt Kenya), *mountain* Kenya, **147** C4
Kirkūk, Iraq, **133** C2
Kirkcudbright, Scotland, **109** C4
Kirkenes, Norway, **107** E1
Kirkland Lake, *Ontario*, Canada, **81** B3
Kirksville, *Missouri*, U.S.A., **85** D4
Kirkwall, Scotland, **109** D2
Kirkwood, South Africa, **149** C5
Kirovohrad, Ukraine, **129** B2
Kiruna, Sweden, **107** D2
Kirundu, Democratic Republic of the Congo, **145** D5
Kisangani, Democratic Republic of the Congo, **145** D5
Kisarazu, Japan, **165** D3
Kishi, Nigeria, **141** D4
Kishiwada, Japan, **165** D4
Kiskőrös, Hungary, **123** D5
Kiskunmajsa, Hungary, **123** D5
Kismaayo, Somalia, **147** D4
Kissidougou, Guinea, **141** B4
Kisumu, Kenya, **147** C4
Kisvárda, Hungary, **123** E4
Kita, Mali, **141** B3
Kitakyūshū, Japan, **165** C4
Kitale, Kenya, **147** C4
Kitami, Japan, **165** E1
Kitgum, Uganda, **147** B3
Kittilä, Finland, **107** D2
Kitwe, Zambia, **149** C2
Kızılırmak, *river*, Turkey, **133** A1
Klagenfurt, Austria, **123** C5
Klaipėda, Lithuania, **121** A3
Klamath Falls, *Oregon*, U.S.A., **83** A3
Klatovy, Czech Republic, **123** B4
Klerksdorp, South Africa, **149** C4
Klichaw, Belarus, **121** D4
Klimavichy, Belarus, **121** E4
Ključ, Bosnia and Herzegovina, **125** B2
Kłodzko, Poland, **123** C3
Kluczbork, Poland, **123** D3
Klyuchevskaya Sopka, *mountain*, Russian Federation, **153** E2
Knighton, Wales, **109** D6
Knin, Croatia, **125** A2
Knittelfeld, Austria, **123** C4
Knoxville, *Tennessee*, U.S.A., **87** B5
Ko Chang, *island*, Thailand, **167** C5
Ko Kut, *island*, Thailand, **167** C5
Ko Phangan, *island*, Thailand, **167** C5
Ko Phuket, *island*, Thailand, **167** B6
Ko Samui, *island*, Thailand, **167** C5
Kościan, Poland, **123** C2
Kočevje, Slovenia, **125** A1
Koba, Indonesia, **170** C5
Kobe, Japan, **165** C4
København (Copenhagen), Denmark, **107** B6
Koblenz, Germany, **111** C3
Kobryn, Belarus, **121** C5
Koch Pk, *mountain*, *Montana*, U.S.A., **83** C2
Kōchi, Japan, **165** C4
Kochi (Cochin), India, **157** C6
Kodinar, India, **157** B4
Kodiak, *Alaska*, U.S.A., **79** B2
Kodiak Island, *Alaska*, U.S.A., **79** B2
Koforidua, Ghana, **141** C4
Kōfu, Japan, **165** D3
Køge, Denmark, **107** B6
Kohtla-Järve, Estonia, **121** C1
Kokkola, Finland, **107** D3
Kökshetaū, Kazakhstan, **155** C1
Kokstad, South Africa, **149** D5
Kolaka, Indonesia, **171** F6
Kolhāpur, India, **157** B4
Kolka, Latvia, **121** B2
Köln (Cologne), Germany, **111** B3
Kolo, Poland, **123** D2
Kołobrzeg, Poland, **123** C2
Kolwezi, Democratic Republic of the Congo, **145**, D7
Komatsu, Japan, **165** D3
Komotini, Greece, **125** D4
Kompasberg, *mountain*, South Africa, **149** C5
Komsomol'sk-na-Amure, Russian Federation, **153** E3
Kon Tum, Vietnam, **167** E4
Kondoa, Tanzania, **147** C4
Kongolo, Democratic Republic of the Congo, **145** D6
Kongsberg, Norway, **107** B5
Kongsvinger, Norway, **107** B4
Kongur Shan, *mountain peak*, China, **155** D4
Konin, Poland, **123** D2
Konitsa, Greece, **125** C4
Konjic, Bosnia and Herzegovina, **125** B2
Konotop, Ukraine, **129** C1
Kontagora, Nigeria, **141** D3
Konya, Turkey, **129** B4
Koplik, Albania, **125** B3
Koppang, Norway, **107** B4
Korba, India, **157** D4
Korbach, Germany, **111** C3
Korçë, Albania, **125** C4
Korea Bay, *gulf*, North Korea, **165** A2
Korea Strait, *gulf*, Japan, **161** E3
Korea Strait, *gulf*, South Korea, **165** B4
Korhogo, Côte d'Ivoire, **141** B4
Korinthos (Corinth), Greece, **125** C5
Kōriyama, Japan, **165** D3
Korkuteli, Turkey, **129** B4
Korla, China, **161** B3
Köroğlu Dağları, *mountain*, Turkey, **129** B3
Korosten, Ukraine, **129** B1
Kortrijk, Belgium, **111** A3
Kosŏng, North Korea, **165** B3
Košice, Slovakia, **123** E4
Kosovska Mitrovica, Yugoslavia, **125** C3
Kostryzn, Poland, **123** C2
Koszalin, Poland, **123** C2
Kota, India, **157** C3
Kota Baharu, Malaysia, **170** B4
Kota Kinabalu, Malaysia, **170** E4
Kotlas, Russian Federation, **153** B2
Kotlik, *Alaska*, U.S.A., **79** C1
Kotovs'k, Ukraine, **129** B2
Kotto, *river*, Central African Republic, **145** D3
Kotuy, *river*, Russian Federation, **153** C2
Koubia, Guinea, **141** A3
Koudougou, Burkina Faso, **141** C3
Koulamoutou, Gabon, **145** B5
Koulikoro, Mali, **141** B3
Koumogo, Chad, **145** C3
Kouroussa, Guinea, **141** B3
Kouvola, Finland, **107** E4
Kovel', Ukraine, **129** A1
Koyukuk, *river*, *Alaska*, U.S.A., **79** C2
Kozani, Greece, **125** C4
Kozhikode (Calicut), India, **157** C5
Krāslava, Latvia, **121** C3
Kraśnik, Poland, **123** E3
Kragujevac, Yugoslavia, **125** C2
Krakatau, *mountain*, Indonesia, **170** C6
Kraków, Poland, **123** D3
Kraljevo, Yugoslavia, **125** C2
Kralovice, Czech Republic, **123** B3
Kranj, Slovenia, **125** A1
Krasnoyarsk, Russian Federation, **153** C3
Krasnystaw, Poland, **123** E3
Krau, Indonesia, **171** K, 6
Kremenchuk, Ukraine, **129** C1
Krems an der Donau, Austria, **123** C4
Kribi, Cameroon, **145** A4
Krishna, *river*, India, **157** C5
Kristiansand, Norway, **107** A5
Kristianstad, Sweden, **107** B6
Kriti (Crete), *island*, Greece, **125** D6
Kroonstad, South Africa, **149**, C4
Krosno, Poland, **123** E3
Krui, Indonesia, **170** C6
Krung Thep (Bangkok), Thailand, **167** C4
Kruševac, Yugoslavia, **125** C3
Krychaw, Belarus, **121** E4
Krygystan, *country*, **155** D3
Kryvyy Rih, Ukraine, **129** C2
K2, *mountain*, China, **157** C1
Kuala Dungun, Malaysia, **170** B4
Kuala Lumpur, Malaysia, **170** B4
Kuala Terengganu, Malaysia, **170** B4
Kualakurun, Indonesia, **170** E5

Kuantan, Malaysia, **170** B4
Kuban', *river,* Russian Federation, **129** C2
Kuching, Malaysia, **170** D5
Kudat, Malaysia, **170** E3
Kufstein, Austria, **123** B4
Kugluktuk, *Nunavut,* Canada, **79** E3
Kūh-e Hazār, *mountain,* Iran, **133** D3
Kūh-e Taftān, *mountain peak,* Iran, **133** E3
Kūh-e Taftān, *mountain,* Iran, **157** A2
Kuh-e Qaysar, *mountain peak* Afghanistan, **155** C5
Kūhhā-ye Zāgros, *mountain,* Iran, **133** C2
Kuhmo, Finland, **107** E3
Kuito, Angola, **149** B2
Kujjuaraapik, *Québec,* Canada, **81** B2
Kukës, Albania, **125** C3
Kula Kangri, *mountain peak,* Bhutan, **157** D2
Kuldīga, Latvia, **121** B2
Kumagaya, Japan, **165** D3
Kumamoto, Japan, **165** C4
Kumanovo, Macedonia, **125** C3
Kumasi, Ghana, **141** C4
Kumbo, Cameroon, **145** A4
Kumi, South Korea, **165** B3
Kumo, Nigeria, **141** E3
Kumon Taungdan, *mountain,* Myanmar (Burma), **167** B1
Kunashir, *island,* Russian Federation, **165** E1
Kungsbacka, Sweden, **107** B5
Kunhing, Myanmar (Burma), **167** B2
Kunlun Shan, *mountain,* China, **161** A3
Kunming, China, **161** C4
Kunsan, South Korea, **165** B3
Kuopio, Finland, **107** E4
Kupang, Indonesia, **171** G7
Kupiano, Papua New Guinea, **175** E2
Kuqa, China, **161** B3
Kure, Japan, **165** C4
Kuressaare, Estonia, **121** B2
Kurgan, Russian Federation, **153** B3
Kurikka, Finland, **107**, D4
Kuril Islands, Russian Federation, **179** B1
Kuril'skiye Ostrova (Kuril Islands), Russian Federation, **153** E3
Kurnool, India, **157** C5
Kurshskiy Zaliv, *lake,* Russian Federation, **121** A3
Kursk, Russian Federation, **153** A2
Kurtalan, Turkey, **129** D4
Kuruman, South Africa, **149** C4
Kurume, Japan, **165** B4
Kurunegala, Sri Lanka, **157** C6
Kushiro, Japan, **165** E1
Kuskokwim, *river, Alaska,* U.S.A., **79** C2
Kūsti, Sudan, **147** B2
Kütahya, Turkey, **129** B4
K'ut'aisi, Georgia, **129** D3
Kutu, Democratic Republic of the Congo, **145** C5
Kuujjuaq, *Québec,* Canada, **81** C2
Kuusamo, Finland, **107** E3
Kuybyshevskoye Vodokhranilishche, *lake,* Russian Federation, **155** A1
Kvikkjokk, Sweden, **107** C2
Kwa Mashu, South Africa, **149** D5
Kwangju, South Korea, **165** B3
Kwekwe, Zimbabwe, **149** D3
Kwenge, *river,* Democratic Republic of the Congo, **145** C6
Kwidzyn, Poland, **123** D2
Kyōto, Japan, **165** D4
Kyŏngju, South Korea, **165** B3
Kyūshū, *island,* Japan, **165** C4
Kyabé, Chad, **145** C3
Kyaikkami, Myanmar (Burma), **167** B4
Kyaikto, Myanmar (Burma), **167** B4
Kyaukpyu, Myanmar (Burma), **167** A3
Kyklades (Cyclades), *island,* Greece, **125** D5
Kyrgyz Ala Too, *mountain,* Kyrgyzstan, **155** D3
Kyrgyzstan, *country,* **153** B4
Kythira, *island,* Greece, **129** A4
Kyyiv (Kiev), Ukraine, **129** B1
Kyyjärvi, Finland, **107** D4
Kyzyl, Russian Federation, **153** C4

L'Aquila, Italy, **117** C4
Lago Viedma, *lake,* Argentina, **103** B6
La Blanquilla, *island,* Venezuela, **93** D4
La Carolina, Spain, **115** C3
La Ceiba, Honduras, **91** B2
La Croisière, France, **113** C3
La Grande, *Oregon,* U.S.A., **83** B2
La Grange, *Georgia,* U.S.A., **87** B5
La Habana (Havana), Cuba, **93** A2
La Nava de Ricomalillo, Spain, **115** B3
La Orchila, *island,* Venezuela, **93** D4
La Oroya, Peru, **101** B3
La Paz, Mexico, **89** B2
La Paz, Bolivia, **101** C4
La Paz, Argentina, **103** D3
La Perouse Strait, *gulf,* Russian Federation, **165** D1
La Plata, Argentina, **103** D4
La Quiaca, Argentina, **103** B1
La Rioja, Argentina, **103** B3
La Rochelle, France, **113** B3
La Roche-sur-Yon, France, **113** B3
La Roda, Spain, **115** C3
La Serena, Chile, **103** B3
La Spezia, Italy, **117** B3
La Tortuga, *island,* Venezuela, **93** D4
La Vega, Dominican Republic, **93** C3
Labé, Guinea, **141** A3
Lábrea, Brazil, **97** B2
Labuan, Malaysia, **170** E4
Labuha, Indonesia, **171** G5
Labuhanbilik, Indonesia, **170** B4
Lac de Kossou, *lake,* Côte dşlvoire, **141** B4
Lac de Mbakaou, *lake,* Cameroon, **145** B4
Lac du Bonnet, *Manitoba,* Canada, **79** F5
Lac Faguibine, *lake,* Mali, **141** B2
Lac Minto, *lake, Québec,* Canada, **81** C2
Lac Tchad, *lake,* Chad, **145** B2
Lac-Gatineau, *Québec,* Canada, **81** C4
Ladozhskoye Ozero, *lake,* Russian Federation, **107** E4
Ladysmith, South Africa, **149** D4
Lae, Papua New Guinea, **175** D1
Lafayette, *Louisiana,* U.S.A., **85** D6
Lafayette, *Indiana,* U.S.A., **87** B3
Lafia, Nigeria, **141** D4
Laghouat, Algeria, **141** D1
Lago Argentino, *lake,* Argentina, **103** B6
Lago Buenos Aires, *lake,* Argentina, **103** B6
Lago Colhué Huapi, *lake,* Argentina, **103** B5
Lago de Cahora Bassa, *lake,* Mozambique, **149** D2
Lago de Chapala, *lake,* Mexico, **89** C3
Lago de Managua, *lake,* Nicaragua, **91** A3
Lago de Maracaibo, *lake,* Venezuela, **97** B2
Lago de Nicaragua, *lake,* Nicaragua, **91** B3
Lago General Carrera, *lake,* Chile, **103** B6
Lago Poopó, *lake,* Bolivia, **101** D4
Lago Titicaca, *lake,* Bolivia, **101** C4
Lago Mar Chiquita, *lake,* Argentina, **103** C3
Lago Musters, *lake,* Argentina, **103** B5
Lagoa dos Patos, *lake,* Brazil, **99** C5
Lagoa Mirim, *lake,* Brazil, **97** C5
Lagos, Portugal, **115** A4
Lagos, Nigeria, **141** D4
Laguna, Brazil, **97** C5
Laguna de Términos, *lake,* Mexico, **89** E3
Lahad Datu, Malaysia, **171** F4
Laḩij, Yemen, **133** B6
Lahore, Pakistan, **157** B2
Lahti, Finland, **107** D4
Lai Châu, Vietnam, **167** C2
Laihia, Finland, **107** D4
Lairg, Scotland, **109** C2
Lajes, Brazil, **97** C5
Lake Albert, Uganda, **147** B4
Lake Athabasca, *Saskatchewan,* Canada, **79** E4
Lake Bangweulu, Zambia, **149** D2
Lake Barlee, Australia, **175** A4
Lake Carnegie, Australia, **175** B4
Lake Charles, *Louisiana,* U.S.A., **85** D6
Lake Coleridge, New Zealand, **177** B5
Lake Erie, *Ohio,* U.S.A., **87** C3
Lake Eyasi, Tanzania, **147** C4
Lake Eyre North, Australia, **175** C4
Lake Frome, Australia, **175** D4
Lake Gairdner, Australia, **175** C5
Lake George, *Florida,* U.S.A., **87** C6
Lake Havasu City, *Arizona,* U.S.A., **83** C5
Lake Hawea, New Zealand, **177** B6
Lake Huron, *Michigan,* U.S.A., **87** C2
Lake Kariba, Zimbabwe, **149** C3
Lake Kivu, Democratic Republic of the Congo, **145** E5
Lake Macfarlane, Australia, **175** C5
Lake Mackay, Australia, **175** B3
Lake Mai-Ndombe, Democratic Republic of the Congo, **145** C5
Lake Malawi, Malawi, **149** D2
Lake Manapouri, New Zealand, **177** A6
Lake Manitoba, *Manitoba,* Canada, **79** F5
Lake Marion, *South Carolina,* U.S.A., **87** C5
Lake Michigan, *Michigan,* U.S.A., **85** E3
Lake Moore, Australia, **175** A4
Lake Murray, Papua New Guinea, **175** D1
Lake Mweru, Democratic Republic of the Congo, **145** E6
Lake Mweru, Tanzania, **145** E6
Lake Mweru, Zambia, **149** C1
Lake Nasser, Egypt, **137** E4
Lake Natron, Tanzania, **147** C4
Lake Nipigon, *Ontario,* Canada, **87** B1
Lake Nipissing, *Ontario,* Canada, **81** B4
Lake Ohau, New Zealand, **177** B6
Lake Okeechobee, *Florida,* U.S.A., **87** C7
Lake Ontario, *New York,* U.S.A., **87** C3
Lake Powell, *Utah,* U.S.A., **83** C5
Lake Pukaki, New Zealand, **177** B5
Lake Rotorua, New Zealand, **177** D3
Lake Rukwa, Tanzania, **145** E6
Lake Sumner, New Zealand, **177** C5
Lake Superior, *Michigan,* U.S.A, **87** A2
Lake Tahoe, *California,* U.S.A., **83** A4
Lake Tanganyika, Democratic Republic of the Congo, **145** E6
Lake Tarawera, New Zealand, **177** D3
Lake Taupo, New Zealand, **177** D3
Lake Te Anau, New Zealand, **177** A6
Lake Tekapo, New Zealand, **177** B5
Lake Texoma, *Oklahoma,* U.S.A., **85** C5
Lake Torrens, Australia, **175** D4
Lake Tumba, Democratic Republic of the Congo, **145** C5
Lake Turkana, Kenya, **147** C3
Lake Victoria, Uganda, **147** B4
Lake Volta, Ghana, **141** C4
Lake Wakatipu, New Zealand, **177** B6
Lake Wanaka, New Zealand, **177** B6
Lake Winnipeg, *Manitoba,* Canada, **79** F5
Lakewood, *Colorado,* U.S.A., **83** E4
Lakota, Côte d'Ivoire, **141** B4
Lakselv, Norway, **107** D1
Lakshadweep Island (Laccadive I.) India, **157** B5
Laliki, Indonesia, **171** G7
Lamakera, Indonesia, **171** G7
Lambaréné, Gabon, **145** A5
Lamesa, *Texas,* U.S.A., **85** B5
Lamia, Greece, **125** C5
Lamitan, Philippines, **171** F3
Lampang, Thailand, **167** C3
Lamphun, Thailand, **167** B3
Lamu, Kenya, **147** D4
Lancang, *river,* China, **161** C4
Lancaster, *South Carolina,* U.S.A., **87** C5
Lancaster, *Pennsylvania,* U.S.A., **87** D4
Lancaster, England, **109** D5
Landeck, Austria, **123** A4
Lander, *Wyoming,* U.S.A., **83** D3
Land's End, *point,* England, **109** B7
Landshut, Germany, **111**, D5
Lang Shan, *mountain,* China, **161** C3
Lạng Sơn, Vietnam, **167** D2
Langres, France, **113** D2
Länkäran, Azerbaijan, **129** E4
Lannion, France, **113** A2
Lansing, *Michigan,* U.S.A., **87** B3
Lanzarote, *island,* Islas Canarias/Spain, **141** A2
Lanzhou, China, **161** C3
Laon, France, **113** C2
Laos, *country,* **167** C3
Lappeenranta, Finland, **107** E4
Lapua, Finland, **107** D4
Lapväärtti, Finland, **107** D4
Laramie, *Wyoming,* U.S.A., **83** E3
Laredo, *Texas,* U.S.A., **85** B7
Larisa, Greece, **125** C4
Lārkāna, Pakistan, **157** B3
Larne, Northern Ireland, **109** C4
Larvik, Norway, **107** B5
Las Cruces, *New Mexico,* U.S.A., **83** D6
Las Palmas de Gran Canaria, Islas Canarias/Spain, **141** A3
Las Piedras, Uruguay, **103** D3
Las Tablas, Panama, **91** C4
Las Vegas, *Nevada,* U.S.A., **83** C5
Las Vegas, *New Mexico,* U.S.A., **83** E5
Latina, Italy, **117** C4
Lātūr, India, **157** C4
Latvia, *country,* **121** B2
Launceston, England, **109** C7
Launceston, Australia, **175** E6
Laurel, *Mississippi,* U.S.A., **85** E6
Lauria, Italy, **117** D5
Lausanne, Switzerland, **117** A2
Laval, *Québec,* Canada, **81** C4
Laval, France, **113** B2
Lawton, *Oklahoma,* U.S.A., **85** C5
Le Creusot, France, **113** C3
Le Havre, France, **113** B2
Le Mans, France, **113** B2
Le Puy-en-Velay, France, **113** C4
Lebak, Philippines, **171** G4
Lebanon, *Missouri,* U.S.A., **85** D4
Lebanon, *country,* **137** E2
Lębork, Poland, **123** C1
Lebu, Chile, **103** A4
Lecce, Italy, **117** E4
Ledesma, Spain, **115** B2
Leeds, England, **109** D5
Leesburg, *Florida,* U.S.A., **87** C6
Leeuwarden, Netherlands, **111** B2
Leeward Island, Caribbean Sea, **105** A3
Lefkosia (Nicosia), Cyprus, **129** C4
Leganés, Spain, **115** C2
Legazpi, Philippines, **171** G2
Legnica, Poland, **123** C3
Leh, India, **157** C2
Leicester, England, **109** D5
Leiden, Netherlands, **111** B2
Leipzig, Germany, **111** D3
Leiria, Portugal, **115** A3
Leirvik, Norway, **107** A4
Lempdes, France, **113** C4
Lena, *river,* Russian Federation, **153** D3
Lengshui Jiang, China, **161** D4
Lensk, Russian Federation, **153** D3
León, Mexico, **89** C3
León, Nicaragua, **91** B3
León, Spain, **115** B1
Lermoos, Austria, **123** A4
Lerwick, Scotland, **109** D1
Les Sables-d'Olonne, France, **113** B3
Leskovac, Yugoslavia, **125** C3
Lesosibirsk, Russian Federation, **153** C3
Lesotho, *country,* **149** C5
Lesser Antilles, *island,* Venezuela, **97** C1
Lesvos (Lesbos), *island,* Greece, **125** E5
Leszno, Poland, **123** C3
Lethem, Guyana, **97** D3
Leticia, Colombia, **97** A2
Letpadan, Myanmar (Burma), **167** B3
Letterkenny, Ireland, **109** B4
Leuven, Belgium, **111** B3
Levadeia, Greece, **125** C5
Levanger, Norway, **107** B3
Levelland, *Texas,* U.S.A., **85** B5
Lewiston, *Idaho,* U.S.A., **83** B2
Lewistown, *Montana,* U.S.A., **83** D2
Lexington, *Kentucky,* U.S.A., **87** B4
Leyte, *island,* Philippines, **171** G3
Lezhë, Albania, **125** B3
Lhasa, China, **161** B4
Lianyungang, China, **161** D3
Liaoyuan, China, **161** E2
Liard, *river, Yukon Territory,* Canada, **79** D3
Libenge, Democratic Republic of the Congo, **145** C4
Liberal, *Kansas,* U.S.A., **85** B4
Liberec, Czech Republic, **123** C3
Liberia, *country,* **141** A4
Libourne, France, **113** B4
Libreville, Gabon, **145** A5
Libya, *country,* **137** B3
Libyan Desert, Sudan, **137** C3
Libyan Desert, Egypt, **137** C3
Libyan Desert, Libya, **137** C3
Libyan Plateau, *mountain,* Libya, **137** C2
Licata, Italy, **117** C6
Lichinga, Mozambique, **149** E2
Lida, Belarus, **121** C4
Liechtenstein, *country,* **117** B1
Liège, Belgium, **111** B3
Lieksa, Finland, **107** E3
Lienz, Austria, **123** B5
Liepāja, Latvia, **121** A3
Liezen, Austria, **123** C4
Liffey, *river,* Ireland, **109** B5
Lifford, Ireland, **109** B4
Likasi, Democratic Republic of the Congo, **145** D7
Lille, France, **113** C1
Lillehammer, Norway, **107** B4
Lilongwe, Malawi, **149** D2
Lima, Peru, **101** B3
Limbe, Cameroon, **145** A4
Limburg an der Lahn, Germany, **111** C3
Limerick, Ireland, **109** A5
Limnos, *island,* Greece, **125** D4
Limoeiro, Brazil, **97** E2
Limoges, France, **113** C3
Limpopo, *river,* Mozambique, **149** D4
Linares, Mexico, **89** C2
Linares, Spain, **115** C3
Lincang, China, **161** C4
Lincoln, *Nebraska,* U.S.A., **85** C3
Lincoln, England, **109** D5
Linden, Guyana, **97** D2
Lindi, Tanzania, **147** C5
Lindsay, *Ontario,* Canada, **81**, B4
Linfen, China, **161** D3
Linhe, China, **161** C3
Linköping, Sweden, **107** C5
Linz, Austria, **123** C4
Lipetsk, Russian Federation, **153** A2
Lisala, Democratic Republic of the Congo, **145** C4
Lisboa (Lisbon), Portugal, **115** A3
Lismore, Australia, **175** E4
Lithuania, *country,* **121** B3
Little Andaman, *island,* India, **157** E5
Little Cayman, *island,* Cayman Islands, **93** A2
Little Colorado, *river, Arizona* U.S.A., **83** C5
Little Falls, *Minnesota,* U.S.A., **85** D2
Little Inagua Island, Bahamas, **93** C2
Little Nicobar, *island,* India, **167** A6
Little Rock, *Arkansas,* U.S.A., **85** D5
Liupanshui, China, **161** C4
Liuzhou, China, **161** D4
Liverpool, England, **109** D5
Livingston, *Montana,* U.S.A., **83** D2
Livingstone, Zambia, **149** C3
Livingstonia, Malawi, **149** D2
Livno, Bosnia and Herzegovina, **125** B2
Livorno, Italy, **117** B3
Liwale, Tanzania, **147** C5
Ljubljana, Slovenia, **125** A1
Ljungby, Sweden, **107** B6
Ljusdal, Sweden, **107** C4
Lleida, Spain, **115** D2
Loano, Italy, **117** B3
Lobito, Angola, **149** A2
Loch Lomond, *lake,* Scotland, **109** C3
Loch Ness, *lake,* Scotland, **109** C3
Locri, Italy, **117** D5
Lodwar, Kenya, **147** C3
Łódź, Poland, **123** D3
Lofoten, *island,* Norway, **107** B2
Logan, *Utah,* U.S.A., **83** C3
Logone, *river,* Chad, **145** B3
Logroño, Spain, **115** C1
Loi-kaw, Myanmar (Burma), **167** B3
Loire, *river,* France, **113** B3
Loja, Ecuador, **101** A2
Lokofe, Democratic Republic of the Congo, **145** D5
Lokoja, Nigeria, **141** D4
Lokomo, Cameroon, **145** B4
Lom Sak, Thailand, **167** C4
Lomami, *river,* Democratic Republic of the Congo, **145** D5
Lomas de Zamora, Argentina, **103** D4
Lombok, *island,* Indonesia, **170** E7
Lomé, Togo, **141** C4
Lompoc, *California,* U.S.A., **83** A5
Łomża, Poland, **123** E2
London, *Ontario,* Canada, **81** B4
London, England, **109** E6
Londonderry, Northern Ireland, **109** B4
Londrina, Brazil, **97** C4
Long Bay, *gulf,* U.S.A., **87** C5
Long Beach, *California,* U.S.A., **83** B6
Long Island, *New York,* U.S.A., **87** E3
Long Island, *island,* Bahamas, **93** B2
Long Xuyên, Vietnam, **167** D5
Longford, Ireland, **109** B5
Longnawan, Indonesia, **170** E5
Longreach, Australia, **175** D3
Longview, *Texas,* U.S.A., **85** C6
Lop Buri, Thailand, **167** C4
Lop Nur, *lake,* China, **161** B3
Lorca, Spain, **115** C4
Lordsburg, *New Mexico,* U.S.A., **83** D6
Lorengau, Papua New Guinea, **175** E1
Lorient, France, **113** A2
Los Alamos, *New Mexico,* U.S.A., **83** E5
Los Angeles, *California,* U.S.A., **83** B6
Los Angeles, Chile, **103** B4
Los Mochis, Mexico, **89** B2
Louang Namtha, Laos, **167** C3
Louangphrabang, Laos, **167** C3
Loubomo, Congo, **145** B6
Loudéac, France, **113** A2
Louga, Senegal, **141** A2
Lough Derg, *lake,* Ireland, **109** B5
Lough Neagh, *lake,* Northern Ireland, **109** B4
Louisiade Arch., *island,* Papua New Guinea, **175** E2
Louisiana, *state,* U.S.A., **85** D6
Louisville, *Kentucky,* U.S.A., **87** B4
Lourdes, France, **113** B5
Louth, England, **109** E5
Louviers, France, **113** C2
Lovelock, *Nevada,* U.S.A., **83** B4
Lower Hutt, New Zealand, **177** D4
Lowestoft, England, **109** E5
Łowicz, Poland, **123** D2
Loxton, South Africa, **149** C5
Lučenec, Slovakia, **123** D4
Lualuba, *river,* Democratic Republic of the Congo, **145** D5
Luama, *river,* Democratic Republic of the Congo, **145** D6
Luanda, Angola, **149** A1
Luanguinga, *river,* Zambia, **149** B2
Luangwa, *river,* Zambia, **149** D2
Luanshya, Zambia, **149** D2
Lubang Island, Philippines, **171** F2
Lubango, Angola, **149** A2
Lubbock, *Texas,* U.S.A., **85** B5
Lübeck, Germany, **111** D2
Lubin, Poland, **123** C3
Lublin, Poland, **123** E3
Lubny, Ukraine, **129** C1
Lubumbashi, Democratic Republic of the Congo, **145** D7
Lucca, Italy, **117** B3
Luckenwalde, Germany, **111** E3
Lucknow, India, **157** C3
Lucusse, Angola, **149** B2
Lüderitz, Namibia, **149** B4
Ludhiāna, India, **157** C2
Ludvika, Sweden, **107** C5
Ludwigslust, Germany, **111** D2
Ludza, Latvia, **121** C2
Luena, Angola, **149** B2
Luga, *river,* Russian Federation, **121** D1
Lugo, Spain, **115** B1
Luhans'k, Ukraine, **129** C2
Luiza, Democratic Republic of the Congo, **145** D6
Łuków, Poland, **123** E2
Luleå, Sweden, **107** D3
Lumbala N'guimbo, Angola, **149** B2
Lumsden, New Zealand, **177** B6
Lunde, Sweden, **107** C4
Lüneburg, Germany, **111** D2
Luninyets, Belarus, **121** D4
Lunsar, Sierra Leone, **141** A4
Luoyang, China, **161** D3
Luozi, Democratic Republic of the Congo, **145** B6
Lurgan, Northern Ireland, **109** B4
Lusaka, Zambia, **149** C2
Lusambo, Democratic Republic of the Congo, **145** D6
Lushoto, Tanzania, **147** C4
Lutherstadt Wittenberg, Germany, **111** D3
Luton, England, **109** E6
Luts'k, Ukraine, **129** A1
Luxembourg, *country,* **111** B4
Luzern, Switzerland, **117** B1
Luzhou, China, **161** C4
Luzon, *island,* Philippines, **171** F1
L'viv, Ukraine, **129** A1
Lycksele, Sweden, **107** C3
Lyepyel', Belarus, **121** D3
Lynn Lake, *Manitoba,* Canada, **79** F4
Lyon, France, **113** D3
Lysychans'k, Ukraine, **129** C1
Lyuban', Belarus, **121** D4

Mā, *river,* Vietnam, **167** D3
Ma'ān, Jordan, **133** A3
Maanselkä, Finland, **107** E3
Maba, Indonesia, **171** H5
Mabote, Mozambique, **149** D3
Macao, China, **161** D4
Macapá, Brazil, **97** C1
Macas, Ecuador, **101** A2
MacDonnell Ranges, *mountain,* Australia, **175** C4
Macedonia, *country,* **125**, C3
Maceió, Brazil, **97** E3
Macerata, Italy, **117** C3
Machakos, Kenya, **147** C4
Machala, Ecuador, **101** A2
Machanga, Mozambique, **149** D3
Mackay, Australia, **175** E3
Mackenzie, *river, Northwest Territories* Canada, **79** D2
Mackenzie Mountains, *mountain range, Northwest Territories,* Canada, **79** D3
Macon, *Georgia,* U.S.A., **87** B5
Mâcon, France, **113** D3
Macquarie Island, Antarctica, **183** B4
Madagascar, *country,* **151** A3
Madang, Papua New Guinea, **175** D1
Madeira, *river,* Brazil, **99** B2
Madeira, *island,* Portugal, **141** A1
Madison, *Wisconsin,* U.S.A., **85** E3
Madona, Latvia, **121** C2
Madre de Dios, *river,* Peru, **99** A3
Madrid, Spain, **115** C2
Madura, *island,* Indonesia, **170** D6
Madurai, India, **157** C6
Mae Hong Son, Thailand, **167** B3
Mae Nam Ping, *river,* Thailand, **167** B4
Mae Sariang, Thailand, **167** B3
Mae Sot, Thailand, **167** B4
Mafia Island, *island,* Tanzania, **147** D5
Mafinga, Tanzania, **147** C5
Magadan, Russian Federation, **153** E2
Magdagachi, Russian Federation, **153** D3
Magdalena, Mexico, **89** B1
Magdalena, *river,* Colombia, **97** A3
Magdalena, Bolivia, **101** D3
Magdeburg, Germany, **111** D3
Magelang, Indonesia, **170** D6
Maglić, *mountain peak,* Yugoslavia, **125** B3
Magwe, Myanmar (Burma), **167** A3
Maha Sarakham, Thailand, **167** C4
Mahakam, *river,* Indonesia, **170** E5
Mahalapye, Botswana, **149** C4
Mahdia, Tunisia, **141** E1
Mahe, India, **157** B5
Mahia Pen., *point,* New Zealand, **177** E3
Mahilyow, Belarus, **121** D3
Mahina, Mali, **141** A3
Mahoenui, New Zealand, **177** D3
Mahón, Spain, **115** E2
Maidi, Indonesia, **171** G5
Maidstone, England, **109** E6
Maiduguri, Nigeria, **141** E3
Maine, *state,* U.S.A., **87** E2
Mainland, *island,* Scotland, **109** D1
Maitland, Australia, **175** E5
Majene, Indonesia, **171** F6
Makeni, Sierra Leone, **141** A4
Makiyivka, Ukraine, **129** C2
Makkah (Mecca), Saudi Arabia, **133** B5
Makokou, Gabon, **145** B5
Makoua, Congo, **145** B5
Makurdi, Nigeria, **141** D4
Malāyer, Iran, **133** C2
Malabo, Equatorial Guinea, **145** A4
Maladzyechna, Belarus, **121** C3
Málaga, Spain, **115** B4
Malakāl, Sudan, **147** B2
Malang, Indonesia, **170** D7
Malanje, Angola, **149** B2
Malaryta, Belarus, **121** C5
Malatya, Turkey, **129** C4
Malawi, *country,* **149** D2
Malaysia, *country,* **170** B4
Malbork, Poland, **123** D2
Maldives, *country,* **151** B2
Maldonado, Uruguay, **103** D4
Male, Maldives, **157** B6
Malè, Italy, **117** B2
Mālegaon, India, **157** B4
Mali, *country,* **141** C2
Malin Head, *point,* Ireland, **109** B4
Malindi, Kenya, **147** D4
Mallorca, *island,* Spain, **115** E2
Mallow, Ireland, **109** A6
Malmesbury, South Africa, **149** B5
Malmö, Sweden, **107** B6
Måløy, Norway, **107** A4
Malta, *country,* **117** D6
Malta, Latvia, **121** C2
Malung, Sweden, **107** B4
Maluso, Philippines, **171** F4
Mamburao, Philippines, **171** F2
Mamoré, *river,* Bolivia, **101** D3
Mamou, Guinea, **141** A3
Man, Côte d'Ivoire, **141** B4
Mana, French Guiana, **97** E2
Manacor, Spain, **115** E3
Manado, Indonesia, **171** G5
Managua, Nicaragua, **91** B3
Manas Hu, *lake,* China, **155** E2
Manaus, Brazil, **99** B2
Manchester, *New Hampshire* U.S.A., **87** E3
Manchester, England, **109** D5
Mandalay, Myanmar (Burma), **167** B2
Mandalgovĭ, Mongolia, **161** C2
Mandan, *North Dakota,* U.S.A., **85** B2
Mandurah, Australia, **175** A5
Manduria, Italy, **117** E4
Manfredonia, Italy, **117** D4
Mangakino, New Zealand, **177** D3
Mangalore, India, **157** B5
Manggar, Indonesia, **170** C5
Mango, Togo, **141** C3
Manhattan, *Kansas,* U.S.A., **85** C4
Manila, Philippines, **171** F2
Manisa, Turkey, **129** B4
Manistee, *Michigan,* U.S.A., **87** B3
Manitoba, *province,* Canada, **79** F5
Manizales, Colombia, **97** A3
Manna, Indonesia, **170** B6
Mannheim, Germany, **111** C4
Manokwari, Indonesia, **171** J5
Manono, Democratic Republic of the Congo, **145** D6
Mansa, Zambia, **149** D2
Mansel Island, *Québec,* Canada, **81** B1
Manta, Ecuador, **101** A1
Mantova, Italy, **117** B2
Mäntsälä, Finland, **107** D4
Manukau, New Zealand, **177** D2
Manunui, New Zealand, **177** D3
Manzanillo, Mexico, **89** C3
Mapi, Indonesia, **171** K6
Maputo, Mozambique, **149** D4
Mar del Plata, Argentina, **103** D4
Mara, South Africa, **149** D4
Maracaibo, Venezuela, **97** B1
Maracay, Venezuela, **97** C2
Marādah, Libya, **137** B2
Maradi, Niger, **141** D3
Marāgheh, Iran, **133** C2
Maralal, Kenya, **147** C4
Marañón, *river,* Peru, **101** B2
Marapanim, Brazil, **97** D1
Marathon, *Texas,* U.S.A., **85** A6
Marau Point, *point,* New Zealand, **177** E3
Marbella, Spain, **115** B4
Marburg, South Africa, **149** D5
Marcona, Peru, **101** B4
Mardin, Turkey, **129** D4
Margate, England, **109** E6
Marhoum, Algeria, **141** C1
Mariazell, Austria, **123** C4
Maribor, Slovenia, **125** A1
Mariental, Namibia, **149** B4
Mariestad, Sweden, **107** B5
Marijampolė, Lithuania, **121** B3
Marinette, *Wisconsin,* U.S.A., **87** B2
Maringá, Brazil, **97** C4
Mariscal Estigarribia, Paraguay, **103** C1
Mariupol', Ukraine, **129** C2
Marka, Somalia, **147** D4
Marmande, France, **113** B4
Marmaris, Turkey, **129** B4
Maroua, Cameroon, **145** B3
Marquette, *Michigan,* U.S.A., **87** B2
Marrakech (Marrakesh), Morocco, **141** B2
Marrupa, Mozambique, **149** E2
Marsá al Burayqah, Libya, **137** C2
Marsá Maţrūḩ, Egypt, **137** D2
Marsabit, Kenya, **147** C3
Marsala, Italy, **117** C6
Marseille, France, **113** D5
Marshall, *Minnesota,* U.S.A., **85** C3
Marshall Islands, *country,* **179** B2
Martapura, Indonesia, **170** C6
Martinique, French Department, **93** E3
Mary, Turkmenistan, **155** B4
Maryborough, Australia, **175** E4
Maryland, *state,* U.S.A., **87** D4
Marysville, *California,* U.S.A., **83** A4
Masaka, Uganda, **147** B4
Masallı, Azerbaijan, **129** E4
Masan, South Korea, **165** B3
Masasi, Tanzania, **147** C5
Masbate, Philippines, **171** G2
Masbate Island, Philippines, **171** G2
Mascara, Algeria, **141** D1
Maseru, Lesotho, **149** C5
Mashava, Zimbabwe, **149** D3
Mashhad, Iran, **133** E2
Masjed Soleymān, Iran, **133** C3
Mason City, *Iowa,* U.S.A., **85** D3
Masqaţ (Muscat), Oman, **133** E4
Massachusetts, *state,* U.S.A., **87** D3
Massawa, Eritrea, **147** C2
Massenya, Chad, **145** B3
Massif de l'Adamaoua, *mountain,* Cameroon, **145** B3
Masterton, New Zealand, **177** D4
Masty, Belarus, **121** C4
Masvingo, Zimbabwe, **149** D3
Matadi, Democratic Republic of the Congo, **145** B6
Matagalpa, Nicaragua, **91** B3
Matam, Senegal, **141** A2
Matamoros, Mexico, **89** D2
Matane, *Québec,* Canada, **81** D3
Matanzas, Cuba, **93** A2
Matara, Sri Lanka, **157** C6
Mataram, Indonesia, **170** E7
Mataró, Spain, **115** E2
Matata, New Zealand, **177** D3
Matehuala, Mexico, **89** C3
Matera, Italy, **117** D4
Matola, Mozambique, **149** D4
Matsue, Japan, **165** C3
Matsumoto, Japan, **165** D3
Matsuyama, Japan, **165** C4
Matterhorn, *mountain peak,* Switzerland, **117** A2
Maturín, Venezuela, **97** C2
Maués, Brazil, **97** C2
Maun, Botswana, **149** C3
Mauritania, *country,* **141** A2
Mauritius, *country,* **151** A3
Mavinga, Angola, **149** B3
Mawasangka, Indonesia, **171** F6
Mawson, Antarctica (Australia), **183** C2
Mayaguana, *island,* Bahamas, **93** C2
Mayagüez, U.S.A., **93** D3
Maymyo, Myanmar (Burma), **167** B2
Mayraira Pt, *point,* Philippines, **171** F1
Mayumba, Gabon, **145** A5
Mazār-e Sharīf, Afghanistan, **155** C4
Mazatlán, Mexico, **89** B3
Mažeikiai, Lithuania, **121** B3
Mazyr, Belarus, **121** D4
Mbabane, Swaziland, **149** D4
Mbaïki, Central African Republic, **145** C4
Mbala, Zambia, **149** D1
Mbale, Uganda, **147** C4
Mbalmayo, Cameroon, **145** B4
Mbandaka, Democratic Republic of the Congo, **145** C5
M'banza Congo, Angola, **149** A1
Mbeya, Tanzania, **147** C5
Mbour, Senegal, **141** A3
Mbuji-Mayi, Democratic Republic of the Congo, **145** D6
McAllen, *Texas,* U.S.A., **85** B7
McCook, *Nebraska,* U.S.A., **85** B4
McGill, *Nevada,* U.S.A., **83** C4
McKenzie, *Tennessee,* U.S.A., **87** A4
M'Clure Strait, *gulf,* Canada, **79** E2
McMurdo, Antarctica (U.S.A.), **183** B3
Mdandu, Tanzania, **147** C5
Mechelen, Belgium, **111** B3
Mecheria, Algeria, **141** C1
Medan, Indonesia, **170** A4
Medellín, Colombia, **97** A2
Medford, *Oregon,* U.S.A., **83** A3
Medinaceli, Spain, **115** C2
Meekatharra, Australia, **175** A4
Meerut, India, **157** C2
Mega, Ethiopia, **147** C3
Meiktila, Myanmar (Burma), **167** B3
Mek'elē, Ethiopia, **147** C2
Meknès, Morocco, **141** C1
Mekong, *river,* Laos, **167** C3
Mekong, *river,* Cambodia, **170** C2
Melaka, Malaysia, **170** B4
Melbourne, Florida, U.S.A., **87** C6
Melbourne, Australia, **175** D5
Melilla, Spain, **141** C1
Melitopolş, Ukraine, **129** C2
Melville Island, *Northwest Territories,* Canada, **79** F2
Melville Island, Australia, **175** C2
Melville Pen., *point, Nunavut,* Canada, **79** G3
Membalong, Indonesia, **170** C6
Memingen, Germany, **111** C5
Memphis, *Tennessee,* U.S.A., **87** A5
Mende, France, **113** C4
Mendoza, Argentina, **103** B3
Menongue, Angola, **149** B2
Menorca, *island,* Spain, **115** E2
Meoqui, Mexico, **89** B2
Meppen, Germany, **111** C2
Merano, Italy, **117** C2
Merauke, Indonesia, **171** K7
Merced, *California,* U.S.A., **83** A5
Mercedes, Argentina, **103** C3
Mercury Bay, *gulf,* New Zealand, **177** D2
Mereeg, Somalia, **147** E3
Mergui, Myanmar (Burma), **167** B5
Mergui Archipelago, *island,* Myanmar (Burma), **167** B5
Mérida, Mexico, **89** E3
Mérida, Venezuela, **97** B2
Mérida, Spain, **115** B3
Meridian, *Mississippi,* U.S.A., **85** E6
Merkinė, Lithuania, **121** C4
Merredin, Australia, **175** A5
Méru, France, **113** C2
Merzifon, Turkey, **129** C3
Mesa, *Arizona,* U.S.A., **83** C6
Mescit Tepe, *mountain,* Turkey, **133** B1
Mesolongi, Greece, **125** C5
Messina, Italy, **117** D5
Messina, South Africa, **149** D4
Mestre, Italy, **117** C2
Meszah Peak, *mountain, British Columbia,* Canada, **79** D3
Meta, *river,* Venezuela, **97** A1
Metairie, *Louisiana,* U.S.A., **85** D6
Metković, Croatia, **125** B3
Metu, Ethiopia, **147** C3
Metz, France, **113** D2
Mexicali, Mexico, **89** A1
Mexico, *country,* **89** C3
México, Mexico, **89** C3
Meymaneh, Afghanistan, **155** C4
Mezőkövesd, Hungary, **123** D4
Mezőtúr, Hungary, **123** E4
Mi'rātah, Libya, **137** B2
Miami, *Florida,* U.S.A., **87** C7
Michigan, *state,* U.S.A., **87** B3
Micronesia, *country,* **179** A2
Middelburg, Netherlands, **111** A3
Middle Andaman, *island,* India, **157** E5
Middlesboro, *Kentucky,* U.S.A., **87** B4
Middlesbrough, England, **109** D4
Midland, *Texas,* U.S.A., **85** B6
Midland, *Michigan,* U.S.A., **87** B3
Midway Islands, U.S.A., **179** B1
Mieres, Spain, **115** B1

Palembang, Indonesia, **170** C6
Palencia, Spain, **115** B2
Palermo, Italy, **117** C5
Palinuro, Italy, **117** D5
Palliser Bay, *gulf*, New Zealand, **177** D4
Palm Springs, *California*, U.S.A., **83** B6
Palma de Mallorca, Spain, **115** E3
Palmer, *Alaska*, U.S.A., **79** C2
Palmerston North, New Zealand, **177** D4
Palmi, Italy, **117** D5
Palmira, Colombia, **97** A3
Palmyras Pt, *point*, India, **157** D4
Palu, Indonesia, **171** F5
Pamdai, Indonesia, **171** J5
Pamekasan, Indonesia, **170** E6
Pamiers, France, **113** C5
Pamirs, *mountain range*, Tajikistan, **155** D4
Pampa, *Texas*, U.S.A., **85** B5
Pampas, *mountain*, Argentina, **103** C4
Pamplona, Spain, **115** C1
Panagyurishte, Bulgaria, **129** A3
Panaji, India, **157** B5
Panama, *country*, **91** C4
Panamá, Panama, **91** C4
Panama Canal, *river*, Panama, **91** C4
Panama City, *Florida*, U.S.A., **87** B6
Panay, *island*, Philippines, **171** F3
Panevėžys, Lithuania, **121** B3
Pangkalpinang, Indonesia, **170** C5
Panzhihua, China, **161** C4
Paola, Italy, **117** D5
Papua New Guinea, *country*, **175** E1
Papun, Myanmar (Burma), **167** B3
Paraguay, *country*, **103** C2
Paraguay, *river*, Paraguay, **103** D2
Parakou, Benin, **141** C4
Paramaribo, Suriname, **97** C1
Parana, *river*, Argentina, **103** C3
Paraná, Argentina, **103** C3
Paraná, *river*, Brazil, **103** E1
Paranaíba, Brazil, **97** C4
Parbhani, India, **157** C4
Parczew, Poland, **123** E3
Parepare, Indonesia, **171** F6
Paris, *Texas*, U.S.A., **85** C5
Paris, France, **113** C2
Parkano, Finland, **107** D4
Parkes, Australia, **175** E5
Parma, Italy, **117** B2
Parnaíba, Brazil, **97** D2
Parnaíba, *river*, Brazil, **97** D2
Pärnu, Estonia, **121** B2
Paroo, *river*, Australia, **175** D4
Paros, *island*, Greece, **129** A4
Parthenay, France, **113** B3
Pasadena, *California*, U.S.A., **83** B5
Pasadena, *Texas*, U.S.A., **85** C6
Pasco, *Washington*, U.S.A., **83** B2
Paso de los Toros, Uruguay, **103** D3
Passau, Germany, **111** E5
Passo Fundo, Brazil, **97** C5
Pastavy, Belarus, **121** C3
Pasto, Colombia, **97** A3
Patagonia, *mountain*, Argentina, **103** B6
Patna, India, **157** D3
Patos, Brazil, **97** E2
Patos de Minas, Brazil, **97** D4
Patra, Greece, **125** C5
Pattani, Thailand, **167** C6
Pattaya, Thailand, **167** C5
Pau, France, **113** B4
Pauillac, France, **113** B4
Paungde, Myanmar (Burma), **167** B3
Pavlodar, Kazakhstan, **155** D1
Pavlohrad, Ukraine, **129** C2
Peć, Yugoslavia, **125** C3
Peace, *river*, *Alberta*, Canada, **79** D4
Pearl, *river*, *Mississippi*, U.S.A., **85** D6
Pecos, *river*, *New Mexico*, U.S.A., **83** E5
Pecos, *Texas*, U.S.A., **85** A6
Pécs, Hungary, **123** D5
Pedra Azul, Brazil, **97** D3
Pedro Afonso, Brazil, **97** D2
Peg. Barisan, *mountain*, Indonesia, **170** B5
Peg. Maoke, *mountain*, Indonesia, **171** J6
Peg. Muller, *mountain*, Indonesia, **170** E5
Peg. Muratus, *mountain*, Indonesia, **170** E6
Peg. Van Rees, *mountain*, Indonesia, **171** J5
Pegasus Bay, *gulf*, New Zealand, **177** C5
Pegu, Myanmar (Burma), **167** B4
Pegu Yoma, *mountain*, Myanmar (Burma), **167** B3
Peipsi Järv, *lake*, Estonia, **121** C1
Peiraias (Piraeus), Greece, **125** D5
Pekanbaru, Indonesia, **170** B5
Pello, Finland, **107** D2
Pelly, *river*, *Yukon Territory*, Canada, **79** D3
Pelly Bay, Canada, **79** F3
Pelotas, Brazil, **97** C5
Pematangsiantar, Indonesia, **170** B4
Pemba, Mozambique, **149** E2
Pemba Island, Tanzania, **147** D4
Pend Oreille Lake, *Idaho*, U.S.A., **83** B1
Pendleton, *Oregon*, U.S.A., **83** B2
Península de Guajira, *island*, Colombia, **97** B1
Península de Guajira, *point*, Colombia, **93** C4
Península de Osa, *point*, Costa Rica, **91** B4
Península de Yucatán, *point*, Mexico, **89** E3
Péninsule d'Ungava, *point*, *Québec*, Canada, **79** H4
Pennines, *mountain*, England, **109** D4
Pennsylvania, *state*, U.S.A., **87** C3
Pensacola, *Florida*, U.S.A., **87** B6
Penza, Russian Federation, **153** A3
Penzance, England, **109** C7
Peoria, *Illinois*, U.S.A., **87** A3
Pereira, Colombia, **97** A3
Pergamino, Argentina, **103** C3
Périgueux, France, **113** B4
Perm', Russian Federation, **153** B3
Přerov, Czech Republic, **123** C4
Perpignan, France, **113** C5
Perryton, *Texas*, U.S.A., **85** B5
Persian Gulf, *gulf*, Iran, **133** C3
Perth, Scotland, **109** C3
Perth, Australia, **175** A5
Peru, *country*, **101** B3
Perugia, Italy, **117** C3
Pescara, Italy, **117** D4
Peshāwar, Pakistan, **157** B2
Peski Kyzylkum, *desert*, Uzbekistan, **155** B3
Pesqueira, Brazil, **97** E2
Peterborough, England, **109** E5
Peterhead, Scotland, **109** D3
Petersburg, *Alaska*, U.S.A., **79** C4
Peto, Mexico, **89** E3
Petoskey, *Michigan*, U.S.A., **87** B2
Petroșani, Romania, **129** A2
Petropavl, Kazakhstan, **155** C1
Petropavlovsk-Kamchatskiy, Russian Federation, **153** E3
Pevek, Russian Federation, **153** E1
Pforzheim, Germany, **111** C4
Phalaborwa, South Africa, **149** D4
Phalodi, India, **157** B3
Phan Rang, Vietnam, **167** E5
Phan Thiết, Vietnam, **167** E5
Phangnga, Thailand, **167** B6
Phayao, Thailand, **167** C3
Phetchabun, Thailand, **167** C4
Phetchaburi, Thailand, **167** C5
Phichit, Thailand, **167** C4
Philadelphia, *Pennsylvania*, U.S.A., **87** D4
Philippines, *country*, **171** G2
Phitsanulok, Thailand, **17** C4
Phnum Pénh (Phnom Penh), Cambodia, **167** D5
Phoenix, *Arizona*, U.S.A., **83** C
Phôngsali, Laos, **167** C2
Phou Bia, *mountain peak*, Laos, **167** C3
Phra Nakhon Si Ayutthaya, Thailand, **167** C4
Phrae, Thailand, **167** C3
Phú Thọ, Vietnam, **167** D2
Phuket, Thailand, **167** B6
Piła, Poland, **123** C2
Piacenza, Italy, **117** B2
Pic de Tibé, *mountain*, Guinea, **141** B4
Pic Toussidé, *mountain peak*, Chad, **145** B1
Picacho del Centinela, *mountain peak*, Mexico, **89** C2
Pickle Lake, *Ontario*, Canada, **81** A3
Pico Basile, *mountain peak*, Equatorial Guinea, **145** A4
Pico Bolívar, *mountain peak*, Venezuela, **97** B2
Pico de Aneto, *mountain peak*, Spain, **115** D1
Pico de Teide, *mountain peak*, Islas Canarias/Spain, **141** A3
Pico Duarte, *mountain peak*, Dominican Republic, **93** C3
Picos, Brazil, **97** E2
Picton, New Zealand, **177** C4
Pidurutalagala, *mountain*, Sri Lanka, **157** C6
Piedras Negras, Mexico, **89** C2
Pieksämäki, Finland, **107** E4
Pierre, *South Dakota*, U.S.A., **85** B2
Pietarsaari, Finland, **107** D3
Pietermaritzburg, South Africa, **149** D5
Pietersburg, South Africa, **149** D4
Pihtipudas, Finland, **107** D3
Pik imeni Ismail Samani, *mountain*, Tajikistan, **155** D4
Pilar, Argentina, **103** D3
Pilbara, *mountain*, Australia, **175** A3
Pilcomayo, *river*, Bolivia, **101** D5
Pilcomayo, *river*, Paraguay, **103** D2
Pimpri-Chinchwad, India, **157** B4
Pinar del Río, Cuba, **93** A2
Pine Bluff, *Arkansas*, U.S.A., **85** D5
Pinerolo, Italy, **117** A2
Piney, France, **113** C2
Pinsk, Belarus, **121** C5
Piombino, Italy, **11** B3
Piotrków Trybunalski, Poland, **123** D3
Piracicaba, Brazil, **97** D4
Pirapora, Brazil, **97** D3
Pirot, Yugoslavia, **125** C3
Pisa, Italy, **117** B3
Pisco, Peru, **101** B4
Písek, Czech Republic, **123** C4
Pissos, France, **113** B4
Pisticci, Italy, **117** D4
Pita, Guinea, **141** A3
Pitanga, Brazil, **97** C4
Pitcairn Islands, U.K. Dependency, **179** D3
Pitești, Romania, **129** A2
Piteå, Sweden, **107** D3
Pittsburgh, *Pennsylvania*, U.S.A., **87** C3
Příbram, Czech Republic, **123** B3
Piura, Peru, **101** A2
Pk Jaya, *mountain*, Indonesia, **171** J6
Pk Mandala, *mountain*, Indonesia, **171** K6
Pk Yamin, *mountain*, Indonesia, **171** K6
Plainview, *Texas*, U.S.A., **85** B5
Plampang, Indonesia, **170** E7
Planalto do Mato Grosso, *mountain*, Brazil, **97** C3
Plasencia, Spain, **115** B3
Plateau du Djado, *mountain*, Niger, **137** A4
Plateau du Tademaït, *mountain*, Algeria, **141** D2
Plato Ustyurt, *mountain*, Kazakhstan, **155** B3
Plauen, Germany, **111** D3
Plây Cu (Pleiku), Vietnam, **167** E4
Pleven, Bulgaria, **129** A3
Pljevlja, Yugoslavia, **125** B3
Ploërmel, France, **113** A2
Plovdiv, Bulgaria, **129** A3
Plungė, Lithuania, **121** B3
Plymouth, England, **109** C7
Plzeň (Pilsen), Czech Republic, **123** B3
Po, *river*, Italy, **117** B2
Požarevac, Yugoslavia, **125** C2
Pocatello, *Idaho*, U.S.A., **83** C3
Podgorica, Yugoslavia, **125** B3
Pofadder, South Africa, **149** B5
P'ohang, South Korea, **165** B3
Pointe de Barfleur, *point*, France, **109** D7
Pointe de Saint-Mathieu, *point*, France, **113** A2
Pointe-à-Pitre, France, **93** E3
Pointe-Noire, Congo, **145** B6
Poitiers, France, **113** B3
Pokaran, India, **157** B3
Pokhara, Nepal, **157** D3
Poland, *country*, **123** D2
Polatlı, Turkey, **129** B4
Polatsk, Belarus, **111** D3
Poltava, Ukraine, **129** C1
Põltsamaa, Estonia, **121** C1
Poluostrov Kamchatka, *point*, Russian Federation, **182** C1
Poluostrov Rybachiy, *island*, Russian Federation, **107** E1
Poluostrov Taymyr, *point*, Russian Federation, **153** C2
Poluostrov Yamal, *point*, Russian Federation, **153** B2
Ponca City, *Oklahoma*, U.S.A., **85** C5
Ponce, U.S.A., **93** D3
Pond Inlet, Canada, **79** G2
Pondicherry, India, **157** C5
Ponferrada, Spain, **115** B1
Ponta Albina, *point*, Angola, **149** A3
Ponta das Palmeirinhas, *point*, Angola, **149** A2
Ponta do Padrão, *point*, Angola, **149** A1
Ponta Grossa, Brazil, **97** C4
Pontevedra, Spain, **115** A1
Pontianak, Indonesia, **170** D5
Pontivy, France, **113** A2
Poole, England, **109** D7
Popayán, Colombia, **97** A3
Popokabaka, Democratic Republic of the Congo, **145** B6
Porbandar, India, **157** B4
Pori, Finland, **107** D4
Porirua, New Zealand, **177** D4
Porjus, Sweden, **107** C2
Porlamar, Venezuela, **97** C1
Poronaysk, Russian Federation, **153** E3
Porpoise Bay, *gulf*, Antarctica, **183** C3
Port Alfred, South Africa, **149** C5
Port Antonio, Jamaica, **93** B3
Port Augusta, Australia, **175** C5
Port Blair, India, **167** A5
Port Elizabeth, South Africa, **149** C5
Port Hardy, *British Columbia*, Canada, **79** C4
Port Headland, Australia, **175** A3
Port Laoise, Ireland, **109** B5
Port Lavaca, *Texas*, U.S.A., **85** C7
Port Lincoln, Australia, **175** C5
Port Macquarie, Australia, **175** E5
Port Moresby, Papua New Guinea, **175** E2
Port of Spain, Trinidad & Tobago, **93** E4
Port Pirie, Australia, **175** C5
Port Stephens, Falkland Islands, **103** C6
Portadown, Northern Ireland, **109** B4
Portalegre, Portugal, **115** B3
Port-au-Prince, Haiti, **93** C3
Portel, Portugal, **115** A3
Port-Gentil, Gabon, **145** A5
Port-Harcourt, Nigeria, **141** D4
Porthmadog, Wales, **109** C5
Portimão, Portugal, **115** A4
Portland, *Oregon*, U.S.A., **83** A2
Port-Menier, *Newfoundland*, Canada, **81** D3
Porto, Portugal, **115** A2
Porto Alegre, Brazil, **97** C5
Porto Amboim, Angola, **149** A2
Pôrto Murtinho, Brazil, **97** C4
Porto Tolle, Italy, **117** C2
Pôrto Velho, Brazil, **97** B2
Porto-Novo, Benin, **141** C4
Portoviejo, Ecuador, **101** A1
Portree, Scotland, **109** B3
Portsmouth, *Virginia*, U.S.A., **87** D4
Portsmouth, *New Hampshire*, U.S.A., **87** E3
Portsmouth, England, **109** D6
Portugal, *country*, **115** A3
Porvoo, Finland, **107** D4
Posadas, Argentina, **103** D2
Postojna, Slovenia, **125** A1
Poteau, *Oklahoma*, U.S.A., **85** C5
Potenza, Italy, **117** D4
P'ot'i, Georgia, **129** D3
Potosí, Bolivia, **101** D5
Potsdam, Germany, **111** D2
Póvoa de Varzim, Portugal, **115** A2
Powder, *river*, *Montana*, U.S.A., **83** D2
Poznań, Poland, **123** C2
Pozo Alcón, Spain, **115** C4
Prachin Buri, Thailand, **167** C4
Prachuap Khiri Khan, Thailand, **167** C5
Pradelles, France, **113** C4
Praha (Prague), Czech Republic, **123** C3
Prato, Italy, **117** B3
Prazaroki, Belarus, **121** D3
Preparis Island, Myanmar (Burma), **167** A4
Preparis North Channel, *gulf*, Myanmar (Burma), **167** A4
Prescott, *Arizona*, U.S.A **83** C5
Presidencia Roque Sáenz Peña, Argentina, **103** C2
Presidente Prudente, Brazil, **97** C4
Presidiente Frei, Antarctica (Chile), **183** A2
Presque Isle, *Maine*, U.S.A., **87** E2
Preston, England, **109** D5
Pretoria, South Africa, **149** C4
Preveza, Greece, **125** C5
Priboj, Yugoslavia, **125** B2
Prieska, South Africa, **149** C5
Prijedor, Bosnia and Herzegovina, **125** A2
Prikaspiyskaya Nizmennostș, *valley*, Kazakhstan, **155** A2
Prince Albert, *Saskatchewan*, Canada, **79** E5
Prince Charles Island, *Nunavut*, Canada, **79** G3
Prince Edward Island, *province*, Canada, **81** D3
Prince Edward Island, South Africa, **151** A4
Prince George, *British Columbia*, Canada, **79** D4
Prince of Wales Island, Canada, **79** F2
Prince Rupert, *British Columbia*, Canada, **79** C4
Príncipe, *island*, Príncipe, **145**, A4
Priština, Yugoslavia, **125** C3
Privolzhskaya Vozvyshennostș, *mountain*, Russian Federation, **129** D1
Prizren, Yugoslavia, **125** C3
Prokuplje, Yugoslavia, **115** C3
Prorva, Kazakhstan, **155** A2
Proserpine, Australia, **175** E3
Providence, *Rhode Island*, U.S.A., **87** E3
Providence Island, Seychelles, **147** E5
Providencia, *island*, Columbia, **91** C3
Provo, *Utah*, U.S.A., **83** C4
Pruzhany, Belarus, **121** C4
Pryluky, Ukraine, **129** B1
Prypyats', *river*, Belarus, **129** B1
Przemyśl, Poland, **123** E3
Pt Arena, *point*, *California*, U.S.A., **83** A4
Pt Barrow, *island*, *Alaska*, U.S.A., **79** D1
Pt Reyes, *point*, *California*, U.S.A., **83** A4
Pta Gallinas, *point*, Colombia, **97** B1
Pta Lengua de Vaca, *point*, Chile, **103** A3
Pta Negra, *point*, Peru, **101** A2
Pta Norte, *point*, Argentina, **103** C5
Pta Norte del Cabo San Antonio, *point*, Argentina, **103** D4
Pta Pariñas, *point*, Peru, **101** A2
Ptuj, Slovenia, **125** A1
Puławy, Poland, **123** E3
Pucallpa, Peru, **101** B3
Pudasjärvi, Finland, **107** E3
Puebla de Sanabria, Spain, **115** B2
Puebla de Zaragoza, Mexico, **89** D3
Pueblo, *Colorado*, U.S.A., **83** E4
Puerto Aisen, Chile, **103** B5
Puerto Ayacucho, Venezuela, **97** C2
Puerto Barrios, Guatemala, **91** A2
Puerto Bermúdez, Peru, **101** B3
Puerto Berrío, Colombia, **97** A2
Puerto Cabezas, Nicaragua, **91** B3
Puerto Deseado, Argentina, **103** C6
Puerto Inírida, Colombia, **97** C3
Puerto Limón, Costa Rica, **91** B4
Puerto Madryn, Argentina, **103** C5
Puerto Maldonado, Peru, **101** C3
Puerto Montt, Chile, **103** B5
Puerto Natales, Chile, **103** B6
Puerto Páez, Venezuela, **97** C2
Puerto Pinasco, Paraguay, **103** D1
Puerto Plata, Dominican Republic, **93** C2
Puerto Princesa, Philippines, **171** F3
Puerto Rico, U.S. Territory, **93** D3
Puerto San Julián, Argentina, **103** C6
Puerto Santa Cruz, Argentina, **103** B6
Puerto Varas, Chile, **103** B5
Puertollano, Spain, **115** C3
Pukch'ŏng, North Korea, **165** B2
Pula, Croatia, **125** A2
Pulai, Indonesia, **171** F5
Pumpėnai, Lithuania, **121** B3
Punata, Bolivia, **101** D4
Pune, India, **157** B4
Puno, Peru, **101** C4
Punta Alta, Argentina, **103** C4
Punta Arenas, Chile, **103** B7
Punta Baja, *point*, Mexico, **89** A1
Punta Burica, *point*, Costa Rica, **91** B4
Punta Eugenia, *point*, Mexico, **89** A2
Punta Mariato, *point*, Panama, **91** C4
Punta Mita, *point*, Mexico, **89** B3
Punta Patuca, *point*, Honduras, **91** B2
Puntarenas, Costa Rica, **91** B3
Puri, India, **157** D4
Purus, *river*, Brazil, **99** B2
Pusan, South Korea, **165** B4
Püspökladány, Hungary, **123** E4
Putaruru, New Zealand, **177** D3
Putorino, New Zealand, **177** D3
Putumayo, *river*, Colombia, **97** A2
Pweto, Democratic Republic of the Congo, **145** E6
P'yŏngyang, North Korea, **165** B2
Pyapon, Myanmar (Burma), **167** B4
Pyè (Prome), Myanmar (Burma), **167** A3
Pyinmana, Myanmar (Burma), **167** B3
Pyramid Lake, *Nevada*, U.S.A., **83** B4
Pyrenees, *mountain range*, France, **113** B5
Pyrgos, Greece, **125** C5
Pyrzyce, Poland, **123** C2
Pyu, Myanmar (Burma), **167** B3

Qaanaag (Thule), Greenland, **182** A3
Qābis, Tunisia, **141** E1
Qā'en, Iran, **133** E2
Qalāt, Afghanistan, **155** C5
Qandahār, Afghanistan, **155** C5
Qandala, Somalia, **147** E2
Qapshaghay, Kazakhstan, **155** D3
Qaragandy (Karaganda), Kazakhstan, **155** D2
Qaraghayly, Kazakhstan, **155** D2
Qardho, Somalia, **147** E2
Qarshi, Uzbekistan, **155** C4
Qa'r al Farāfirah, Egypt, **137** D3
Qattara Depression, *valley*, Egypt, **137** D2
Qazvīn, Iran, **133** C2
Qeqertarsuaq, Greenland, **182** A3
Qeqertarsuaq (Disko), *island*, Greenland, **79** H2
Qilian Shan, *mountain*, China, **161** C3
Qinā, Egypt, **137** E3
Qingdao, China, **161** D3
Qinghai Hu, *lake*, China, **161** C3
Qingzang Gaoyuan (Plateau of Tibet), *mountain*, China, **161** A3
Qiqihar, China, **161** E2
Qitaihe, China, **161** E2
Qolleh-ye Damāvand, *mountain*, Iran, **133** D2
Qom, Iran, **133** C2
Qostanay (Kustanay), Kazakhstan, **155** C1
Quảng Ngãi, Vietnam, **167** E4
Quanzhou, China, **161** E4
Quba, Azerbaijan, **129** E3
Qūchān, Iran, **133** E2
Qünghirot, Uzbekistan, **155** B3
Queanbeyan, Australia, **175** E5
Québec, Canada, **81** C3
Qued Zem, Morocco, **141** B2
Queen Charlotte Islands, *British Columbia*, Canada, **79** C4
Queen Elizabeth Islands, Canada, **79** F1
Queensland, *state*, Australia, **175** D3
Queenstown, South Africa, **149** C5
Queenstown, New Zealand, **177** B6
Queenstown, Australia, **175** D6
Quelimane, Mozambique, **149** E3
Querétaro, Mexico, **89** C3
Quesnel, *British Columbia*, Canada, **79** D4
Quetta, Pakistan, **157** A2
Quevedo, Ecuador, **101** A1
Quezon, Philippines, **170** E3
Quezon City, Philippines, **171** F2
Qui Nho'n, Vietnam, **167** E4
Quibdó, Colombia, **97** A2
Quiberon, France, **113** A2
Quillan, France, **113** C5
Quilpue, South America, **103** B3
Quimper, France, **113** A2
Quincy, *Missouri*, U.S.A., **85** D4
Quinzau, Angola, **149** A1
Quitapa, Angola, **149** B2
Quito, Ecuador, **101** A1
Qujing, China, **161** C4
Qulsary, Kazakhstan, **155** A2
Quryq, Kazakhstan, **155** A3
Qyzylorda (Kzyl-Orda), Kazakhstan, **155** C3

Raahe, Finland, **107** D3
Raas Macbar, *point*, Somalia, **147** E2
Raas Xaafuun, *point*, Somalia, **147** E2
Rabat, Morocco, **141** B1
Rabaul, Papua New Guinea, **175** E1
Rābigh, Saudi Arabia, **133** A4
Racine, *Wisconsin*, U.S.A., **87** B3
Radom, Poland, **123** D3
Radomsko, Poland, **123** D3
Raga, Sudan, **147** A3
Ragusa, Italy, **117** D6
Rahīmyār Khān, Pakistan, **157** B3
Raha, Indonesia, **171** F6
Raipur, India, **157** C4
Rājkot, India, **157** B4
Rajshahi, Bangladesh, **157** D3
Rakaia, *river*, New Zealand, **177** B5
Rakvere, Estonia, **121** C1
Raleigh, *North Carolina*, U.S.A., **87** C5
Rambouillet, France, **113** C2
Râmnicu Vâlcea, Romania, **129** A2
Rāmpur, India, **157** C3
Ramree Island, Myanmar (Burma), **167** A3
Ramsjö, Sweden, **107** C4
Rancagua, Chile, **103** B3
Rānchī, India, **157** D3
Ranfurly, New Zealand, **177** B6
Rangiriri, New Zealand, **177** D3
Rangitaiki, *river*, New Zealand, **177** D3
Rangpur, Bangladesh, **157** D3
Rankin Inlet, *Nunavut*, Canada, **79** F4
Ranong, Thailand, **167** B5
Ransiki, Indonesia, **171** J5
Rantepao, Indonesia, **171** F6
Rantsila, Finland, **107** D3
Rapallo, Italy, **117** B3
Rapid City, *South Dakota*, U.S.A., **85** B3
Ra's al Ḩadd, *point*, Oman, **133** E4
Ra's al Hilāl, *point*, Libya, **137** C2
Ra's al Kalb, *point*, Yemen, **133** C6
Ra's al Madrakah, *point*, Oman, **133** E5
Ra's at Tīn, *point*, Libya, **137** C2
Ra's Banās, *point*, Egypt, **137** E4
Ras Dashen Terara, *mountain peak*, Ethiopia, **147** C2
Ra's Mirbāț, *point*, Oman, **133** D6
Raseiniai, Lithuania, **121** B3
Rasht, Iran, **133** C2
Raška, Yugoslavia, **125** C3
Ratchaburi, Thailand, **167** C4
Ratnāgiri, India, **157** B4
Raton, *New Mexico*, U.S.A., **83** E5
Raukumara Range, *mountain*, New Zealand, **177** E3
Rauma, Finland, **107** D4
Raurkela, India, **157** D4
Rāvar, Iran, **133** D3
Ravenna, Italy, **117** C3
Ravensburg, Germany, **111** C5
Ravensthorpe, Australia, **175** A5
Rāwalpindi, Pakistan, **157** B2
Rawlins, *Wyoming*, U.S.A., **83** D3
Rawson, Argentina, **103** C5
Rčch GiÛ, Vietnam, **167** D5
Reading, England, **109** D6
Rebun-tō, *island*, Japan, **165** D1
Rechytsa, Belarus, **121** E4
Recife, Brazil, **97** E3
Reconquista, Argentina, **103** C3
Red, *river*, *Oklahoma*, U.S.A., **85** B5
Red Bluff, *California*, U.S.A., **83** A4
Red Deer, *Alberta*, Canada, **79** E5
Redding, *California*, U.S.A., **83** A4
Reefton, New Zealand, **177** C5
Regensburg, Germany, **111** D4
Reggane, Algeria, **141** C3
Reggio di Calabria, Italy, **117** D5
Reggio nell' Emilia, Italy, **117** B3
Regina, *Saskatchewan*, Canada, **79** E5
Rehoboth, Namibia, **149** B4
Reims, France, **113** C2
Reindeer Lake, *lake*, *Saskatchewan*, Canada, **79** E4
Reinosa, Spain, **115** C1
Relizane, Algeria, **141** D1
Remanso, Brazil, **97** D3
Rena, Norway, **107** B4
Renam, Myanmar (Burma), **167** B1
Rendsburg, Germany, **111** C1
Rengat, Indonesia, **170** B5
Renmark, Australia, **175** D5
Rennes, France, **113** B2
Reno, *Nevada*, U.S.A., **83** B4
Requena, Spain, **115** C3
Resistencia, Argentina, **103** D2
Resolute, *Nunavut*, Canada, **79** F2
Resolution Island, Canada, **81** D1
Resolution Island, New Zealand, **177** A6
Rethymno, Greece, **125** D6
Réunion, French Department, **151** A3
Reus, Spain, **115** D2
Reutlingen, Germany, **111** C5
Rewa, India, **157** C3
Rexburg, *Idaho*, U.S.A., **83** C3
Reykjavík, Iceland, **107** A1
Reynosa, Mexico, **89** D2
Rēzekne, Latvia, **121** C2
Rhein (Rhine), *river*, Germany, **111** B3
Rheine, Germany, **111** C2
Rhinelander, *Wisconsin*, U.S.A., **87** A2
Rhode Island, *state*, U.S.A., **87** E3
Rhône, *river*, France, **113** D4
Rhône, *river*, Switzerland, **117** A2
Ribeirão Prêto, Brazil, **97** D4
Riberalta, Bolivia, **101** D3
Richmond, *Virginia*, U.S.A., **87** D4
Richmond, New Zealand, **177** C4
Richmond Range, *mountain*, New Zealand, **177** C4
Ridgecrest, *California*, U.S.A., **83** B5
Rieti, Italy, **117** C4
Rīga, Latvia, **121** B2
Rijeka, Croatia, **125** A2
Rimini, Italy, **117** C3
Rimouski, *Québec*, Canada, **81** C3
Rio Branco, Brazil, **97** A3
Río Colorado, Argentina, **103** C4
Río Cuarto, Argentina, **103** C3
Rio de Janeiro, Brazil, **97** D4
Río de la Plata, *gulf*, Argentina, **103** D4
Río Gallegos, Argentina, **103** B6
Rio Grande, *river*, *Texas*, U.S.A., **85** A6
Rio Grande, Brazil, **97** C5
Río Grande, Argentina, **103** C7
Rio Tuba, Philippines, **170** E3
Rio Verde, Brazil, **97** C3
Riobamba, Ecuador, **101** A1
Ríohacha, Colombia, **97** B1
Rishiri-tō, *island*, Japan, **165** D1
Risør, Norway, **107** B5
Riva del Garda, Italy, **117** B2
Riverside, *California*, U.S.A., **83** B6
Rivne, Ukraine, **129** B1
Rjukan, Norway, **107** A4
Rožňava, Slovakia, **123** D4
Rožaj, Yugoslavia, **125** C3
Road Town, U.K., **93** D3
Roanne, France, **113** C3
Roanoke, *Virginia*, U.S.A., **87** C4
Rochester, *Minnesota*, U.S.A., **85** D3
Rochester, *New York*, U.S.A., **87** C3
Rock Springs, *Wyoming*, U.S.A., **83** D3
Rockford, *Illinois*, U.S.A., **87** A3
Rockhampton, Australia, **175** E3
Rocky Mountains, *mountain range*, *British Columbia*, Canada, **79** D4
Rocky Mountains, *mountain range*, *Colorado*, U.S.A., **83** D4
Rødby, Denmark, **107** B6
Rodez, France, **113** C4
Rodos, Greece, **125** E6
Rodos (Rhodes), *island*, Greece, **125** E6
Rogliano, Italy, **117** D5
Roi Et, Thailand, **167** D4
Roja, Latvia, **121** B2
Rokiškis, Lithuania, **121** C3
Rolla, *Missouri*, U.S.A., **85** D4
Roma, Australia, **175** E4
Roma (Rome), Italy, **117** C4
Romania, *country*, **125** D1
Romny, Ukraine, **129** C1
Ronda, Spain, **115** B4
Rong, *river*, China, **167** E2
Rongklang, *mountain*, Myanmar (Burma), **167** A2
Roosevelt Island, Antarctica, **183** B3
Røros, Norway, **107** B4
Rørvik, Norway, **107** B3
Rosario, Argentina, **103** C3
Roscoff, France, **113** A2
Roscrea, Ireland, **109** B5
Roseau, Dominica, **93** E3
Roseburg, *Oregon*, U.S.A., **83** A3
Rosenheim, Germany, **111** D5
Ross Island, Antartica, **183** B3
Rossano, Italy, **117** D5
Rossel, *island*, Papua New Grunea, **175** E2
Rosso, Mauritania, **141** A2
Rostock, Germany, **111** D1
Rostov-na-Donu, Russian Federation, **153** A3
Roswell, *New Mexico*, U.S.A., **83** E6
Rothera, Antarctica (U.K.), **183** A2
Roti, *island*, Indonesia, **171** G7
Rotomanu, New Zealand, **177** C5
Rotorua, New Zealand, **177** D3
Rotterdam, Netherlands, **111** B2
Rouen, France, **113** C2
Rovaniemi, Finland, **107** D2
Rovereto, Italy, **117** B2
Rovigo, Italy, **117** C2
Roxas, Philippines, **171** F3
Royan, France, **113** B3
Roye, France, **113** C2
Ružomberok, Slovakia, **123** D4
Ruapuke Island, New Zealand, **17** B7
Rubtsovsk, Russian Federation, **153** B4
Rūdnyy, Kazakhstan, **155** C1
Rugby, *North Dakota*, U.S.A., **85** C1
Rum Cay, *island*, Bahamas, **93** B2
Ruma, Yugoslavia, **125** C2
Rumbek, Sudan, **147** B3
Rundu, Namibia, **149** B3
Ruse, Bulgaria, **129** A3
Russas, Brazil, **97** E2
Russian Federation, *country*, **153** C3
Rustefjelbma, Norway, **107** E1
Rustenburg, South Africa, **149** C4
Ruteng, Indonesia, **171** F7
Rwanda, *country*, **147** B4
Rybnik, Poland, **123** D3
Rzeszów, Poland, **123** E3

Sāgar, India, **157** C3
Sāhīwāl, Pakistan, **157**, B2
Sāngli, India, **157** B4
Sārī, Iran, **133** D2
Sātāra, India, **157** B4
Sīkar, India, **157** B3
Sīrjān, Iran, **133** D3
Sīwah, Egypt, **137** C3
Sŏul (Seoul), South Korea, **165** B3
Sūhāj, Egypt, **137** E3
Słupsk, Poland, **123** C1
Saarbrücken, Germany, **111** B4
Sääre, Estonia, **121** B2
Saaremaa, *island*, Estonia, **121** B2
Saarijärvi, Finland, **107** D4
Šabac, Yugoslavia, **125** B2
Sabadell, Spain, **115** D2
Sabhā, Libya, **137** B3
Sabsevār, Iran, **133** D2
Sachs Harbour, *Northwest Territories*, Canada, **79** E2
Sacramento, *California*, U.S.A., **83** A4
Sacramento, *river*, *California*, U.S.A., **83** A4
Sado-shima, *island*, Japan, **165** D3
Safi, Morocco, **141** B2
Saga, Japan, **165** B4
Sagaing, Myanmar (Burma), **167** B2
Saginaw, *Michigan*, U.S.A., **87** B3
Sagua la Grande, Cuba, **93** A2
Sagunto, Spain, **115** D3
Sahara, *desert*, Algeria, **141** C1
Sahara, *desert*, Chad, **145** C2
Sahara, *desert*, Libya, **137** C4
Sahara, *desert*, Mali, **141** C4
Sahara, *desert*, Mauritania, **141** C4
Sahara, *desert*, Sudan, **147** A1
Şahrā' Murzuq, *desert*, Niger, **137** A3
Saija, Finland, **107** E2
Saimaa, *lake*, Finland, **107** E4
Saint Arnaud, New Zealand, **177** C4
Saint Helena Bay, *gulf*, South Africa, **149** B5
Saint John, *New Brunswick*, Canada, **81** D4
Saint Johnșs, Antigua and Barbuda, **93** E3
Saint Moritz, Switzerland, **117** B2
Saint-Brieuc, France, **113** A2
Saint-Dizier, France, **113** D2
Saint-Étienne, France, **113** C4
Saint-Lô, France, **113** B2
Saint-Louis, Senegal, **141** A2
Saint-Malo, France, **113** B2
Saint-Nazaire, France, **113** A3
Saint-Quentin, France, **113** C2
St Andrews, Scotland, **109** D3
St Augustine, *Florida*, U.S.A., **87** C6
St Austell, England, **109** C7
St George, *Utah*, U.S.A., **83** C5
St George's, Grenada, **93** E4
St George's Channel, *gulf*, Ireland, **109** B6
St Helena, U.K. Dependency, **105** C4
St Helens, *Oregon*, U.S.A., **83** A2
St John's, *Newfoundland*, Canada, **81** E3
St Joseph, *Missouri*, U.S.A., **85** C4
St Joseph Point, *point*, *Florida*, U.S.A., **87** B6
St Kilda, *island*, Scotland, **109** B2
St Kitts and Nevis, *country*, **93** D3
St Lawrence, *river*, *Québec*, Canada, **87** E1
St Lawrence Island, *Alaska*, U.S.A., **79** B1
St Louis, *Missouri*, U.S.A., **85** D4
St Lucia, *country*, **93** E4
St Marys, *Ohio*, U.S.A., **87** B3
St Paul, *Minnesota*, U.S.A., **85** D2
St Petersburg, *Florida*, U.S.A., **87** C7
St Pierre and Miquelon, French Territorial, Collectivity, **105** A1
St Pierre Island, Seychelles, **147** E5
St Vincent and the Grenadines, *country*, **93** D4
Sakākah, Saudi Arabia, **133** B3
Sakata, Japan, **165** D3
Saketa, Indonesia, **171** H5
Saki, Nigeria, **141** D4
Şäki, Azerbaijan, **129** E3
Sakon Nakhon, Thailand, **167** D4
Sala, Sweden, **107** C5
Salado, *river*, Argentina, **103** C2
Şalālah, Oman, **133** D6
Salamanca, Spain, **115** B2
Salar de Arizaro, *lake*, Argentina, **103** B2
Salar de Atacama, *lake*, Chile, **103** B1
Salar de Coipasa, *lake*, Bolivia, **101** C5
Salar de Uyuni, *lake*, Bolivia, **101** D5
Salas, Spain, **115** B1
Salau, France, **113** B5
Salavat, Russian Federation, **153** B3
Salbris, France, **113** C3
Saldanha, South Africa, **149** B5
Saldus, Latvia, **121** B2
Sale, Australia, **175** E6
Salekhard, Russian Federation, **153** B2
Salem, *Oregon*, U.S.A., **83** A2
Salem, India, **157** C5
Salerno, Italy, **117** D4
Salgótarján, Hungary, **123** D4
Salihorsk, Belarus, **121** D4
Salina, *Kansas*, U.S.A., **85** C4
Salina Cruz, Mexico, **89** D4
Salinas, California, U.S.A., **83** A5
Salinas, Ecuador, **101** A2
Salinas Grandes, *lake*, Argentina, **103** C1
Salisbury, England, **109** D6
Sallūm, Sudan, **147** C1
Salmon, *river*, *Idaho*, U.S.A., **83** B2
Salo, Finland, **107** D4
Salt Lake City, *Utah*, U.S.A., **83** C4
Salta, Argentina, **103** C2
Saltillo, Mexico, **89** C2
Salto, Uruguay, **103** D3
Salvador, Brazil, **97** E3
Salzburg, Austria, **123** B4
Salzgitter, Germany, **111** D3
Salzwedel, Germany, **111** D2
Samar, *island*, Philippines, **171** G2
Samara, Russian Federation, **153** A3
Samarai, Papua New Guinea, **175** E2
Samarinda, Indonesia, **170** E5
Samarqand, Uzbekistan, **155** C4
Sambalpur, India, **157** D4
Samch'ŏk, South Korea, **165** B3
Samoa, *country*, **179** B3
Samos, *island*, Greece, **125** E5
Samothraki, *island*, Greece, **129** A3
Sampit, Indonesia, **170** D5
Samsun, Turkey, **129** C3
Samut Prakan, Thailand, **167** C4
San, *river*, Cambodia, **167** D4
San Andrés, *island*, Colombia, **91** B3
San Andrés Tuxtla, Mexico, **89** D4
San Angelo, *Texas*, U.S.A., **85** B6
San Antonio, *Texas*, U.S.A **85** B6
San Benedetto del Tronto, Italy, **117** C3
San Bernardino, *California*, U.S.A., **83** B6
San Bernardo, Chile, **103** B3

San Carlos, Philippines, **171** F1
San Carlos de Bariloche, Argentina, **103** B5
San Cristóbal, Venezuela, **97** B2
San Diego, *California*, U.S.A., **83** B6
San Esteban de Gormaz, Spain, **115** C2
San Felipe, Mexico, **89** A1
San Fernando, Trinidad & Tobago, **93** E4
San Fernando, Argentina, **103** D3
San Fernando, Philippines, **171** F1
San Fernando, Philippines, **171** F2
San Fernando de Apure, Venezuela, **97** C2
San Fernando del Valle de Catamarca, Argentina, **103** C2
San Francisco, *California*, U.S.A., **83** A4
San Ignacio, Bolivia, **101** E4
San Joaquin, *river, California*, U.S.A., **83** A4
San Jose, *California*, U.S.A., **83** A4
San Jose, Philippines, **171** F2
San José, Costa Rica, **91** B4
San José del Cabo, Mexico, **89** B3
San José del Guaviare, Colombia, **97** B3
San Juan, U.S.A., **93** D3
San Juan, Argentina, **103** B3
San Juan de los Morros, Venezuela, **97** C2
San Juan del Norte, Nicaragua, **91** B3
San Lorenzo, Ecuador, **101** A1
San Luis, Argentina, **103** B3
San Luis Obispo, *California*, U.S.A., **83** A5
San Luis Potosí, Mexico, **89** C3
San Marino, San Marino, **117** C3
San Martín de los Andes, Argentina, **103** B5
San Miguel, El Salvador, **91** A3
San Miguel de Tucumán, Argentina, **103** C2
San Miguelito, Panama, **91** C4
San Nicolás de los Arroyos, Argentina, **103** C3
San Pablo, Philippines, **171** F2
San Pedro, Argentina, **103** C2
San Pedro, Paraguay, **103** D2
San Pedro Sula, Honduras, **91** A2
San Ramón, Bolivia, **101** D3
San Remo, Italy, **117** A3
San Salvador, El Salvador, **91** A3
San Salvador, *island*, Bahamas, **93** C2
San Salvador de Jujuy, Argentina, **103** C2
Şan'ā', Yemen, **133** B6
Sanae, Antarctica (South Africa), **183** B2
Sanaga, *river*, Cameroon, **145** B4
Sanana, *island*, Indonesia, **171** G5
Sanandaj, Iran, **133** C2
Sandakan, Malaysia, **170** E4
Sanday, *island*, Scotland, **109** D2
Sandbukta, Norway, **107** D1
Sandia, Peru, **101** C4
Sandnes, Norway, **107** A5
Sandomierz, Poland, **123** E3
Sanford, *Maine*, U.S.A., **87** E3
Sangar, Russian Federation, **153** D3
Sangmélima, Cameroon, **145** B4
Sankt-Peterburg (St Petersburg), Russian Federation, **153** A2
Sanluri, Italy, **117** B5
Sanok, Poland, **123** E3
Sant' Antioco, Italy, **117** A5
Santa Ana, *California*, U.S.A., **83** B6
Santa Ana, El Salvador, **91** A3
Santa Ana, Ecuador, **101** A1
Santa Barbara, *California*, U.S.A., **83** B5
Santa Clara, Cuba, **93** A2
Santa Cruz, *California*, U.S.A., **83** A5
Santa Cruz, Bolivia, **101** D4
Santa Cruz de la Palma, Islas Canarias/Spain, **141** A2
Santa Cruz de Tenerife, Islas Canarias/Spain, **141** A2
Santa Eugenia, Spain, **115** A1
Santa Fe, *New Mexico*, U.S.A., **83** E5
Santa Fe, Argentina, **103** C3
Santa Maria, *California*, U.S.A., **83** A5
Santa Maria, Brazil, **97** C5
Santa Marta, Colombia, **97** A1
Santa Rosa, *California*, U.S.A., **83** A4
Santa Rosa, Ecuador, **101** A2
Santa Rosa, Argentina, **103** C4
Santa Rosalía, Mexico, **89** A2
Santander, Spain, **115** C1
Santander, Philippines, **171** G3
Santarém, Brazil, **97** C2
Santarém, Portugal, **115** A3
Santiago, Brazil, **97** C5
Santiago, Chile, **99** A5
Santiago, Dominican Republic, **93** C2
Santiago, Panama, **91** C4
Santiago del Estero, Argentina, **103** C2
Santiago de Compostela, Spain, **115** A1
Santiago de Cuba, Cuba, **93** B2
Santo Amaro, Brazil, **97** E3
Santo Angelo, Brazil, **97** C5
Santo Domingo, Mexico, **89** A2
Santo Domingo, Dominican Republic, **93** C3
Sanya, China, **161** D5
São Bento, Brazil, **97** D2
São Carlos, Brazil, **97** D4
São Francisco, Brazil, **97** D3
São Francisco, *river*, Brazil, **97** D3
São Luís, Brazil, **97** D2
São Luis Gonzaga, Brazil, **97** C5
São Paulo, Brazil, **97** D4
São Paulo de Olivença, Brazil, **97** A2
São Tomé, *island*, São Tomé and Príncipe, **145** A5
São Tomé and Príncipe, *country*, **145** A5
Saône, *river*, France, **113** D3
Sapele, Nigeria, **141** D4
Sapporo, Japan, **165** E2
Sapulut, Malaysia, **170** E4
Sarāvān, Iran, **133** E4
Saraburi, Thailand, **167** C4
Sarajevo, Bosnia and Herzegovina, **125** B2
Saransk, Russian Federation, **153** A3
Sarasota, *Florida*, U.S.A., **87** C7
Saravan, Laos, **167** D4
Sardegna, *island*, Italy, **117** A4
Sargodha, Pakistan, **157** B2
Sarh, Chad, **145** C3
Sariwon, North Korea, **165** B3
Sarmi, Indonesia, **171** K5
Särna, Sweden, **107** B4
Sarny, Ukraine, **129** B1
Sarqan, Kazakhstan, **155** E2
Sarriá, Spain, **115** B1
Saryshagan, Kazakhstan, **155** D2
Sasak, Indonesia, **170** B5
Sasebo, Japan, **165** B4
Saskatchewan, *province*, Canada, **79** E4
Saskatoon, *Saskatchewan*, Canada, **79** E5
Sassandra, Côte d'Ivoire, **141** B4
Sassari, Italy, **117** B4
Sassnitz, Germany, **111** E1
Sätbaev, Kazakhstan, **155** C2
Satu Mare, Romania, **129** A2
Sauda, Norway, **107** A4
Saudi Arabia, *country*, **133** B4
Saulgau, Germany, **111** C5
Saulkrasti, Latvia, **121** B2
Sault Ste Marie, *Ontario*, Canada, **81** A3
Saurimo, Angola, **149** B2
Sava, *river*, Croatia, **125** B2
Savannah, *Georgia*, U.S.A., **87** C5
Savannah, *river, South Carolina*, U.S.A., **87** C5
Savannakhét, Laos, **167** D4
Save, *river*, Mozambique, **149** D3
Savona, Italy, **117** B3
Savonlinna, Finland, **107** E4
Savukoski, Finland, **107** E2
Sawankhalok, Thailand, **167** C3
Sayḩūt, Yemen, **133** C6
Saynshand, Mongolia, **161** D2
Saywūn, Yemen, **133** C6
Scarborough, Trinidad & Tobago, **93** E4
Scarborough, England, **109** D4
Schefferville, *Québec*, Canada, **81** D2
Schleswig, Germany, **111** C1
Schroffenstein, *mountain*, Namibia, **149** B4
Schwedt, Germany, **111** E2
Schwerin, Germany, **111** D2
Sciacca, Italy, **117** C6
Scotland, *country*, **109** C3
Scott Base, Antarctica (New Zealand), **183** B3
Scottsbluff, *Nebraska*, U.S.A., **85** B3
Searcy, *Arkansas*, U.S.A., **85** D5
Seattle, *Washington*, U.S.A., **83** A1
Seaward Kaikruoa Range, *mountain*, New Zealand, **177** C5
Sebkha Azzel Matti, *lake*, Algeria, **141** C3
Sebkha Mekerrhane, *lake*, Algeria, **141** D3
Secretary Island, New Zealand, **177** A6
Sedan, France, **113** D2
Ségou, Mali, **141** B3
Segovia, Spain, **115** C2
Séguéla, Côte d'Ivoire, **141** B4
Seinäjoki, Finland, **107** D4
Seine, *river*, France, **113** C2
Sekondi, Ghana, **141** C4
Selat Karimata, *gulf*, Indonesia, **170** C5
Selat Makasar, *gulf*, Indonesia, **170** E6
Sélibabi, Mauritania, **141** A3
Selkirk, *Manitoba*, Canada, **79** F5
Selma, *Alabama*, U.S.A., **87** B5
Semara, Western Sahara/Morocco, **141** B3
Semarang, Indonesia, **170** D6
Semey, Kazakhstan, **155** E2
Semnān, Iran, **133** D2
Senanga, Zambia, **149** C3
Sendai, Japan, **165** E3
Senegal, *country*, **141** A3
Sénégal, *river*, Senegal, **141** A2
Sengerema, Tanzania, **147** B4
Senj, Croatia, **125** A2
Senlis, France, **113** C2
Sens, France, **113** C2
Sepasu, Indonesia, **170** E5
Sepik, *river*, Papua New Guinea, **175** D1
Sept-Îles, *Québec*, Canada, **81** D3
Seram, *island*, Indonesia, **175** B1
Serang, Indonesia, **170** C6
Seremban, Malaysia, **170** B4
Serov, Russian Federation, **153** B3
Serowe, Botswana, **149** C4
Serpa, Portugal, **115** A3
Serres, Greece, **125** D4
Sesheke, Zambia, **149** C3
Sète, France, **113** C4
Sete Lagoas, Brazil, **97** D4
Sétif, Algeria, **141** D1
Settat, Morocco, **141** B2
Setúbal, Portugal, **115** A3
Sevana Lich, *lake*, Armenia, **133** C1
Sevastopol', Ukraine, **129** C2
Severn, *river*, *Ontario*, Canada, **81** A2
Severnaya Zemlya, *island*, Russian Federation, **153** C2
Sevilla, Spain, **115** B4
Seward, *Alaska*, U.S.A., **79** C2
Seward Peninsula, *point*, *Alaska*, U.S.A., **79** C1
Seychelles, *country*, **151** A3
Seyðisfjörður, Iceland, **107** B1
Sfax, Tunisia, **141** E1
's-Gravenhage (The Hague), Netherlands, **111** B2
Shāhjahānpur, India, **157** C3
Shīndand, Afghanistan, **155** B5
Shīrāz, Iran, **133** D3
Shū, Kazakhstan, **155** D3
Shū, *river*, Kazakhstan, **155** D3
Shaţţ al Jarīd, *lake*, Algeria, **139** E1
Shache, China, **161** A3
Shaghan, Kazakhstan, **155** D2
Shandī, Sudan, **147** B1
Shanghai, China, **161** E4
Shantou, China, **161** D4
Shaoguan, China, **161** D4
Shaoxing, China, **161** E4
Shaqrā', Yemen, **133** B6
Shaqrā', Saudi Arabia, **133** C4
Shar, Kazakhstan, **155** E2
Shark Bay, *gulf*, Australia, **175** A4
Shchūchinsk, Kazakhstan, **155** C1
Sheboygan, *Wisconsin*, U.S.A., **85** E3
Shelqar, Kazakhstan, **155** B2
Shenyang, China, **161** E3
Shenzhen, China, **161** D4
Shepetivka, Ukraine, **129** B1
Shepparton, Australia, **175** D5
Sherbro Island, Sierra Leone, **141** A4
Sherbrooke, *Québec*, Canada, **81** C4
Sheridan, *Wyoming*, U.S.A., **83** D2
Sherman, *Texas*, U.S.A., **85** C5
Shetland Islands, Scotland, **109** D1
Shihezi, China, **161** B2
Shijiazhuang, China, **161** D3
Shikārpur, Pakistan, **157** B3
Shikoku, *island*, Japan, **165** C4
Shiliguri, India, **157** D3
Shilka, *river*, Russian Federation, **161** D2
Shillong, India, **157** E3
Shimbiris, *mountain*, Somalia, **147** E2
Shimla, India, **157** C2
Shimoga, India, **157** B5
Shinyanga, Tanzania, **147** C4
Shiono-misaki, *point*, Japan, **165** D4
Shiretoko-misaki, *point*, Japan, **165** E1
Shiyan, China, **161** D4
Shizuishan, China, **161** C3
Shizuoka, Japan, **165** D4
Shklow, Belarus, **121** D3
Shkodër, Albania, **125** B3
Shoshone Mountains, *mountain*, *Nevada*, U.S.A., **83** B4
Shoyna, Russian Federation, **153** B2
Shreveport, *Louisiana*, U.S.A., **85** D6
Shubarqudyq, Kazakhstan, **155** B2
Shumen, Bulgaria, **129** B3
Shumilina, Belarus, **121** D3
Shurugwi, Zimbabwe, **149** D3
Shwebo, Myanmar (Burma), **167** B2
Shymkent, Kazakhstan, **155** C3
Si Sa Ket, Thailand, **167** D4
Siargao Island, Philippines, **171** G3
Šiauliai, Lithuania, **121** B3
Šibenik, Croatia, **125** A2
Sibi, Pakistan, **157** B2
Sibiti, Congo, **145** B5
Sibolga, Indonesia, **170** A5
Sibu, Malaysia, **170** D4
Sibut, Central African Republic, **145** C4
Sicilia (Sicily), *island*, Italy, **117** D6
Sidaouet, Niger, **141** D2
Sidi Bel Abbès, Algeria, **141** C1
Sidi Ifni, Morocco, **141** B2
Sidi Okba, Algeria, **141** D1
Siegen, Germany, **111** C3
Siembra, Indonesia, **171** H6
Siena, Italy, **117** C3
Sierpc, Poland, **123** D2
Sierra Grande, Argentina, **103** C5
Sierra Leone, *country*, **141** A4
Sierra Madre Del Sur, *mountain*, Mexico, **89** C3
Sierra Madre Oriental, *mountain range*, Mexico, **89** C2
Sierra Morena, *mountain*, Spain, **115** B3
Sierra Nevada, *mountain*, California, U.S.A**83** A4
Sierra Nevada del Cocuy, *mountain*, Colombia, **97** B2
Sierra Vista, *Arizona*, U.S.A., **83** D6
Sierre, Switzerland, **117** A2
Sigli, Indonesia, **170** A4
Signy, Antarctica (U.K.), **183** A1
Siguiri, Guinea, **141** B3
Siilinjärvi, Finland, **107** E4
Siirt, Turkey, **129** D4
Sikasso, Mali, **141** B3
Sikea, Greece, **125** D4
Sikeston, *Missouri*, U.S.A., **85** E5
Sikhote-Alin', *mountain*, Russian Federation, **161** E2
Siktyakh, Russia Federation, **153** D2
Silifke, Turkey, **129** C4
Šilutė, Lithuania, **121** B3
Silver City, *New Mexico*, U.S.A., **83** D6
Şirnak, Turkey, **129** D4
Simav, Turkey, **129** B4
Simferopolş, Ukraine, **129** C2
Simpson Desert, Australia, **175** C4
Simrishamn, Sweden, **107** B6
Sinŭiju, North Korea, **165** A2
Sinabang, Indonesia, **170** A4
Sincelejo, Colombia, **97** A2
Sindangan, Philippines, **171** F3
Sines, Portugal, **115** A3
Singapore, *country*, **170** C5
Singaraja, Indonesia, **170** E7
Singida, Tanzania, **147** C4
Singkawang, Indonesia, **170** D5
Sinj, Croatia, **125** A2
Sinjah, Sudan, **147** C2
Sinjai, Indonesia, **171** F6
Sinop, Turkey, **129** C3
Siófok, Hungary, **123** D5
Sion, Switzerland, **117** A2
Sioux City, *Iowa*, U.S.A., **85** C3
Sioux Falls, *South Dakota*, U.S.A., **85** C3
Siple Island, Antarctica, **183** A3
Siracusa, Italy, **117** D6
Sisŏphŏn, Cambodia, **167** C4
Sisak, Croatia, **125** A2
Sisian, Armenia, **129** E3
Siteia, Greece, **125** E6
Sitka, *Alaska*, U.S.A., **79** C3
Sittang, *river*, Myanmar (Burma), **167** B3
Sittwe (Akyab), Myanmar (Burma), **167** A3
Sivas, Turkey, **129** C4
Siverek, Turkey, **129** D4
Sivrihisar, Turkey, **129** B4
Skagerrak, *gulf*, Denmark/Norway, **107** A5
Skagway, *Alaska*, U.S.A., **79** C3
Skarżysko-Kamienna, Poland, **123** D3
Skaudvilė, Lithuania, **121** B3
Skegness, England, **109** E5
Skellefteå, Sweden, **107** D3
Skien, Norway, **107** B5
Skikda, Algeria, **141** E1
Skive, Denmark, **107** A6
Skopje, Macedonia, **125** C3
Skrunda, Latvia, **121** B2
Skye, *island*, Scotland, **109** B3
Slave, *river*, *Northwest Territories*, Canada, **79** E4
Slavonski Brod, Croatia, **125** B2
Slawharad, Belarus, **121** E4
Sligo, Ireland, **109** B4
Slonim, Belarus, **121** C4
Slovakia, *country*, **123** D4
Slovenia, *country*, **125** A1
Smallwood Reservoir, *lake*, *Newfoundland*, Canada, **81** D2
Smøla, *island*, Norway, **107** A3
Snake, *river*, *Washington*, U.S.A., **83** B2
Snake, *river*, *Idaho*, U.S.A., **83** C3
Snina, Slovakia, **123** E4
Snowdon, *mountain*, Wales, **109** C5
Snyder, *Texas*, U.S.A., **85** B6
Sobral, Brazil, **97** E2
Socorro, *New Mexico*, U.S.A., **83** D6
Socorro, Colombia, **97** B2
Sodankylä, Finland, **107** D2
Söderhamn, Sweden, **107** C4
Sodo, Ethiopia, **147** C3
Soe, Indonesia, **171** G7
Sofiya (Sofia), Bulgaria, **125** D3
Sogamoso, Colombia, **97** B2
Sokch'o, South Korea, **165** B3
Söke, Turkey, **129** B4
Sokhumi, Georgia, **129** D3
Sokółka, Poland, **123** E2
Sokodé, Togo, **141** C4
Sokoto, Nigeria, **141** D3
Solāpur, India, **157** C4
Sollefteå, Sweden, **107** C4
Solomon Islands, *country*, **179** B3
Soltau, Germany, **111** C2
Solwezi, Zambia, **149** C2
Soma, Turkey, **129** B4
Somalia, *country*, **147** E3
Sombor, Yugoslavia, **125** B2
Somerset, *Kentucky*, U.S.A., **87** B4
Somerset East, South Africa, **149** C5
Somerset Island, *Nunavut*, Canada, **79** F2
Sondrio, Italy, **117** B2
Songea, Tanzania, **147** C5
Songhua, *river*, China, **165** B1
Songkhla, Thailand, **167** C6
Songnim, North Korea, **165** B3
Sopron, Hungary, **123** C4
Sora, Italy, **117** C4
Soria, Spain, **115** C2
Sorocaba, Brazil, **97** D4
Sorong, Indonesia, **171** H5
Soroti, Uganda, **147** C4
Sorrento, Italy, **117** D4
Sorsele, Sweden, **107** C3
Souk-el-Arba-du-Rharb, Morocco, **141** C1
Sousse, Tunisia, **141** E1
South, U.K., **183** A1
South Africa, *country*, **149** B4
South Andaman, *island*, India, **157** E5
South Australia, *state*, Australia, **175** C4
South Bend, *Indiana*, U.S.A., **87** B3
South Cape, *point*, New Zealand, **177** A7
South Carolina, *state*, U.S.A., **87** C5
South Dakota, *state*, U.S.A., **85** B2
South Georgia, *island*, Antarctica, **183** A1
South Georgia Islands, U.K. Dependency, **105** B5
South Korea, *country*, **165** C3
South Orkney Islands, Antarctica (U.K.), **183** A2
South Platte, *river*, *Colorado*, U.S.A., **83** E4
South Ronaldsay, *island*, Scotland, **109** D2
South Sandwich Islands, Argentina, **183** A1
South Taranaki Bight, *gulf*, New Zealand, **177** C4
South Uist, *island*, Scotland, **109** B3
Southampton, England, **109** D6
Southampton Island, *Québec*, Canada, **81** B1
Southend-on-Sea, England, **109** E6
Southern Alps, *mountain*, New Zealand, **177** B5
Southern Uplands, *mountain*, Scotland, **109** C4
Sovetsk, Russian Federation, **121** B3
Sowa Pan, *lake*, Botswana, **149** C3
Soweto, South Africa, **149** C4
Spain, *country*, **115** C3
Sparti (Sparta), Greece, **125** C5
Spencer, *Iowa*, U.S.A., **85** C3
Spencer Gulf, *gulf*, Australia, **175** C5
Spittal an der Drau, Austria, **123** B5
Split, Croatia, **125** A2
Špoģi, Latvia, **121** C3
Spokane, *Washington*, U.S.A., **83** B1
Spoleto, Italy, **117** C3
Springbok, South Africa, **149** B5
Springfield, *Missouri*, U.S.A., **85** D4
Springfield, *Illinois*, U.S.A., **87** A4
Springfield, *Massachusetts*, U.S.A., **87** D3
Springhill, *Louisiana*, U.S.A., **85** D6
Springs Junction, New Zealand, **177** C5
Sprova, Norway, **107** B3
Spruce Knob, *mountain*, *West Virginia*, U.S.A., **87** C4
Srīnagar, India, **157** B2
Sredne-Russkaya vozvyshennostş, *mountain*, Russian Federation, **129** C1
Srêpôk, *river*, Cambodia, **167** D5
Sri Jayawardanapura-Kotte, Sri Lanka, **157** C6
Sri Lanka, *country*, **157** C6
Stafford, England, **109** D5
Stanger, South Africa, **149** D5
Stanley, Falkland Islands, **103** D6
Stanley, *mountain peak*, Democratic Republic of the Congo, **145** E5
Stara Planina, *mountain range*, Bulgaria, **125** D3
Statesboro, *Georgia*, U.S.A., **87** C5
Stavanger, Norway, **107** A5
Staveley, New Zealand, **177** C5
Steinkjer, Norway, **107** B3
Stellenbosch, South Africa, **149** B5
Stendal, Germany, **111** D2
Stephenville, *Newfoundland*, Canada, **81** E3
Stephenville, *Texas*, U.S.A., **85** C6
Sterling, *Colorado*, U.S.A., **83** E3
Stewart Island, New Zealand, **177** B7
Steyr, Austria, **123** C4
Štip, Macedonia, **125** C3
Stirling, Scotland, **109** C3
Stockholm, Sweden, **107** C5
Stockton-on-Tees, England, **109** D4
Stoke-on-Trent, England, **109** D5
Stolac, Bosnia and Herzegovina, **125** B3
Stolin, Belarus, **121** D5
Stonehaven, Scotland, **109** D3
Støren, Norway, **107** B3
Storjord, Norway, **107** C2
Stornoway, Scotland, **109** B2
Storuman, Sweden, **107** C3
Strait of Dover, *gulf*, England, **109** E7
Strait of Gibraltar, *gulf*, Spain, **115** B4
Strait of Hormuz, *gulf*, Oman, **133** D4
Strait of Malacca, *gulf*, Indonesia, **170** A4
Strait of Sicily, *gulf*, Italy, **137** A1
Straits of Florida, *gulf*, U.S.A., **87** C7
Stralsund, Germany, **111** E1
Stranda, Norway, **107** A4
Stranraer, Scotland, **109** C4
Strasbourg, France, **113** E2
Strömsund, Sweden, **107** C3
Stronsay, *island*, Scotland, **109** D2
Stryy, Ukraine, **129** A1
Strzelecki Desert, Australia, **175** D4
Stuben, Austria, **123** A5
Stutterheim, South Africa, **149** C5
Stuttgart, Germany, **111** C4
Stykkishólmur, Iceland, **107** A1
Subotica, Yugoslavia, **125** C1
Suceava, Romania, **129** A2
Sucre, Bolivia, **101** D4
Sudan, *country*, **147** B2
Sudbury, *Ontario*, Canada, **81** B4
Sudety, *mountain range*, Czech Republic, **123** C3
Şuḩār, Oman, **133** D4
Sühbaatar, Mongolia, **161** C2
Suhl, Germany, **111** D3
Suihua, China, **161** E2
Sukadana, Indonesia, **170** D5
Sukeva, Finland, **107** E3
Sukkur, Pakistan, **157** B3
Sulaimān Range, *mountain range*, Pakistan, **157** B3
Sulawesi (Celebes), *island*, Indonesia, **171** F5
Sulechów, Poland, **123** C2
Sullana, Peru, **101** A2
Sulmona, Italy, **117** C4
Sumatera (Sumatra), *mountain*, Indonesia, **170** B5
Sumatera (Sumatra), *island*, Indonesia, **151** C2
Sumba, *island*, Indonesia, **171** F7
Sumbawa, *island*, Indonesia, **170** E7
Sumbawanga, Tanzania, **147** B5
Sumbe, Angola, **149** A2
Sumqayıt, Azerbaijan, **129** E3
Sumy, Ukraine, **129** C1
Sunchşŏn, South Korea, **165** B4
Sunderland, England, **109** D4
Sundsvall, Sweden, **107** C4
Sunyani, Ghana, **141** C4
Suomussalmi, Finland, **107** E3
Suquţrá (Socotra), *island*, Yemen, **133** D6
Şūr, Oman, **133** E4
Şūr (Tyre), Lebanon, **133** A2
Surabaya, Indonesia, **170** D6
Surat, India, **157** B4
Surat Thani, Thailand, **167** B6
Surgut, Russian Federation, **153** B3
Surigao, Philippines, **171** G3
Surin, Thailand, **167** D4
Suriname, *country*, **97** C1
Surt, Libya, **137** B2
Surulangun, Indonesia, **170** B5
Susanville, *California*, U.S.A., **83** A4
Sutlej, *river*, Pakistan, **157** B2
Suwałki, Poland, **123** E1
Suwon, South Korea, **165** B3
Svalbard, Norwegian, Dependency, **153** B1
Sveg, Sweden, **107** C4
Svendborg, Denmark, **107** B6
Svetlyy, Russian Federation, **121** A3
Svidník, Slovakia, **123** E3
Svir, Belarus, **121** C3
Svitavy, Czech Republic, **123** C3
Svolvær, Norway, **107** C2
Swakopmund, Namibia, **149** A4
Swan, *river*, Australia, **175** A5
Swansea, Wales, **109** C6
Swaziland, *country*, **149** D4
Sweden, *country*, **107** C5
Swift Current, *Saskatchewan*, Canada, **79** E5
Świnoujście, Poland, **123** C2
Switzerland, *country*, **117** A2
Sydney, *Nova Scotia*, Canada, **81** E3
Sydney, Australia, **175** E5
Syktyvkar, Russian Federation, **153** B2
Sylhet, Bangladesh, **157** E3
Syowa, Antarctica (Japan), **183** C2
Syracuse, *New York*, U.S.A., **87** D3
Syrdar'ya, *river*, Kazakhstan, **155** B3
Syria, *country*, **133** B2
Szczecin, Poland, **123** C2
Szczecinek, Poland, **123** C2
Szczytno, Poland, **123** D2
Szeged, Hungary, **123** D5
Székesfehérvár, Hungary, **123** D4
Szekszárd, Hungary, **123** D5
Szombathely, Hungary, **123** C4

Ţabas, Iran, **133** D2
Tábor, Czech Republic, **123** C4
Tabora, Tanzania, **147** B4
Tabou, Côte d'Ivoire, **141** B4
Tabrīz, Iran, **133** C1
Tabūk, Saudi Arabia, **133** A3
Tacheng, China, **161** B2
Tacloban, Philippines, **171** G2
Tacna, Peru, **101** C4
Tacoma, *Washington*, U.S.A., **83** A2
Taegu, South Korea, **165** B3
Taejŏn, South Korea, **165** B3
Tafalla, Spain, **115** C1
Tagula, *island*, Papua New Guinea, **175** E2
Tagum, Philippines, **171** G3
Tahat, *mountain peak*, Algeria, **139** D1
Tahoua, Niger, **141** D3
Tşai-chung, Taiwan, **161** E4
Taihape, New Zealand, **177** D4
Tain, Scotland, **109** C2
T'ai-pei, Taiwan, **161** E4
Taiping, Malaysia, **170** B4
Tais, Indonesia, **170** B6
Taivalkoski, Finland, **107** E3
Taiwan, *country*, **161** E4
Taiwan Strait, *gulf*, Taiwan, **161** E4
Taiyuan, China, **161** D3
Taşizz, Yemen, **133** B6
Tajikistan, *country*, **155** C4
Tajo, *river*, Spain, **115** B3
Tak, Thailand, **167** B4
Takabba, Kenya, **147** D3
Takamatsu, Japan, **165** C4
Takengon, Indonesia, **170** A4
Takêv, Cambodia, **167** D5
Takikawa, Japan, **165** E1
Talachyn, Belarus, **121** D3
Talangbatu, Indonesia, **170** C6
Talara, Peru, **101** A2
Talavera de la Reina, Spain, **115** B3
Talca, Chile, **103** B4
Talcahuano, Chile, **103** B4
Taldyqorghan (Taldykorgan), Kazakhstan, **155** D3
Talladega, *Alabama*, U.S.A., **87** B5
Tallahassee, *Florida*, U.S.A., **87** B6
Tallinn, Estonia, **121** B1
Talsi, Latvia, **121** B2
Tam Kỳ, Vietnam, **167** E4
Tamale, Ghana, **141** C4
Tamanrasset, Algeria, **141** D4
Tamboura, Central African Republic, **145** D4
Tambura, Sudan, **147** B3
Tampa, *Florida*, U.S.A., **87** C6
Tampere, Finland, **107** D4
Tampico, Mexico, **89** D3
Tamworth, Australia, **175** E4
Tana, *river*, Kenya, **147** D4
T'ana Hāyk' (Lake Tana), *lake*, Sudan, **133** A6
T'ana Hāyk' (Lake Tana), *lake*, Ethiopia, **147** C2
Tanabe, Japan, **165** C4
Tanahmerah, Indonesia, **171** K6
Tanami Desert, Australia, **175** C3
Tanana, *river*, *Alaska*, U.S.A., **79** C2
Tanch'ŏn, North Korea, **165** B2
Tandil, Argentina, **103** D4
Tanga, Tanzania, **147** C4
Tanger (Tangier), Morocco, **141** C1
Tanisapata, Indonesia, **171** H5
Tanjungkarang-Telukbetung, Indonesia, **170** C6
Tanjungredeb, Indonesia, **170** E4
Tanout, Niger, **141** D3
Ţanţā, Egypt, **137** D2
Tan-Tan, Morocco, **141** B2
Tanzania, *country*, **147** B5
Taormina, Italy, **117** D6
Taoudenni, Mali, **141** C1
Tapa, Estonia, **121** C1
Tapachula, Mexico, **89** E4
Tapajós, *river*, Brazil, **99** C2
Tapan, Indonesia, **170** B5
Tapi, *river*, India, **157** B4
Tapolca, Hungary, **123** D5
Tapuae-o-Uenuku Mtn, *mountain*, New Zealand, **177** C5
Tapul Group, *island*, Philippines, **171** F4
Tapurucuara, Brazil, **97** B1
Taquari, *river*, Brazil, **103** D1
Tara, Russian Federation, **153** B3
Tara, *river*, Russian Federation, **155** D1
Ţarābulus (Tripoli), Lebanon, **133** A2
Ţarābulus(Tripoli), Libya, **137** B2
Taradale, New Zealand, **177** D4
Tarakan, Indonesia, **170** E4
Taranto, Italy, **117** E4
Taraz, Kazakhstan, **155** D3
Tarbes, France, **113** B5
Taree, Australia, **175** E5
Tarfaya, Morocco, **141** A3
Târgu Jiu, Romania, **129** A2
Târgu Mureş, Romania, **129** A2
Tarija, Bolivia, **101** D5
Tarim, *river*, China, **161** A3
Tarim Pendi, *valley*, China, **161** A3
Taripa, Indonesia, **171** F5
Taritatu, *river*, Indonesia, **171** K6
Tarlac, Philippines, **171** F2
Tarnobrzeg, Poland, **123** E3
Tarnów, Poland, **123** E3
Taroudannt, Morocco, **141** B2
Tarragona, Spain, **115** D2
Tarso Emissi, *mountain*, Chad, **145** C1
Tartu, Estonia, **121** C1
Ţarţūs, Syria, **133** A2
Tasböget, Kazakhstan, **155** C3
Tasikmalaya, Indonesia, **170** C6
Tasmania, *state*, Australia, **175** E6
Tasman Bay, *gulf*, New Zealand, **177** C4
Tata, Morocco, **141** B2
Tatabánya, Hungary, **123** D4
Taţāwīn, Tunisia, **141** E2
Tatvan, Turkey, **129** D4
Taungdwingyi, Myanmar (Burma), **167** B3
Taunggyi, Myanmar (Burma), **167** B3
Taungup, Myanmar (Burma), **167** A3
Taunton, England, **109** D6
Taupo, New Zealand, **177** D3
Tauragė, Lithuania, **121** B3
Tauranga, New Zealand, **177** D3
Tauroa Peninsula, *point*, New Zealand, **177** C2
Tavoy (Dawei), Myanmar (Burma), **167** B4
Tavoy Pt, *point*, Myanmar (Burma), **167** B4
Ţawkar, Sudan, **147** C1
Tây Ninh, Vietnam, **167** D5
Taypaq, Kazakhstan, **155** A2
Tayshet, Russian Federation, **153** C3
Taytay, Philippines, **171** F3
Ţayyebāt, Iran, **133** E2
Taz, *river*, Russian Federation, **153** C2
Taza, Morocco, **141** C1
Tāzirbū, Libya, **137** C3
T'bilisi, Georgia, **129** D3
Tchibanga, Gabon, **145** A5
Tczew, Poland, **123** D2
Te Anau, New Zealand, **177** A6
Te Kuiti, New Zealand, **177** D3
Třebíč, Czech Republic, **123** C4
Tebingtinggi, Indonesia, **170** B4
Tegucigalpa, Honduras, **91** A3
Tehrān, Iran, **155** A4
Tehrān (Teheran), Iran, **133** D2
Tejen, Turkmenistan, **155** B4
Tejo, *river*, Portugal, **115** A3
Tekeli, Kazakhstan, **155** D3
Tekirdağ, Turkey, **129** B3
Tel Aviv-Yafo, Israel, **133** A2
Tel. Cenderawasih, *gulf*, Indonesia, **171** J5
Telč, Czech Republic, **123** C4
Teles Pires (São Manuel), *river*, Brazil, **99** C2
Telšiai, Lithuania, **121** B3
Teluk Tomini, *gulf*, Indonesia, **171** F5
Telukdalam, Indonesia, **170** A5
Tema, Ghana, **141** C4
Tembito, Indonesia, **171** F5
Tembo, Democratic Republic of the Congo, **145** C6
Temirtaū, Kazakhstan, **155** D2
Tempio Pausania, Italy, **117** B4
Tempué, Angola, **149** B2
Temuco, Chile, **103** B4
Temuka, New Zealand, **177** B6
Tenāli, India, **157** C5
Tenerife, *island*, Islas Canarias/Spain, **141** A3
Ténès, Algeria, **141** D1
Tennant Creek, Australia, **175** C3
Tennessee, *river*, *Tennessee*, U.S.A., **87** A5
Tennessee, *state*, U.S.A., **87** A5
Tepa, Indonesia, **171** H7
Tepic, Mexico, **89** B3
Teresina, Brazil, **97** D2
Termoli, Italy, **117** D4
Terni, Italy, **117** C3
Ternopilş, Ukraine, **129** A1
Terra Nova Bay, Antarctica (New Zealand), **183** B3
Terracina, Italy, **117** C4
Terrassa, Spain, **115** D2
Teruel, Spain, **115** C2
Teseney, Eritrea, **147** C2
Teshio, *river*, Japan, **165** E1
Tessalit, Mali, **141** C2
Tessaoua, Niger, **141** D3
Tete, Mozambique, **149** D3
Tetouan (Tetuán), Morocco, **141** C1
Tetovo, Macedonia, **125** C3
Texarkana, *Texas*, U.S.A., **85** D5
Texarkana, *Arkansas*, U.S.A., **85** D5
Texas, *state*, U.S.A., **85** B6
Tg Datu, *point*, Malaysia, **170** D4
Tg Jambuair, *point*, Indonesia, **167** B6
Tg Kandi, *point*, Indonesia, **171** F5
Tg Puting, *point*, Indonesia, **170** D6
Tg Selatan, *point*, Indonesia, **170** E6
Tg Vals, *point*, Indonesia, **171** J7
Thái Nguyên, Vietnam, **167** D2
Thailand, *country*, **167** C4
Thames, *river*, England, **109** E6
Thanh Hóa, Vietnam, **167** D3
Thanh Phố Hồ Chí Minh (Saigon), Vietnam, **167** D5
Thanlwin (Salween), *river*, Myanmar (Burma), **167** B3
Thasos, *island*, Greece, **125** D4
Thaton, Myanmar (Burma), **167** B4
The Grenadines, *island*, Grenada, **93** E4
The Pas, *Manitoba*, Canada, **79** F5
Thessaloniki (Salonica), Greece, **125** D4
Thetford, England, **109** E5
Thief River Falls, *Minnesota*, U.S.A., **85** C2
Thimphu, Bhutan, **157** D3
Thionville, France, **113** D2
Thiruvananthapuram (Trivandrum), India, **157** C6
Thisted, Denmark, **107** A5
Thiva, Greece, **125** D5
Thiviers, France, **113** B4
Thomasville, *Georgia*, U.S.A., **87** B6
Thompson, *Manitoba*, Canada, **79** F4
Thouars, France, **113** B3
Three Forks, *Montana*, U.S.A., **83** C2
Thunder Bay, *Ontario*, Canada, **81** A3
Thung Song, Thailand, **167** C6
Thurso, Scotland, **109** C2
Thurston Island, Antarctica, **183** A3
Tian Shan, *mountain*, Kyrgyzstan, **161** A2
Tian Shan, *mountain*, China, **161** A2
Tianjin, China, **161** D3
Tianshui, China, **161** C3
Tibesti, *mountain range*, Chad, **145** B1
Tidjikja, Mauritania, **141** A2
Tielongtan, India, **157** C1
Tifariti, Western Sahara/Morocco, **141** B3
Tifu, Indonesia, **171** G6
Tijuana, Mexico, **89** A1
Tiksi, Russian Federation, **153** D2
Tillabéri, Niger, **141** C3
Ţimā, Egypt, **137** D3
Timaru, New Zealand, **177** B6
Timber Creek, Australia, **175** C2
Timişoara, Romania, **129** A2
Timimoun, Algeria, **141** C2
Timor, *island*, Indonesia, **171** G7
Tindouf, Algeria, **141** B3
Tinombo, Indonesia, **171** F5
Tinos, *island*, Greece, **129** A4
Tinsukia, India, **157** E2
Tipperary, Ireland, **109** B5
Tiranë (Tirana), Albania, **125** B3
Tiraspol, Moldova, **129** B2
Tirebolu, Turkey, **129** D3
Tirua Point, *point*, New Zealand, **177** C3
Tiruchchirāppalli, India, **157** C5
Tisza, *river*, Hungary, **123** D4
Tiverton, England, **109** C6
Tizi Ouzou, Algeria, **141** D1
Tizimín, Mexico, **89** E3
Tiznit, Morocco, **141** E2
Tlemcen, Algeria, **141** C1
Tobago, *island*, Trinidad & Tobago, **93** E4
Tobelo, Indonesia, **171** H5

Tobermory, Scotland, 109 B3
Toboali, Indonesia, 170 C6
Tocantins, river, Brazil, 97 D3
Tocopilla, Chile, 103 B1
Togo, country, 141 C4
Tokara-rettō, island, Japan, 165 B5
Tokat, Turkey, 129 C3
Tokelau, N.Z. Territory, 179 C3
Tokmak, Kyrgyzstan, 155 D3
Tokuno-shima, island, Japan, 165 B5
Tokushima, Japan, 165 C4
Tōkyō, Japan, 165 D3
Toledo, Ohio, U.S.A., 87 B3
Toledo, Spain, 115 C3
Toledo, Philippines, 171 G3
Tolitoli, Indonesia, 171 F5
Tolmezzo, Italy, 117 C1
Toluca, Mexico, 89 C3
Tom Price, Australia, 175 A3
Tomakomai, Japan, 165 E2
Tomaszów Lubelski, Poland, 123 E3
Tombouctou, Mali, 141 C2
Tombstone, Arizona, U.S.A., 83 D6
Tombua, Angola, 149 A3
Tome, Chile, 103 B5
Tomsk, Russian Federation, 153 C3
Tondano, Indonesia, 171 G5
Tønder, Denmark, 107 A6
Tonga, country, 179 B3
Tongchuan, China, 161 D3
Tongliao, China, 161 E2
Tônlé Sab, lake, Cambodia, 167 C5
Tønsberg, Norway, 107 B5
Toowoomba, Australia, 175 E4
Topeka, Kansas, U.S.A., 85 C4
Topol'çany, Slovakia, 123 D4
Torgau, Germany, 111 D3
Torghay, Kazakhstan, 155 C2
Torino (Turin), Italy, 117 A2
Tornal'a, Slovakia, 123 D4
Toronto, Ontario, Canada, 81 B4
Tororo, Uganda, 147 C4
Toros Dağları, mountain range, Turkey, 129 B4
Torre del Grecco, Italy, 117 D4
Torrelavega, Spain, 115 C1
Torreón, Mexico, 89 C2
Torrens Strait, gulf, Australia, 175 D2
Torrevieja, Spain, 115 D5
Tortosa, Spain, 115 D2
Toruń, Poland, 123 D2
Toshkent (Tashkent), Uzbekistan, 155 C3
Tottori, Japan, 165 C3
Touggourt, Algeria, 141 D2
Toulon, France, 113 D5
Toulouse, France, 113 C5
Toungoo, Myanmar (Burma), 167 B2
Tourlaville, France, 113 B2
Tours, France, 113 B3
Toussiana, Burkina Faso, 141 B3
Townsville, Australia, 175 D3
Toyama, Japan, 165 D3
Trabzon, Turkey, 129 D3
Tralee, Ireland, 109 A6
Tranås, Sweden, 107 B5
Trang, Thailand, 167 C6
Transantarctic Mountains, Antarctica, 183 B2
Trapani, Italy, 117 C5
Trat, Thailand, 167 C5
Treinta-y-Tres, Uruguay, 103 D3
Trelew, Argentina, 103 C5
Trenčín, Slovakia, 123 D4
Trento, Italy, 117 C2
Tres Arroyos, Argentina, 103 C4
Tres Isletas, Argentina, 103 C2
Tricase, Italy, 117 E5
Trieste, Italy, 117 C2
Trikala, Greece, 125 C4
Trincomalee, Sri Lanka, 157 C6
Trindade, island, Brazil, 105 B4
Trinidad, Colorado, U.S.A., 83 E5
Trinidad, island, Trinidad & Tobago, 93 E4
Trinidad, Bolivia, 101 D4
Trinidad and Tobago, country, 93 E4
Trinity, river, Texas, U.S.A., 85 C6
Tripoli, Greece, 125 C5
Trnava, Slovakia, 123 D4
Trobriand Island, Papua New Guinea, 175 E1
Trogir, Croatia, 125 A2
Tromsø, Norway, 107 C1
Trondheim, Norway, 107 B3
Troyes, France, 113 C2
Trujillo, Venezuela, 97 B2
Trujillo, Peru, 101 A3
Tsetserleg, Mongolia, 161 C2
Tshabong, Botswana, 149 C4
Tshela, Democratic Republic of the Congo, 145 B6
Tshibwika, Democratic Republic of the Congo, 145 C6
Tshikapa, Democratic Republic of the Congo, 145 C6
Tsimlyanskoye Vodokhranilishche, lake, Russian Federation, 129 D2
Tsumeb, Namibia, 149 B3
Tsuruga, Japan, 165 D3
Tsuruoka, Japan, 165 D3
Tsushima, island, Japan, 165 B4
Tsuyama, Japan, 165 C4
Tuai, New Zealand, 177 E3
Tuakau, New Zealand, 177 D3
Tuam, Ireland, 109 A5
Tubruq, Libya, 137 C2
Tucano, Brazil, 97 E3
Tucson, Arizona, U.S.A., 83 C6
Tucumcari, New Mexico, U.S.A., 83 E5
Tucupita, Venezuela, 97 D2
Tucuruí, Brazil, 97 D2
Tudela, Spain, 115 A2
Tufi, Papua New Guinea, 175 E2
Tui, Spain, 115 A2
Tuktoyaktuk, Canada, 182 A2
Tukums, Latvia, 121 B2
Tula, Mexico, 89 C3
Tulcán, Ecuador, 101 A1
Tulcea, Romania, 129 B2
Tulita, Northwest Territories, Canada, 79 D3
Tullahoma, Tennessee, U.S.A., 87 B5
Tulle, France, 113 C4
Tulsa, Oklahoma, U.S.A., 85 C5
Tuluá, Colombia, 97 A3
Tumaco, Colombia, 97 A3
Tumbes, Peru, 101 A2
Tunduru, Tanzania, 147 C5
Tundzha, river, Bulgaria, 125 E3
Tunis, Tunisia, 117 B6
Tūnis, Tunisia, 139 E1
Tunisia, country, 137 A2
Tunja, Colombia, 97 B2
Tupelo, Mississippi, U.S.A., 85 E5
Tupiza, Bolivia, 101 D5
Tupungato, mountain, Chile, 103 B3
Tura, Russian Federation, 153 C3
Ţurayf, Saudi Arabia, 133 B3
Turbat, Pakistan, 157 A3
Turbo, Colombia, 97 A2
Turhal, Turkey, 129 C3
Turkey, country, 129 C3
Türkistan, Kazakhstan, 155 C3
Türkmenbashi, Turkmenistan, 155 A3
Turkmenistan, country, 155 B3
Turks and Caicos Islands, U.K. Dependency, 93 C2
Turku, Finland, 107 D4
Turpan, China, 161 B2
Turpan Pendi, valley, China, 161 B3
Türtkül, Uzbekistan, 155 B3
Tuscaloosa, Alabama, U.S.A., 87 B5
Tuticorin, India, 157 C6
Tutóia, Brazil, 97 D2
Tutuala, Indonesia, 171 G7
Tutume, Botswana, 149 C3
Tuturumuri, New Zealand, 177 D4
Tuvalu, country, 179 B3
Tuxpan, Mexico, 89 D3
Tuxtla Gutiérrez, Mexico, 89 D4
Tuy Hòa, Vietnam, 167 E5
Tuz Gölü, lake, Turkey, 129 B4
Tuzla, Bosnia and Herzegovina, 125 B2
Tver', Russian Federation, 153 B3
Twin Falls, Idaho, U.S.A., 83 C3
Twizel, New Zealand, 177 B6
Tyler, Texas, U.S.A., 85 C6
Tynda, Russian Federation, 153 D3
Tynset, Norway, 107 B4
Tyrnavos, Greece, 125 C4

U.S.A., country, 83 C3; 85 C4; 87 B4
U'ak, Turkey, 129 B4
Ubangi, river, Congo, 145 C4
Ube, Japan, 165 B4
Úbeda, Spain, 115 C3
Uberaba, Brazil, 97 D4
Uberlândia, Brazil, 97 D4
Ubon Ratchathani, Thailand, 167 D4
Ucayali, river, Peru, 101 B3
Uchquduq, Uzbekistan, 155 C3
Udachnyy, Russian Federation, 153 D3
Udaipur, India, 157 B3
Uddevalla, Sweden, 107 B5
Uddjaure, lake, Sweden, 107 C3
Udine, Italy, 117 C2
Udon Thani, Thailand, 167 C4
Uele, river, Democratic Republic of the Congo, 145 D4
Uelzen, Germany, 111 D2
Ufa, Russian Federation, 153 B3
Ugâle, Latvia, 121 B2
Uganda, country, 147 B4
Ugento, Italy, 117 E5
Uherské Hradiště, Czech Republic, 123 C4
Uíge, Angola, 149 A1
Uitenhage, South Africa, 149 C5
Ujungpandang (Makassar), Indonesia, 171 F6
Ukhta, Russian Federation, 153 B2
Ukiah, California, U.S.A., 83 A4
Ukmergė, Lithuania, 121 C2
Ukraine, country, 129 B1
Ulaanbaatar (Ulan Bator), Mongolia, 161 C2
Ulaangom, Mongolia, 161 B2
Ulanhot, China, 161 D2
Ulan-Ude, Russian Federation, 153 D4
Uliastay, Mongolia, 161 C2
Ullŭngdo, island, South Korea, 165 C3
Ullapool, Scotland, 109 C2
Ulm, Germany, 111 C5
Ulsan, South Korea, 165 B3
Ulungur Hu, lake, China, 155 E2
Uluru (Ayers Rock), mountain, Australia, 175 C4
Uman', Ukraine, 129 B2
Umeå, Sweden, 107 C3
Umeälven, river, Sweden, 107 C3
Umm Durmān (Omdurman), Sudan, 147 B2
Umm Lajj, Saudi Arabia, 133 A4
Umm Saşad, Libya, 137 C2
Umtata, South Africa, 149 C5
Umuarama, Brazil, 97 C4
'Unayzah, Saudi Arabia, 133 B4
Ungana Bay, gulf, Kenya, 147 D4
Ungava Bay, gulf, Canada, 81 C1
United Kingdom, country, 109 A3
Unst, island, Scotland, 109 D1
Upington, South Africa, 149 B4
Upper Hutt, New Zealand, 177 D4
Uppsala, Sweden, 107 C5
Ural, river, Russian Federation, 155 B1
Ural Skiy Khrebet, mountain, Russian Federation, 153 B3
Urambo, Tanzania, 147 B5
Urbino, Italy, 117 C3
Urdos, France, 113 B5
Urdzhar, Kazakhstan, 155 E2
Urfa, Turkey, 129 D4
Urganch, Uzbekistan, 155 B3
Uruapan, Mexico, 89 C3
Uruguaiana, Brazil, 97 C5
Uruguay, country, 103 D3
Uruguay, river, Argentina, 103 D3
Ürümqi, China, 161 B2
Urung, Indonesia, 171 H6
Uşče, Yugoslavia, 125 C3
Üshtöbe, Kazakhstan, 155 D3
Usol'ye-Sibirskoye, Russian Federation, 153 C4
Ussel, France, 113 C3
Ussuriysk, Russian Federation, 153 E4
Ust'-Kamchatsk, Russian Federation, 153 F3
Ústí nad Labem, Czech Republic, 123 B3
Ust'-Ilim'sk, Russian Federation, 153 C3
Ust'-Kut, Russian Federation, 153 C3
Ust'-Tsil'ma, Russian Federation, 153 B2
Usumacinta, river, Mexico, 89 E4
Utah, state, U.S.A., 83 C4
Utena, Lithuania, 121 C3
Uthai Thani, Thailand, 167 C4
Utrecht, Netherlands, 111 B2
Utsjoki, Finland, 107 D1
Utsunomiya, Japan, 165 D3
Uttaradit, Thailand, 167 C3
Uvira, Democratic Republic of the Congo, 145 E5
Uwajima, Japan, 165 C4
Uyo, Nigeria, 141 D4
Uzbekistan, country, 155 B3
Uzhhorod, Ukraine, 129 A2

Vārānasi (Benares), India, 157 D3
Vũng Tàu, Vietnam, 167 D5
Vinh Long, Vietnam, 167 D5
Vaal, river, South Africa, 149 C4
Vaasa, Finland, 107 D4
Vadodara, India, 157 B4
Vadsø, Norway, 107 E1
Vaduz, Liechtenstein 117 B1
Valdepeñas, Spain, 115 C3
Valdivia, Chile, 103 B4
Val-d'Or, Québec, Canada, 81 B3
Valença, Brazil, 97 E3
Valence, France, 113 D4
Valencia, Venezuela, 97 C2
Valencia, Spain, 115 D3
Valentine, Nebraska, U.S.A., 85 B3
Valera, Venezuela, 97 B2
Valga, Estonia, 121 C2
Valjevo, Yugoslavia, 125 C2
Valka, Latvia, 121 C2
Valladolid, Spain, 115 B2
Valledupar, Colombia, 97 B1
Vallejo, California, U.S.A., 83 A4
Vallenar, South America, 103 B2
Valletta, Malta, 117 D6
Valmiera, Latvia, 121 C2
Valozhyn, Belarus, 121 C4
Valparaíso, South America, 103 B3
Valverde del Camino, Spain, 115 B4
Van, Turkey, 129 D4
Van Gölü, lake, Turkey, 129 D4
Vancouver, British Columbia, Canada, 79 D5
Vancouver Island, British Columbia, Canada, 79 C5
Vänern, lake, Sweden, 107 B5
Vänersborg, Sweden, 107 B5
Vanino, Russian Federation, 153 E3
Vannes, France, 113 A2
Vanuatu, country, 179 B3
Varaždin, Croatia, 125, A1
Varangerhalvøya, island, Norway, 107 E1
Varberg, Sweden, 107 B5
Varde, Denmark, 107 A6
Vardø, Norway, 107 E1
Varese, Italy, 117 B2
Varkaus, Finland, 107 E4
Varna, Bulgaria, 129 B3
Värnamo, Sweden, 107 B5
Vaslui, Romania, 129 B2
Västansjö, Sweden, 107 C3
Västerås, Sweden, 107 C5
Västervik, Sweden, 107 C5
Vasto, Italy, 117 D4
Vatican City, country, 117 B4
Vaughn, New Mexico, U.S.A., 83 E5
Vaupés, river, Colombia, 97 B3
Vawkavysk, Belarus, 121 C4
Växjö, Sweden, 107 B6
Vechta, Germany, 111 C2
Vega, island, Norway, 107 B3
Vegreville, Alberta, Canada, 79 E5
Vejle, Denmark, 107 A6
Velika Kapela, mountain range, Croatia, 125 A2
Velika Plana, Yugoslavia, 125 C2
Velletri, Italy, 117 C4
Vellore, India, 157 C5
Vendôme, France, 113 B3
Venezia (Venice), Italy, 117 C2
Venezuela, country, 97 C2
Veracruz, Mexico, 89 D3
Verdun, France, 113 D2
Verín, Spain, 115 B2
Verkhoyansk, Russian Federation, 153 D2

Vermillion, South Dakota, U.S.A., 85 C3
Vermont, state, U.S.A., 87 D3
Vernadsky, Antarctica (Ukraine), 183 A2
Vernon, Texas, U.S.A., 85 B5
Veroia, Greece, 125 C4
Verona, Italy, 117 B2
Versailles, France, 113 C2
Vesoul, France, 113 D3
Vesterålen, island, Norway, 107 C2
Vesuvio, mountain, Italy, 117 D4
Veszprém, Hungary, 123, C4
Veteli, Finland, 107 D3
Vetlanda, Sweden, 107 B5
Việt Tri, Vietnam, 167 D2
Viana do Castelo, Portugal, 115 A2
Viangchan (Vientiane), Laos, 167 C3
Viborg, Denmark, 107 A6
Vic, Spain, 115 D2
Vice Comodoro Marambio, Antarctica (Argentina), 183 A2
Vicenza, Italy, 117 C2
Vichy, France, 113 C3
Victoria, British Columbia, Canada, 79 C5
Victoria, river, Australia, 175 C2
Victoria, state, Australia, 175 D5
Victoria Island, Northwest Territories, Canada, 79 E2
Vidin, Bulgaria, 129 A3
Viedma, Argentina, 103 C5
Vierzon, France, 113 C3
Viesīte, Latvia, 121 C3
Vieste, Italy, 117 D4
Vietnam, country, 167 D3
Vigan, Philippines, 171 F1
Vigo, Spain, 115 A2
Vijayawāda, India, 157 C5
Vík, Iceland, 107 A1
Vila Real, Portugal, 115 A2
Vilanova i la Geltrú, Spain, 115 D2
Vilhelmina, Sweden, 107 C3
Viljandi, Estonia, 121 C2
Villa María, Argentina, 103 C3
Villablino, Spain, 115 B1
Villach, Austria, 123 B5
Villahermosa, Mexico, 89 D4
Villajoyosa, Spain, 115 D3
Villarrica, Paraguay, 103 D2
Villazón, Bolivia, 101 D5
Vilefranche-sur-Saône, France, 113 D3
Villena, Spain, 115 D3
Villeurbanne, France, 113 D3
Vilnius, Lithuania, 121 C3
Vilyuy, river, Russian Federation, 153 D3
Vimianzo, Spain, 115 A1
Viña del Mar, South America, 103 B3
Vinaròs, Spain, 115 D2
Vincennes, Indiana, U.S.A., 87 B4
Vincennes Bay, gulf, Antarctica, 183 C3
Vinh, Vietnam, 167 D3
Vinnytsya, Ukraine, 129 B1
Vinson Massif, mountain, Antarctica, 183 A2
Virac, Philippines, 171 G2
Viranşehir, Turkey, 129 D4
Virgin Islands, U.K. Dependency, 93 D2
Virgin Islands, U.S. Territory, 93 D2
Virginia, Minnesota, U.S.A., 85 D2
Virginia, state, U.S.A., 87 C4
Virovitica, Croatia, 125 B1
Visby, Sweden, 107 C5
Viseu, Portugal, 115 A2
Vishākhapatnam, India, 157 D4
Viterbo, Italy, 117 C4
Vitoria-Gasteiz, Spain, 115 C1
Vitry-le-François, France, 113 D2
Vitsyebsk, Belarus, 121 D3
Vittangi, Sweden, 107 D2
Vizianagaram, India, 157 D4
Vladivostok, Russian Federation, 153 E4
Vlorë, Albania, 125 B4
Vol. Citlaltépetl (Pico de Orizaba), mountain, Mexico, 89 D3
Vol. Llullaillaco, mountain peak, Chile, 103 B2
Vol. Maipú, mountain peak, Chile, 103 B3
Vol. Ollagüe, mountain peak, Bolivia, 101 D5
Vol. San Pedro, mountain peak, Bolivia, 103 B1
Vol. Tajumulco, mountain peak, Guatemala, 91 A2
Volcán Barú, mountain peak, Panama, 91 B4
Volga, river, Russian Federation, 155 A2
Volgograd (Stalingrad), Russian Federation, 153 A3
Volksrust, South Africa, 149 D4
Vologda, Russian Federation, 153 A2
Volos, Greece, 125 C4
Volterra, Italy, 117 B3
Vorkuta, Russian Federation, 182 C3
Võrtsjärv, lake, Estonia, 121 C2
Vosges, mountain, France, 117 A1
Voss, Norway, 107 A4
Vostok, Antarctica (Russian Federation), 183 C3
Vranje, Yugoslavia, 125 C3
Vršac, Yugoslavia, 125 C2
Vryburg, South Africa, 149 C4
Vuotso, Finland, 107 D2

Wa, Ghana, 141 C3
Wabash, river, Indiana, U.S.A., 87 B3
Wabé Gestro, river, Ethiopia, 147 D3
Wabé Shabelē, river, Ethiopia, 147 D3
Wabush, Newfoundland, Canada, 81 D2
Waco, Texas, U.S.A., 85 C6
Wad Medani, Sudan, 147 B2
Waddān, Libya, 137 B2
Wādī Ḩalfā, Sudan, 147 B1
Wagga Wagga, Australia, 175 E5
Wahai, Indonesia, 171 H5
Waiau, New Zealand, 177 C5
Waihi, New Zealand, 177 D3
Waikabubak, Indonesia, 171 F7
Waikato, river, New Zealand, 177 D3
Waimate, New Zealand, 177 B6
Waingapu, Indonesia, 171 F7
Wairoa, New Zealand, 177 E3
Waitakere, New Zealand, 177 D2
Waitaki, river, New Zealand, 177 B6
Waitotara, New Zealand, 177 D4
Wake Island, U.S.A., 179 B2
Wakkanai, Japan, 165 E1
Waku-Kungo, Angola, 149 A2
Wałbrzych, Poland, 123 C3
Wałcz, Poland, 123 C2
Wales, country, 109 C6
Wallis and Futuna, French Territory, 179 B3
Walpole, Australia, 175 A5
Walvis Bay, Namibia, 149 A4
Wamba, Democratic Republic of the Congo, 145 E4
Wan Xian, China, 161 D4
Wanaka, New Zealand, 177 B6
Wanda Shan, mountain, China, 165 C1
Wanganui, New Zealand, 177 D4
Warangal, India, 157 C4
Warka, Poland, 123 D2
Warm Springs, Nevada, U.S.A., 83 B4
Warmandi, Indonesia, 171 H5
Warmbad, Namibia, 149 B4
Warnambool, Australia, 175 D6
Warrego, river, Australia, 175 D4
Warren Landing, Manitoba, Canada, 79 F5
Warri, Nigeria, 141 D4
Warszawa (Warsaw), Poland, 123 D2
Warwick, England, 109 D6
Warwick, Australia, 175 E4
Washake Needles, mountain peak, Wyoming, U.S.A., 83 D3
Washington, state, U.S.A., 83 A2
Washington D. C., Washington D. C., U.S.A., 87 D4
Waterford, Ireland, 109 B6
Waterloo, Iowa, U.S.A., 85 D3
Watertown, South Dakota, U.S.A., 85 C2
Waterville, Maine, U.S.A., 87 E3
Watford, England, 109 E6
Watmuri, Indonesia, 171 H6
Watsa, Democratic Republic of the Congo, 145 E4
Watson Lake, Yukon Territory, Canada, 79 D3
Wausau, Wisconsin, U.S.A., 87 A2
Wāw, Sudan, 147 B3
Waycross, Georgia, U.S.A., 87 C6
Weiden in der Oberpfalz, Germany, 111 D4
Weiner Neustadt, Austria, 123 C5
Weipa, Australia, 175 D2
Weißenburg in Bayern, Germany, 111 D4
Wellington, island, Chile, 103 A6
Wellington, New Zealand, 177 D4

Wellsford, New Zealand, 177 D2
Wenatchee, Washington, U.S.A., 83 B2
Wenzhou, China, 161 E4
Werfen, Austria, 123 B4
Wesel, Germany, 111 B3
Wessel Island, Australia, 175 C2
West Falkland, island, Falkland Islands, 103 C6
West Palm Beach, Florida, U.S.A., 87 C7
West Virginia, state, U.S.A., 87 C4
Western Australia, state, Australia, 175 B4
Western Ghats, mountain, India, 157 B4
Western Sahara, country, 141 A3
Westport, Ireland, 109 A5
Westport, New Zealand, 177 C4
Wetar, island, Indonesia, 171 G6
Wete, Mozambique, 147 D4
Wewak, Papua New Guinea, 175 D1
Wexford, Ireland, 109 B6
Weyburn, Saskatchewan, Canada, 79 E5
Whakapara, New Zealand, 177 D2
Whangamomona, New Zealand, 177 D3
Whanganui, river, New Zealand, 177 D3
Whangarei Inlet, gulf, New Zealand, 177 D2
Wheeler Pk, mountain, Nevada, U.S.A., 83 C4
Wheeler Pk, mountain peak, New Mexico, U.S.A., 83 E5
White, river, South Dakota, U.S.A., 85 B3
White Butte, mountain, North Dakota, U.S.A., 85 B2
Whitehaven, England, 109 C4
Whitehorse, Yukon Territory, Canada, 79 D3
Whitsunday Group, island, Australia, 175 E3
Whyalla, Australia, 175 C5
Wichita, Kansas, U.S.A., 85 C4
Wichita Falls, Texas, U.S.A., 85 C5
Wick, Scotland, 109 C2
Wicklow Mts, mountain, Ireland, 109 B6
Wieluń, Poland, 123 D3
Wien (Vienna), Austria, 117 D1
Wiesbaden, Germany, 111 C4
Wilhelmshaven, Germany, 111 C2
Willemstad, Netherlands, 93 C4
Willemstad, Venezuela, 97 B1
Williston, North Dakota, U.S.A., 85 B1
Willmar, Minnesota, U.S.A., 85 C2
Wilmington, North Carolina, U.S.A., 87 C5
Wilsons Promontory, point, Australia, 175 D6
Windhoek, Namibia, 149 B4
Windorah, Australia, 175 D4
Windsor, Ontario, Canada, 81 B4
Windward Island, Caribbean Sea, 105 A3
Windward Passage, gulf, Cuba/Haiti, 93 B3
Winnemucca, Nevada, U.S.A., 83 B3
Winnipeg, Manitoba, Canada, 79 F5
Winston-Salem, North Carolina, U.S.A., 87 C5
Winterthur, Switzerland, 117 B1
Winton, New Zealand, 177 B6
Wisła, river, Poland, 123 D3
Wisconsin, state, U.S.A., 85 C3
Wittenberge, Germany, 111 D2
Włocławek, Poland, 123 D2
Wodonga, Australia, 175 E5
Wolfsburg, Germany, 111 C4
Wollaston Lake, lake, Saskatchewan, Canada, 79 F4
Wollongong, Australia, 175 E5
Wonsan, North Korea, 165 B2
Woodlark, island, Papua New Guinea, 175 E2
Woodward, Oklahoma, U.S.A., 85 B5
Woomera, Australia, 175 C4
Worcester, England, 109 D6
Workington, England, 109 C4
Worland, Wyoming, U.S.A., 83 D3
Worms, Germany, 111 C4
Worthington, Minnesota, U.S.A., 85 C3
Wotu, Indonesia, 171 F6
Wrangell, Alaska, U.S.A., 79 C4
Wrocław, Poland, 123 C3
Wuhai, China, 161 C3
Wuhan, China, 161 D4
Wuhu, China, 161 E4
Wuliang Shan, mountain range, China, 161 C3
Würzburg, Germany, 111 C4
Wuwei, China, 161 C3
Wuxi, China, 161 E4
Wyndham, Australia, 175 B2
Wyoming, state, U.S.A., 83 D3
Wyszków, Poland, 123 D2

Xaafuun, Somalia, 147 E2
Xai-Xai, Mozambique, 149 D4
Xankändi', Azerbaijan, 129 E3
Xanthi, Greece, 125 D4
Xert, Spain, 115 D2
Xiamen, China, 161 E4
Xi'an, China, 161 D3
Xiangfan, China, 161 D4
Xianggang (Hong Kong), China, 161 D4
Xiangkhoang, Laos, 167 C3
Xichang, China, 161 C4
Xigazê, China, 161 B4
Xiliao, river, China, 165 A1
Xilin Hot, China, 161 D2
Xingkai Hu, lake, China, 165 C1
Xingtai, China, 161 D3
Xingu, river, Brazil, 99 C2
Xining, China, 161 C3
Xinyang, China, 161 D4
Xique-Xique, Brazil, 97 D3
Xisha Qundao (Paracel I.), island, (Sovereignty, disputed), 170 D1
Xuzhou, China, 161 D4

Yildiseli, Turkey, 129 C3
Yāsūj, Iran, 133 D3
Yŏsu, South Korea, 165 B4
Yablonovyy Khrebet, mountain, Russian Federation, 161 D2
Yafran, Libya, 137 A2
Yakeshi, China, 161 D2
Yakima, Washington, U.S.A., 83 B2
Yakutsk, Russian Federation, 153 D3
Yala, Thailand, 167 C6
Yalta, Ukraine, 129 C2
Yalu, river, China, 165 B2
Yamagata, Japan, 165 D3
Yamaguchi, Japan, 165 B4
Yamoussoukro, Côte d'Ivoire, 141 B4
Yamuna, river, India, 157 C3
Yana, river, Russian Federation, 153 D2
Yan'an, China, 161 D3
Yanbu' al Baḩr, Saudi Arabia, 133 A4
Yangambi, Democratic Republic of the Congo, 145 D5
Yangon (Rangoon), Myanmar (Burma), 167 B4
Yanji, China, 161 E2
Yantai, China, 161 E3
Yaoundé, Cameroon, 145 B4
Yarkant, river, China, 161 A3
Yasothon, Thailand, 167 D4
Yatsushiro, Japan, 165 B4

Yawri Bay, gulf, Sierra Leone, 141 A4
Yazd, Iran, 133 D3
Ye, Myanmar (Burma), 167 B4
Yekaterinburg, Russian Federation, 153 B3
Yell, island, Scotland, 109 D1
Yellowknife, Northwest Territories, Canada, 79 E3
Yellowstone, river, Montana, U.S.A., 83 D2
Yel'sk, Belarus, 121 D5
Yemen, country, 133 C6
Yên Bái, Vietnam, 167 D2
Yendi, Ghana, 141 C4
Yeovil, England, 109 D6
Yerevan, Armenia, 129 D3
Yerushalayim (Jerusalem), Israel, 137 E2
Yevpatoriya, Ukraine, 129 C2
Yibin, China, 161 C4
Yichang, China, 161 D4
Yichun, China, 161 E2
Yinchuan, China, 161 C3
Yingkou, China, 161 E3
Yining, China, 161 B2
Ylitornio, Finland, 107 D2
Ylivieska, Finland, 107 D3
Yody, Belarus, 121 C3
Yogyakarta, Indonesia, 170 D7
Yokohama, Japan, 165 D3
Yola, Nigeria, 141 E4
York, England, 109 D5
York Factory, Manitoba, Canada, 79 F4
Yorkton, Saskatchewan, Canada, 79 F5
Yoro, Honduras, 91 A2
Youghal, Ireland, 109 B6
Youngstown, Ohio, U.S.A., 87 C3
Youssoufia, Morocco, 141 B2
Yozgat, Turkey, 129 C4
Yŏnghŭng, North Korea, 165 B2
Ystad, Sweden, 107 B6
Ysyk-Köl, lake, Kyrgyzstan, 161 A2
Yucatán Channel, gulf, Mexico, 91 B1
Yucatán Channel, gulf, Cuba, 91 B1
Yugoslavia, country, 125 C2
Yukon, river, Alaska, U.S.A., 79 C2
Yukon, river, Yukon Territory, Canada, 79 C3
Yukon Territory, Canada, 79 D2
Yuma, Arizona, U.S.A., 83 C6
Yumen, China, 161 C3
Yunkai Dashan, mountain, China, 167 C2
Yurimaguas, Peru, 101 B2
Yushu, China, 161 C3
Yuty, Paraguay, 103 D2
Yuzhno-Sakhalinsk, Russian Federation, 153 E3

Zābol, Iran, 133 E3
Zähedän, Iran, 133 E3
Złoczew, Poland, 123 D3
Zabīd, Yemen, 133 B6
Zacharo, Greece, 125 C5
Zadar, Croatia, 125 A2
Zafra, Spain, 115 B3
Zagreb, Croatia, 125 A1
Zaïre, river, Zaire, 145 C5
Zaječar, Yugoslavia, 125 C2
Zaliv Aniva, gulf, Russian Federation, 165 E1
Zambezi, river, Zambia, 149, D3
Zamboanga, Philippines, 171 F3
Zamość, Poland, 123 E3
Zamora, Spain, 115 B2
Zanjān, Iran, 133 C2
Zanzibar, Tanzania, 147 C5
Zanzibar Island, Tanzania, 147 D5
Zapadno Sibirskaya Ravnina, valley, Russian Federation, 153 B2
Zapadnyy Sayan, mountain, Russian Federation, 161 B2
Zapala, Argentina, 103 B4
Zaporizhzhya, Ukraine, 129 C2
Zarafshon, Uzbekistan, 155 C3
Zaragoza, Spain, 115 C2
Zaranj, Afghanistan, 155 B5
Zaraza, Venezuela, 97 C2
Zaria, Nigeria, 141 D3
Zarzaïtine, Algeria, 141 E2
Zawiercie, Poland, 123 D3
Zaysan, Kazakhstan, 155 E2
Zaysan Köli, lake, Kazakhstan, 155 E2
Zelenogradsk, Russian Federation, 121 A3
Zemlya Frantsa-Iosifa, island, Russian Federation, 153 C1
Zenica, Bosnia and Herzegovina, 125 B2
Zeven, Germany, 111 C2
Zeya, river, Russian Federation, 161 E1
Zgierz, Poland, 123 D2
Zgorzelec, Poland, 123 C3
Zhanatas, Kazakhstan, 155 C3
Zhangaözen, Kazakhstan, 155 A3
Zhangaqala, Kazakhstan, 155 A2
Zhangaqorghan, Kazakhstan, 155 C3
Zhangguangcai Ling, mountain, China, 165 B3
Zhangjiakou, China, 161 D3
Zhangye, China, 161 C3
Zhanjiang, China, 161 D4
Zhaotong, China, 161 C4
Zharkent, Kazakhstan, 155 E3
Zharma, Kazakhstan, 155 E2
Zhayyq, river, Kazakhstan, 155 A2
Zhengzhou, China, 161 D4
Zhetibay, Kazakhstan, 155 A3
Zhetiqara, Kazakhstan, 155 B1
Zhezqazghan, Kazakhstan, 155 C2
Zhigansk, Russian Federation, 153 D2
Zhlobin, Belarus, 121 E4
Zhob, Pakistan, 157 B2
Zhodzina, Belarus, 121 D4
Zhongshan, Antarctica (China), 183 C2
Zhytomyr, Ukraine, 129 B1
Zibo, China, 161 D3
Zielona Góra, Poland, 123 C3
Zigong, China, 161 C4
Ziguinchor, Senegal, 141 A3
Žilina, Slovakia, 123 D4
Zima, Russian Federation, 153 C3
Zimbabwe, country, 149 C3
Zinder, Niger, 141 D3
Zixing, China, 161 D4
Zlītan, Libya, 137 B2
Znojmo, Czech Republic, 123 C4
Zoetermeer, Netherlands, 111 B2
Zomba, Malawi, 149 E2
Zonguldak, Turkey, 129 B3
Zorita, Spain, 115 B3
Zouar, Chad, 145 B1
Zrenjanin, Yugoslavia, 125 C2
Zunyi, China, 161 C4
Zürich, Switzerland, 117 B1
Zuo, river, China, 167 C2
Zuwārah, Libya, 137 A2
Zwedru, Liberia, 141 B4
Zwickau, Germany, 111 D3
Zyryanovsk, Kazakhstan, 155 E2

Acknowledgements

The publishers wish to thank the following people and organisations for the use of their photographs:

Yancey Walker and Kellie Leigh; African wild dogs, page 47
WIRES; platypus, page 50
Mandy King and Fabio Cavadini; Panguna copper mine, Bougainville, page 52
UNICEF; child in Rio de Janeiro, page 52
Community Aid Abroad-Oxfam Australia (J. V. Higgins); Pune, India, page 53
Colin Hesse; Jabiluka protest, page 54